A Complete Guide to

INTERIM FINANCIAL REPORTING

with Illustrative statements

A Complete Guide to

INTERIM FINANCIAL REPORTING

with Illustrative statements

Deepa Agarwal, CA

Technical Reviewer

Sunil Gupta, CA, CPA (USA)

B L O O M S B U R Y

NEW DELHI • LONDON • OXFORD • NEW YORK • SYDNEY

First published in India 2017

Disclaimer

ISBN 9789386349309

10 9 8 7 6 5 4 3 2 1

Bloomsbury Publishing India Pvt. Ltd
DDA Complex, LSC Building No.4
Second Floor, Pocket C–6 & 7, Vasant Kunj
New Delhi 110070
www.bloomsbury.com

Printed and bound in India by Rajkamal Electric Press, Kundli

To find out more about our authors and books visit www.bloomsbury.com. Here you will find extracts, author interviews, details of forthcoming events and the option to sign up for our newsletters.

Dedication

This book is dedicated to my beloved parents
and my husband who have encouraged
me to become a better professional
each day!

Acknowledgement

I wish to acknowledge the contribution made by Mr. Toby Thomas, Ms Nikita Jain, Mr. Mahesh Koirala and Ms. Divya Malhotra for their continuous efforts in reviewing and providing additional inputs in preparation of this publication.

Valuable suggestions and constructive feedback from the users are welcome and would be gratefully acknowledged. I invite comments and suggestions from the esteemed professionals at deepaagarwal@icai.org.

Deepa Agarwal, CA

About the author

Deepa Agarwal, B.Com, CA with 13th Rank in all over India and 5th Rank in NIRC, has more than 15 years of experience in serving national and multi-national companies in the areas of Auditing and Accounting, Corporate Laws and other related matters.

She has completed Information Systems Audit (ISA) course from ICAI in September 2006 (and certified course on IFRS from the Institute of Chartered Accountants of India, New Delhi in March 2011.

She has worked with the Technical Directorate of ICAI for around 5 years and has assisted ICAI in various publications such as background material on AS 16, Technical guide on Accounting and Auditing issues in Chit Fund, Technical guide on internal auditing in case of intangible assets. She worked with BSR & Co. LLP in the technical department for a period of 9 years. Presently, she is leading the technical department of a renowned consultancy firm.

She has authored 'The Law & Practice of Financial Reporting Requirements and Auditor's Responsibilities under Companies Act, 2013' published by Bloomsbury Professional.

She has worked extensively on preparation of comments, guidance and presentations on Companies Bill and Companies Act, 2013.

She acted as a faculty member for the ICAI course organised by Ind-AS IFRS Implementation Committee. She has been a speaker in numerous seminars on accounting, auditing and companies act matters at various forums. She has imparted trainings to chartered accountants on Accounting Standards, Indian Accounting Standards, Auditing Standards and other updates.

She regularly provides comments on various drafts on documents related to accounting, auditing and corporate laws issued by ICAI and MCA and worked extensively on issuance of interpretations, opinions and guidance on related matters.

Technical reviewer's profile

Sunil Gupta, B.Com, CA, LL.B, CPA (California Board of Accountancy, USA), has more than 13 years of experience in the areas of Corporate Reporting, Income Tax, Transfer Pricing, Tax Accounting, International Taxation, Tax litigations, Mergers, Acquisitions & Restructuring, Service tax, VAT/CST, etc. He has worked with many corporates and has vast experience in Information Technology, Mining and Oil & Gas Industries.

Preface

Indian Accounting Standards (Ind AS) have already been applicable for phase I companies from 1 April 2016. The companies covered in phase I are required to prepare and present their financial statements, including financial results, under Ind AS 34.

It would have been a mammoth exercise for the listed companies to present all the reviewed/audited Ind AS comparative figures and all the reconciliations along with quarterly financial results in the first year of adoption of Ind AS. To provide relief to the companies during transition phase, SEBI has relaxed some of the requirements with respect to comparative periods and reconciliations to be presented. Similarly, other regulators/bodies have also issued various clarifications. This publication brings together the key requirements for preparation and submission of interim financial reports and results, and the relevant circulars and clarifications along with key features of the 'Implementation Guide on Auditor's Reports under Indian Accounting Standards for Transition Phase' released by the Auditing and Assurance Standards Board of the ICAI for ready reference to the preparers of financial results and auditors.

Various formats for publishing financial results required by SEBI are also annexed in the publication for both equity listed companies and debt listed companies. This publication also analyses the impact of adoption of Ind AS on the profits of 31 Nifty 50 companies and highlights key areas contributing to the impacts on the profit of these companies, by comparing the reported results for the quarter ended 30 September 2015 under the previous GAAP with the restated results for the same quarter under Ind AS, that have been published as comparatives for the quarter ended 30 September 2016. This would help the companies operating in various industrial sectors that would be covered in phase II of the implementation, to evaluate what impact transition to Ind AS could have on revenue, profit and some other key line items of the financial statements.

Numerous examples have been provided to explain the concepts given in Ind AS 34. The publication also presents key requirements emanating from internal financial reporting framework and various SEBI circulars in tabular format in an easy-to-understand manner. Therefore the publication is a comprehensive material, which places all the requirements in respect of interim financial reporting including financial results by listed companies at one place. A comprehensive checklist on internal financial reporting as per the provisions of Ind AS 34 has also been provided to help users understand the requirements of Ind AS 34. The last chapter provides illustrative condensed standalone interim financial statements as required under Ind AS 34 which will serve as an important reference for the preparers of interim financial statements.

Contents at a glance

Table of contents

LEGAL FRAMEWORK

Appendices

Chapter 1

Introduction

1.1 BACKGROUND

Interim financial statement refers to the financial statements covering a period less than one year. Often interim financial statements are issued for the *quarters* between the annual financial statements. The objective of preparation of these financial statements is to give investors, stakeholders and other users updated information on the company's operations. Annual data available by way of annual financial statements do not suffice to evaluate developments in industry and general economy. Investors may require updated information for making or revising projections of earnings, financial position and valuation of the company while making their investment decisions. The Financial Accounting Standards Board (FASB), recognised by the Securities and Exchange Commission as the designated accounting standard setter for public companies has listed down the following five possible objectives and uses for interim reporting:

- to estimate annual earnings
- to make projections
- to identify turning points
- to evaluate management performance
- to supplement the annual report

Unlike the annual financial statements, interim financial statements can be condensed. The condensed financial statements may or may not be audited. The interim financial report is intended to provide an update on the latest complete set of annual financial statements. Accordingly, it focuses on new activities, events, and circumstances and does not duplicate information previously reported. Therefore, the users should refer to the previously issued and complete annual financial statements and reports.

1.2 ACCOUNTING FRAMEWORK FOR INTERIM FINANCIAL REPORTING

AS 25, *Interim Financial Reporting* issued by the Accounting Standards Board of the ICAI observes that 'Timely and reliable interim financial reporting improves the ability of investors, creditors and others to understand an enterprise's capacity to generate earnings and cash flows, its financial condition and liquidity'. AS 25 is effective in respect of accounting periods commencing on or after 1 April 2002. An interim financial report as defined by AS 25 is a financial report containing either a complete set of financial statements or a set of condensed financial statements for an interim period. AS 25 prescribes the minimum content of an interim financial report and the principles for recognition and measurement in complete or condensed financial statements for an interim period.

1.2.1 Convergence with IFRSs

In order to minimize differences in the Accounting Standards (ASs) internationally, compliance with Indian Accounting Standards (Ind ASs) has been made mandatory in a phased approach for the companies by the MCA so that there is rigorous participation and better understanding of business reporting on the global front. The notification of Ind AS would fill significant gaps that exist in the current accounting guidance.

The MCA through its notification dated 16 February 2015 has issued the Companies (Indian Accounting Standards) Rules, 2015 and later amended these rules by notification dated 30 March 2016 referred to as the Companies (Indian Accounting Standards) (Amendment) Rules, 2016. The amended rules have laid down a roadmap for NBFC and confirmed the roadmap for bank and insurance companies.

1.2.2 Obligation to comply with Ind AS

Rule 4 of the Companies (Indian Accounting Standards) Rules, 2015 as amended by the Companies (Indian Accounting Standards) (Amendment) Rules, 2016, states as below:

> "(1) *The Companies and their auditors shall comply with the Ind AS specified in Annexure to these rules in preparation of their financial statements and audit respectively, in the following manner, namely:-*
>
> (i) *any company and its holding, subsidiary, joint venture or associate company may comply with the Indian Accounting Standards (Ind AS) for financial statements for accounting periods beginning on or after 1st April, 2015, with the comparatives for the periods ending on 31st March, 2015, or thereafter;*
>
> (ii) *the following companies shall comply with the Indian Accounting Standards (Ind AS) for the accounting periods beginning on or after 1st April, 2016, with the comparatives for the periods ending on 31st March, 2016, or thereafter, namely:-*

(a) companies whose equity or debt securities are listed or are in the process of being listed on any stock exchange in India or outside India and having net worth of rupees five hundred crore or more;

(b) companies other than those covered by sub-clause (a) of clause (ii) of sub-rule (1) and having net worth of rupees five hundred crore or more;

(c) holding, subsidiary, joint venture or associate companies of companies covered by sub-clause (a) of clause (ii) of sub-rule (1) and sub-clause (b) of clause (ii) of sub- rule (1) as the case may be; and

(iii) the following companies shall comply with the Indian Accounting Standards (Ind AS) for the accounting periods beginning on or after 1st April, 2017, with the comparatives for the periods ending on 31st March, 2017, or thereafter, namely:-

(a) companies whose equity or debt securities are listed or are in the process of being listed on any stock exchange in India or outside India and having net worth of less than rupees five hundred crore;

(b) companies other than those covered in clause (ii) of sub- rule (1) and sub-clause (a) of clause (iii) of sub-rule (1), that is, unlisted companies having net worth of rupees two hundred and fifty crore or more but less than rupees five hundred crore.

(c) holding, subsidiary, joint venture or associate companies of companies covered under sub-clause (a) of clause (iii) of sub-rule (1) and sub-clause (b) of clause (iii) of sub- rule (1), as the case may be.

……………………………

(iv) Notwithstanding the requirement of clauses (i) to (iii), Non-Banking Financial Companies (NBFCs) shall comply with the Indian Accounting Standards (Ind ASs) in preparation of their financial statements and audit respectively, in the following manner, namely:-

(a) The following NBFCs shall comply with the Indian Accounting Standards (Ind AS) for accounting periods beginning on or after the 1st April, 2018, with comparatives for the periods ending on 31st March, 2018, or thereafter—

(A) NBFCs having net worth of rupees five hundred crore or more;

(B) holding, subsidiary, joint venture or associate companies of companies covered under item (A), other than those already covered under clauses (i), (ii) and (iii) of sub-rule (1) of rule 4.

(b) The following NBFCs shall comply with the Indian Accounting Standards (Ind AS) for accounting periods beginning on or after the 1st April, 2019, with comparatives for the periods ending on 31stMarch, 2019, or thereafter—

(A) NBFCs whose equity or debt securities are listed or in the process of listing on any stock exchange in India or outside India and having net worth less than rupees five hundred crore;

(B) NBFCs, that are unlisted companies, having net worth of rupees two-hundred and fifty crore or more but less than rupees five hundred crore; and

(C) holding, subsidiary, joint venture or associate companies of companies covered under item (A) or item (B) of sub-clause (b), other than those already covered in clauses (i), (ii) and (iii) of sub-rule (1) or item (B) of sub-clause (a) of clause (iv).

……………………….."

"(2) For the purposes of calculation of net worth of companies under sub-rule (1), the following principles shall apply, namely:-

(a) the net worth shall be calculated in accordance with the stand-alone financial statements of the company as on 31 March 2014 or the first audited financial statements for accounting period which ends after that date;

(b) for companies which are not in existence on 31 March 2014 or an existing company falling under any of thresholds specified in sub-rule (1) for the first time after 31 March 2014, the net worth shall be calculated on the basis of the first audited financial statements ending after that date in respect of which it meets the thresholds specified in sub-rule (1).

Explanation - For the purposes of sub-clause (b), the companies meeting the specified thresholds given in sub-rule (1) for the first time at the end of an accounting year shall apply Ind AS from the immediate next accounting year in the manner specified in sub-rule (1).

Illustration - (i) The companies meeting threshold for the first time as on 31st March, 2017 shall apply Ind AS for the financial year 2017-18 onwards.

…………………"

Rule 5 of the Companies (Indian Accounting Standards) Rules, 2015 as amended by the Companies (Indian Accounting Standards) (Amendment) Rules, 2016 states as below:

> *"The Banking Companies and Insurance Companies shall apply the Ind ASs as notified by the Reserve Bank of India (RBI) and Insurance Regulatory Development Authority (IRDA) respectively. An insurer or insurance company shall however, provide Ind AS compliant financial statement data for the purposes of preparation of consolidated financial statements by its parent or investor or venturer, as required by the parent or investor or venturer to comply with the requirements of these rules."*

MCA had issued a press release on 18 January 2016 outlining the roadmap for implementation of Ind AS for scheduled commercial banks (excluding Regional Rural Banks (RRBs)), insurance companies and NBFCs. In response to the above mentioned press release, in February 2016, RBI has issued notification for implementation of Ind AS for scheduled commercial banks (excluding RRBs) setting forth the guidance and additional compliance requirements. Further, in March 2016, IRDA has issued notification for implementation of Ind AS for insurance companies setting forth the implementation guidance and additional compliance requirements. Similarly, the roadmap for implementation of Ind AS for NBFCs was notified by the MCA vide the Companies (Indian Accounting Standards) (Amendment) Rules, 2016 on 30 March 2016, as already stated above.

The notification issued by RBI on 11 February 2016 states as follows:

> *"Banks shall comply with the Indian Accounting Standards (Ind AS) for financial statements for accounting periods beginning from April 1, 2018 onwards, with comparatives for the periods ending March 31, 2018 or thereafter. Ind AS shall be applicable to both standalone financial statements and consolidated financial statements. "Comparatives" shall mean comparative figures for the preceding accounting period."*

Similarly, the circular issued by the IRDAI on 01 March 2016 states as follows:

> *"Insurers shall comply with the Indian Accounting Standards (Ind AS) for financial statements for accounting periods beginning from April 1, 2018 onwards, with comparatives for the periods ending March 31, 2018. Ind AS shall be applicable to both standalone financial statements and consolidated financial statements. "Comparatives" shall mean comparative figures for the preceding accounting period."*

1.2.3 Obligation to comply with Ind AS for companies other than banks, NBFCs and insurer/insurance companies

<table>
<tr><th rowspan="2">Phases</th><th rowspan="2">Companies covered*</th><th colspan="2">Year of adoption</th></tr>
<tr><th>Mandatory</th><th>Voluntary</th></tr>
<tr><td>Phase I</td><td>All companies with net worth >= INR 500 crore</td><td>FY 2016-17</td><td>FY 2015-16</td></tr>
<tr><td>Phase II</td><td>All companies listed or in the process of being listed
Companies having a net worth >= INR 250 crore</td><td>FY 2017-18</td><td>FY 2015-16 or thereafter</td></tr>
</table>

**As per the Companies (Indian Accounting Standards) Rules, 2016, the holding, subsidiary and fellow subsidiary companies, associates and joint ventures, of the respective companies shall also be covered.*

1.2.4 Obligation to comply with Ind AS for banks, NBFCs and insurer/insurance companies

<table>
<tr><th rowspan="2">Phases</th><th rowspan="2">NBFCs*</th><th colspan="2">Year of adoption</th></tr>
<tr><th>Mandatory</th><th>Voluntary</th></tr>
<tr><td>Phase I</td><td>All NBFCs with net worth >= INR 500 crore</td><td>FY 2018-19</td><td rowspan="2">Not permitted</td></tr>
<tr><td>Phase II</td><td>All NBFCs listed or in the process of being listed
Unlisted NBFCs having a net worth >= INR 250 crore</td><td>FY 2019-20</td></tr>
</table>

**As per the Companies (Indian Accounting Standards) Rules, 2016, the holding, subsidiary and fellow subsidiary companies, associates and joint ventures, of the respective companies shall also be covered.*

<table>
<tr><th rowspan="2">Particulars</th><th colspan="2">Year of adoption</th></tr>
<tr><th>Mandatory</th><th>Voluntary</th></tr>
<tr><td>Scheduled commercial banks (excluding RRBs, All-India Term-lending Refinancing Institutions)</td><td>FY 2018-19</td><td rowspan="2">Not permitted</td></tr>
<tr><td>Insurance companies</td><td>FY 2018-19</td></tr>
</table>

As per the roadmap:

- Voluntarily the companies can adopt Ind AS for accounting periods beginning on or after 1 April 2015 with comparatives for the period ended 31 March 2015 or thereafter.
- The applicability of Ind AS is made mandatory under phase I for companies whose net worth is of INR 500 crore or more for period beginning on or after 1 April 2016, with comparatives for the period ended 31 March 2016, or thereafter.
- Under phase II Ind AS is made mandatory for periods beginning on or after 1 April 2017, with comparatives beginning for the period ending 31 March 2017 or thereafter for the companies having net worth more than INR 250 crore but less than INR 500 crore.
- Under phase II, Ind AS would be mandatorily applicable to companies whose equity and debt securities are listed or are in the process of listing on any stock exchange in India or outside India and were not covered in phase I.
- Ind AS would also apply to the holding, subsidiary, joint venture (JV) or associate companies of companies covered above.
- Companies whose securities are listed or are in the process of listing on the small and medium enterprises exchanges as referred to in Chapter XB or on the Institutional Trading Platform without initial public offering in accordance with the provisions of Chapter XC of the Securities and Exchange Board of India (Issue of Capital and Disclosure Requirements) Regulations, 2009 are not required to apply Ind AS and can continue to comply with the Companies (Accounting Standards) Rules, 2006.
- It is worthwhile to note that Ind AS would be applicable to both stand-alone and consolidated financial statements.
- Also, the net worth for implementation of Ind AS should be calculated based on the stand-alone financial statements of the company as on 31 March 2014 or the first audited financial statements for accounting period ending subsequently. For companies falling under any of thresholds specified in rule 4(1) of the Companies (Indian Accounting Standards) Rules, 2015 for the first time after 31 March 2014, the net worth should be calculated on the basis of the first audited financial statements ending after that date.
- Once a company applies Ind AS voluntarily, it will be required to follow the Ind AS for all the subsequent financial statements.

With the notification of Ind AS converged accounting standards (as discussed below), Ind AS 34, *Interim Financial Reporting* is effective from financial year 2016-17 for Phase I companies and will be applicable from financial year 2017-18 for Phase II companies in accordance with the roadmap notified by MCA. Like AS 25, Ind AS 34 also prescribed the minimum content for an interim financial report and the principles for recognition and measurement in complete or condensed financial statements for an interim period. Also, it does not mandate which entities are required to publish interim financial reports, how frequently or how soon after the end of the interim period. This standard applies if an entity is required or elects to publish an interim financial report in accordance with Ind AS.

1.3 LEGAL FRAMEWORK OF INTERIM FINANCIAL REPORTING

SEBI had issued the SEBI (Listing Obligations and Disclosure Requirements) Regulations ('SEBI Listing Regulations') on 2 September 2016, which came into force on 1 December 2016. With the applicability of SEBI Listing Regulations, the erstwhile Listing Agreement was rescinded. As per clause 41 of the erstwhile Listing Agreement, an equity listed company was required to prepare quarterly financial results and submit to the stock exchange(s). Similarly, clause 29 of the erstwhile Listing Agreement required a debt listed company to prepare and submit half-yearly financial results to the stock exchange(s). The corresponding regulations in the SEBI Listing Regulations for clause 41 and clause 29 are reg 33 and reg 52 respectively.

1.3.1 Regulation 33 of the SEBI Listing Regulations

Regulation 33 of the SEBI Listing Regulations requires a company which has listed its specified securities (equity shares and convertible securities) to prepare and submit the quarterly financial results to the stock exchange(s). Regulation 33 further states that the quarterly and year to date results shall be prepared in accordance with the recognition and measurement principles laid down in Accounting Standard 25 or Indian Accounting Standard 34 (AS 25/Ind AS 34 – Interim Financial Reporting), as applicable, specified in sec 133 of the *Companies Act, 2013* read with relevant rules framed thereunder or as specified by the Institute of Chartered Accountants of India, whichever is applicable.

1.3.2 Regulation 52 of the SEBI Listing Regulations

Regulation 52 of the SEBI Listing Regulations requires a company which has listed its non-convertible debt securities or non-convertible redeemable preference shares or both to prepare and submit un-audited or audited financial results on a half yearly basis to the stock exchange(s).

1.3.3 Regulation 23 of the SEBI (Infrastructure Investment Trusts) Regulations

Regulation 23 of the SEBI (Infrastructure Investment Trusts) Regulations, 2014 prescribe disclosures to be made by an InvIT to the Stock Exchange(s) where its units are listed. The said disclosures, inter-alia, include disclosures for financial as well as non-financial information. A recent circular dated 29 November 2016 on Continuous disclosures and compliances by InvITs states that the financial information presented by the InvIT can be in the form of condensed financial statements. Such financial information shall comply with the minimum requirements for condensed financial statements as described in Ind AS 34 on 'Interim Financial Reporting', to the extent applicable.

In addition, the insurance companies are also required to prepare and publish quarterly/half-yearly financial statements as per notifications issued by the IRDAI. The master circular on "Preparation of financial statements and filing returns of life insurance business –Life Insurance Business" issued by the IRDAI on 11 December 2013 state that insurers shall publish, in at least one English daily newspaper, the Balance Sheet, Profit & Loss Account, Revenue Account and Key Analytical Ratios on an half yearly basis and the insurers shall host all the forms including Revenue Account, Profit & Loss Account, Balance Sheet, segmental reporting, schedules to accounts and other forms, on their website on quarterly/half yearly/yearly basis on their websites.

Ind AS 34, *Interim Financial Reporting* does not mandate which entities should be required to publish interim financial reports, how frequently, or how soon after the end of an interim period. However, a company may be required to prepare condensed interim financial statements in various situations discussed above, which are dealt in detail in separate chapters of this publication.

Chapter 2

Accounting framework for companies to which Ind ASs are applicable

As stated in previous chapters, Indian Accounting Standards (Ind ASs) are applicable to entities in a phased manner with effect from accounting periods commencing on or after 1 April 2016. An entity needs to apply the requirements of Ind AS 34, *Interim Financial Reporting* if an entity is required or elects to publish an interim financial report in accordance with Ind ASs.

2.1 IND AS 34, INTERIM FINANCIAL REPORTING

As per Ind AS 34, an interim financial report means a financial report containing either a complete set of financial statements or a set of condensed financial statements. Ind AS 34 does not mandate which entities should be required to publish interim financial reports, how frequently, or how soon after the end of an interim period. However, governments, securities regulators, stock exchanges, and accountancy bodies often require entities whose debt or equity securities are publicly traded to publish interim financial reports.

2.1.1 Minimum components of an interim financial report

An interim financial report shall include, at a minimum, the following components:

(a) a condensed balance sheet;

(b) a condensed statement of profit and loss;

(c) a condensed statement of changes in equity;

(d) a condensed statement of cash flows; and

(e) selected explanatory notes.

SEBI regulations require the following statements to be submitted as part of financial results:

- Quarterly and year-to-date financial results (including segment reporting)
- Statement of Assets and Liabilities as at the end of the half-year end

2.1.2 Periods required to be presented in an interim financial report

Ind AS 34 requires interim financial reports to include interim financial statements (whether condensed or complete) for the periods listed below:

Statement	Current	Comparative
Balance Sheet	End of current interim period	End of immediately preceding financial year
Statement of profit or loss	Current interim period and cumulatively for the year-to-date	Comparable interim period and year-to-date of immediately preceding financial year
Statement of changes in equity	Cumulative for the current financial year-to-date	Comparable year-to-date of immediately preceding financial year
Statement of cash flows	Cumulatively for the current financial year-to-date	Comparable year-to-date of immediately preceding financial year

The selected explanatory notes and additional information should contain comparative information for each of the periods presented.

Entities with seasonal businesses

For an entity whose business is highly seasonal, financial information for the twelve months up to the end of the interim period and comparative information for the prior twelve-month period may be useful. Accordingly, entities whose business is highly seasonal are encouraged to consider reporting such information in addition to the information called for in the preceding paragraph.

2.1.3 Basis of preparation of interim financial reports

Ind AS 34 requires the use of discrete period approach; i.e. items of income and expenses should be recognised and measured on a basis consistent with that used in preparing the annual financial statements. The standard states that the frequency (annual, half-yearly or quarterly) of an entity's interim reporting should not affect the measurement of its annual results.

2.1.4 Recognition and measurement principles

2.1.4.1 Same accounting policies as annual

An entity shall apply the same accounting policies in its interim financial statements as are applied in its annual financial statements, except for accounting policy changes made after the date of the most recent annual financial statements that are to be reflected in the next annual financial statements. However, the frequency of an entity's reporting (annual, half-yearly, or quarterly) shall not affect the measurement of its annual results. To achieve that objective, measurements for interim reporting purposes shall be made on a year-to-date basis.

Requiring that an entity apply the same accounting policies in its interim financial statements as in its annual statements may seem to suggest that interim period measurements are made as if each interim period stands alone as an independent reporting period. However, by providing that the frequency of an entity's reporting shall not affect the measurement of its annual results, Ind AS 34 acknowledges that an interim period is a part of a larger financial year. Year to date measurements may involve changes in estimates of amounts reported in prior interim periods of the current financial year. But the principles for recognising assets, liabilities, income, and expenses for interim periods are the same as in annual financial statements.

2.1.4.2 Recognition and measurement principle of a new standard

The recognition and measurement requirements of any new standard should be applied to all interim periods within the annual period in which the new standards are adopted unless the transitional requirements of the standard permit or require different transition.

Example

- The principles for recognising and measuring losses from inventory write-downs, restructurings, or impairments in an interim period are the same as those that an entity would follow if it prepared only annual financial statements. However, if such items are recognised and measured in one interim period and the estimate changes in a subsequent interim period of that financial year, the original estimate is changed in the subsequent interim period either by accrual of an additional amount of loss or by reversal of the previously recognised amount
- a cost that does not meet the definition of an asset at the end of an interim period is not deferred in the balance sheet either to await future information as to whether it has met the definition of an asset or to smooth earnings over interim periods within a financial year

- income tax expense is recognised in each interim period based on the best estimate of the weighted average annual income tax rate expected for the full financial year. Amounts accrued for income tax expense in one interim period may have to be adjusted in a subsequent interim period of that financial year if the estimate of the annual income tax rate changes.

2.1.4.3 *Change in accounting policy*

Any change in accounting policy on adoption of a new or revised standard should be accounted for in accordance with the transitional requirements specified in the standard. In the absence of such specific transitional requirements, the change in accounting policy should be accounted for in accordance with the general guidance on changes in accounting policies in Ind AS 8, *Accounting Policies, Changes in Accounting Estimates and Errors*.

2.1.4.4 *Levies*

Appendix C to Ind AS 37, *Provisions, Contingent Liabilities and Contingent Assets* provides guidance on when to recognise a liability for a levy imposed by a government; it applies both for levies that are accounted for in accordance with Ind AS 37 and those for which the timing and amount of the levy is certain. In interim financial report, a liability to pay a levy should not be recognised if there is no present obligation to pay the levy at the end of the interim reporting period and should be recognised if a present obligation to pay the levy exists at the end of the interim reporting period.

2.1.4.5 *Seasonal, cyclical or occasional revenue*

Revenues that are received seasonally, cyclically, or occasionally within a financial year shall not be anticipated or deferred as of an interim date if anticipation or deferral would not be appropriate at the end of the entity's financial year.

Examples include dividend revenue, royalties, and government grants. Additionally, some entities consistently earn more revenues in certain interim periods of a financial year than in other interim periods, for example, seasonal revenues of retailers. Such revenues are recognised when they occur.

Example

Company A engaged in retail business should not divide the figure of its forecasted revenue by two to arrive at its half-year revenue figures. Instead, the company reports its actual results for the half year. If the company wishes to demonstrate the cyclicality nature of its revenues, it may include by way of additional information, revenue for the 12 months up to the end of the interim reporting period and comparative information for the corresponding 12 months period.

2.1.4.6 Uneven cost

Costs that are incurred unevenly during an entity's financial year shall be anticipated or deferred for interim reporting purposes if, and only if, it is also appropriate to anticipate or defer that type of cost at the end of the financial year. Therefore, a cost that does not meet the definition of an asset should be expensed off immediately.

2.1.4.7 Use of estimates

Ind AS 34 requires that measurement procedures used in interim financial reports should be designed to ensure that the resulting information is reliable, with all material relevant financial information being appropriately disclosed. It nevertheless acknowledges that, while reasonable estimates are often used for both annual and interim financial reports, interim reports generally will require a greater use of estimation methods than annual financial reports.

Ind AS 34 does not include Appendix C to IAS 34 which provides a number of examples to the use of estimates in interim financial reports, which are reproduced below for reference:

Examples to the use of estimates for interim reporting purposes

[Appendix C to IAS 34]

Inventories: Full stock-taking and valuation procedures may not be required for inventories at interim dates, although it may be done at financial year end. It may be sufficient to make estimates at interim dates based on sales margins. Classifications of current and non-current assets and liabilities: Entities may do a more thorough investigation for classifying assets and liabilities as current or non-current at the end of annual reporting periods than at interim dates.

Provisions: Determination of the appropriate amount of a provision (such as a provision for warranties, environmental costs, and site restoration costs) may be complex and often costly and time-consuming. Entities sometimes engage outside experts to assist in the annual calculations. Making similar estimates at interim dates often entails updating of the prior annual provision rather than the engaging of outside experts to do a new calculation.

Pensions: IAS 19, *Employee Benefits* requires that an entity determine the present value of defined benefit obligations and the market value of plan assets at the end of each reporting period and encourages an entity to involve a professionally qualified actuary in measurement of the obligations. For interim reporting purposes, reliable measurement is often obtainable by extrapolation of the latest actuarial valuation.

Income taxes: Entities may calculate income tax expense and deferred income tax liability at annual dates by applying the tax rate for each individual jurisdiction to measures of income for each jurisdiction. IAS 34.B14 acknowledges that while that degree of precision is desirable at the end of interim reporting periods as well, it may not be achievable in all cases, and a weighted average of rates across jurisdictions or across categories of income is used if it is a reasonable approximation of the effect of using more specific rates.

Contingencies: The measurement of contingencies may involve the opinions of legal experts or other advisers. Formal reports from independent experts are sometimes obtained with respect to contingencies. Such opinions about litigation, claims, assessments, and other contingencies and uncertainties may or may not also be needed at interim dates.

Revaluations and fair value accounting: IAS 16, *Property, Plant and Equipment* allows an entity to choose as its accounting policy the revaluation model whereby items of property, plant and equipment are revalued to fair value. Similarly, IAS 40 Investment Property requires an entity to determine the fair value of investment property. For those measurements, an entity may rely on professionally-qualified valuers at the end of annual reporting periods, though not at the end of interim reporting periods.

Intercompany reconciliations: Some intercompany balances that are reconciled on a detailed level in preparing consolidated financial statements at financial year end might be reconciled at a less detailed level in preparing consolidated financial statements at an interim date.

Specialised industries: Because of complexity, costliness and time, interim period measurements in specialised industries might be less precise than at financial year-end. An example would be calculation of insurance reserves by insurance companies.

2.1.4.8 Transitional provisions

Unlike AS 25, Ind AS 34 does not provide any exemption from presentation of comparative financial information in the first interim financial statements presented by an entity. However, additional reconciliations would be required to be prepared and presented in accordance with Ind AS 101 when a first-time adopted presents an interim financial report (refer Chapter 3 for details).

2.1.4.9 Inventory losses and variations in manufacturing costs

The losses on inventories and variations in manufacturing costs should be recognised using the same principles as would have been used at the annual reporting date. Such losses/variations should not be deferred on the basis that they will be restored or absorbed by the annual reporting date.

2.1.4.10 Major periodic maintenance and periodic costs

The costs of periodic maintenance and overhaul costs are not anticipated for the purpose of interim financial reporting. However, if the requirement to recognise a provision is met at the end of the interim period, then it needs be considered in preparation of interim financial reporting.

> **Example**
>
> Company Pee Ltd. produces packed food using vegetables. The annual reporting period ends on 31 December. The production takes place from 1 January to 31 July and most of the labour work on a temporary basis. The plant is closed during the period 1 August to 31 December and some maintenance work is performed.
>
> The costs such as salary and wages of labour and other direct overheads are mainly incurred over the first six-month period, but other significant costs on cleaning and maintenance of the plant is incurred during the second six-month period. Depreciation is also a direct cost for production.
>
> In this example, maintenance and repair costs are recognised as they are incurred. Pee Ltd. does not recognise a provision for the costs to be incurred during the period of August to December.
>
> The depreciation cost is allocated on a systematic basis that reflects the pattern in which the asset is used in production. It may be appropriate to charge unit of production method instead of a straight line method since the plant will be non-operational for a period of 5 months.

2.1.4.11 Amortisation and depreciation charges

Intangible assets that have a finite useful life are often amortised on a straight-line basis. Therefore, it would not be appropriate to allocate amortisation to interim periods on the basis of seasonal revenues when an entity's accounting policy is to amortise intangible assets on a straight-line basis.

2.1.4.12 Employee benefits

Ind AS 19 requires that re-measurements should be recognised in the period in which they arise. Determining as to whether there is a need to re-measure the net defined benefit liability for interim reporting purposes requires judgement. Thus, the potential materiality of the re-measurements should be assessed in determining whether an updated valuation is necessary.

It is not necessary to obtain an updated actuarial valuation at each interim reporting date; however entities may choose to update their actuarial valuation at more frequent intervals than that required by Ind AS.

2.1.4.13 Employer payroll taxes and insurance contributions

If employer payroll taxes or contributions to government-sponsored insurance funds are assessed on an annual basis, the employer's related expense is recognised in interim periods using an estimated average annual effective payroll tax or contribution rate, even though a large portion of the payments may be made early in the financial year.

A common example could be an employer payroll tax or insurance contribution that is imposed up to a certain maximum level of earnings per employee. For higher income employees, the maximum income is reached before the end of the financial year, and the employer makes no further payments through the end of the year.

Example – Capped social contributions

An employer is required to pay 5% of annual salaries into an insurance fund. Contributions are capped at INR 5,00,000, which means that no contributions for salaries in excess of this amount are required. For an employee with a monthly salary of INR 40,000 (annual salary of 4,80,000) the employer would recognise an expense of INR 12,000 (6*40,000*5%) in its half year interim financial statements.

2.1.4.14 Reversal of impairment loss on goodwill

Ind AS 36, *Impairment of Assets* requires an entity to assess goodwill for impairment at the end of each reporting date and if required, to recognise an impairment loss. However, it prohibits reversal of impairment of goodwill. Similarly, Appendix A to Ind AS 25 prohibits reversal of impairment loss recognised in a previous interim period in respect of goodwill.

2.1.4.15 Taxation

Ind AS 34 states that income tax expense is recognised in each interim period based on the best estimate of the weighted average annual income tax rate expected for the full financial year. Amounts accrued for income tax expense in one interim period may have to be adjusted in a subsequent interim period of that financial year if the estimate of the annual income tax rate changes.

This is consistent with the basic concept set out in the standard that the same accounting recognition and measurement principles should be applied in an interim financial report as are applied in annual financial statements. Income taxes are assessed on an annual basis.

Therefore, interim period income tax expense is calculated by applying, to an interim period's pre-tax income, the tax rate that would be applicable to expected total annual earnings, that is, the estimated average annual effective income tax rate. That estimated average annual income tax rate would reflect the tax rate structure expected to be applicable to the full year's earnings including enacted or substantively enacted changes in the income tax rates scheduled to take effect later in the financial year. The estimated average annual income tax rate would be re-estimated on a year-to-date basis

To the extent practicable, a separate estimated average annual effective income tax rate is determined for each governing taxation law and applied individually to the interim period pre-tax income under such laws. Similarly, if different income tax rates apply to different categories of income (such as capital gains or income earned in particular industries), to the extent practicable a separate rate is applied to each individual category of interim period pre-tax income. While that degree of precision is desirable, it may not be achievable in all cases, and a weighted average of rates across such governing taxation laws or across categories of income is used if it is a reasonable approximation of the effect of using more specific rates.

Example: Calculation of tax for interim period

Guidance

Ind AS 34

30(c) income tax expense is recognised in each interim period based on the best estimate of the weighted average annual income tax rate expected for the full financial year. Amounts accrued for income tax expense in one interim period may have to be adjusted in a subsequent interim period of that financial year if the estimate of the annual income tax rate changes.

AS 25

29(c) income tax expense is recognised in each interim period based on the best estimate of the weighted average annual income tax rate expected for the full financial year. Amounts accrued for income tax expense in one interim period may have to be adjusted in a subsequent interim period of that financial year if the estimate of the annual income tax rate changes.

Example

An enterprise that reports quarterly has following estimated pre-tax income (after considering estimated depreciation on the probable acquisition of fixed assets during the year):

(INR in Lakhs)

Quarter I	(5)
Quarter II	50
Quarter III	70
Quarter IV	(20)
Estimated annual pre-tax income	**95**

Carried forward losses from earlier accounting periods, the deferred tax asset in respect of which was not recognised as it did not meet the requirements specified in Ind AS 12, is INR 35 lakhs at the beginning of the year. During this year, in view of the expected taxable income, this loss is expected to be set off there against.

Additional estimated depreciation as per tax laws as compared to the accounting depreciation after considering depreciation on probable capital expenditure on acquisition of fixed assets during the year is INR 10 lakhs.

Case I: If there are no other differences between accounting income and taxable income and if the applicable rate of tax is 30%, calculate the tax expense for each quarter.

(INR in Lakhs)

Estimated annual pre-tax income			**95**
Carried forward losses from earlier accounting periods			(35)
Additional estimated depreciation as per tax laws as compared to the accounting depreciation			(10)
Estimated taxable income on which tax payable			**50**
Applicable tax rate			30%
Estimated current tax expense for the year			**15.00**
Estimated deferred tax expense for the year (10 X 30%)			**3.00**
Weighted average annual effective tax rate (current tax) 15/95 X 100			15.79%
Weighted Average Annual Effective Tax Rate (deferred tax) 3/95 X 100			3.16%
Tax expense for the interim period			
	Current tax	**Deferred tax**	**Total**
Quarter I	(5) X 15.79% = (0.79)	(5) X 3.16% = (0.16)	(0.95)
Quarter II	50 X 15.79% = 7.90	50 X 3.16% = 1.58	9.48
Quarter III	70 X 15.79% = 11.05	70 X 3.16% = 2.21	13.26
Quarter IV	(20) X 15.79% = (3.16)	(20) X 3.16% = (0.63)	(3.79)
Total	**15**	**3**	**18**

Case II: If in above case estimated income for quarter III includes estimated capital gains of INR 20 lakhs, on which tax of 10% is applicable, calculate the tax expense for each quarter.

(INR in Lakhs)

Estimated annual pre-tax income			**95**
Carried forward losses from earlier accounting periods			(35)
Additional estimated depreciation as per tax laws as compared to the accounting depreciation			(10)
Estimated taxable income on which tax payable			**50**
Estimated current tax expense for the year			
On Capital Gains portion of annual income (20 X 10%)			2
On other income ((50-20) X 30%)			9
Total			**11**
Estimated deferred tax expense for the year (10 X 30%)			**3**
Weighted average annual effective tax rate (current tax) 2/20 X 100 %			10%
Weighted average annual effective tax rate (current tax) 9/75 X 100 %			12%
Weighted Average Annual Effective Tax Rate (deferred tax) 3/75 X 100 %			4%
Tax expense for the interim period			
	Current tax	Deferred tax	Total
Quarter I	(5) X 12% = (0.60)	(5) X 4% = (0.20)	(0.93)
Quarter II	50 X 12% = 6	50 X 4% = 2.00	9.33
Quarter III	50 X 12% = 6 20 X 10% = 2	70 X 4% = 2.00	9.33
Quarter IV	(20) X 12% = (2.40)	(20) X 4% = (0.80)	(3.73)

Total	11	3	14

2.1.4.16 *Current tax and deferred tax*

It is noteworthy that the standard does not differentiate between current income tax and deferred tax, referring only to income tax expense. Under a year-to-date basis, the estimated rate is based on tax rates and laws that are enacted or substantively enacted by the end of the interim period. The changes in legislation expected to occur before the end of the current year are not recognised in preparing the interim financial report.

Even if the disclosure requirements of interim results requires for a "net amount of tax expense", there is no requirement to split tax expense between current tax and deferred tax.

However in case split of tax expense is required, an appropriate method may be to split current and deferred tax based on the relative proportions expected at the annual reporting date. Same guidance has been provided in the guidance note on measurement of taxes in interim financials to AS 25.

Since the income tax expense is calculated by applying the estimated annual effective tax rate to the pre-tax profit or loss for the interim period, the resulting deferred tax asset or liability does not reflect the effect of temporary differences that do not impact profit or loss – e.g. temporary differences on the revaluation of property, plant and equipment.

2.1.4.17 *Impairment*

Ind AS 34 requires that the recognition and measurement of impairments (including reversals of impairments) should be determined by the same criteria that are applied at the year end, which are laid out in Ind AS 36. However, it is not necessary for an entity to perform detailed impairment calculations at each interim date. The entity should review its assets for indicators of significant impairment since the end of the most recent financial year to determine whether such calculations are required.

2.1.4.18 *Contingent lease payments*

Contingent lease payments can create legal or constructive obligations that are recognised as liabilities. If contingent lease payments are based on a particular threshold which is expected to be met, an obligation can arise in an interim period and therefore the entity should recognise a liability.

2.1.4.19 *Change in financial year-end*

A change in an entity's annual financial reporting period-end may impact the periods presented for interim reporting.

Example

ABC Limited has financial year starting from 1 July and ending on 30 June. After the end of financial year beginning on 1 July 2014 and ending on 30 June 2015, the company changed its financial year to make it year ended on 31 March. What comparative periods shall the company present for submitting along with quarterly results to SEBI under Regulation 33 for the year 2016-17, if the company does not take any exemption given by the SEBI circular dated 5 July 2016?

What are the comparative periods if the financial year was 1 January to 31 December and the previous year was for a period of 15 months from 1 January 2015 to 31 March 2016, as the company changed the financial year to make it March ended?

Solution:

FY 2016-17	Comparative financial results (When previous year is 9 months ended 31 March 2016)	Comparative financial results (When previous year is 15 months ended 31 March 2016)
Quarter I	Comparative figures for corresponding quarter of previous year (3 months ended 30 June 2015) – Not required to be given*	YTD comparative financial results: Six months period ended 30 June 2015**
Quarter II	YTD comparative financial results: Three months period ended 30 September 2015*	YTD comparative financial results: Nine months period ended 30 September 2015**
Quarter III	YTD comparative financial results: Six months period ended 31 December 2015*	YTD comparative financial results: Twelve months period ended 31 December 2015**

*Financial results of all quarters including quarter IV (i.e. quarter ending 31 March 2017) to include comparative financial results for the previous year which is 9 months ended 31 March 2016.

**Financial results of all quarters including quarter IV (i.e. quarter ending 31 March 2017) to include comparative financial results for the previous year which is 15 months ended 31 March 2016.

In these cases, the company shall disclose with due prominence, that the comparative amounts presented are not entirely comparable.

2.1.4.20 Consolidated financial statements

An interim financial report is prepared on a consolidated basis if the entity's most recent annual financial statements were consolidated statements. The parent's separate financial statements are not consistent or comparable with the consolidated statements in the most recent annual financial report.

If an entity's annual financial report included the parent's separate financial statements in addition to consolidated financial statements, this Standard neither requires nor prohibits the inclusion of the parent's separate statements in the entity's interim financial report.

> Where the entity has disposed of all its subsidiaries during the interim period, and it has no subsidiaries as at the end of the interim reporting period, it should prepare its interim financial report on a consolidated basis since it had subsidiaries at some point during the interim period.

2.1.4.21 Materiality

Ind AS 34 states that in deciding how to recognise, measure, classify, or disclose an item for interim financial reporting purposes, materiality shall be assessed in relation to the interim period financial data. In making assessments of materiality, it shall be recognised that interim measurements may rely on estimates to a greater extent than measurements of annual financial data.

Materiality is as defined in Ind AS 1, Presentation of Financial Statements as below:

Omissions or misstatements of items are material if they could, individually or collectively, influence the economic decisions that users make on the basis of the financial statements. Materiality depends on the size and nature of the omission or misstatement judged in the surrounding circumstances. The size or nature of the item, or a combination of both, could be the determining factor.

Therefore, it is important to apply the principle of materiality to ensure that an interim financial report includes all the information that is relevant to understanding the financial position and financial performance of the entity during the interim period.

2.1.4.22 Business combination

Business combinations during the reporting period

> If a business combination has occurred during the interim period, Ind AS 34 requires the entity to disclose all the details prescribed for annual financial statements by Ind AS 103, Business Combinations.
>
> To meet the objective specified in Ind AS 103, the acquirer shall disclose the

following information for each business combination that occurs during the reporting period:

(a) the name and a description of the acquiree.

(b) the acquisition date.

(c) the percentage of voting equity interests acquired.

(d) the primary reasons for the business combination and a description of how the acquirer obtained control of the acquiree.

(e) a qualitative description of the factors that make up the goodwill recognised, such as expected synergies from combining operations of the acquiree and the acquirer, intangible assets that do not qualify for separate recognition or other factors.

(f) the acquisition-date fair value of the total consideration transferred and the acquisition-date fair value of each major class of consideration, such as:

  (i) cash;

  (ii) other tangible or intangible assets, including a business or subsidiary of the acquirer;

  (iii) liabilities incurred, for example, a liability for contingent consideration; and

  (iv) equity interests of the acquirer, including the number of instruments or interests issued or issuable and the method of measuring the fair value of those instruments or interests.

(g) for contingent consideration arrangements and indemnification assets:

  (i) the amount recognised as of the acquisition date;

  (ii) a description of the arrangement and the basis for determining the amount of the payment; and

  (iii) an estimate of the range of outcomes (undiscounted) or, if a range cannot be estimated, that fact and the reasons why a range cannot be estimated. If the maximum amount of the payment is unlimited, the acquirer shall disclose that fact.

(h) for acquired receivables:

  (i) the fair value of the receivables;

  (ii) the gross contractual amounts receivable; and

  (iii) the best estimate at the acquisition date of the contractual cash flows not expected to be collected.

  The disclosures shall be provided by major class of receivable, such as loans, direct finance leases and any other class of receivables.

(i) the amounts recognised as of the acquisition date for each major class of assets acquired and liabilities assumed.

(j) for each contingent liability recognised in accordance with paragraph 23, the information required in paragraph 85 of Ind AS 37, Provisions, Contingent

Liabilities and Contingent Assets. If a contingent liability is not recognised because its fair value cannot be measured reliably, the acquirer shall disclose:

 (i) the information required by paragraph 86 of Ind AS 37; and

 (ii) the reasons why the liability cannot be measured reliably.

(k) the total amount of goodwill that is expected to be deductible for tax purposes.

(l) for transactions that are recognised separately from the acquisition of assets and assumption of liabilities in the business combination

 (i) a description of each transaction;

 (ii) how the acquirer accounted for each transaction;

 (iii) the amounts recognised for each transaction and the line item in the financial statements in which each amount is recognised; and

 (iv) if the transaction is the effective settlement of a pre-existing relationship, the method used to determine the settlement amount.

(m) the disclosure of separately recognised transactions required by (l) shall include the amount of acquisition-related costs and, separately, the amount of those costs recognised as an expense and the line item or items in the statement of profit and loss in which those expenses are recognised. The amount of any issue costs not recognised as an expense and how they were recognised shall also be disclosed.

(n) in a bargain purchase:

 (i) the amount of any gain recognised in other comprehensive income;

 (ii) the amount of any gain directly recognised in equity ;and

 (iii) a description of the reasons why the transaction resulted in a gain in case of (i) above.

(o) for each business combination in which the acquirer holds less than 100 per cent of the equity interests in the acquiree at the acquisition date:

 (i) the amount of the non-controlling interest in the acquiree recognised at the acquisition date and the measurement basis for that amount; and

(ii) for each non-controlling interest in an acquiree measured at fair value, the valuation technique(s) and significant inputs used to measure that value.

(p) in a business combination achieved in stages:

(i) the acquisition-date fair value of the equity interest in the acquiree held by the acquirer immediately before the acquisition date; and

(ii) the amount of any gain or loss recognised as a result of remeasuring to fair value the equity interest in the acquiree held by the acquirer before the business combination (see paragraph 42) and the line item in the statement of profit and loss in which that gain or loss is recognised.

(q) the following information:

(i) the amounts of revenue and profit or loss of the acquiree since the acquisition date included in the consolidated statement of profit and loss for the reporting period; and

(ii) the revenue and profit or loss of the combined entity for the current reporting period as though the acquisition date for all business combinations that occurred during the year had been as of the beginning of the annual reporting period.

If disclosure of any of the information required by this subparagraph is impracticable, the acquirer shall disclose that fact and explain why the disclosure is impracticable. This Ind AS uses the term 'impracticable' with the same meaning as in Ind AS 8, Accounting Policies, Changes in Accounting Estimates and Errors.

2.1.4.23 Business combinations after the reporting period

Ind AS 103 states that if the acquisition date of a business combination is after the end of the reporting period but before the financial statements are approved for issue, the acquirer shall disclose the information required by Ind AS 103 unless the initial accounting for the business combination is incomplete at the time the financial statements are approved for issue. In that situation, the acquirer shall describe which disclosures could not be made and the reasons why they cannot be made.

Illustrative examples in IAS 34

The illustrative examples in IAS 34 provide guidance on certain key issues. Though the examples have not been included in Ind AS 34, they will be relevant to understand the practical issues.

Given below are the examples:

7.1 Employer payroll taxes and insurance contributions

If employer payroll taxes or contributions to government-sponsored insurance funds are assessed on an annual basis, the employer's related expense is recognised in interim periods using an estimated average annual effective payroll tax or contribution rate, even though a large portion of the payments may be made early in the financial year. A common example is an employer payroll tax or insurance contribution that is imposed up to a certain maximum level of earnings per employee. For higher income employees, the maximum income is reached before the end of the financial year, and the employer makes no further payments through the end of the year. [IAS 34.B1]

7.2 Major planned periodic maintenance or overhaul

The cost of a planned major periodic maintenance or overhaul or other seasonal expenditure that is expected to occur late in the year is not anticipated for interim reporting purposes, unless an event has caused the entity to have a legal or constructive obligation. The mere intention or necessity to incur expenditure related to the future is not sufficient to give rise to an obligation. [IAS 34.B2]

7.3 Provisions

A provision is recognised when an entity has no realistic alternative but to make a transfer of economic benefits as a result of an event that has created a legal or constructive obligation. The amount of the obligation is adjusted upward or downward, with a corresponding loss or gain recognised in profit or loss, if the entity's best estimate of the amount of the obligation changes.

IAS 34 requires that an entity apply the same criteria for recognising and measuring a provision at an interim date as it would at the end of its financial year. The existence or non-existence of an obligation to transfer benefits is not a function of the length of the reporting period. It is a question of fact. [IAS 34.B3 & B4]

7.4 Year-end bonuses

The nature of year-end bonuses varies widely. Some are earned simply by continued employment during a time period. Some bonuses are earned based on a monthly, quarterly, or annual measure of operating result. They may be purely discretionary, contractual, or based on years of historical precedent.

A bonus is anticipated for interim reporting purposes if, and only if: [IAS 34.B5 & B6]

- the bonus is a legal obligation, or past practice would make the bonus a constructive obligation and the entity has no realistic alternative but to make the payments; and
- a reliable estimate of the obligation can be made.

IAS 19 *Employee Benefits* provides guidance on the application of the recognition rules to year-end bonuses.

7.5 Contingent lease payments

Contingent lease payments can be an example of a legal or constructive obligation that is recognised as a liability. If a lease provides for contingent payments based on the lessee achieving a certain level of annual sales, an obligation can arise in the interim period of the financial year before the required annual level of sales has been achieved, if that required level of sales is expected to be achieved and the entity, therefore, has no realistic alternative but to make the future lease payment. [IAS 34.B7]

7.6 Intangible assets

Entities are required to apply the definition and recognition criteria for an intangible asset in the same way in an interim period as in an annual period. Costs incurred before the recognition criteria for an intangible asset are met are recognised as an expense. Costs incurred after the specific point in time at which the criteria are met are recognised as part of the cost of an intangible asset. 'Deferring' costs as assets in an interim statement of financial position in the hope that the recognition criteria will be met later in the financial year is not justified. [IAS 34.B8]

7.7 Pensions

The pension cost for an interim period is calculated on a year-to-date basis by using the actuarially-determined pension cost rate at the end of the prior financial year, adjusted for significant market fluctuations since that time and for significant curtailments, settlements or other significant one- time events. [IAS 34.B9]

7.8 Vacations, holidays, and other short-term compensated absences

Accumulating compensated absences are those that are carried forward and can be used in future periods if the current period's entitlement is not used in full. IAS 19 *Employee Benefits* requires that an entity measure the expected cost of and obligation for accumulating compensated absences at the amount the entity expects to pay as a result of the unused entitlement that has accumulated at the end of the reporting period. That principle is also applied at the end of interim financial reporting periods. Conversely, an entity recognises no expense or liability for non-accumulating compensated absences at the end of an interim reporting period, just as it recognises none at the end of an annual reporting period. [IAS 34.B10]

7.9 Other planned but irregularly occurring costs

An entity's budget may include certain costs expected to be incurred irregularly during the financial year, such as charitable contributions and employee-training costs. Those costs generally are discretionary, even though they are planned and tend to recur from year to year. Recognising an obligation at the end of an interim financial reporting period for such costs that have not yet been incurred generally is not consistent with the definition of a liability. [IAS 34.B11]

7.10 Contractual or anticipated purchase price changes

Volume rebates or discounts and other contractual changes in the prices of raw materials, labour, or other purchased goods and services are anticipated in interim periods, by both the payer and the recipient, if it is probable that they have been earned or will take effect. Thus, contractual rebates and discounts are anticipated, but discretionary rebates and discounts are not anticipated because the definitions of asset and liability (requiring *control* over resources to be received, or an *obligation* to pay out resources) would not be met. [IAS 34.B23]

7.11 Depreciation and amortisation

Depreciation and amortisation charges for an interim period are based only on assets owned during that interim period. They should not take into account asset acquisitions or disposals planned for later in the financial year. [IAS 34.B24]

7.12 Inventories

7.12.1 Measurement of inventories – general

Inventories are measured for interim financial reporting using the same principles as at financial year end. IAS 2 *Inventories* establishes requirements for recognising and measuring inventories. Inventories pose particular problems at the end of any financial reporting period because of the need to determine inventory quantities, costs and net realisable values. Nonetheless, the same measurement principles are applied for inventories at the end of interim reporting periods. To save cost and time, entities often use estimates to measure inventories at interim dates to a greater extent than at the end of annual reporting periods. The following sections set out examples of how to apply the net realisable value test at an interim date and how to treat manufacturing variances at interim dates. [IAS 34.B25]

7.12.2 Net realisable value of inventories

The net realisable value of inventories is determined by reference to selling prices and related costs to complete and dispose at interim dates. [IAS 34.B26]

An entity will reverse a write-down to net realisable value in a subsequent reporting period only if it would be appropriate to do so at the end of the financial year. [IAS 34.B26]

7.12.3 Interim period manufacturing cost variances

Price, efficiency, spending and volume variances of a manufacturing entity are recognised in income at the end of interim reporting periods to the same extent that those variances are recognised in income at financial year end. Deferral of variances that are expected to be absorbed by the year end is not appropriate because it could result in reporting inventory at the interim date at more or less than its portion of the actual cost of manufacture. [IAS 34.B28]

7.13 Foreign currency translation gains and losses

Foreign currency translation gains and losses are measured for interim financial reporting using the same principles as at financial year end. [IAS 34.B29]

IAS 21 *The Effects of Changes in Foreign Exchange Rates* specifies how to translate the financial statements for foreign operations into the presentation currency, including guidelines for using average or closing foreign exchange rates and guidelines for including the resulting adjustments in profit or loss or in other comprehensive income. Consistent with IAS 21, the actual average and closing rates for the interim period are used. Entities do not anticipate changes in foreign exchange rates in the remainder of the current financial year when translating foreign operations at an interim date. [IAS 34.B30]

If IAS 21 requires that translation adjustments are recognised as income or as expenses in the period in which they arise, that principle is applied during each interim period. Entities do not defer some foreign currency translation adjustments at an interim date if the adjustment is expected to reverse before the end of the financial year. [IAS 34.B31]

7.14 Interim financial reporting in hyperinflationary economies

Interim financial reports in hyperinflationary economies are prepared following the same principles as at financial year end. IAS 29 *Financial Reporting in Hyperinflationary Economies* requires that the financial statements of an entity that reports in the currency of a hyperinflationary economy be stated in terms of the measuring unit current at the end of the reporting period, and the gain or loss on the net monetary position is included in net income. Also, comparative financial data reported for prior periods is restated to the current measuring unit. [IAS 34.B32 & B33]

Entities are required to follow the same principles at interim dates, thereby presenting all interim data in the measuring unit as of the end of the interim period, with the resulting gain or loss on the net monetary position included in the interim period's net income. Entities should not annualise the recognition of the gain or loss. Nor do they use an estimated annual inflation rate in preparing an interim financial report in a hyperinflationary economy. [IAS 34.B34]

2.2 CONDENSED OR COMPLETE INTERIM FINANCIAL STATEMENTS

If an entity presents the minimum required information for interim financial statements prescribed by Ind AS 34, the resultant financial statements are described as 'condensed'. Ind AS 34 also permits the entities to include a complete set of financial statements in their interim financial reports. If an entity chooses to adopt this alternative, the form and content of the financial statements must confirm to the requirements of Ind AS 1, *Presentation of financial statements* for a complete set of financial statements, in addition to complying with the requirements of Ind AS 34. It may also be noted that the requirements of Ind AS 1 are generally not applicable to condensed interim financial statements.

2.2.1 Items to appear on the face of the condensed financial statements

Ind AS 34 requires that if an entity publishes a set of condensed financial statements in its interim financial report, those condensed statements shall include, at a minimum, each of the headings and subtotals that were included in its most recent annual financial statements and the selected explanatory notes as required by this Standard. Additional line items or notes shall be included if their omission would make the condensed interim financial statements misleading.

The phrase 'each of the headings and subtotals, seem to imply that not all of the line items that were presented in the most recent annual financial statements are necessarily required. However, it would be appropriate to include additional line items if their omission would make the condensed interim financial statements misleading. Therefore, a new category of asset, liability, income, expense, equity or cash flow arising for the first time in the interim items that were included in the entity's most recent annual financial statements. Also, Ind AS period may require presentation as an additional line item in the condensed financial statements.

2.2.2 Selected explanatory notes

Ind AS 34 requires that an interim financial report should contain selected explanatory notes. Further, entities are not required to repeat or provide insignificant updates to information already reported in the most recent annual financial statements.

Explanatory notes in condensed financial statements

Explanatory notes to the condensed financial statement include the following information if it is material, unless it is disclosed elsewhere in the interim financial report:

Ind AS 34 requires that the following information should be disclosed in the notes to the interim financial statements, if material to an understanding of the interim period and if not disclosed elsewhere in the interim financial report. The information shall normally be reported on a financial year-to-date basis:

(a) a statement that the same accounting policies and methods of computation are followed in the interim financial statements as were followed in the most recent annual financial statements or, if those policies or methods have been changed, a description of the nature and effect of the change;

(b) explanatory comments about the seasonality or cyclicality of interim operations;

(c) the nature and amount of items affecting assets, liabilities, equity, net income or cash flows, that are unusual because of their size, nature or incidence;

(d) the nature and amount of changes in estimates of amounts reported in prior interim periods of the current financial year, or changes in estimates of amounts reported in prior financial years, if those changes have a material effect in the current interim period;

(e) issuances, repurchases and repayments of debt and equity securities;

(f) dividends paid (aggregate or per share), separately for ordinary shares and other shares;

(g) the following segment information:

  (i) revenues from external customers, if included in the measure of segment profit or loss reviewed by the chief operating decision maker or otherwise regularly provided to the chief operating decision maker;

  (ii) intersegment revenues, if included in the measure of segment profit or loss reviewed by the chief operating decision maker or otherwise regularly provided to the chief operating decision maker;

  (iii) a measure of segment profit or loss;

  (iv) total assets for which there has been a material change from the amount disclosed in the last annual financial statements;

  (v) a description of differences from the last annual financial statements in the basis of segmentation or in the basis of measurement of segment profit or loss; and

  (vi) a reconciliation of the total of the reportable segments' measures of profit or loss to the entity's profit or loss before tax expense (tax income) and discontinued operations. However, if an entity allocates to reportable segments items such as tax expense (tax income), the entity may reconcile the total of the segments' measures of profit or loss to profit or loss after those items. Material reconciling items should be separately identified and described in that reconciliation;

(h) material events subsequent to the end of the interim period that have not been reflected in the interim financial statements;

(i) the effect of changes in the composition of the entity during the interim period, including business combinations, obtaining or losing control of subsidiaries and long-term investments, restructurings and discontinued operations; and

(j) changes in contingent liabilities or contingent assets since the end of the last reporting period.

Ind AS 34 provides the following examples of the kinds of disclosures that are required:

(a) the write-down of inventories to net realisable value and the reversal of such a write-down;

(b) recognition of a loss from the impairment of financial assets, property, plant and equipment, intangible assets, assets arising from contracts with customers, or other assets, and the reversal of such an impairment loss;

(c) the reversal of any provisions for the costs of restructuring;

(d) acquisitions and disposals of items of property, plant and equipment;

(e) commitments for the purchase of property, plant and equipment;

(f) litigation settlements;

(g) corrections of prior period errors; changes in the business or economic circumstances that affect the fair value of the entity's financial assets and financial liabilities, whether those assets or liabilities are recognised at fair value or amortised cost;

(h) any loan default or breach of a loan agreement that has not been remedied on or before the end of the reporting period;

(i) related party transactions;

(j) transfers between levels of the fair value hierarchy used in measuring the fair value of financial instruments;

(k) changes in the classification of financial assets as a result of a change in the purpose or use of those assets; and

(l) changes in contingent liabilities or contingent assets.

While making disclosures of related party transactions, care should be taken in determining the level of disclosure that is necessary in condensed financial statements. If the nature and amounts of related party transactions are consistent with those previously reported, then no disclosure may be necessary in the condensed financial statements. However, if related party transactions are significant, then disclosure may be necessary even if the nature and amounts of those transactions are consistent with previous periods.

Other examples of items that may be material to an understanding of the interim period include:

- changes in significant judgements and assumptions made by management, as well as areas of estimation uncertainty;
- disclosures required by Ind AS 107, if changes in an entity's financial risk management objectives and policies or in the nature and extent of risks arising from financial instruments occur during the interim period;

Any significant changes in estimates made during the final interim period are disclosed in the annual financial statements, unless separate interim financial statements are published for this period.

Additional disclosures are required in the interim financial statements in the year that an entity adopts IFRS.

2.3 SIGNIFICANT DIFFERENCES WITH AS 25, INTERIM FINANCIAL REPORTING

AS 25, notified under Companies (Accounting Standards) Rules, 2006 is applicable to entities to which Ind ASs is not applicable.

2.3.1 Interim financial report – Definition

Under AS 25, a condensed interim financial report should contain the following:

- Condensed balance sheet
- Condensed statement of profit and loss,
- Condensed cash flow statement, and
- Selected explanatory notes and key disclosures such as EPS.

There is no requirement to prepare Statement of Changes in Equity and Other Comprehensive Income under AS 25.

2.3.2 Inclusion of separate financial statements of parent in interim financial report

Under AS 25, if an entity's annual financial report included the consolidated financial statements in addition to the separate financial statements, the interim financial report should include both the consolidated financial statements and separate financial statements, complete or condensed. However, Ind AS 34 states that if the entity's interim report has been prepared on a consolidated basis, it neither requires nor prohibits the inclusion of the parent's separate statements.

2.3.3 Change in accounting policy

Ind AS 34 states that a change in accounting policy, other than one for which the transition is specified by a new Ind AS, should be reflected by:

(a) restating the financial statements of prior interim periods of the current financial year and the comparable interim periods of any prior financial years that will be restated in the annual financial statements in accordance with Ind AS 8; or

(b) when it is impracticable to determine the cumulative effect at the beginning of the financial year of applying a new accounting policy to all prior periods, adjusting the financial statements of prior interim periods of the current financial year, and comparable interim periods of prior financial years to apply the new accounting policy prospectively from the earliest date practicable.

However, AS 25 states that a change in accounting policy, other than one for which the transition is specified by an Accounting Standard, should be reflected by restating the financial statements of prior interim periods of the current financial year. It also states that one objective of the preceding principle is to ensure that a single accounting policy is applied to a particular class of transactions throughout an entire financial year. The effect of the principle stated above is to require that within the current financial year any change in accounting policy be applied retrospectively to the beginning of the financial year.

It may also be noted that SEBI Listing Regulations refer to AS 5, Net profit or loss for the period, Prior Period Items and Changes in Accounting Policies in case of change in accounting policy. AS 5 states that any change in an accounting policy which has a material effect should be disclosed. The impact of, and the adjustments resulting from, such change, if material, should be shown in the financial statements of the period in which such change is made, to reflect the effect of such change. Where the effect of such change is not ascertainable, wholly or in part, the fact should be indicated. If a change is made in the accounting policies which has no material effect on the financial statements for the current period but which is reasonably expected to have a material effect in later periods, the fact of such change should be appropriately disclosed in the period in which the change is adopted. Therefore, AS 5 does not permit restatement of prior interim periods of the current financial year.

2.3.4 Disclosure of compliance with accounting standards

Ind AS 34 requires that if an entity's interim financial report is in compliance with this Standard, that fact shall be disclosed. An interim financial report shall not be described as complying with Ind ASs unless it complies with all of the requirements of Ind ASs.

However, AS 25 does not contain any specific requirement for providing explicit statement of compliance with AS 25.

2.3.5 Reversal of impairment loss on goodwill

Appendix A (Para-4) to Ind AS states that:

> *"Ind AS 36 paragraph 124 states that 'An impairment loss recognised for goodwill shall not be reversed in a subsequent period.' "*

Therefore, an entity shall not reverse an impairment loss recognised in a previous interim period in respect of goodwill. An entity shall not extend this accounting principle by analogy to other areas of potential conflict between Ind AS 34 and other Indian Accounting Standards.

AS 25 does not contain any such prohibition. Reference may be made to AS 28, Impairment of Assets, which permits reversal of impairment on goodwill in a situation where the impairment loss was caused by a specific external event of an exceptional nature that is not expected to recur; and subsequent external events have occurred that reverse the effect of that event.

2.3.6 Transitional provisions

Ind AS 34 does not provide any exemption from presentation of comparative financial information in the first interim financial statements presented by an entity. Reference should be made to Chapter 3, First time adoption and challenges in preparation of interim results as per Ind AS 34 for preparation of additional reconciliation requirements, if a first-time adopted presents an interim financial report under Ind AS 34 for part of the period covered by its first Ind AS financial statements.

Whereas, AS 25 as part of transitional provisions states a on the first occasion that an interim financial report is presented in accordance with this Standard, the following need not be presented in respect of all the interim periods of the current financial year:

(a) comparative statements of profit and loss for the comparable interim periods (current and year-to-date) of the immediately preceding financial year; and

(b) comparative cash flow statement for the comparable year-to-date period of the immediately preceding financial year.

2.4 SIGNIFICANT DIFFERENCES WITH IAS 34, INTERIM FINANCIAL REPORTING

Under IAS 34, entities have an option to either follow the single statement approach or the two statements approach, i.e. for preparation of statement of profit or loss and other comprehensive income. If an entity presents items of profit or loss in a separate statement in its annual financial statement, it will also be required to present interim condensed information in a separate statement. Further, if an entity presents a separate statement of profit or loss, then basic and diluted EPS should be presented in that statement.

Ind AS 1 allows only the single statement approach, it requires that an entity shall present a single statement of profit and loss, with profit or loss and other comprehensive income presented in two sections. Under Ind AS 34, it should present basic and diluted EPS for the interim period in the statement that presents the components of profit or loss for that period.

2.5 IND AS 34 – INTERIM FINANCIAL REPORTING

Scope

- Does not mandate which entities are required to publish interim financial reports.
- Applies to entities required by governments, securities regulators, stock exchanges, and accountancy bodies or that elect to publish interim financial reports.

Definitions

- **Interim period:** financial reporting period shorter than a full financial year
- **Interim financial report:** either a complete set of financial statements (as described in Ind AS 1) or a set of condensed financial statements for an interim period.

Minimum components of an interim financial report

a. a condensed balance sheet;
b. a condensed statement of profit and loss;
c. a condensed statement of changes in equity;
d. a condensed statement of cash flows; and
e. selected explanatory notes

If a complete set is published, the form and content shall conform to the requirements of Ind AS 1.

If condensed set is published, the condensed statements to include at a minimum

- headings and subtotals included in its most recent annual financial statements;
- the selected explanatory notes as required by this Standard;
- additional line items or notes if their omission would make the condensed interim financial statements misleading;
- basic and diluted earnings per share if the entity is within the scope of Ind AS 33.

Periods to be presented

Current periods (Ind AS 34)	Comparative periods (Ind AS 34)	SEBI requirements – Current periods (First year of Ind AS implementation)	SEBI requirements – Comparative periods (First year of Ind AS implementation)
Balance sheet as of the end of the current interim period.	A comparative balance sheet as of the end of the immediately preceding financial year.	Statement of assets and liabilities as of the end of the second and fourth quarters	A comparative statement of assets and liabilities as of the immediately preceding financial year is mandatory for fourth quarter only.
Statements of profit and loss for the current interim period and cumulatively for the current financial year to date.	Comparative statements of profit and loss for the comparable interim periods (current and year-to-date) of the immediately preceding financial year.	Financial results for the current interim period and cumulatively for the current financial year to date.	Comparative financial results for the comparable interim periods (current and year-to-date) of the immediately preceding financial year. Comparative financial results for the previous accounting year are mandatory for fourth quarter only.
Statement of changes in equity cumulatively for the current financial year to date.	A comparative statement for the comparable year-to-date period of the immediately preceding financial year.	Not required	Not required
Statement of cash flows cumulatively for the current financial year to date.	A comparative statement for the comparable year-to-date period of the immediately preceding financial year.	Not required	Not required

Minimum components of an interim financial report

Significant events and transactions

- The interim financial report is intended to provide an update on the latest complete set of annual financial statements, hence focuses on new activities, events, and circumstances and does not duplicate information previously reported.
- Disclose significant events and transactions since the end of the last annual reporting period.

Recognition and measurement

Accounting policy

- Same accounting policies to be applied as are applied in its annual financial statements
- except for accounting policy changes that are to be reflected in the next annual financial statements.
- Like annual period, at the interim date also, tests of future economic benefits to be applied for assets and an existing obligation a must be represented by a liability.
- Tax expense is recognised based on the best estimate of the weighted average annual income tax rate expected for the full financial year.

Revenues received seasonally, cyclically, or occasionally

Not be anticipated or deferred as of an interim date if anticipation or deferral would not be appropriate at the end of the financial year.

Recognise such revenues when they occur.

Costs incurred unevenly during the financial year

Anticipated or deferred if, and only if, it is also appropriate to anticipate or defer that type of cost at the end of the financial year.

Estimates

Interim reports generally require a greater use of estimation methods than annual financial reports.

Accounting policy

Restatement of previously reported interim periods

- If accounting policy is changed (other than one for which the transition is specified by a new Ind AS)
  - restate the financial statements of:
  - prior interim periods of the current financial year and
- the comparable interim periods of any prior financial years

if the annual financial statements will be restated in accordance with Ind AS 8.

- Adjust the financial statements of prior interim periods of the current financial year, and comparable interim periods of prior financial years to apply the new accounting policy prospectively from the earliest date practicable
  - when it is impracticable to determine the cumulative effect at the beginning of the financial year of applying a new accounting policy to all prior periods.

Impairment (Appendix A)

- Ind AS 36 does not allow the reversal of an impairment loss recognised for goodwill in a subsequent period'
- Hence an impairment loss recognised in a previous interim period in respect of goodwill not to be reversed.

Other provisions

- Disclose the fact that the interim financial statements comply with Ind AS 34.
- If an interim financial report is described as complying with Ind ASs, all of the requirements of Ind ASs to be complied.
- Materiality to be assessed in relation to the interim period financial data, in deciding how to recognise, measure, classify, or disclose an item for interim financial reporting purposes.
- The nature and amount of changes in estimates reported in prior interim periods or reported in prior financial years to be disclosed.

Chapter 3

First time adoption and challenges in preparation of interim results as per Ind AS 34

Clause 33 of the SEBI Listing regulations deals with preparation and presentation of interim financial information for companies whose equity shares are listed on a recognised stock exchange in India. Among other matters, Clause 33 also requires that the quarterly and year-to-date results will be prepared in accordance with the recognition and measurement principle laid down in AS 25, Interim financial reporting or Ind AS 34, Interim Financial reporting, as applicable.

SEBI has prescribed a specific format for submission of financial results and will be in compliance with the recognition and measurement principles of AS 25/Ind AS 34. An entity, may on voluntary basis, prepare full interim financial statements (condensed or complete) which comply with recognition and measurement principles, presentation and disclosure principles of Ind AS 34. This will be in addition to interim financial results required to be prepared and filed with stock exchanges by listed companies.

In accordance with the principles of Ind AS 101, an entity is required to apply Ind AS 101 in each interim financial report that it presents in accordance with Ind AS 34 for part of the period covered by its first Ind AS financial statements.

If a first time adopter presents an interim financial report under Ind AS 34 for part of the period covered by its first Ind AS financial statements, the following are required to be presented in addition to requirements of Ind AS 34:

(i) a reconciliation of its equity in accordance with previous GAAP at the end of that comparable interim period to its equity under Ind ASs at that date; and

(ii) a reconciliation to its total comprehensive income in accordance with Ind ASs for that comparable interim period (current and year to date). The starting point for that reconciliation shall be total comprehensive income in accordance with previous GAAP for that period or, if an entity did not report such a total, profit or loss in accordance with previous GAAP.

If an entity changes its accounting policies or its use of the exemptions contained in Ind AS 101, it shall explain the changes in each such interim financial report.

In addition to the reconciliations required above, an entity's first interim financial report in accordance with Ind AS 34 for part of the period covered by its first Ind AS financial statements shall include the following reconciliations:

- reconciliations of its equity reported in accordance with previous GAAP to its equity in accordance with Ind ASs for both of the following dates:
  - (i) the date of transition to Ind ASs; and
  - (ii) the end of the latest period presented in the entity's most recent annual financial statements in accordance with previous GAAP.
- a reconciliation to its total comprehensive income in accordance with Ind ASs for the latest period in the entity's most recent annual financial statements. The starting point for that reconciliation shall be total comprehensive income in accordance with previous GAAP

Further an entity's first interim financial report should also contain the following:

- Explanation of significant adjustments to the statement of cash flows
- Explanation of errors made under previous GAAP, whether correction of errors should have been presented separately from changes in accounting policies.

3.1 EXEMPTION FROM RECONCILIATION

SEBI circular dated 5 July 2016 provides exemption from preparation of reconciliations specified by Ind AS 101. It states as below:

The listed entities in order to comply with the requirements of paragraph 32 of Ind AS 101 – First time Adoption of Ind AS, shall provide a reconciliation of its equity and net profit/loss, in the following manner, for enabling the investors to understand the material adjustments to the Balance Sheet and Statement of Profit and Loss on account of transition from the previous Indian GAAP to Ind-AS:

(i) Reconciliation of its equity for the previous year ended March 31, 2016, shall be provided while submitting the Audited Yearly Balance Sheet for the period ended March 31, 2017.

Reconciliation of its equity for the previous year ended March 31, 2016, shall be provided in case the listed entity intends to provide the same while submitting the Unaudited/Audited Ind-AS compliant Half-Yearly Balance Sheet for the period ended September 30, 2016.

(ii) Reconciliation of its net profit/loss as mentioned in the Unaudited/Audited quarterly financial results shall be provided only for the corresponding quarter of the previous year.

Therefore, the following position emerges:

- Profit reconciliation required for comparative periods
- Equity reconciliation for comparative period mandatory only for annual reporting.

Reconciliations required to be included in interim financial report under Ind AS 34

Quarter	**Reconciliation of total comprehensive income**	**Reconciliation of equity**
Quarter ending June 2016	Reconciliation of total comprehensive income for quarter ending 30 June 2015 and year ending March 2016	Reconciliation of equity as on 30 June 2015, as on 1 April 2015 and as on 31 March 2016
Quarter ending September 2016	Reconciliation of total comprehensive income for quarter ending 30 September 2015, year-to-date ending September 2015	Reconciliation of equity as on 30 September 2015
Quarter ending 31 December 2016	Reconciliation of total comprehensive income for quarter ending 31 December 2015, year-to-date ending December 2015	Reconciliation of equity as on 31 December 2015
Quarter ending 31 March 2017	Reconciliation of total comprehensive income for quarter ending 31 March 2016 and year ending 31 March 2016*	Reconciliation of equity as on 1 April 2015* and as on 31 March 2016*

*To be included in entity's first Ind AS financial statements (Paragraph 24(a) and 24(b) of Ind AS 101)

A listed company which adopts Ind AS in preparation of its annual financial statements will start publishing Ind AS financial information from the first quarter of the financial year. Therefore, companies covered in Phase I, i.e. from the financial year commencing on 1 April 2016 will be required to prepare financial results for the quarter ended 30 June 2016 in accordance with Ind AS 34. These results will also contain comparative information in accordance with Ind AS.

3.2 TRANSITIONAL PROVISIONS – ILLUSTRATIONS

A company is adopting Ind AS from financial year 2016-17 and its date of transition to Ind AS is 1 April 2015. If the company publishes quarterly reports in accordance with Ind AS 34, what reconciliations are to be presented in its interim reports for various quarters of the year ending 31 March 2017 and in its first Ind AS financial statements?

Quarter	**Reconciliation of equity**	**Reconciliation of comprehensive income or profit or loss**	**Explanation of material adjustments to statement of cash flows**
Quarter 1			
1 April 2015	Yes		
31 March 2016	Yes		Yes
30 June 2016 • 3 Months ended	Yes	 Yes	
Quarter 2			
30 September 2015 • 3 Months ended • 6 months ended	Yes	 Yes Yes	
Quarter 3			
31 December 2015 • 3 Months ended • 9 months ended	Yes	 Yes Yes	
First Ind AS financial statements			
1 April 2015	Yes		
31 March 2016	Yes	Yes	Yes

In this example, if the company is preparing Ind AS compliant financial results for various quarters for the year ending 31 March 2017 under Regulation 33 of the SEBI (Listing Obligation and Disclosure) Requirements, 2015:

(a) What are the reconciliations to be given mandatorily as per the SEBI circular dated 5 July 2016?

Quarter	Reconciliation of equity	Reconciliation of comprehensive income or profit or loss	Explanation of material adjustments to statement of cash flows
Quarter 1			
1 April 2015			
31 March 2016			
30 June 2016 • 3 Months ended		 Yes	
Quarter 2			
30 September 2015 • 3 Months ended • 6 months ended		 Yes Yes	
Quarter 3			
31 December 2015 • 3 Months ended • 9 months ended		 Yes Yes	
First Ind AS financial statements			
1 April 2015	Refer note below		
31 March 2016	Yes	Yes	Refer note below

Note: Though a company is not required to prepare reconciliation of equity as on the date of transition and explanation of material adjustments to statement of cash flow in annual financial statements prepared under Regulation 33 to be submitted to SEBI, the aforesaid reconciliation and explanation are required in the financial statements prepared under the Companies Act, 2013, for compliance with the provisions of AS 101, First-time Adoption of Indian Accounting Standards.

(b) What are the Ind AS compliant results including comparatives to be given mandatorily as per the SEBI circular dated 5 July 2016?

Quarter	Balance sheet/Statement of Assets and Liabilities	Financial results
Quarter I		3 months ended 30 June 2016 **Mandatory comparative period:** 3 months ended 30 June 2015 **Non-mandatory comparative period:** 3 months ended 31 March 2016 Year ended 31 March 2016
Quarter II	As at 30 September 2016 **Comparative periods:** Not mandatory - As at 31 March 2016	3 months ended 30 September 2016 6 months ended 30 September 2016 **Mandatory comparative period:** 3 months ended 30 June 2016 3 months ended 30 September 2015 6 months ended 30 September 2015 **Non-mandatory comparative period:** Year ended 31 March 2016
Quarter III		3 months ended 31 December 2016 9 months ended 31 December 2016 **Comparative periods:** 3 months ended 30 September 2015 3 months ended 31 December 2015 9 months ended 31 December 2015 **Non-mandatory comparative period:** Year ended 31 March 2016
Quarter IV	No exemption given	No exemption given

Please refer the Annexure at the end of this chapter for the financial results of some sample companies.

Annexures

Annexure I: Financial results

RELIANCE CAPITAL LIMITED [NBFC]

Statement of Standalone Unaudited Financial Results for the quarter and half year ended September 30, 2016

PART I (INR in crore except per share data)

Sr. No.	Particulars	Quarter Ended			Half year ended		Year ended
		30-Sep-16	30-Jun-16	30-Sep-15	30-Sep-16	30-Sep-15	31-Mar-16
		Unaudited	Unaudited	Unaudited	Unaudited	Unaudited	Audited
1	**Income from operations**						
	(a) Income from operations	860	928	837	1 788	1 740	3 945
	(b) Other operating income	38	56	33	94	64	131
	Total income from operations	**898**	**984**	**870**	**1 882**	**1 804**	**4 076**
2	**Expenses**						
	(a) Cost of materials consumed	-	-	-			-
	(b) Purchases of stock-in-trade	-	-	-	-	-	-
	(c) Changes in inventories of finished goods. work-in-progress	-	-	-	-	-	-
	(d) Employee benefits expense	52	45	51	97	91	194
	(e) Depreciation and amortisation expense	10	10	10	20	20	37
	(f) Professional fees	27	46	31	73	64	136
	(g) Provision for NPA and doubtful debts/Written off (Net)	29	67	38	96	78	100
	(h) Provision/(Reversal) for Diminution in the Value of Investments/written	15	(3)	6	12	10	(11)

Sr. No.	Particulars	Quarter Ended			Half year ended		Year ended
		30-Sep-16	30-Jun-16	30-Sep-15	30-Sep-16	30-Sep-15	31-Mar-16
		Unaudited	Unaudited	Unaudited	Unaudited	Unaudited	Audited
	off (net)						
	(i) Other expenses	76	47	46	123	101	216
	Total expenses	**209**	**212**	**182**	**421**	**364**	**672**
3	**Profit/(Loss) from Operations before other income, finance** costs and exceptional items (1-2)	**689**	**772**	**688**	**1 461**	**1 440**	**3 404**
4	Other Income	42	23	30	65	42	69
5	**Profit/(Loss) from ordinary activities before finance costs** and exceptional items (3 + 4)	**731**	**795**	**718**	**1 526**	**1 482**	**3 473**
6	Finance costs	565	553	570	1 118	1 137	2 297
7	**Profit/(Loss) from ordinary activities after finance costs but** before exceptional items (5 - 6)	**166**	**242**	**148**	**408**	**345**	**1 176**
3	Exceptional items	-	-	-	-	-	-
9	**Profit/(Loss) from ordinary activities before Tax (7-8)**	**166**	**242**	**148**	**408**	**345**	**1 176**
10	Tax expense (Net)	36	29	40	65	62	199
11	**Net Profit (+)/Loss (-) from ordinary activities after tax (9-10)**	**130**	**213**	**108**	**343**	**283**	**977**
12	Extraordinary items	-	-	-	-	-	-
13	**Net Profit/(Loss) for the period (11-12)**	**130**	**213**	**108**	**343**	**283**	**977**
14	Paid-up equity share capital (Face value of INR 10 each)	253	253	253	253	253	253
15	Reserves excluding revaluation reserves as per balance sheet of previous accounting year						13 028
16	**Earnings Per Share of INR 10 each (not annualised)**						
	i. Before extraordinary items						
	(a) Basic	5.13	8.44	4.30	13.57	11.22	38.67
	(b) Diluted	5.13	8.44	4.30	13.57	11.22	38.67

Sr. No.	Particulars	Quarter Ended			Half year ended		Year ended
		30-Sep-16	30-Jun-16	30-Sep-15	30-Sep-16	30-Sep-15	31-Mar-16
		Unaudited	Unaudited	Unaudited	Unaudited	Unaudited	Audited
	ii After extraordinary items						
	(a) Basic	5.13	8.44	4.30	13.57	11.22	38.67
	(b) Diluted	5.13	8.44	4.30	13.57	11.22	38.67

RELIANCE CAPITAL LIMITED

Unaudited Standalone Segment Reporting for the quarter and half year ended September 30, 2016

(INR in crore)

Sr. No.	Particulars	Quarter Ended			Half year ended		Year ended
		30-Sep-16	30-Jun-16	30-Sep-15	30-Sep-16	30-Sep-15	31-Mar-16
		Unaudited	Unaudited	Unaudited	Unaudited	Unaudited	Audited
1	**Segment Revenue**						
a	Finance & Investments	445	523	443	967	966	2 309
b	Commercial Finance (Refer Note No. 3)	496	485	458	981	882	1 839
	Total	**941**	**1008**	**901**	**1 948**	**1 848**	**4 148**
	Inter segment	(1)	(1)	(1)	(2)	(2)	(3)
	Net Income	**940**	**1007**	**900**	**1 947**	**1 846**	**4 145**
2	**Segment Results**						
a	Finance & Investments	93	185	78	278	233	866
b	Commercial Finance (Refer Note No. 3)	74	57	71	131	113	312
	Total Segment Profit before Tax	**167**	**242**	**149**	**409**	**346**	**1 178**
	Unallocated expenses (**INR41 25 000)	(1)	(**)	(1)	(1)	(1)	(2)
	Profit before Tax	**166**	**242**	**148**	**408**	**345**	**1 176**
3	**Segment Assets**						
a	Finance & Investments	25 167	23 592	24 540	25 167	24 540	23 317
b	Commercial Finance	13 350	14 014	11 897	13 350	11 897	13 037
	Total	**38 517**	**37 606**	**36 437**	**38 517**	**36 437**	**36 354**

Sr. No.	Particulars	Quarter Ended			Half year ended		Year ended
		30-Sep-16	30-Jun-16	30-Sep-15	30-Sep-16	30-Sep-15	31-Mar-16
		Unaudited	Unaudited	Unaudited	Unaudited	Unaudited	Audited
4	**Segment Liabilities**						
a	Finance & Investments	13 658	12138	13 459	13 658	13 459	12 020
b	Commercial Finance	11 235	11973	10 112	11 235	10 112	11 053
	Total	**24 893**	**24111**	**23 571**	**24 893**	**23 571**	**23 073**

Notes:

1 Previous Period/Year figures have been regrouped/rearranged wherever necessary.

2 The Company has reported segment wise information as per Accounting Standard (AS 17), in terms of Companies (Accounts) Rules, 2014. The operations of the

Company are conducted within India, there is no separate reportable geographical segment and the Company reported the following business segments:

(i) Finance and Investments comprising of the investments and corporate lending business of the Company.

(ii) Commercial finance comprising of the commercial finance business of the Company.

3 The Board of Directors of the Company at its Meeting held on February 25, 2016 had approved the Scheme of Arrangement under Sections 391 to 394 of the Companies Act, 1956 (the 'Scheme') for demerger of Commercial Finance Business of the Company to its wholly owned subsidiary viz. Reliance Commercial Finance Limited (Formerly Reliance Gilts Limited). The Appointed Date for the Scheme is April 1, 2016. The Scheme is subject to requisite approvals, including sanction of the Hon'ble High Court of Judicature at Bombay. Accordingly, aforesaid Commercial Finance Division has been considered as discontinuing operations. The related income tax for concerned Commercial Finance Business is INR16 crore and profit after tax is INR58 crore for the quarter ended September 30, 2016 and is INR31 crore and profit after tax is INR100 crore for the half year ended September 30, 2016.

Post Demerger the Company would be applying to the Reserve Bank of India for registering itself as a Core Investment Company.

4 The Listed Secured Non-Convertible Debentures of the Company aggregating to INR11,385 crore as on September 30, 2016 are secured by way of first pari passu mortgage/charge on the Company's immovable property and on present and future boot debts/business receivables of the Company as specifically mentioned in the respective Trust Deeds and the asset cover thereof exceeds hundred percent of the principal amount of the said Debentures.

5 Disclosures under Regulation 52(4) of the Securities and Exchange Board of India (Listing Obligations and Disclosure Requirements) Regulations, 2015 are given in Annexure A.

6 The financial results for the quarter and half year ended September 30, 2016 of the Company have been subjected to a “Limited Review” by the Statutory Auditors of the Company.

7 The above results were reviewed the Audit Committee. The Board of Directors at its meeting held on October 24, 2016 approved the above results and its release.

For Reliance Capital Limited

Soumen Ghosh

Executive Director & Group CEO

Dated: October 24, 2016

RELIANCE CAPITAL LIMITED

Standalone Statement of Assets and Liabilities

(INR in crore)

Sr. No.	Particulars	As at September 30, 2016	As at March 31,2016
		Unaudited	**Audited**
A	**EQUITY AND LIABILITIES**		
1	**Shareholders' funds**		
	(a) Share capital	253	253
	(b) Reserves and surplus	13 371	13 028
	Sub-total - Shareholders' funds	**13 624**	**13 281**
2	**Non-Current Liabilities**		
	(a) Long-term borrowings	16 486	13615
	(b) Other Long-term liabilities	171	121
	(c) Long-Term provisions	61	59
	Sub-total - Non-current liabilities	**16 718**	**13 795**
3	**Current Liabilities**		
	(a) Short-term borrowings	3 472	3 812
	(b) Trade payables	1	6
	(c) Other current liabilities	4 654	5 167
	(d) Short-term provisions	48	293
	Sub-total - Current liabilities	**8 175**	**9 278**
	TOTAL - EQUITY AND LIABILITIES	**38 517**	**36 354**
B	**ASSETS**		
1	**Non-current assets**		
	(a) Fixed assets	176	179
	(b) Non-Current investments	11 277	11 109
	(c) Long-term loans and advances	18 569	16 426
	(d) Other non-current assets	586	743
	Sub-total - Non-current assets	**30 607**	**28 457**
2	**Current assets**		
	(a) Current investments	460	137
	(b) Trade receivables		
	'(Previous year INR 15 01 520)		
	(c) Cash & Bank balances	756	1 670
	(d) Short-term loans and advances	5417	5 643
	(e) Other current assets	1 278	447
	Sub-total - Current assets	**7 910**	**7 897**
	TOTAL - ASSETS	**38 517**	**36 354**

Annexure A

Disclosures pursuant to Regulation 52(4) of the Securities and Exchange Board of India (Listing Obligations and Disclosure Requirements) Regulations, 2015 for the six months ended September 30, 2016

1. **Credit Rating**

Particulars	Rating Agency	Rating
Long Term Debt Programme	CARE Ratings	CARE AAA Credit Watch
Market Linked Debentures	CARE Ratings	CARE PP- MLD AAA Credit Watch
Subordinated Tier II NCD	Brickwork Ratings	BWR AAA/Stable Ratings under watch with developing implications
Secured NCD	Brickwork Ratings	BWR AAA/Stable Ratings under watch with developing implications
Subordinated Debt	CARE Ratings	CARE AA+ Credit Watch

2. **Debt Equity Ratio**

   Debt Equity Ratio of the Company as on September 30, 2016 is 1.75 as per Standalone Unaudited Financials of the Company.

3. **Previous due date for the payment of Principal/Interest - Interest and Principal have been paid on due dates.**

SI. No.	ISIN	Series Id	From (1-04-2016 to 30-09-2016)	
			Interest	Principal
1	INE013A07004	947992	12-Apr-16	
2	INE013A07V09	949106	17-Apr-16	
3	INE013A070Q9	947993	18-Apr-16	
4	INE013A08291	949105	18-Apr-16	
5	INE013A08226	948743	20-Apr-16	
6	INE013A07A33	950229	22-Apr-16	
7	INE013A070S5	947994	23-Apr-16	
8	INE013A07VP6	949107	23-Apr-16	
9	INE013A070U1	947984	07-May-16	
10	INE013A07SN7	948755	09-May-16	

SI. No.	ISIN	Series Id	From (1-04-2016 to 30-09-2016)	
			Interest	Principal
11	INE013A07MQ3	947263	12-May-16	12-May-16
12	INE013A07OZ0	948051	16-May-16	
13	INE013A07YZ9	949916	17-May-16	17-May-16
14	INE013A08093	947509	20-May-16	
15	INE013A08101	947508	20-May-16	
16	INE013A07WB4	949236	24-May-16	
17	INE013A08234	948744	25-May-16	
18	INE013A08317	949669	25-May-16	
19	INE013A07MU5	947312	26-May-16	26-May-16
20	INE013A07WG3	949237	27-May-16	
21	INE013A07NU3	947798	30-May-16	
22	INE013A07PH5	948059	01-Jun-16	
23	INE013A07PJ1	948057	06-Jun-16	
24	INE013A08242	948746	13-Jun-16	
25	INE013A07PM5	948060	15-Jun-16	
26	INE013A07PP8	948061	20-Jun-16	
27	INE013A07PR4	948062	21-Jun-16	
28	INE013A08309	949319	27-Jun-16	
29	INE013A07003	952365	29-Jun-16	
30	INE013A08259	948747	29-Jun-16	
31	INE013A08333	949783	02-JUI-16	
32	INE013A08341	949797	07-Jul-16	
33	INE013A07037	952394	08-Jul-16	
34	INE013A08358	949798	14-Jul-16	
35	INE013A08119	947510	14-Jul-16	
36	INE013A07NC1	947480	19-Jul-16	19-Jul-16
37	INE013A07QE0	948501	25-Jul-16	
38	INE013A07ND9	947481	26-Jul-16	26-Jul-16

SI. No.	ISIN	Series Id	From (1-04-2016 to 30-09-2016)	
			Interest	Principal
39	INE013A07052	952513	01-Aug-16	
40	INE013A07QJ9	948497	01-Aug-16	
41	INE013A07A66	950619	04-Aug-16	
42	INE013A07060	952561	05-Aug-16	
43	INE013A07QN1	948496	08-Aug-16	
44	INE013A07QQ4	948494	08-Aug-16	
45	INE013A07QR2	948487	09-Aug-16	
46	INE013A07NF4	947495	12-Aug-16	
47	INE013A08127	947511	12-Aug-16	
48	INE013A08135	947512	12-Aug-16	
49	INE013A07094	952601	13-Aug-16	
50	INE013A07QY8	948486	17-Aug-16	
51	INE013A07QX0	948503	22-Aug-16	
52	INE013A07WU4	949431	22-Aug-16	
53	INE013A07P02	952677	25-Aug-16	
54	INE013A07RA6	948485	31-Aug-16	
55	INE013A07RF5	948483	06-Sep-16	
56	INE013A07C56	950853	11-Sep-16	
57	INE013A07NJ6	947500	13-Sep-16	13-Sep-16
58	INE013A07RN9	948481	21-Sep-16	
59	INE013A07E21	950906	26-Sep-16	
60	INE013A07OL0	947990	27-Sep-16	
61	INE013A07RS8	948479	27-Sep-16	
62	INE013A08267	948748	27-Sep-16	
63	INE013A07RT6	948478	28-Sep-16	
64	INE013A08143	947513	30-Sep-16	
65	INE013A07YJ3	949728	NA	08-Apr-16
66	INE013A07K49	951583	NA	21-Apr-16

SI. No.	ISIN	Series Id	From (1-04-2016 to 30-09-2016)	
			Interest	Principal
67	INE013A07G60	951119	NA	22-Apr-16
68	INE013A07Y03	949785	NA	25-Apr-16
69	INE013A07YS4	949843	NA	26-Apr-16
70	INE013A07M54	951901	NA	27-Apr-16
71	1NE013A07TK1	948734	NA	17-May-16
72	INE013A07ZK8	949995	NA	14-Jun-16
73	INE013A07ZM4	949987	NA	20-Jun-16
74	INE013A07ZO0	950007	NA	23-Jun-16
75	INE013A07ZQ5	950019	NA	24-Jun-16
76	INE013A07ZV5	950070	NA	28-Jun-16
77	INE013A07ZS1	950035	NA	29-Jun-16
78	INE013A07UZ7	949023	NA	27-Sep-16
79	INE013A07VF7	949067	NA	01-Aug-16
80	INE013A07VG5	949066	NA	04-Aug-16
81	INE013A07VJ9	949088	NA	08-Aug-16
82	INE013A07VK7	949090	NA	09-Aug-16
83	INE013A07VN1	949097	NA	16-Aug-16
84	INE013A07VQ4	949127	NA	22-Aug-16
85	INE013A07A41	950069	NA	04-Jul-16
86	INE013A07W4	949177	NA	01-Sep-16
87	INE013A07VW2	949178	NA	01-Sep-16
88	INE013A07WE8	949225	NA	20-Sep-16
89	INE013A07WF5	949223	NA	18-Sep-16
90	INE013A07WH1	949238	NA	25-Sep-16
91	INE013A07E62	950984	NA	30-Sep-16
92	INE013A07F20	951031	NA	01-Jun-16
93	INE013A07G78	951120	NA	25-J ul-16
94	INE013A07H10	951148	NA	30-Jun-16

SI. No.	ISIN	Series Id	From (1-04-2016 to 30-09-2016)	
			Interest	Principal
95	INE013A07K56	951585	NA	26-Apr-16
96	INE013A07M62	952000	NA	19-Apr-16

4. Next due date for the payment of interest/principal along with amount of Interest

SI. No.	ISIN	Series Id	From (1-10-2016 to 31-03-2017)	
			Interest	Principal
1	INE013A07RW0	948751	10-Oct-16	
2	INE013A07RX8	948752	10-Oct-16	
3	INE013A070 04	947992	12-Oct-16	
4	INE013A07G11	951054	16-Oct-16	
5	INE013A07NP3	947792	18-Oct-16	18-Oct-16
6	INE013A07Q19	952915	20-Oct-16	
7	INE013A07Q27	952916	20-Oct-16	
8	INE013A07G52	951117	21-Oct-16	21-Oct-16
9	INE013A07Q43	952909	24-Oct-16	
10	INE013A07Q50	952910	24-Oct-16	
11	INE013A070S5	947994	24-Oct-16	
12	INE013A07NT5	947793	31-Oct-16	31-Oct-16
13	INE013A07H36	951177	31-Oct-16	
14	INE013A07SK3	948754	02-Nov-16	
15	INE013A07SJ5	948753	05-Nov-16	
16	INE013A07H77	951224	10-Nov-16	29-Dec-16
17	INE013A07I01	951248	21-Nov-16	
18	INE013A07PH5	948059	01-Dec-16	
19	INE013A07NV1	947799	09-Dec-16	09-Dec-16
20	INE013A07S41	953117	12-Dec-16	
21	INE013A07TA2	948621	13-Dec-16	
22	INE013A07TC8	948666	17-Dec-16	

SI. No.	ISIN	Series Id	From (1-10-2016 to 31-03-2017)	
			Interest	Principal
23	INE013A07NX7	947800	19-Dec-16	19-Dec-16
24	INE013A07TD6	948667	20-Dec-16	
25	INE013A07YF1	949729	20-Dec-16	
26	INE013A07YK1	949730	20-Dec-16	20-Dec-16
27	INE013A07NY5	947801	21-Dec-16	
28	INE013A07TF1	948691	28-Dec-16	
29	INE013A08358	949798	16-Jan-17	
30	INE013A070A3	947802	16-Jan-17	16-Jan-17
31	INE013A07TN5	948805	24-Jan-17	
32	INE013A07T03	948806	24-Jan-17	
33	INE013A07TV8	948821	31-Jan-17	
34	INE013A07NF4	947495	13-Feb-17	
35	INE013A070D4	954693	13-Feb-17	
36	INE013A07V46	953488	17-Feb-17	
37	INE013A07QX0	948503	22-Feb-17	
38	INE013A075D3	954753	22-Feb-17	
39	INE013A07ZR3	949998	13-Mar-17	13-Mar-17
40	INE013A070K2	947989	16-Mar-17	16-Mar-17
41	INE013A07W11	953642	17-Mar-17	
42	INE013A07UW4	948989	18-Mar-17	
43	INE013A07RN9	948481	21-Mar-17	
44	INE013A07UY0	949019	22-Mar-17	
45	INE013A07W37	953671	22-Mar-17	
46	INE013A07W29	953692	23-Mar-17	
47	INE013A07H51	951176	25-Mar-17	
48	INE013A07OL0	947990	27-Mar-17	27-Mar-17
49	INE013A07W60	953719	29-Mar-17	
50	INE013A07VY8	949175	NA	07-Nov-16

Sl. No.	ISIN	Series Id	From (1-10-2016 to 31-03-2017)	
			Interest	Principal
51	INE013A07WI9	949256	NA	07-Oct-16
52	INE013A07WL3	949278	NA	13-Oct-16
53	INE013A07WR0	949427	NA	21-Dec-16
54	INE013A07WY6	949479	NA	10-Mar-17
55	INE013A07XA4	949502	NA	20-Jan-17
56	INE013A07XB2	949505	NA	20-Jan-17
57	INE013A07XC0	949503	NA	22-Mar-17
58	INE013A07XF3	949560	NA	03-Feb-17
59	INE013A07XP2	949619	NA	06-Mar-17
60	INE013A07XV0	949630	NA	02-Feb-17
61	INE013A07XY4	949672	NA	02-Mar-17
62	INE013A07YI5	949727	NA	20-Mar-17
63	INE013A07A58	950607	NA	24-Oct-16
64	INE013A07A74	950608	NA	24-Oct-16
65	INE013A07B40	950653	NA	08-Nov-16
66	INE013A07B57	950654	NA	08-Nov-16
67	INE013A07B81	950714	NA	25-NOV-16
68	INE013A07B99	950758	NA	23-NOV-16
69	INE013A07D30	950844	NA	12-Dec-16
70	INE013A07D71	950913	NA	13-Jan-17
71	INE013A07F46	951035	NA	01-Jan-17
72	INE013A07F61	951055	NA	10-Jan-17
73	INE013A07G86	951121	NA	27-Oct-16
74	INE013A07G94	951178	NA	31-Oct-16
75	INE013A07H93	951252	NA	25-Nov-16
76	INE013A07I43	951329	NA	28-Nov-16
77	INE013A07J00	951359	NA	06-Dec-16
78	INE013A07J34	951400	NA	14-Dec-16

SI. No.	ISIN	Series Id	From (1-10-2016 to 31-03-2017)	
			Interest	Principal
79	INE013A07K23	951584	NA	20-Jan-17
80	INE013A07L06	951670	NA	10-Feb-17
81	INE013A07L97	951762	NA	09-Mar-17
82	INE013A07M39	951835	NA	10-Mar-17
83	INE013A07M47	951836	NA	20-Mar-17
84	INE013A07M88	952049	NA	03-Oct-16
85	INE013A07N87	952317	NA	13-Dec-16
86	INE013A07029	952366	NA	27-Jan-17
87	INE013A07P51	952785	NA	20-Mar-17
88	INE013A07P69	952805	NA	23-Dec-16
89	INE013A07Q01	952878	NA	09-Jan-17
90	INE013A07Q35	952908	NA	21-Mar-17

5. **Outstanding redeemable preference shares:** Nil

6. **Debenture Redemption Reserve (DRR)**

   No DRR is required in respect of privately placed debentures in terms of Rule 18(7)(b)(ii) of Companies (Share Capital and Debenture) Rules, 2014.

7. **Net Worth:** INR 13,466 crore

   - Includes INR846 crore created pursuant to the Scheme of Amalgamation approved by High Court which shall for all regulatory purposes be considered to be part of owned funds/net worth of the Company.
   - Includes INR 3,837 crore created pursuant to the Scheme of Amalgamation approved by High Court.

8. **Net Profit After Tax:** INR 343 crore

9. **Earnings Per Share:** INR 13.57 per share

SUNDARAM FINANCE

STATEMENT OF UNAUDITED RESULTS FOR THE QUARTER AND HALF YEAR ENDED 30.09.2016

(INR in Lakhs)

SI. No	Particulars	Quarter Ended			Half year ended		Year Ended
		30.09.2016	30.06.2016	30.09.2015	30.09.2016	30.09.2015	31.03.2016
		Unaudited	Unaudited	Unaudited	Unaudited	Unaudited	Audited
1	**Income from operations**	59185.05	55766.63	58405.74	114951.68	113921.17	231244.14
2	**Expenses** (a) Employee benefits	5802.40	5739.77	5291 64	11542.17	10614.89	21258.88
	(b) Depreciation and amortisation expense	2040.15	1918.07	2090.69	3958.22	4130.03	8419.68
	(c) Contingent Provision against Standard Assets	116.78	281.79	157.11	398.57	314.22	131.68
	(d) Provisions and write off	1166.07	1166.18	1806.33	2332 25	3406.58	7974.30
	(e) Administrative and Other expenses	4692.21	4728.40	5355.21	9420.61	9988 27	19620.43
	Total expenses	**13817.61**	**13834.21**	**14700.98**	**27651.82**	**28453.99**	**57404.97**
3	**Profit from Operations before other income, finance costs and exceptional items**	**45367.44**	**41932.42**	**43704.76**	**87299.86**	**85467.18**	**173839.17**
4	Other Income	3365.18	393.22	8755.20	3758 40	10348.69	16258 19
5	**Profit from ordinary activities before finance** costs and exceptional items	**48732.62**	**42325.64**	**52459.96**	**91058.26**	**95815.87**	**190097.36**
6	Finance costs	30297.68	29072.21	30475.75	59369.89	59362.33	121774.01
7	**Profit from ordinary activities after finance costs but before exceptional items**	**18434.94**	**13253.43**	**21984.21**	**31688.37**	**36453.54**	**68323.35**
8	Exceptional items	-	-	*	-	*	*
9	**Profit from ordinary activities before tax**	**18434.94**	**13253.43**	**21984.21**	**31688.37**	**36453.54**	**68323.35**
10	Tax expense	5666.84	4235.78	6585.38	9902.62	11154.79	20595.60
11	Net Profit from ordinary activities after tax	12768.10	9017.65	15398.83	21785.75	25298.75	47727.75
12	Extraordinary items	-	-	-	*	-	-
13	**Net profit for the period - (Refer Note 2)**	**12768.10**	**9017.65**	**15398.83**	**21785.75**	**25298.75**	**47727.75**
14	Paid-up Equity Share Capital (Face value of INR 10 each)	11110.39	11110.39	11110.39	11110.39	11110.39	11110.39
15	Reserves excluding Revaluation Reserves						320152.10
16	**Basic and Diluted**	**11.49**	**8.12**	**13.86**	**19.61**	**22.77**	**42.96**

Sl. No	Particulars	Quarter Ended			Half year ended		Year Ended
		30.09.2016	30.06.2016	30.09.2015	30.09.2016	30.09.2015	31.03.2016
		Unaudited	Unaudited	Unaudited	Unaudited	Unaudited	Audited
	Earnings per Share (before extraordinary items) (INR)						
	Basic and Diluted Earnings per Share (after extraordinary items) (INR)	**11.49**	**8.12**	**13.86**	**19.61**	**22.77**	**42.96**

Notes:

1. The above results were approved by the Board of Directors at their meeting held on 31st October 2016.
2. **Profit for the quarter and half year ended 30.09.2016 is not comparable with that of the corresponding periods of the previous year, which includes a one time profit of INR 4064.68 lakhs, arising from the sale of equity shares of BNP Paribas Sundaram Global Securities Operations Private Limited.**
3. Income deferment and provision for Non-Performing Assets have been made on an estimated basis, as in earlier years. For this purpose, the Company has followed the 3 months overdue norms for classification of NPA , as compared to 120 days norms followed for the quarter and half year ended 30th September, 2015.
4. The Company is engaged primarily in the business of financing and accordingly there is no separate reportable segment as per Accounting Standard (AS-17) 'Segment Reporting'.
5. Previous year's figures have been regrouped wherever necessary to conform to current year's classification.
6. The Statutory Auditors have carried out a Limited Review of the financial results for the quarter ended 30th September 2016.
7. The Company's Secured Non - Convertible Debentures are secured by mortgage of immovable property ranking pari passu and Hypothecation of specific Loan receivables/Hire purchase/ Lease agreements with a cover of 100% /125%, as per the terms of issue.

By Order of the Board
T T SRINIVASARAGHAVAN
Managing Director

Chennai
31.10.2016

STATEMENT OF UNAUDITED RESULTS FOR THE QUARTER AND HALF YEAR ENDED 30.09.2016 (*Contd.*)

Statement of Assets and Liabilities

(*INR in Lakhs*)

Sl. No.	Particulars	30.09.2016	30.09.2015	31.03.2016 (Audited)
A	**EQUITY AND LIABILITIES**			
1	**Shareholders' Funds**			
	(a) Share Capital	11110.39	11110.39	11110.39
	(b) Reserves and Surplus	342035.32	312084.71	320152.10
	Sub-total - Shareholders' Funds	**353145.71**	**323195.10**	**331262.49**
2	**Non-current Liabilities**			
	(a) Long-term borrowings	558936.75	568621.20	486517.11
	(b) Deferred tax liabilities (net)			
	(c) Other long-term liabilities	15956.96	11640.75	15568.60
	(d) Long-term provisions	9413.36	8784.35	8908.39
	Sub-total - Non-current Liabilities	**584307.07**	**589046.30**	**510994.10**
3	**Current Liabilities**			
	(a) Short-term borrowings	326400.82	361301.62	222774.39
	(b) Trade payables	9680.10	8032.80	8782.63
	(c) Other current liabilities	533253.28	547236.80	646542.99
	(d) Short-term provisions	18432.08	15030.91	18899.63
	Sub-total - Current liabilities	**887766.28**	**931602.13**	**896999.64**
	TOTAL - EQUITY AND LIABILITIES	**1825219.06**	**1843843.53**	**1739256.23**
B	**ASSETS**			
1	**Non-current Assets**			
	(a) Fixed Assets	28075.13	30039.16	27844.00
	(b) Goodwill on consolidation			
	(c) Non-current investments	160294.96	149884.68	150465.62
	(d) Deferred tax assets (net)	13201.57	11982.42	12159.35
	(e) Long-term loans and advances	834250.01	818611.70	788754.93
	(f) Other non-current assets	3128.42	1976.12	3051.46
	Sub-total - Non-current assets	**1038950.09**	**1012494.08**	**982275.36**
2	**Current Assets**			
	(a) Current investments	10924.08	21166.60	33158.46
	(b) Inventories			
	(c) Trade receivables			
	(d) Cash and cash equivalents	68223.29	42307.55	55256.41
	(e) Short-term loans and advances	690871.28	749364.56	652961.60
	(f) Other current assets	16250.32	18510.74	15604.40
	Sub-total - Current assets	**786268.97**	**831349.45**	**756980.87**
	TOTAL - ASSETS	**1825219.06**	**1843843.53**	**1739256.23**

INFOSYS LIMITED

Audited financial results of Infosys Limited for the quarter and half-year ended September 30,2016 prepared in compliance with the Indian Accounting Standard (Ind-AS)

(in INR crore, except per equity share data)

Particulars	Quarter ended September 30,	Quarter ended June 30,	Quarter ended September 30,	Half-year ended September 30,		Year ended March 31,
	2016	2016	2015	2016	2015	2016
	Audited	Audited	Audited	Audited	Audited	Audited
Revenue from operations	15,000	14,420	13,525	29,420	26,263	53,983
Other income, net	763	761	775	1,525	1,496	3,006
Total income	**15,763**	**15,181**	**14,300**	**30,945**	**27,759**	**56,989**
Expenses Employee benefit expenses	7,939	7,605	6,987	15,544	13,794	28,207
Deferred consideration pertaining to acquisition	-	-	64	-	124	149
Cost of technical sub-contractors	1,183	1,135	1,035	2,319	2,000'	4,417
Travel expenses	364	576	425	940	857	1,655
Cost of software packages and others	312	224	335	536	626	1,049
Communication expenses	90	82	80	172	160	311
Consultancy and professional charges	119	119	123	238	255	563
Depreciation and amortisation expense	338	319	272	657	524	1,115
Other expenses	606	661	426	1,268	876	1,923
Total expenses	**10,951**	**10,721**	**9,747**	**21,674**	**19,216**	**39,389**
Profit before tax	**4,812**	**4,460**	**4,553**	**9,271**	**8,543**	**17,600**
Tax expense: Current tax	1,327	1,314	1,333	2,640	2,385	4,898
Deferred tax	9	(34)	(28)	(25)	19	9
Profit for the period	**3,476**	**3,180**	**3,248**	**6,656**	**6,139**	**12,693**
Other comprehensive income *Items that will not be reclassified subsequently to profit or loss* Remeasurement of the net defined benefit liability/asset	(35)	(17)	1	(52)	(7)	(2)
Equity instruments through other comprehensive income	-	-	-	-	-	-
Fair value changes on cash flow hedges	2	-	-	2	-	-
Items that will be reclassified subsequently to profit or loss	-	-	-	-	-	-

Particulars	Quarter ended September 30,	Quarter ended June 30,	Quarter ended September 30,	Half-year ended September 30,		Year ended March 31,
	2016	2016	2015	2016	2015	2016
	Audited	Audited	Audited	Audited	Audited	Audited
Total other comprehensive income, net of tax	**(33)**	**(17)**	**1**	**(50)**	**(7)**	**(2)**
Total comprehensive income, for the period	**3,443**	**3,163**	**3,249**	**6,606**	**6,132**	**12,691**
Paid-up share capital (par value INR 5/- each fully paid)	1,148	1,148	1,148	1,148	1,148	1,148
Other Equity	59,934	59,934	51,617	59,934	51,617	59,934
Earnings per equity share (par value INR 5 /- each)						
Basic (INR)	15.13	13.85	14.14	28.98	26.73	55.26
Diluted (INR)	15.13	13.85	14.14	28.98	26.73	55.26

Notes:

1. The audited financial statements for the quarter and half-year ended September 30, 2016 have been taken on record by the Board of Directors at its meeting held on October 14, 2016. The statutory auditors have expressed an unqualified audit opinion. The information presented above is extracted from the audited standalone financial statements. The financial statements are prepared in accordance with the Indian Accounting Standard (Ind-AS) as prescribed under Section 133 of the Companies Act, 2013 read with Rule 3 of the Companies (Indian Accounting Standards) Rules, 2015 and Companies (Indian Accounting Standards) Amendment Rules, 2016.
2. The Company has adopted all the Ind-AS standards on April 1, 2016 with April 1, 2015 as the transition date, and the adoptions were carried out in accordance with Ind-AS 101- First time adoption of Indian Accounting Standards. The transition was carried out from Indian Accounting Principles generally accepted in India as prescribed under Section 133 of the Companies Act, 2013 read with Rule 7 of the Companies (Accounts) Rules, 2014 (I GAAP), which was the previous GAAP.
3. The Board, at the meeting held on October 14,2016 appointed D. N. Prahlad as Independent Director effective from that date.
4. The Board of Directors in their meeting held on October 14, 2016, on recommendation of the Nomination and Remuneration Committee, have approved the revised annual compensation of U.B. Pravin Rao, Chief Operating Officer and Whole Time Director of the Company, with effect from November 1,2016, subject to the approval of the shareholders. The compensation includes fixed compensation of INR 4.62 crore per annum and a variable compensation of up to INR 3.88 crore per annum. Additionally, based on fiscal 2016 performance, 27,250 restricted stock units (RSU) and 43,000 stock options would be granted under the 2015 Stock Incentive Compensation Plan (2015

plan), as approved by the shareholders vide postal ballot dated March 31, 2016. These RSUs and stock options would vest over a period of 4 years and shall be exercisable within the period as approved by the committee. The exercise price of the RSUs will be equal to the par value of the shares and the exercise price of the stock options would be the market price as on the date of grant, as approved by shareholders. RSUs and stock options, in future periods, will be granted on achievement of performance conditions, as may be decided by the Nomination and Remuneration Committee.

5. The Board of Directors in their meeting held on October 14, 2016, on recommendation of the Nomination and Remuneration Committee, have approved the revised compensation structure of M.D Ranganath, Mohit Joshi, Sandeep Dadlani, Rajesh K Murthy, Ravikumar S, David Kennedy, Krishnamurthy Shankar and Manikantha AGS with effect from November 1, 2016. The revised aggregate compensation of the above individuals includes fixed compensation of 24 crore and variable compensation of upto 20 crore.

   Additionally, based on fiscal 2016 performance, restricted stock units (RSU) of 245,750 and stock options of 502,550 will be granted on November 1,2016 under the 2015 Stock Incentive Compensation Plan (2015 plan), as approved by the shareholders vide postal ballot dated March 31, 2016. These RSUs and stock options would vest over a period of 4 years and shall be exercisable within the period as approved by the committee. The exercise price of RSUs will be equal to the par value of the shares and the exercise price of the stock options would be the market price as on the date of grant. The Audit committee in their meeting held on October 13, 2016, resolved to include Mohit Joshi, Sandeep Dadlani, Rajesh K Murthy, Ravi Kumar S, Krishnamurthy Shankar and David Kennedy as key managerial personnel as defined under Ind-AS 24 - Related Party Disclosures effective from the date of the meeting. Dr. Vishal Sikka, U.B. Pravin Rao, M.D. Ranganath and Manikantha AGS are key managerial personnel as defined under Section 2 (51) of the Companies Act, 2013.

6. The Nomination and Remuneration Committee of the Board of Directors of Infosys Limited at its meeting held on October 13,2016, based on fiscal 2016 performance approved the grant of upto 906,275 RSUs and upto 943,810 stock options with effect from November 1, 2016, to a total of upto 425 eligible and identified high-performing executives of the Company and its subsidiaries under the 2015 Stock Incentive Compensation Plan (2015 plan), as approved by the shareholders vide postal ballot dated March 31, 2016. These RSUs and stock options shall vest over a period of 4 years from the date of grant, and shall be exercisable within the period as approved by the committee. The exercise price of the RSUs will be equal to the par value of the shares and the exercise price of the stock options would be the market price as on the date of grant.

7. **Information on dividends for the quarter and half-year ended September 30, 2016**

   The Board declared an interim dividend of INR 11/- per equity share . The record date for the payment of interim dividend is October 24, 2016. The interim dividend will be paid on October 26, 2016. The interim dividend declared in the previous year was INR10/- (not adjusted for bonus issue) per equity share.

(*in INR*)

Particulars	Quarter ended September 30,	Quarter ended June 30,	Quarter ended September 30,	Half-year ended September 30,		Year ended March 31,
	2016	2016	2015	2016	2015	2016
Dividend per share (par value INR 5/- each) Interim dividend	11.00	-	10.00	11.00	10.00	10.00
Final dividend	-	-	-	-	-	14.25

8. Statement of assets and liabilities (Standalone-Audited)

(*in INR crore*)

Particulars	As at	
	September 30, 2016	March 31, 2016
ASSETS		
Non-current assets Property, plant and equipment	8,470	8,248
Capital work-in-progress	1,053	934
Intangible assets	-	-
Financial assets		
Investments	11,253	11,076
Loans	5	5
Other financial assets	206	192
Deferred tax assets (net)	428	405
Other non-current assets	834	755
Income tax assets (net)	4,981	5,020
Total non - current assets	**27,230**	**26,635**
Current assets		
Financial assets		
Investments	1,905	2
Trade receivables	10,168	9,798
Cash and cash equivalents	27,967	29,176
Loans	321	355
Other financial assets	6,286	4,801
Other current assets	1,800	1,965
Total current assets	**48,447**	**46,097**
Total assets	**75.677**	**72.732**
EQUITY AND LIABILITIES		
Equity		
Equity share capital	1,148	1,148
Other equity	62,632	59,934
Total equity	**63,780**	**61,082**
LIABILITIES	39	62

Particulars	As at	
	September 30, 2016	March 31, 2016
Non-current liabilities		
Financial liabilities		
Other financial liabilities		
Deferred tax liabilities (net)	-	-
Total non - current liabilities	**39**	**62**
Current liabilities		
Financial liabilities		
Trade payables	272	623
Other financial liabilities	5,128	5,132
Other current liabilities	2,178	2,093
Provisions	556	436
Income tax liabilities (net)	3,724	3,304
Total current liabilities	**11,858**	**11,588**
Total equity and liabilities	**75.677**	**72.732**

The disclosure is an extract of the audited Balance Sheet as at September 30, 2016 and March 31, 2016 prepared in compliance with the Indian Accounting Standards (Ind-AS).

9. Reconciliation of Statement of Profit and Loss as previously reported under IGAAP to Ind-AS

(in INR crore)

Particulars	Note	Three months ended September 30, 2015		
		IGAAP	Effects of transition to Ind-AS	Ind-AS
Revenue from operations		13,525	-	13,525
Other income, net	1.2	774	1	775
Total income		**14,299**	**1**	**14,300**
Expenses Employee benefit expenses	1.1	6,985	2	6,987
Deferred consideration pertaining to acquisition	1.2	46	18	64
Cost of technical sub-contractors		1,035	-	1,035
Travel expenses		425	-	425
Cost of software packages and others		335	-	335
Communication expenses		80	-	80
Consultancy and professional charges		123	-	123
Depreciation and amortization expenses		272	-	272
Other expenses	1.2	423	3	426
Total expenses		**9,724**	**23**	**9,747**
Profit before exceptional items and tax		**4,575**	**(22)**	**4,553**
Profit on transfer of business	1.3	3,036	(3,036)	-
Profit before tax		**7,611**	**(3,058)**	**4,553**

Particulars	Note	Three months ended September 30, 2015		
		IGAAP	Effects of transition to Ind-AS	Ind-AS
Tax expense:				
Current tax		1,333	-	1,333
Deferred tax		(28)	-	(28)
Profit for the period		**6,306**	**(3,058)**	**3,248**
Other comprehensive income *Items that will not be reclassified subsequently to profit or loss* Remeasurement of the net defined benefit liability/asset	1.1		1	1
Equity instruments through other comprehensive income			-	-
		-	1	**1**
Items that will be reclassified subsequently to profit or loss		-	-	-
Total other comprehensive income, net of tax		**-**	**1**	**1**
Total comprehensive income for the period		**6,306**	**(3,057)**	**3,249**

This reconciliation statement has been provided in accordance with circular C1R/CFD/FAC/62/201 6 issued by SEBI dated July 05, 2016 on account of implementation of lnd-AS by listed companies.

Explanations for reconciliation of profit and loss as previously reported under IGAAP to Ind-AS

1.1 a) As per Ind-AS 19 - Employee Benefits, actuarial gains and losses are recognized in other comprehensive income and not reclassified to profit and loss in a subsequent period.

b) Adjustments reflect unamortized negative past service cost arising on modification of the gratuity plan in an earlier period. Ind-AS 19 requires such gains and losses to be adjusted to retained earnings.

1.2. Adjustments reflect impact of discounting pertaining to deferred consideration and contingent consideration payable for business combinations.

1.3. Profit on transfer of business between entities under common control has been reversed and taken to business transfer reserve on account of transition to Ind-AS.

10. Reconciliation of equity as previously reported under IGAAP to Ind-AS

(*in INR crore*)

Particulars	Note	Balance Sheet as at March 31, 2016		
		IGAAP	Effects of transition to Ind-AS	Ind-AS
ASSETS **Non-current assets** Property, plant and equipment		8,248		8,248

Particulars	Note	Balance Sheet as at March 31, 2016		
		IGAAP	Effects of transition to Ind-AS	Ind-AS
Capital work-in-progress		934	-	934
Intangible assets		-	-	-
Financial assets				
Investments	1.1	11,111	(35)	11,076
Loans		5	-	5
Other financial assets		192	-	192
Deferred tax assets (net)		405	-	405
Other non-current assets		755	-	755
Income tax assets (net)		5,020	-	5,020
Total non-current assets		**26,670**	**(35)**	**26,635**
Current assets Financial assets:				
Investments	1.1	2		2
Trade receivables		9,798	-	9,798
Cash and cash equivalents		29,176	-	29,176
Loans		355	-	355
Other financial assets		4,801.	-	4,801
Other current assets		1,965	-	1,965
Total current assets		**46,097**	**-**	**46,097**
Total assets		**72,767**	**(35)**	**72,732**
EQUITY AND LIABILITIES Equity Equity share capital		1,148		1,148
Other equity	1.5	56,009	3,925	59,934
Total equity		**57,157**	**3,925**	**61,082**
Non-current liabilities Financial liabilities Other financial liabilities	1.2	73	(11)	62
Deferred tax liabilities (net)		-	-	-
Other non-current liabilities		-	-	-
Total non-current liabilities		**73**	**(ID**	**62**
Current liabilities Financial liabilities				
Trade payables		623		623
Other financial liabilities	1.2	5,138	(6)	5,132
Other current liabilities	1.3	2,097	(4)	2,093
Provisions	1.4	4,375	(3,939)	436
Other current liabilities		3,304	-	3,304
Total current liabilities		**15,537**	**(3,949)**	**11,588**
Total liabilities and equity		**72,767**	**(35)**	**72,732**

This reconciliation statement has been provided in accordance with circular CIR/CFD/FAC/62/2016 issued by SEBI dated July 05, 2016 on account of implementation of Ind-AS by listed companies.

Explanations for reconciliation of balance sheet as previously reported under IGAAP to IND-AS

1.1. Investment

a) Tax free bonds are carried at amortized cost both under Ind-AS and IGAAP. Investment in equity instruments are carried at fair value through OCI in Ind-AS compared to being carried at cost under IGAAP.

b) Investments include discounted value of contingent consideration payable on acquisition of business under Ind-AS as compared to undiscounted value of contingent consideration under IGAAP.

1.2. Other financial liabilities

Other financial liabilities - adjustments includes impact of discounting the deferred and contingent consideration payable for acquisitions under Ind-AS.

1.3. Other current liabilities

Adjustments that reflect unamortised negative past service cost arising on modification of the gratuity plan in an earlier period. Ind-AS 19 requires such gains and losses to be adjusted to retained earnings.

1.4. Provisions

Adjustments reflect final dividend (including corporate dividend tax), declared and approved post reporting period.

1.5. Other equity

a) Adjustments to retained earnings and other comprehensive income has been made in accordance with Ind-AS, for the above mentioned line items.

b) In addition, as per Ind-AS 19, actuarial gain and losses are recognized in other comprehensive income as compared to being recognized in the statement of profit and loss under IGAAP.

c) Profit on transfer of business between entities under common control which were earlier recognized in statement of profit and loss under IGAAP are adjusted to reserves on transition to Ind-AS.

11. Segment reporting (Standalone-Audited)

Particulars	Quarter ended September 30,	Quarter ended June 30,	Quarter ended September 30,	Half-year ended September 30,		Year ended March 31,
	2016	2016	2015	2016	2015	2016
Revenue by business segment Financial services (FS)	3,998	3,873	3,692	7,871	7,343	14,846
Manufacturing (MFG)	1,506	1,472	1,445	2,978	2,693	5,434

Particulars	Quarter ended September 30,	Quarter ended June 30,	Quarter ended September 30,	Half-year ended September 30,		Year ended March 31,
	2016	2016	2015	2016	2015	2016
Energy & utilities, communication and services (ECS)	3,510	3,341	2,981	6,851	5,824	12,124
Retail, consumer packaged goods and logistics (RCL)	2,598	2,583	2,377	5,181	4,556	9,411
Life sciences, healthcare and insurance (HILIFE)	1,736	1,627	1,611	3,364	3,119	6,392
Hi-Tech	1,275	1,270	1,184	2,545	2,302	4,736
All Other Segments	377	254	235	630	426	1,040
Total	**15,000**	**14,420**	**13,525**	**29,420**	**26,263**	**53,983**
Less: Inter-segment revenue	-	-	-	-	-	-
Net revenue from operations	**15,000**	**14,420**	**13,525**	**29,420**	**26,263**	**53,983**
Segment profit before tax Financial services (FS)	1,064	1,026	1,093	2,090	2,145	4,185
Manufacturing (MFG)	449	410	349	859	673	1,436
Energy & utilities, communication and services (ECS)	1,114	1,022	959	2,136	1,815	3,829
Retail, consumer packaged goods and logistics (RCL)	816	771	727	1,586	1,367	2,817
Life sciences, healthcare and insurance (HILIFE)	500	451	480	951	876	1,844
Hi-Tech	365	341	377	706	655	1,373
All other segments	81	-	68	80	44	239
Total	**4,389**	**4,021**	**4,053**	**8,408**	**7,575**	**15,723**
Less: Other unallocable expenditure	340	322	275	662	528	1,129
Add: Unallocable other income	763	761	775	1,525	1,496	3,006
Profit before tax	**4,812**	**4,460**	**4,553**	**9,271**	**8,543**	**17,600**

Notes on segment information:

Business segments

Based on the "management approach" as defined in Ind-AS 108 - Operating Segments, the Chief Operating Decision Marker evaluates the Company's performance and allocates resources based on an analysis of various performance indicators by business segments. Accordingly, information has been presented along these business segments. The accounting principles used in the preparation of the financial statements are consistently applied to record revenue and expenditure in individual segments

Segment Assets/Liabilities

Assets and liabilities used in the company's business are not identified to any of the reportable segments, as these are used interchangeably between segments. The Management believes that it is not practicable to provide segment disclosures relating to total assets and liabilities since a meaningful segregation of the available data is onerous.

By order of the Board

for Infosys Limited

Bangalore, India **Dr. Vishal Sikka**

October 14, 2016

Chief Executive Officer and Managing Director

Certain statements in these results concerning our future growth prospects are forward-looking statements regarding our future business expectations intended to qualify for the 'safe harbor' under the Private Securities Litigation Reform Act of1995, which involve a number of risks and uncertainties that could cause actual results to differ materially from those in such forward-looking statements. The risks and uncertainties relating to these statements include, but are not limited to, risks and uncertainties regarding fluctuations in earnings, fluctuations in foreign exchange rates, our ability to manage growth, intense competition in IT services including those factors which may affect our cost advantage, wage increases in India, our ability to attract and retain highly skilled professionals, time and cost overruns on fixed-price, fixed-time frame contracts, client concentration, restrictions on immigration, industry segment concentration, our ability to manage our international operations, reduced demand for technology in our key focus areas, disruptions in telecommunication networks or system failures, our ability to successfully complete and integrate potential acquisitions, liability for damages on our service contracts, the success of the companies in which Infosys has made strategic investments, withdrawal or expiration of governmental fiscal incentives, political instability and regional conflicts, an inability to accurately predict economic or industry trends, legal restrictions on raising capital or acquiring companies outside India, and unauthorized use of our intellectual property and general economic conditions affecting our industry. Additional risks that coidd affect our future operating results are more fully described in our United States Securities and Exchange Commission filings including our Annual Report on Form 20-F for the fiscal year ended March 31, 2016. These filings are available at www.sec.gov. Infosys may, from time to time, make additional written and oral forward-looking statements, including statements contained in the company's filings with the Securities and Exchange Commission and our reports to shareholders. In addition, please note that the date of this release is October 14, 2016, and any forward-looking statements contained herein are based on assumptions that we believe to be reasonable as of this date. The company does not undertake to update any forward-looking statements that may be made from time to time by or on behalf of the company unless it is required by law.

RELIANCE INDUSTRIES

Unaudited standalone financial results for the quarter/half year ended 30th September 2016

(*INR in crore, except per share data*)

Sr. No.		Particulars	Quarter Ended			Half Year Ended		Year Ended
			30 Sep'16	30 June'16	30 Sep'15	30 Sep'16	30 Sep'15	31 Mar'16
1		**Income from operations**	**64,344**	**59,493**	**64,515**	**123,837**	**135,927**	**251,241**
2		**Expenses**						
	(a)	Cost of materials consumed	39,506	35,801	39,976	75,307	88,952	152,769
	(b)	Purchases of stock-in-trade	1,944	802	1,134	2,746	2,434	4,241
	(c)	Changes in inventories of finished goods, work-in-progress and stock-in-trade	(292)	(1,734)	1,957	(2,026)	54	4,171
	(d)	Excise duty and service tax recovered	4,767	5,997	3,698	10,764	9,293	18,083
	(e)	Employee benefits expense	1,016	1,251	940	2,267	2,157	4,262
	(f)	Depreciation, amortization and depletion expense	2,029	1,950	2,085	3,979	4,095	8,590
	(9)	Other expenses	6,848	6,559	7,225	13,407	14,278	28,368
		Total Expenses	**55,618**	**50,626**	**57,015**	**106,444**	**121,263**	**220,484**
3		**Profit from operations before other income and finance costs**	**8,526**	**8,867**	**7,500**	**17,393**	**14,664**	**30,757**
4		Other Income	2,280	2,033	1,683	4,313	3,399	7,821
5		**Profit from ordinary activities before finance costs**	**10,806**	**10,900**	**9,183**	**21,706**	**18,063**	**38,578**
6		Finance costs	633	924	723	1,557	1,340	2,562

Sr. No.	Particulars	Quarter Ended			Half Year Ended		Year Ended
		30 Sep'16	30 June'16	30 Sep'15	30 Sep'16	30 Sep'15	31 Mar'16
7	**Profit from ordinary activities before tax**	**10,173**	**9,976**	**8,460**	**20,149**	**16,723**	**36,016**
8	Tax expense	2,469	2,428	1,926	4,897	3,820	8,590
9	**Net Profit for the Period**	**7,704**	**7,548**	**6,534**	**15,252**	**12,903**	**27,426**
10	Other comprehensive income (after tax)	654	258	968	912	1,265	696
11	**Total comprehensive income (after tax) (OCI)**	**8,358**	**7,806**	**7,502**	**16,164**	**14,168**	**28,122**
12	Paid up Equity Share Capital, Equity Shares of INR 10/- each.	3,243	3,242	3,238	3,243	3,238	3,240
13	Reserves excluding revaluation reserves						2,50,155
14	Earnings per share (Face value of INR 10) (Not Annualised)						
	(a) Basic	23.8	23.3	20.2	47.0	39.9	84.7
	(b) Diluted	23.7	23.2	20.1	47.0	39.8	84.5
15	Capital Redemption reserve/Debenture Redemption Reserve	1,165	1,165	1,165	1,165	1,165	1,165
16	Net Worth	269,689	261,297	242,985	269,689	242,985	253,348
17	(a) Debt Service Coverage Ratio	1.11	3.09	7.06	1.63	4.45	5.39
	(b) Interest Service Coverage Ratio	17.07	11.80	12.71	13.94	13.48	15.06
	(c) Debt - Equity Ratio	0.38	0.40	0.40	0.38	0.40	0.42

Notes:

1. Result for the quarter/half year ended 30th September 2016 are in compliance with Indian Accounting Standards (Ind-AS) notified by the Ministry of Corporate Affairs. Consequently, result for the quarter ended 30th September 2015 , half year ended 30th September 2015 and previous year ended 31st March 2016 have been restated to comply with Ind-AS to make them comparable.

2. The Government of India (GOI), by its letters dated 2nd May, 2012, 14th November, 2013,10th July, 2014 and 3rd June 2016 has communicated that it proposes to disallow certain costs which the Production Sharing Contract (PSC),

relating to Block KG-DWN-98/3 entitles the Company to recover. Based on legal advice received, the Company continues to maintain that a Contractor is entitled to recover all of its costs under the terms of the PSC and there are no provisions that entitle the Government to disallow the recovery of any Contract Cost as defined in the PSC. The Company has already referred the issue to arbitration and already communicated the same to GOI for resolution of disputes. Pending decision of the arbitration, the demand from the GOI of $ 148 million (for INR 987 crore) being the company's share (total demand $ 247 million) towards additional Profit Petroleum has been considered as contingent liability.

3. The listed non-convertible debentures aggregating INR 1,270 crore as on 30th September, 2016 are secured by way of first mortgage/charge on the Company's certain properties and the asset cover thereof exceeds hundred percent of the principal amount of the said debentures.

4. Details of secured non-convertible debentures are as follows;

Sr. No.	Particulars	Previous Due Date (1st April 2016 till 30th Sep 2016)		Next Due Date (1st Oct 2016 till 31st March 2017)	
		Principal	Interest	Principal	Interest
	Reliance Industries Limited				
1.	PPD 177	-	-	24th Nov 2016	24th Nov 2016
2.	PPD 179 Tranche 3	-	-	-	8th Dec 2016
3.	PPD 180 Tranche 1	-	7th May 2016	-	-

Interest and Principal have been paid on the due dates.

5. Formulae for computation of ratios are as follows –

$$\text{Debt Service Coverage Ratio} = \frac{\text{Earnings before interest and tax}}{\text{Interest Expense + Principal Repayments made during the period for long term loans}}$$

$$\text{Interest Service Coverage Ratio} = \frac{\text{Earnings before interest and tax}}{\text{Interest Expense}}$$

$$\text{Debt/Eguity Ratio} = \frac{\text{Total Debt}}{\text{Equity}}$$

6. Transition to Ind-AS:

The Company has adopted Ind AS with effect from 1st April 2016 with comparatives being restated. Accordingly the impact of transition has been provided in the Opening Reserves as at 1st April 2015 and all the periods presented have been restated.

Reconciliation of profit and reserve between Ind AS and previous Indian GAAP for earlier periods and as at March 31, 2016

(INR in crore)

Sr. No	Nature of adjustments	Note ref.	Profit reconciliation			Reserve reconciliation
			Quarter ended	Half Year ended	Year ended	As at
			30-Sep-15	30-Sep-15	31-Mar-16	31-Mar-16
	Net Profit before OCI/Reserves as per Previous Indian GAAP		**6,561**	**12,879**	**27,417**	**236,944**
1	Change in accounting policy for Oil & Gas Activity - From Full Cost Method (FCM) to Successful Efforts Method (SEM)	1	77	229	279	(20,114)
2	Fair valuation as deemed cost for Property, Plant and Equipment	II	-	-	-	41,292
3	Fair Valuation for financial assets	III	47	(72)	167	4,110
4	Deferred Tax	IV	(103)	(52)	(306)	(11,947)
5	Others	V	(46)	(81)	(131)	(130)
	Total		(27)	24	9	13,211
	Net profit before OCI/Reserves as per Ind AS		**6,534**	**12,903**	**27,426**	**250,155**

Notes:

I. **Change in accounting policy for Oil & Gas Activity - From Full cost method (FCM) to Successful Efforts Method (SEM):** The impact on account of change in accounting policy from FCM to SEM is recognised in the Opening Reserves on the date of transition and consequential impact of depletion and write offs is recognized in the Profit and Loss Account. Major differences impacting such change of accounting policy are in the areas of;

- Expenditure on surrendered blocks, unproved wells and abandoned wells, which has been expensed under SEM.
- Depletion on producing property in SEM is calculated using Proved Developed Reserve, as against Proved Reserve in FCM.

II. **Fair valuation as deemed cost for Property, Plant and Equipment:** The Company have considered fair value for property, viz land admeasuring over 30,000 acres, situated in India, with impact of INR 41,292 crore in accordance with stipulations of Ind AS 101 with the resultant impact being accounted for in the reserves.

III. **Fair valuation for Financial Assets:** The Company has valued financial assets (other than Investment in subsidiaries, associate and joint ventures which are accounted at cost), at fair value. Impact of fair value changes as on the date of transition, is recognised in opening reserves and changes thereafter are recognised in Profit and Loss Account or Other Comprehensive Income, as the case may be.

IV. **Deferred Tax:** The impact of transition adjustments together with Ind AS mandate of using balance sheet approach (against profit and loss approach in the previous GAAP) for computation of deferred taxes has resulted in charge to the Reserves, on the date of transition, with consequential impact to the Profit and Loss account for the subsequent periods.

V. **Others:** Other adjustments primarily comprise of:

a. Attributing time value of money to Assets Retirement Obligation: Under Ind AS, such obligation is recognised and measured at present value. Under previous Indian GAAP it was recorded at cost. The impact for the periods subsequent to the date of transition is reflected in the Profit and Loss account.

b. Loan processing fees/transaction cost: Under Ind AS such expenditure are considered for calculating effective interest rate. The impact for the periods subsequent to the date of transition is reflected in the Profit and Loss account.

Further transition adjustments may be required to the financial statements as at 31st March, 2016 including those arising from new or revised standards or interpretations issued by the Ministry of Corporate Affairs or changes in use of one or more optional exemptions from full retrospective application of certain Ind AS standards.

7. The Company retained its domestic credit ratings of "CRISIL AAA" from CRISIL and "Ind AAA" from India Rating and an investment grade rating for its international debt from Moody's as Baa2 and BBB+ from S&P.

8. The Audit Committee has reviewed the above results and the Board of Directors has approved the above results and its release at their respective meetings held on 20th October 2016. The Statutory Auditors of the Company have carried out a Limited Review of the aforesaid results.

Unaudited Standalone Balance Sheet

(INR in crore)

Sr. No.	Particulars	As at 30th September 2016	As at 31st March 2016
A	**ASSETS**		
1	**Non- Current Assets**		
	(a) Property, plant and equipment	131.916	132,662
	(b) Capital work-in-progress	109,800	96,994
	(d) Intangible assets	14,725	14,881
	(e) Intangible Assets under Development	14.796	14,014
	(f) Financial Assets		
	(i) Investments	116,891	115,134
	(ii) Loans	10,368	11,812
	(g) Other Non-current assets	2,638	4,394
	Total Non-Current Assets	**401,134**	**389,891**
2	**Current Assets**		
	(a) Inventories	32,777	28,034
	(b) Financial Assets		
	(i) Investments	43,284	42,116
	(ii) Trade Receivables	4,234	3,495
	(iii) Cash & Bank Balance	4,412	6,892
	(iv) Loans	6,808	4,973
	(v) Others Financial Asset	2,625	2,654
	(c) Other Current Assets	5,156	4,038
	Total Current assets	**99.296**	**92,202**
	Total Assets	**500,430**	**482,093**
B	**EQUITY & LIABILITIES**		
1	**Equity**		
	(a) Equity Share capital	3,243	3,240
	(b) Other Equity	266,494	250,155
	Total Equity	**269,737**	**253,395**
2	**Liabilities**		
	Non - Current Liabilities		
	(a) Financial Liabilities		
	(i) Borrowings	80,004	77,504
	(b) Deferred tax liabilities (net)	25,620	25,106
	(d) Long Term Provisions	1,119	1,066
	Total Non current liabilities	**106,743**	**103,676**
	Current Liabilities		
	(a) Financial Liabilities		
	(i) Borrowings	16,419	14,490

Sr. No.	Particulars	As at 30th September 2016	As at 31st March 2016
	(ii) Trade Payables	58.999	54,521
	(iii) Other Financial Liabilities	34,454	46,493
	(b) Other Current liabilities	12.822	8,348
	(c) Short Term Provisions	1,256	1,170
	Total Current liabilities	**123,950**	**125,022**
	Total Equity And Liabilities	**500,430**	**482,093**

UNAUDITED STANDALONE SEGMENT INFORMATION FOR THE QUARTER/HALF YEAR ENDED 30th SEPTEMBER 2016

(INR in crore)

Sr. No.	Particulars	Quarter Ended			Half Year Ended		Year Ended
		30 Sep'16	30 June'16	30 Sep'15	30 Sep'16	30 Sep'15	31 Mar'16
1.	Segment Revenue						
	- Petrochemicals	21,293	19,409	19,851	40,702	39,403	76,982
	- Refining	51,838	48,946	51,265	100,784	112,623	202,504
	- Oil and Gas	701	783	1,166	1,484	2,366	4,259
	- Others	305	234	278	539	474	1,086
	Gross Turnover (Turnover and Inter Segment Transfers)	**74,137**	**69,372**	**72,560**	**143,509**	**154,866**	**284,831**
	Less: Inter Segment Transfers	9,793	9,879	8,045	19,672	18,939	33,590
	Turnover	**64,344**	**59,493**	**64,515**	**123,837**	**135,927**	**251,241**
2.	**Segment Results**						
	- Petrochemicals	3,464	2,901	2,511	6,365	4,960	10,264
	- Refining	5,901	6,581	5,399	12,482	10,522	23,201
	- Oil and Gas	24	48	137	72	371	373
	- Others	90	99	56	189	119	295
	Total Segment Profit before Interest and Tax	**9,479**	**9,629**	**8,103**	**19,108**	**15,972**	**34,133**
	(i) Interest Expense	(633)	(924)	(723)	(1,557)	(1,340)	(2,562)
	(ii) Interest Income	1,072	1,128	1,093	2,200	2,148	4,169
	(iii) Other Un-allocable Income (Net of Expenditure)	255	143	(13)	398	(57)	276

Sr. No.	Particulars	Quarter Ended			Half Year Ended		Year Ended
		30 Sep'16	30 June'16	30 Sep'15	30 Sep'16	30 Sep'15	31 Mar'16
	Profit before Tax	**10,173**	**9,976**	**8,460**	**20,149**	**16,723**	**36,016**
	(i) Provision for Current Tax	(2,217)	(2,192)	(1,750)	(4,409)	(3,472)	(7,802)
	(ii) Provision for Deferred Tax	(252)	(236)	(176)	(488)	(348)	(788)
	Profit after Tax	**7,704**	**7,548**	**6,534**	**15,252**	**12,903**	**27,426**
3.	**Segment Assets**						
	- Petrochemicals	94,861	88,572	60,686	94,861	60,686	86,280
	- Refining	171,116	174,266	181,643	171,116	181,643	163,123
	- Oil and Gas	24,990	25,234	23,308	24,990	23,308	24,467
	- Others	62,778	59,047	46,877	62,778	46,877	58.977
	- Unallocated	146,685	150,954	140,477	146,685	140,477	149,246
	Total Segment Assets	**500,430**	**498,073**	**452,991**	**500,430**	**452,991**	**482,093**
5.	**Segment Liabilities**						
	- Petrochemicals	15,379	13,902	10,044	15,379	10,044	12,205
	- Refining	60,821	67,790	59,555	60,821	59,555	59,900
	- Oil and Gas	4,599	4,653	3,641	4,599	3,641	4,457
	- Others	638	558	913	638	913	687
	- Unallocated	418,993	411,170	378,838	418,993	378,838	404.844
	Total Segment Liabilities	**500,430**	**498,073**	**452,991**	**500,430**	**452,991**	**482,093**

Notes to Segment Information (Standalone) for the Quarter Ended 30th September 2016

1. As per Indian Accounting Standard 108 'Operating Segment' (Ind-AS 108), the Company has reported 'Segment Information', as described below:

   a) The **petrochemicals** segment includes production and marketing operations of petrochemical products namely, High density Polyethylene, Low density Polyethylene, Linear Low density Polyethylene, Polypropylene, Polyvinyl Chloride, Polyester Yarn, Polyester Fibres, Purified Terephthalic Acid, Paraxylene, Ethylene Glycol, Olefins, Aromatics, Linear Alkyl Benzene, Butadiene, Acrylonitrile, Poly Butadiene Rubber, Styrene Butadiene Rubber, Caustic Soda and Polyethylene Terephthalate.

   b) The **refining** segment includes production and marketing operations of the petroleum products.

   c) The **oil and gas** segment includes exploration, development and production of crude oil and natural gas.

d) The smaller business segments not separately reportable have been grouped under the **others** segment.

e) Other investments/assets and income from the same are considered under **unallocable.**

For Reliance Industries Limited

Mukesh D Ambani

Chairman & Managing Director

October 20, 2016

TATA CONSULTANCY SERVICES LIMITED

Statement of Audited Standalone Financial Results for the Quarter and Six months ended September 30, 2016

(INR in crores)

		Quarter ended			Six months ended		Year ended
		September 30, 2016	June 30, 2016	September 30, 2015	September 30, 2016	September 30, 2015	March 31, 2016
1	**INCOME FROM OPERATIONS (NET)**	**23,016**	**23,087**	**21,636**	**46,103**	**41,985**	**85,864**
2	**EXPENSES**						
	a) Employee costs	11,937	11,891	10,318	23,828	20,422	42,420
	b) Fees to external consultants	1,664	1,719	1,501	3,383	2,811	5,978
	c) Depreciation and amortisation expense	396	386	362	782	710	1,459
	d) Other operating expenses	2,596	2,670	2,746	5,266	5,188	10,412
	Total expenses	**16,593**	**16,666**	**14,927**	**33,259**	**29,131**	**60,269**
3	**PROFIT FROM OPERATIONS BEFORE OTHER INCOME, FINANCE COSTS AND TAX (1-2)**	**6,423**	**6,421**	**6,709**	**12,844**	**12,854**	**25,595**
4	OTHER INCOME (NET)	1,175	979	679	2,154	1,670	3.757
5	**PROFIT BEFORE FINANCE COSTS AND TAX (3+4)**	**7,598**	**7,400**	**7,388**	**14,998**	**14,524**	**29,352**
6	FINANCE COSTS	3	6	3	9	4	13
7	**PROFIT BEFORE TAX (5-6)**	**7,595**	**7,394**	**7,385**	**14,989**	**14,520**	**29,339**
8	TAX EXPENSE	1,637	1,616	1,662	3,253	3,164	6,264
9	**NET PROFIT FOR THE PERIOD (7-8)**	**5,958**	**5,778**	**5,723**	**11,736**	**11,356**	**23,075**
10	**OTHER COMPREHENSIVE INCOME**	**340**	**106**	**29**	**446**	**(143)**	**(132)**
11	TOTAL COMPREHENSIVE INCOME (9+10)	6,298	5,884	5,752	12,182	11,213	22,943
12	Paid up equity share capital (Face Value: INR 1 per share)	197.04	197.04	197.04	197.04	197.04	197.04
13	**Total Reserves**						**64,816**
14	Basle and diluted earnings per share (In INR)	30.24	29.32	29.04	59.56	57.63	117.11

(INR in crores)

		As at September 30,	As at March 31,
		2016	**2016**
1.	**ASSETS**		
	Non - current assets		
(a)	Property, plant and equipment	9,326	9,056
(b)	Capital work-ln-progress	1,363	1,640
(c)	Intangible assets	21	24
(d)	Financial assets		
	(I) Investments	2,210	2,229
	(II) Loans	8	2,432
	(III) Other financial assets	727	1,179
(e)	Income tax asset (net)	4,687	4,230
(0	Deferred tax assets (net)	2,341	2,528
(B)	Other assets	604	720
	Total non-currrent assets	**21,287**	**24,038**
	Current assets		
(a)	Inventories	16	9
(b)	Financial assets		
	(i) Investments	28,343	21,930
	(ii) Trade receivables	19,746	19,058
	(iii) Unbilled revenue	3,499	2,712
	(iv) Cash and cash equivalents	511	4,383
	(v) Other balances with banks	531	423
	(vi) Loans	4,530	2,523
	(vii) Other financial assets	1,264	866
(c)	Other assets	1,097	1,473
	Total current assets	**59,537**	**53,377**
	TOTAL ASSETS	**80,824**	**77,415**
II.	**EQUITY AND LIABILITIES**		
	Equity		
(a)	Share capital	197	197
(b)	Other equity	69,060	64,816
	Total equity	69,257	65,013
	Liabilities		

		As at September 30,	As at March 31,
		2016	**2016**
	Non-current liabilities		
(a)	Financial liabilities		
	(i) Long-term borrowings	46	50
	(ii) Other financial liabilities	239	293
(b)	Employee benefit obligation	56	48
(c)	Provisions	19	40
(d)	Deferred tax liabilities (net)	418	366
(e)	Other liabilities	315	298
	Total non-current liabilities	**1,093**	**1,095**
	Current liabilities		
(a)	Financial liabilities		
	(i) Short-term borrowings	1	113
	(ii) Trade and other payables	4,814	5,373
	(iii) Other financial liabilities	1,101	2,083
(b)	Income received In advance	1,070	1,068
(c)	Current Income tax liabilities (net)	1,025	536
(d)	Employee benefit obligation	1,321	1,164
(e)	Provisions	136	115
(f)	Other liabilities	1,006	855
	Total current liabilities	**10,474**	**11,307**
	TOTAL EQUITY AND LIABILITIES	**80,824**	**77,415**

Select explanatory notes to the Statement of Audited Financial Results for the Quarter and Six months ended September 30, 2016.

1. Particulars of entities consolidated as on September 30, 2016

   a) **Entities held directly**

   APTOnline Limited, C-Edge Technologies Limited, CMC Americas Inc., Diligenta Limited, MahaOnline Limited, MP Online Limited, Tata America International Corporation, Tata Consultancy Services Canada Inc., Tata Consultancy Services (Africa) (PTY) Ltd., Tata Consultancy Services Asia Pacific Pte Ltd., Tata Consultancy Services Belgium S.A., Tata Consultancy Services Deutschland GmbH, Tata Consultancy Services Netherlands BV, Tata Consultancy Services Qatar S.S.C., Tata Consultancy Services Sverige AB, Tata Sons & Consultancy Services Employees' Welfare Trust, TCS e-Serve International Limited, TCS FNS Pty Limited, TCS Foundation, TCS Iberoamerlca SA, TCS e-Serve Limited - Employees' Welfare Trust.

b) Entitles held indirectly

Altl HR S.A.S., Alti Infrastructures Systemes & Reseaux S.A.S., Alt! NV, Alt! S.A., Alti Switzerland S.A.; CMC eBiz Inc., Diligenta 2 Limited, MGDC S.C., MS GV Investments Corporation, Planaxis Technologies Inc., PT Financial Network Services, PT Tata Consultancy Services Indonesia, Tata Consultancy Services (China) Co., Ltd., Tata Consultancy Services (Philippines) Inc., Tata Consultancy Services (South Africa) (PTY) Ltd., Tata Consultancy Services (Thailand) Limited, Tata Consultancy Services Argentina S.A., Tata Consultancy Services Chile S.A., Tata Consultancy Services Danmark ApS, Tata Consultancy Services De Espana S.A., Tata Consultancy Services De Mexico S.A., De C.V., Tata Consultancy Services Do Brasil Ltda, Tata Consultancy Services France S.A.S., Tata Consultancy Services Japan, Ltd., Tata Consultancy Services Luxembourg S.A., Tata Consultancy Services Malaysia Sdn Bhd, Tata Consultancy Services Osterreich GmbH, Tata Consultancy Services Portugal Unipessoal Limitada, Tata Consultancy Services Saudi Arabia , Tata Consultancy Services Switzerland Ltd., TCS Solution Center S.A., TCS e-Serve America, Inc., TCS Financial Solutions Beijing Co., Ltd., TCS Financial Solutions Australia Holdings Pty Limited, TCS Financial Solutions Australia Pty Limited, TCS Inversiones Chile Limitada, TCS Italia SRL, TATASOLUTION CENTER S.A., TCS Uruguay S.A., Teamlink, TECHNOLOGY OUTSOURCING S.A.C., TCS e- Serve International Limited - Employees' Welfare Benefit Trust, Tescom (France) Software Systems Testing S.A.R.L.

2. The audited consolidated financial results and the audited standalone financial res2ults of the Company for the quarter and six months ended September 30, 2016 have been reviewed by the Audit Committee of the Board and approved by the Board of Directors at its meeting held on October 13, 2016.

3. The Company adopted Indian Accounting Standards ("Ind AS") from April 1, 2016 and accordingly these financial results have been prepared in accordance with the recognition and measurement principles laid down in the Ind AS 34 Interim Financial Reporting prescribed under Section 133 of the Companies Act, 2013 read with the relevant rules issued thereunder and the other accounting principles generally accepted in India. Financial results for all the periods presented have been prepared in accordance with the recognition and measurement principles of Ind AS 34.

4. Reconciliations between consolidated and unconsolidated equity and financial results, as previously reported (referred to as 'Previous GAAP') and Ind AS for quarters/year presented are as under:

EQUITY RECONCILIATION

(INR in crores)

	Consolidated			Unconsolidated		
	As at September 30, 2015	As at March 31, 2016	As at April 1, 2015	As at September 30, 2015	As at March 31, 2016	As at April 1, 2015
Equity under Previous GAAP attributable to:						
Tata Consultancy Services Limited	60,307	$5,361	50,635	54,823	58,867	45,416
Amalgamation of CMC/adjusted effect of CMC merger	-	-	(296)	-	-	810
Non-controlling interests	456	502	1,128	-	-	-
Equity under Previous GAAP	**60,763**	**65,863**	**51,467**	**54,823**	**58,867**	**46,226**
Dividend and taxon dividend	1,304	6,406	5,649	1,304	6,403	5,724
Effect of Consolidation of Employee welfare trusts	173	184	168	-	-	-
Depredation and amortisation	(507)	(483)	(537)	(486)	(440)	(537)
Obligation to acquire non-controlling Interests	(222)	(189)	(240)	-	-	-
Reorganisation of entities under common control	(167)	(167)	(167)	-	-	
Fair valuation of investments	19	86	10	16	83	9
Tax adjustments Including deferred tax on undistributed earnings	(68)	(243)	(25)	140	101	133
Impact of retrospective application of Ind AS 103 to past business combinations	(38)	(29)	(47)	-	-	-
Others	-	(1)	(2)	4	(1)	(1)
Equity under Ind AS Attributable to:	**61,257**	**71,427**	**56,276**	**55,801**	**65,013**	**51,554**
Tata Consultancy Services Limited	60,984	71,072	56,053	55,801	65,013	51,554
Non-controlling Interests	273	355	223	-	-	-

TOTAL COMPREHENSIVE INCOME RECONCILIATION

(INR in crores)

	Consolidated			Unconsolidated		
	For the quarter ended September 30, 2015	**For Six months ended September 30, 2015**	**For the year ended March 31, 2016**	**For the quarter ended September 30, 2015**	**For Six months ended September 30, 2015**	**For the year ended March 31, 2016**
Net Profit under Previous GAAP	**6,108**	**11,849**	**24,375**	**5,698**	**11,273**	**22,883**
Actuarial (gain)/toss on employee defined benefit funds recognised In Other Comprehensive Income	32	43	114	16	24	122
Effect of change In depreciation method recognised as change In estimate	IS	32	57	25	51	97
Obligation to acquire non-controlling Interest In a subsidiary	(3)	(6)	(15)	-	-	-
Effect of measuring Investments at fair value through profit and loss	(18)	9	(2)	(18)	8	(3)
Deferred taxes Including taxes on undistributed earnings of subsidiaries	(39)	(66)	(202)	(1)	(12)	(28)
Others	(2)	S	11	3	12	4
Net Profit for the period under Ind AS	**6,093**	**11,866**	**24,338**	**5,723**	**11,356**	**23,075**
Other Comprehensive Income	S7	110	269	29	(143)	(132)
Total Comprehensive Income under Ind AS	**6,150**	**11,976**	**24,607**	**5,752**	**11,213**	**22,943**

5. The Board of Directors at Its meeting held on October 13, 2016, has declared an Interim dividend of INR 6.50 per equity share.

For and on behalf of the Board of Directors

N.Chandrasekaran

CEO & Managing Director

Mumbai

October 13, 2016

Chapter 4

Audit and review report on interim financial results

First time implementation of Ind AS poses many challenges in defining auditor's responsibilities towards the audit of comparative information including opening balance sheet and reconciliations as at the transition date and its implication on the auditor's reporting. Accordingly, ICAI felt that there is a need to define auditor's responsibilities with respect to audit of such financial information. ICAI has issued an implementation guide on auditor's reports under Indian AS for transition phase.

This Implementation Guide provides guidance on reporting responsibilities of the auditors for the audit of:

(a) Ind AS financial statements prepared for the first year in which Ind AS are applicable to the company.

(b) Ind AS financial results prepared by a listed entity under SEBI Listing Regulations during the first year of adoption of Ind AS.

(c) Special purpose financial statements for the corresponding period and opening balance sheet as per Ind AS which will be presented by the company as part of its first Ind AS financial statements.

The implementation guide states that SA 710 'Comparative Information—Corresponding Figures and Comparative Financial Statements' deals with the auditor's responsibilities regarding comparative information in an audit of financial statements. As per this SA, there are two different broad approaches to the auditor's reporting responsibilities in respect of such comparative information:

(1) corresponding figures and

(2) comparative financial statements.

Under corresponding figures approach, the auditor's opinion does not refer to the corresponding figures (except in the limited specified circumstances); it refers to the current period only. The amounts and other disclosures for the prior period are included as an integral part of the current period financial statements, and are intended to be read only in relation to the amounts and other disclosures relating to the current period figures. In contrast, when 'comparative financial statements' are presented, the auditor's opinion refers to each period for which financial statements are presented and on which an audit opinion is expressed.

As per the guide, the audit report on the financial statements/financial results prepared in conformity with Ind AS would also be based on the corresponding figures approach. As per the Standards on Auditing, the current auditor can place reliance on comparative information audited by the predecessor auditor (subject to the requirements of SA 510, 'Initial Audit Engagements-Opening Balances' and SA 710).

With respect to the reporting by the auditor, it is noted that as per the formats of the financial results prescribed by SEBI, the annual figures for the previous year had to be stated as 'audited' even where the quarterly results are reviewed. However, SEBI has relaxed the requirement for the first three quarters of the first year of Ind AS implementation whereby submission of annual financial results for the previous year is not mandatory. There can nevertheless be situations where companies do not avail the relaxation and instead choose to present audited or reviewed results for the previous year and/or relevant quarters of the previous year.

Where the company opts to present audited/reviewed financial results for the corresponding periods, there may be situations where the prior period(s) figures were not reviewed/audited by another auditor (being the predecessor auditor). Further, while the predecessor auditor may have reviewed/audited the financial result of the previous year, such review/audit would have been performed for financial statements prepared under previous GAAP and not Ind AS. In such cases also, the guidance provided in the ICAI technical guide can be applied for review/audit of corresponding financial results prepared as per Ind AS in the first year of transition.

Suggested format of the audit report/limited review report on quarterly financial results has been given below.

4.1 IMPLEMENTATION GUIDE ON AUDITOR'S REPORT UNDER IND AS FOR TRANSITION PHASE

The following formats have been included in the implementation guide on Auditor's Reports under Indian Accounting Standards for Transition Phase:

4.1.1 Illustrative Format of Audit Report on Quarterly Financial Results (Companies other than Banks and Insurance Companies) (Phase 1) - Unmodified Opinion (only for quarterly results in the first year of Ind AS implementation)

Circumstances include the following:

- Only mandatory information as per the SEBI circular CIR/CFD/FAC/62/2016 dated 5th July 2016 is presented in the financial results.
- The results for the corresponding periods in the previous year have not been audited as per the relaxation available in the above referred circular.

Auditor's Report on Quarterly Financial Results and Year to Date Results of the Company Pursuant to the Regulation 33 of the SEBI (Listing Obligations and Disclosure Requirements) Regulations, 2015

To

Board of Directors of....... (Name of the company) We have audited the quarterly standalone financial results of......... (Name of the company) for the quarter ended.......... (date of the quarter end) and the year to date results for the period ...... to ...., attached herewith, being submitted by the company pursuant to the requirement of Regulation 33 of the SEBI (Listing Obligations and Disclosure Requirements) Regulations, 2015. Attention is drawn to the fact that the figures for the corresponding quarter ended and the corresponding year to date from....to ...., including the reconciliation of profit/loss under Ind AS of the corresponding quarter with profit/loss reported under previous GAAP, as reported in these financial results have been approved by company's Board of Directors but have not been subjected to audit[1].

These quarterly standalone financial results as well as the year to date standalone financial results have been prepared on the basis of the interim financial statements, which are the responsibility of the company's management. Our responsibility is to express an opinion on these financial results based on our audit of such interim standalone financial statements, which have been prepared in accordance with the recognition and measurement principles laid down in Indian Accounting Standard (Ind AS) for Interim Financial Reporting (Ind AS 34), prescribed under Section 133 of the Companies Act, 2013 read with relevant rules issued thereunder; or by the Institute of Chartered Accountants of India[2], as applicable and other accounting principles generally accepted in India.

We conducted our audit in accordance with the auditing standards generally accepted in India. Those standards require that we plan and perform the audit to obtain reasonable assurance about whether the financial results are free of material misstatement(s). An audit includes examining, on a test basis, evidence supporting the amounts disclosed as financial results. An audit also includes assessing the accounting principles used and significant estimates made by management. We believe that our audit provides a reasonable basis for our opinion.

Based on our audit conducted as above, in our opinion and to the best of our information and according to the explanations given to us, these quarterly standalone financial results as well as the year to date results:

(i) are presented in accordance with the requirements of Regulation 33 of the SEBI (Listing Obligations and

---

1 This sentence may need to be modified depending on the exemption, if any, available for the relevant quarter.

2 Where, a listed entity is not a company.

Disclosure Requirements) Regulations, 2015 and SEBI circular dated 5th July 2016 in this regard; and

(ii) give a true and fair view of the net profit/loss (financial performance including other comprehensive income)[3] and other financial information for the quarter ended ...... (date of the quarter end) as well as the year to date results for the period from ..... to ....

For XYZ & Co. Chartered Accountants
(Firm's Registration No.)

Signature
(Name of the member signing the audit report)
(Designation)[4]
(Membership Number)

Place of signature:

Date:

3 Whichever is applicable.

4 Partner or proprietor, as the case may be.

4.1.2 Illustrative Format of Limited Review Report on Quarterly Financial Results for Companies (other than banks and insurance companies) (Phase 1) - Unmodified Opinion (only for quarterly results in the first year of Ind AS implementation)

Circumstances include the following:

- Only mandatory information as per the SEBI circular CIR/CFD/FAC/62/2016 dated 5th July 2016 is presented in the financial results.
- The results for the corresponding periods in the previous year have not been reviewed as per the relaxation available in the above referred circular.

Limited Review Report on Quarterly Financial Results and Year to Date Results of the Company Pursuant to the Regulation 33 of the SEBI (Listing Obligations and Disclosure Requirements) Regulations, 2015

To Board of Directors of...... (Name of the Company)

We have reviewed the accompanying statement of unaudited standalone financial results of .... (Name of the Company) for the period ended..... and the year to-date results for the period ..... to..... attached herewith, being submitted by the company pursuant to the requirements of Regulation 33 of the SEBI (Listing Obligations and Disclosure Requirements) Regulations, 2015. Attention is drawn to the fact that the figures for the corresponding quarter ended and the corresponding year to date from ....to..., including the reconciliation of profit/loss under Ind AS of the corresponding quarter with profit/loss reported under previous GAAP, as reported in these financial results have been approved by company's Board of Directors but have not been subjected to review[5].

This statement is the responsibility of the Company's Management and has been approved by the Board of Directors. Our responsibility is to issue a report on these financial statements based on our review.

We conducted our review in accordance with the Standard on Review Engagement (SRE) 2410, *Review of Interim Financial Information Performed by the Independent Auditor of the Entity'* issued by the Institute of Chartered Accountants of India. This standard requires that we plan and perform the review to obtain moderate assurance as to whether the financial statements are free of material misstatement. A review is limited primarily to inquiries of company personnel and analytical procedures applied to

[5] This sentence may need to be modified depending on the exemption, if any, available for the relevant quarter.

financial data and thus provides less assurance than an audit. We have not performed an audit and accordingly, we do not express an audit opinion.

Based on our review conducted as above, nothing has come to our attention that causes us to believe that the accompanying statement of unaudited standalone financial results prepared in accordance with applicable accounting standards i.e. Ind AS prescribed under Section 133 of the Companies Act, 2013 read with relevant rules issued thereunder or by the Institute of Chartered Accountants of India[6] and other recognized accounting practices and policies has not disclosed the information required to be disclosed in terms of Regulation 33 of the SEBI (Listing Obligations and Disclosure Requirements) Regulations, 2015 and SEBI Circular dated 5th July, 2016 including the manner in which it is to be disclosed, or that it contains any material misstatement.

For XYZ & Co.
Chartered Accountants
(Firm's Registration No.)

Signature
(Name of the member signing the report)
(Designation)[7]
(Membership Number)

Place of signature:

Date:

6 Where, a listed entity is not a company.

7 Partner or proprietor, as the case may be.

4.2 OTHER FORMATS

4.2.1 Review Report on Quarterly Financial Results and Year to Date Results of the Company Pursuant to the Regulation 33 of the SEBI (Listing Obligations and Disclosure Requirements) Regulations, 2015

To the Board of Directors of *(Name of the Company)*

(1) We have reviewed the accompanying statement of unaudited financial results ("the Statement") of ***(Name of the Company)*** ("the Company") for the quarter ended ***(date of the quarter end[8])*** and the year to date results for the period .... to .... This Statement is the responsibility of the Company's Management and has been approved by the Board of Directors. Our responsibility is to issue a report on the Statement based on our review.

(2) We conducted our review in accordance with the Standard on Review Engagement (SRE) 2410, Review of Interim Financial Information Performed by the Independent Auditor of the Entity, issued by the Institute of Chartered Accountants of India. This standard requires that we plan and perform the review to obtain moderate assurance as to whether the Statement is free of material misstatement. A review is limited primarily to inquiries of company personnel and analytical procedures, applied to financial data and thus provides less assurance than an audit. We have not performed an audit and accordingly, we do not express an audit opinion.

(3) (Insert qualification(s), if any)[9]

(4) Based on our review conducted as above, {except for the effects of qualification(s) as described in the previous paragraph(s),} [10] nothing has come to our attention that causes us to believe that the accompanying Statement prepared in accordance with applicable accounting standards, as notified under the {Companies (Accounting Standards) Rules, 2006 read with Rule 7 of the Companies (Accounts) Rules, 2014 in respect of Section 133 of the Companies Act, 2013}/{Companies (Indian Accounting Standards) Rules, 2015 as specified in Section 133 of the Companies Act, 2013 read with SEBI Circular CIR/CFD/CMD/15/2015 dated 30 November 2015[11]}*[12]* and other recognised accounting practices and policies has not

---

8 Date format is to be DD/Month/Year (e.g. 31 March 20XX). It shall be used consistently throughout the review report.

9 All the modifications should be drafted as per Standard on Auditing (SA) 705, 'Modifications to the Opinion in the Independent Auditor's Report'. In case of any adverse opinion or disclaimer of opinion, the report should be carefully drafted in accordance with SA 705.

10 The text would be relevant only where qualification is being inserted.

11 As per paragraph 5 of SEBI Circular CIR/CFD/CMD/15/2015 dated 30 November 2015, companies adopting the Ind AS in terms of Companies (Indian Accounting Standards) Rules, 2015 notified by

disclosed the information required to be disclosed in terms of Regulation 33 of the SEBI (Listing Obligations and Disclosure Requirements) Regulations, 2015, including the manner in which it is to be disclosed, or that it contains any material misstatement.

(5) (Insert Emphasis of Matter, if any here)[13]

(6) [14]The review of unaudited financial results for the three months period ended 30 June 20*XX,* [15]{six months period ended 30 September 20*XX* and nine months period ended 31 December 20*XX*} included in the Statement was carried out and reported by .... ***(name of the previous auditor)*** vide their unqualified review report dated .... ***(date of the review report for the first quarter),*** [16]*{*unqualified review report dated .... ***(date of the review report for the second quarter)*** and unqualified review report dated .... ***(date of the review report for the third quarter)}*** respectively, whose review report(s) has/have been furnished to us and which have been relied upon by us for the purpose of our review of the Statement. Our review report is not qualified in respect of this matter. [17] [18]

For XXXXXXXXXXXX
Chartered Accountants
Firm Registration No: XXXXXXXX

per **XXXXXXX**
Partner
Membership No. XXXXXXXX

(Place)

(Date)

MCA on February 16, 2015 while publishing quarterly/annual financial results under Regulation 33 of the Listing Regulations, 2015, should ensure that the comparatives filed along with such quarterly/annual financial results are also Ind AS compliant.

12 Use as applicable.

13 Emphasis of Matter paragraph in the review report should be carefully drafted and placed in the review report as per SA 706, 'Emphasis of Matter Paragraphs and Other Matter Paragraphs in the Independent Auditor's Report'. Also, a statement to the effect that 'Our report is not modified in respect of this matter.' should be mentioned in the paragraph.

14 This paragraph has to be added, if an audit firm has been appointed as auditor during the financial year under audit and the previous quarter(s) have been reviewed by the previous auditor.

15 In cases where the appointment of audit firm has been done for the third or the fourth quarter onwards during the year.

16 In cases where the appointment of audit firm has been done for the third or the fourth quarter onwards during the year.

17 The review report should also refer to the corresponding figures as required by para 10 of SA 710 (R), 'Comparative Information—Corresponding Figures and Comparative Financial Statements' where applicable.

18 Where the previous year was audited by other auditor, the same should be referred to in accordance with paragraph 17 and Example-C of SA 710 (R)

4.2.2 Review Report on Quarterly Consolidated Financial Results and Consolidated Year to Date Results of the Company Pursuant to the Regulation 33 of the SEBI (Listing Obligations and Disclosure Requirements) Regulations, 2015

To the Board of Directors of *(Name of the Company)*

1. We have reviewed the accompanying statement of unaudited consolidated financial results ("the Statement") of ***(Name of the Company)*** ("the Company") and its subsidiaries (the Company and its subsidiaries together referred to as "the Group"), {its associates and jointly controlled entities}[19] for the quarter ended ***(date of the quarter end*** [20]***)*** and the year to date results for the period .... to .... This Statement is the responsibility of the Company's Management and has been approved by the Board of Directors. Our responsibility is to issue a report on the Statement based on our review.

2. We conducted our review in accordance with the Standard on Review Engagement (SRE) 2410, Review of Interim Financial Information Performed by the Independent Auditor of the Entity, issued by the Institute of Chartered Accountants of India. This standard requires that we plan and perform the review to obtain moderate assurance as to whether the Statement is free of material misstatement. A review is limited primarily to inquiries of company personnel and analytical procedures, applied to financial data and thus provides less assurance than an audit. We have not performed an audit and accordingly, we do not express an audit opinion.

3. (Insert qualification(s), if any)[21]

4. Based on our review conducted as above {and upon consideration of the review reports of other auditors}[22], {except for the effects of qualification(s) as described in the previous paragraph(s)}[23], nothing has come to our attention that causes us to believe that the accompanying Statement prepared in accordance with applicable accounting standards, as notified under the {Companies (Accounting Standards) Rules, 2006 read with Rule 7 of the Companies (Accounts) Rules, 2014 in respect of Section 133 of the

---

19 Use as applicable throughout the report

20 Date format is to be DD/Month/Year (e.g. 31 March 20XX). It shall be used consistently throughout the review report.

21 All the modifications should be drafted as per Standard on Auditing (SA) 705, 'Modifications to the Opinion in the Independent Auditor's Report'. In case of any adverse opinion or disclaimer of opinion, the report should be carefully drafted in accordance with SA 705.

22 Add where we are not the auditors of all the components of the group.

23 The text would be relevant only where qualification is being inserted.

Companies Act, 2013}/{Companies (Indian Accounting Standards) Rules, 2015 as specified in Section 133 of the Companies Act, 2013 read with SEBI Circular CIR/CFD/CMD/15/2015 dated 30 November 2015[24]}[25] and other recognised accounting practices and policies has not disclosed the information required to be disclosed in terms of Regulation 33 of the SEBI (Listing Obligations and Disclosure Requirements) Regulations, 2015, including the manner in which it is to be disclosed, or that it contains any material misstatement.

5. (Insert Emphasis of Matter, if any here)[26]

6. [27]We did not review the interim financial results of ***(number)*** subsidiaries, {and ***(number)*** joint ventures }[28], included in the Statement, whose interim financial results reflect [total revenues (after eliminating intra-group transactions) of ₹.........and .... for the quarter and period ended ***(date of the quarter end)***, respectively, net profit/net loss[29] after tax and prior period items (after eliminating intra-group transactions) of ₹ ....and .... for the quarter and period ended ***(date of the quarter end)*** respectively {and total assets of ₹.........as at quarter ended ***(date of quarter end)***}[30]. {The statement also includes the Group's share of net profit/loss of Rs. _____and _________ for the quarter and period ended ____________ as considered in the statement, in respect of *(number)* associates, whose interim financial results have not been reviewed by us}[31]][32]. These interim financial results have been reviewed by other auditors whose review report(s) has/have been furnished to us and our report in respect thereof is based solely on the review report(s) of such other auditors. Our review report is not qualified in respect of this matter.

---

24 As per paragraph 5 of SEBI Circular CIR/CFD/CMD/15/2015 dated 30 November 2015, companies adopting the Ind AS in terms of Companies (Indian Accounting Standards) Rules, 2015 notified by MCA on February 16, 2015 while publishing quarterly/annual financial results under Regulation 33 of the Listing Regulations, 2015, should ensure that the comparatives filed along with such quarterly/annual financial results are also Ind AS compliant.

25 Use as applicable.

26 Emphasis of Matter paragraph in the review report should be carefully drafted and placed in the review report as per SA 706, , 'Emphasis of Matter Paragraphs and Other Matter Paragraphs in the Independent Auditor's Report' . Also, a statement to the effect that 'Our report is not modified in respect of this matter.' should be mentioned in the paragraph.

27 Add where we are not the auditors of all the components of the group.

28 Wherever applicable.

29 Whichever applicable.

30 In case of half yearly and annual financial results.

31 Insert where applicable

32 In case of Companies following Ind AS as notified under the Companies (Indian Accounting Standards) Rules 2015, engagement teams need to amend this as per the terminologies used under the Ind AS.

7. [33]The review of unaudited consolidated financial results for the three months period ended 30 June 20*XX*, [34]{six months period ended 30 September 20*XX* and nine months period ended 31 December 20*XX*} included in the Statement was carried out and reported by ....***(name of the previous auditor)*** vide their unqualified review report dated ....***(date of the review report for the first quarter),*** [35]{unqualified review report dated ....***(date of the review report for the second quarter)*** and unqualified review report dated ....***(date of the review report for the third quarter)}*** respectively whose review report(s) has/have been furnished to us and which have been relied upon by us for the purpose of our review of the Statement. Our review report is not qualified in respect of this matter. [36] [37]

For XXXXXXXXXX

Chartered Accountants

Firm Registration No: XXXXXXXXX

per XXXXXXX

Partner

Membership No. XXXXXXXX

(Place)[38]

(Date)

---

[33] This paragraph has to be added, if audit firm has been appointed as auditor during the financial year under audit and the previous quarter(s) have been reviewed by the previous auditor.

[34] In cases where the appointment of audit firm has been done for the third or the fourth quarter onwards during the year.

[35] In cases where the appointment of audit firm has been done for the third or the fourth quarter onwards during the year.

[36] The review report should also refer to the corresponding figures as required by para 10 of SA 710 (R), 'Comparative Information—Corresponding Figures and Comparative Financial Statements', where applicable.

[37] Where the previous year was audited by other auditor, the same should be referred to in accordance with paragraph 17 and Example-C of SA 710 (R)

[38] City where the review report is being signed.

4.2.3 Independent Auditors' Report on Condensed Consolidated Financial Statements

To the Board of Directors of *(Name of the Company)*

1. We have audited the accompanying Condensed Consolidated Financial Statements of ***(Name of the Company)***, ("the Company") and its subsidiaries, {associates and joint ventures}[39] (collectively referred to as "the Group"), which comprise the Condensed Consolidated Balance Sheet as at ***(Date of Balance Sheet[40])*** , and the Condensed Consolidated Statement of Profit and Loss {and Condensed Consolidated Cash Flow Statement}[41] for the quarter then ended, and a summary of significant accounting policies and other explanatory information[42].

Management's Responsibility for the Condensed Consolidated Financial Statements

2. Management is responsible for the preparation of these Condensed Consolidated Financial Statements that give a true and fair view of the financial position, financial performance and {cash flows}[43] of the Group in accordance with accounting principles generally accepted in India. This responsibility includes the design, implementation and maintenance of internal control relevant to the preparation and presentation of the Condensed Consolidated Financial Statements that give a true and fair view and are free from material misstatement, whether due to fraud or error.

Auditors' Responsibility

3. Our responsibility is to express an opinion on these Condensed Consolidated Financial Statements based on our audit. We conducted our audit in accordance with the Standards on Auditing issued by the Institute of Chartered Accountants of India. Those Standards require that we comply with ethical requirements and plan and perform the audit to obtain reasonable assurance about whether the Condensed Consolidated Financial Statements are free from material misstatement.

4. An audit involves performing procedures to obtain audit evidence about the amounts and disclosures in the Condensed Consolidated Financial Statements. The procedures selected depend on the auditors' judgment,

[39] Wherever applicable.

[40] Date format to be DD Month Year (e.g. 31 March 20XX). It shall be used consistently throughout the auditor's report.

[41] Applicable for all listed companies and to be evaluated for other companies.

[42] Same wordings to be incorporated in the Condensed Consolidated Financial Statements.

[43] Wherever applicable.

including the assessment of the risks of material misstatement of the Condensed Consolidated Financial Statements, whether due to fraud or error. In making those risk assessments, the auditor consider internal control relevant to the Company's preparation and presentation of the Condensed Consolidated Financial Statements that give a true and fair view in order to design audit procedures that are appropriate in the circumstances. An audit also includes evaluating the appropriateness of accounting policies used and the reasonableness of the accounting estimates made by management, as well as evaluating the overall presentation of the Condensed Consolidated Financial Statements.

5. We believe that the audit evidence we have obtained is sufficient and appropriate to provide a basis for our audit opinion.

Basis for Qualified Opinion/Adverse Opinion/Disclaimer of Opinion[44]

6. *(Insert modifications, if any)*[45]

Opinion/Qualified Opinion/Adverse Opinion/Disclaimer of Opinion[46]

7. In our opinion and to the best of our information and according to the explanations given to us {and based on the consideration of the reports of the other auditors on the financial statements of the subsidiaries, (associates and joint ventures) as noted below}[47], *(except for the effects of the matter described in the Basis for Qualified Opinion paragraph)*[48] the Condensed Consolidated Financial Statements give a true and fair view in conformity with the accounting principles generally accepted in India:

    (i) in the case of the Condensed Consolidated Balance Sheet, of the state of affairs of the Group as at (Date of the Balance Sheet);

    (ii) in the case of the Condensed Consolidated Statement of Profit and Loss, of the profit/loss[49] for the quarter ended on that date; and

---

44 As the case may be (Paragraph 16 of SA 705).

45 The modification paragraph in the auditors' report and the effect thereof on auditors' report and on the matters to be reported after this modification paragraph should be carefully drafted and placed in the auditors' report as per SA 705. The 'Basis of Qualified/Adverse/Disclaimer of Opinion' and the respective Opinion paragraphs should be in italics as required by SA 705 (illustration 2). In the case of an adverse opinion, please modify the opening paragraph and paragraph 5 above, in accordance with SA 705.

46 As the case may be (Paragraph 22 of SA 705). In case of any modification the entire opinion paragraph should be in italics and should be carefully drafted as per SA 705.

47 Add where we are not the auditors of all components of the group.

48 Insert where there is a qualification in the auditors' report. In this case the entire Opinion paragraph should also be in italics.

49 Retain whichever is applicable and delete the other.

(iii) {in the case of the Condensed Consolidated Cash Flow Statement, of the cash flows for the quarter ended on that date.}[50]

Emphasis of Matter

8. (Insert matter of emphasis paragraph, if any)[51]

Other Matter[52]

9. [53]We did not audit the Condensed Financial Statements of certain subsidiaries, {associates and joint ventures}[54], whose financial statements reflect total assets (after eliminating intra-group transactions) of INR. ...... as at ....(date of Balance sheet) ; total revenues (after eliminating intra-group transactions) of .... and net cash flows aggregating to .... for the quarter then ended. These financial statements have been audited by other auditors whose audit report(s) has (have) been furnished to us by the management, and our opinion is based solely on the audit report(s) of the other auditors. Our opinion is not qualified in respect of this matter.

For XXXXXXXXXXX
Chartered Accountants
Firm Registration No.: XXXXXXXX

per ABC
Partner
Membership No. XXXX

(Place)[55]
(Date)

---

50 Wherever applicable.

51 Emphasis of Matter paragraph in the auditors' report should be carefully drafted and placed in auditors' report as per SA 706. Also a statement to the effect that 'Our opinion is not modified in respect of this matter' should be mentioned in the paragraph.

52 This matter is given in "Other Matter" paragraph as it is currently permitted in India for an auditor to sign off a consolidated audit opinion, even where he has not performed a substantial part of the audit himself. The other matter paragraph in the auditor's report should be carefully drafted and placed as per SA 706.

53 Add where we are not the auditors of all components of the group.

54 Wherever applicable.

55 City where the auditors' report is being signed.

4.2.4 Independent Auditors' Report on Condensed Financial Statements

To the Members of (*Name of the Company*).

Report on the Condensed Financial Statements

1. We have audited the accompanying Condensed Financial Statements of ***(Name of the Company)***, ("the Company"), which comprise the Condensed Balance Sheet as at ***(Date of Balance Sheet[56])***, and the Condensed Statement of Profit and Loss {and Condensed Cash Flow Statement}[57] for the quarter then ended, and a summary of significant accounting policies and other explanatory information[58].

Management's Responsibility for the Condensed Financial Statements

2. Management is responsible for the preparation of these Condensed Financial Statements that give a true and fair view of the financial position, financial performance {and cash flows}[59] of the Company in accordance with the Accounting Standards referred to in sub-section (3C) of Section 211 of the Companies Act, 1956 ("the Act"). This responsibility includes the design, implementation and maintenance of internal control relevant to the preparation and presentation of the Condensed Financial Statements that give a true and fair view and are free from material misstatement, whether due to fraud or error.

Auditors' Responsibility

3. Our responsibility is to express an opinion on these Condensed Financial Statements based on our audit. We conducted our audit in accordance with the Standards on Auditing issued by the Institute of Chartered Accountants of India. Those Standards require that we comply with ethical requirements and plan and perform the audit to obtain reasonable assurance about whether the Condensed Financial Statements are free from material misstatement.

4. An audit involves performing procedures to obtain audit evidence about the amounts and disclosures in the Condensed Financial Statements. The procedures selected depend on the auditors' judgment, including the assessment of the risks of material misstatement of the Condensed Financial Statements, whether due to fraud or error. In making those risk assessments, the auditor consider internal control relevant to the Company's preparation and fair presentation of the Condensed Financial Statements in order to

---

56 Date format is to be DD/Month/Year (e.g. 31 March 20XX). It shall be used consistently throughout the auditors' report.

57 Wherever applicable.

58 Same wordings to be incorporated in the Condensed Financial Statements.

59 Wherever applicable.

design audit procedures that are appropriate in the circumstances. An audit also includes evaluating the appropriateness of accounting policies used and the reasonableness of the accounting estimates made by management, as well as evaluating the overall presentation of the Condensed Financial Statements.

5. We believe that the audit evidence we have obtained is sufficient and appropriate to provide a basis for our audit opinion.

Basis for Qualified Opinion/Adverse Opinion/Disclaimer of Opinion[60]

6. (*Insert modifications, if any*)[61]

Opinion/Qualified Opinion/Adverse Opinion/Disclaimer of Opinion[62]

7. In our opinion and to the best of our information and according to the explanations given to us, *(except for the effects of the matter described in the Basis for Qualified Opinion paragraph)*[63] the Condensed Financial Statements give the information required by the Act in the manner so required and give a true and fair view in conformity with the accounting principles generally accepted in India:

   (i) in the case of the Condensed Balance Sheet, of the state of affairs of the Company as at (Date of the Balance Sheet);

   (ii) in the case of Condensed Statement of Profit and Loss, of the profit/loss[64] for the quarter ended on that date; and

   (iii) {in the case of the Condensed Cash Flow Statement, of the cash flows for the quarter ended on that date}[65]

60 As the case may be (Paragraph 16 of SA 705).

61 The modification paragraph in the auditors' report and the effect thereof on the auditors' report and on the matters to be reported after this modification paragraph should be carefully drafted and placed in the auditors' report as per SA 705. The 'Basis of Qualified/Adverse/Disclaimer of opinion' and the respective Opinion paragraphs should be in italics as per firm's policy. In the case of an adverse opinion, please modify the opening paragraph and paragraph 5 above, in accordance with SA 705.

62 As the case may be (Paragraph 22 of SA 705). In case of any modification the entire opinion paragraph should be in italics and should be carefully drafted as per SA 705.

63 Insert where there is a qualification in the auditors' report. In this case the entire Opinion paragraph should also be in italics.

64 Retain whichever is applicable and delete the other.

65 Wherever applicable.

Emphasis of Matter[66]

8. (Insert matter of emphasis paragraph, if any)

Other Matter [67]

9. *(Insert other matter, if any)*

For XXXXXXXXXXXXXX
Chartered Accountants
Firm Registration No.: XXXXXXXX

per ABC
Partner
Membership No. XXXX

(Place)[68]
(Date)

66 Emphasis of Matter paragraph in the auditors' report should be carefully drafted and placed in the auditors' report as per SA 706. Also a statement to the effect that 'Our opinion is not modified in respect of this matter' should be mentioned in the paragraph.

67 This paragraph is to be used in rare circumstances. The other matter paragraph in the auditor's report should be carefully drafted and placed as per SA 706 (refer paragraph A5 and A11 for placement).

68 City where the auditors' report is being signed.

Chapter 5

Illustrative disclosure checklist

This checklist is intended to help preparers in the preparation and presentation of interim financial statements in accordance with Ind AS 34 Interim Financial Reporting by identifying the recognition, measurement, presentation and disclosure requirements.

Ind AS 34 - Interim Financial Reporting

Sl. No.	Technical reference	Particulars	Response			Remarks
			Yes	**No**	**N/A**	
1		Whether an entity is required or elects to publish an interim financial report in accordance with Ind AS 34? (If the entity elects to prepare and present interim financial report (without a statutory or regulatory requirement), then this standard will be applicable to the entity. Whether an entity is required to prepare and present interim financial reports pursuant to requirements of statute, e.g. under Regulation 33 and Regulation 52 of the Listing Regulations and such regulations/requirements does not specifically mandate full compliance with Ind AS 34? If yes, please apply Question __________ related to recognition and measurement in addition to the specific requirements of the statute/regulation.				

Sl. No.	Technical reference	Particulars	Response			Remarks
		Form and content of the interim financial statements				
2	**Ind AS 34.9**	If the entity publishes a complete set of financial statements in its interim financial report, whether the form and content of those statements confirm to the requirements of Ind AS 1, Presentation of Financial Statements for a complete set of financial statements?				
3	**Ind AS 34.10**	If the entity publishes a condensed set of financial statements in its interim financial report, whether the condensed statements include, at a minimum, each of the headings and subtotals that were included in its most recent annual financial statements and the selected explanatory notes as required by the standard? (Additional line items or notes shall be included if their omission would make the condensed interim financial statements misleading).				
4	**Ind AS 34.11**	When entity is within the scope of Ind AS 33, *Earnings per Share,* ensure that the interim financial report present basic and diluted earnings per share for that interim period and comparable periods in the statement that presents the components of profit or loss for an interim period.				
5	**Ind AS 34.14**	If the entity's most recent annual financial statements are consolidated statements, whether the entity prepares its interim financial report on a consolidated				

Sl. No.	Technical reference	Particulars	Response			Remarks
		basis? (If the entity's annual financial report included the parent's separate financial statements in addition to consolidated financial statements, then the standard neither requires nor prohibits the inclusion of the parent's separate statements in the entity's interim financial report).				
		Minimum components of an interim financial report				
6	**Ind AS 34.8**	Ensure that interim financial report includes, at a minimum, the following components: (a) a condensed balance sheet; (b) a condensed statement of profit or loss; (c) a condensed statement of changes in equity; (d) a condensed statement of cash flows; and (e) Selected explanatory notes ***Note:***[Ind AS 34.7] Nothing in this standard is intended to prohibit or discourage an entity from publishing a complete set of financial statements (as described in Ind AS 1, *Presentation of Financial Statements*) in its interim financial report, rather than condensed financial statements and selected explanatory notes. Nor does this standard prohibit or discourage an entity from including in condensed interim financial statements more than the minimum line items or selected explanatory notes as set out in this standard.				

Sl. No.	Technical reference	Particulars	Response			Remarks
		Content of an interim financial report				
		Materiality				
7	**Ind AS 34.23**	In deciding how to recognise, measure, classify, or disclose an item for interim financial reporting purposes, entity assesses the materiality in relation to the interim period financial data. ***Note:*** (1) [Ind AS 34.23]: In making assessments of materiality, it shall be recognised that interim measurements may rely on estimates to a greater extent than measurements of annual financial data. (2) [Ind AS 34.24]: Ind AS 1, *Presentation of Financial Statements* and Ind AS 8, *Accounting Policies, Changes in Accounting estimates and errors*, define an item as material if its omission or misstatement could influence the economic decisions of users of the financial statements.				
		Recognition and measurement				
		Same accounting policies as annual				
8	**Ind AS 34.28**	Has the entity applied the same accounting policies in its interim financial statements as are applied in its annual financial statements, except for accounting policy changes made after the date of the most recent annual financial statements that are to be reflected				

Sl. No.	Technical reference	Particulars	Response			Remarks
		in the next annual financial statements. ***Notes:*** (1) [Ind AS 34.28] The frequency of an entity's reporting (annual, half-yearly, or quarterly) shall not affect the measurement of its annual results. To achieve that objective, measurements for interim reporting purposes shall be made on a year-to-date basis. (2) [Ind AS 34.30] To illustrate: (a) the principles for recognising and measuring losses from inventory write-downs, restructurings, or impairments in an interim period are the same as those that an entity would follow if it prepared only annual financial statements. However, if such items are recognised and measured in one interim period and the estimate changes in a subsequent interim period of that financial year, the original estimate is changed in the subsequent interim period either by accrual of an additional amount of loss or by reversal of the previously recognised amount; (b) a cost that does not meet the definition of an asset				

Sl. No.	Technical reference	Particulars	Response			Remarks
		at the end of an interim period is not deferred in the balance sheet either to await future information as to whether it has met the definition of an asset or to smooth earnings over interim periods within a financial year; and (c) income tax expense is recognised in each interim period based on the best estimate of the weighted average annual income tax rate expected for the full financial year. Amounts accrued for income tax expense in one interim period may have to be adjusted in a subsequent interim period of that financial year if the estimate of the annual income tax rate changes. (3) [Ind AS 34.32] For assets, the same tests of future economic benefits apply at interim dates and at the end of an entity's financial year. Costs that, by their nature, would not qualify as assets at financial year-end would not qualify at interim dates either. Similarly, a liability at the end of an interim reporting period must represent an existing obligation at that date, just as it must at the end of an annual reporting period.				

Sl. No.	Technical reference	Particulars	Response			Remarks
		Revenues received seasonally, cyclically, or occasionally				
9	**Ind AS 34.37**	Whether the entity does not anticipate or defer, as of an interim date, those revenues which are received seasonally, cyclically, or occasionally within a financial year when such anticipation or deferral would not be appropriate at the end of the entity's financial year. ***Notes:*** [Ind AS 34.38] Examples include dividend revenue, royalties, and government grants. Additionally, some entities consistently earn more revenues in certain interim periods of a financial year than in other interim periods, for example, seasonal revenues of retailers. Such revenues are recognised when they occur.				
		Costs incurred unevenly during the financial year				
10	**Ind AS 34.39**	Whether the entity anticipates or defers, for interim reporting purposes, those costs that are incurred unevenly during an entity's financial year when it is also appropriate to anticipate or defer that type of cost at the end of the financial year?				
		Use of estimates				
11	**Ind AS 34.41**	Whether the entity has designed the measurement procedures to be followed in an interim financial report to ensure that the resulting information is reliable and that all material financial information that is relevant to an understanding of				

Sl. No.	Technical reference	Particulars	Response			Remarks
		the financial position or performance of the entity is appropriately disclosed?				
		Restatement of previously reported interim periods				
12	**Ind AS 34.43**	If an entity has changed an accounting policy (other than one for which the transition is specified by a new Ind AS), has the entity reflected the change by:				
		(a) restating the financial statements of prior interim periods of the current financial year and the comparable interim periods of any prior financial years that will be restated in the annual financial statements in accordance with Ind AS 8, Accounting Policies, Changes in Accounting Estimates and Errors; or (b) when it is impracticable to determine the cumulative effect at the beginning of the financial year of applying a new accounting policy to all prior periods, adjusting the financial statements of prior interim periods of the current financial year, and comparable interim periods of prior financial years to apply the new accounting policy prospectively from the earliest date practicable?				

Sl. No.	Technical reference	Particulars	Response			Remarks
		Appendix A: Interim financial reporting and impairment				
		Accounting principle				
13	**Ind AS 34. Appendix A.8**	Entity does not reverse an impairment loss recognised in a previous interim period in respect of goodwill. ***Notes*:** [Ind AS 34. Appendix A.9] An entity shall not extend this accounting principle by analogy to other areas of potential conflict between this Standard and other Ind AS.				
		Significant events and transactions				
14	**Ind AS 34.15**	Ensure that the interim financial report include an explanation of events and transactions that are significant to an understanding of the changes in the financial position and performance of the entity since the end of the last annual reporting period. ***Notes:*** [Ind AS 34.6] The interim financial report is intended to provide an update on the latest complete set of annual financial statements. Accordingly, it focuses on new activities, events, and circumstances and does not duplicate information previously reported.				
15	**Ind AS 34.15B**	Ensure that the interim financial statements disclose the following list of events and transactions, if significant (the list is not exhaustive):				
		(a) the write-down of inventories				

Sl. No.	Technical reference	Particulars	Response			Remarks
		to net realisable value and the reversal of such a write-down;				
		(b) recognition of a loss from the impairment of financial assets, property, plant and equipment, intangible assets, or other assets, and the reversal of such an impairment loss;				
		(c) the reversal of any provisions for the costs of restructuring;				
		(d) acquisitions and disposals of items of property, plant and equipment;				
		(c) commitments for the purchase of property, plant and equipment;				
		(f) litigation settlements;				
		(g) corrections of prior period errors;				
		(h) changes in the business or economic circumstances that affect the fair value of the entity's financial assets and financial liabilities are recognised at fair value or amortised cost;				
		(i) any loan default or breach of a loan agreement that has not been remedied on or before the end of the reporting period; and				
		(j) related party transactions;				
		(k) transfers between levels of the fair value hierarchy used in measuring the fair value of				

Sl. No.	Technical reference	Particulars	Response			Remarks
		financial instruments;				
		(l) changes in the classification of financial assets as a result of a change in the purpose or use of those assets; and				
		(m) changes in contingent liabilities or contingent assets.				
		Other disclosures				
17	**Ind AS 34.16A**	Ensure that the interim financial report include the following information, in the notes, normally on a financial year-to – date basis, if not disclosed elsewhere in the interim financial report:				
		(a) a statement that the same accounting policies and methods of computation are followed in the interim financial statements as compared with the most recent annual financial statements or, if those policies or methods have been changed, a description of the nature and effect of the change.				
		(b) explanatory comments about the seasonality or cyclicality of interim operations.				
		(c) the nature and amount of items affecting assets, liabilities, equity, net income or cash flows that are unusual because of their nature, size or incidence.				
		(d) the nature and amount of				

Sl. No.	Technical reference	Particulars	Response			Remarks
		changes in estimates of amounts reported in prior interim periods of the current financial year or changes in estimates of amounts reported in prior financial years.				
		(e) Issues, repurchases and repayments of debt and equity securities				
		(f) dividends paid (aggregate or per share) separately for ordinary shares and other shares				
		(g) dividends paid (aggregate or per share) separately for the following segment information (disclosure of segment information is required in an entity's interim financial report only if Ind AS 108, Operating Segments, requires that entity to disclose segment information in its annual financial statements).				
		(i) revenues from external customers, if included in the measure of segment profit or loss reviewed by the chief operating decision maker or otherwise regularly provided to the chief operating decision maker.				
		(ii) intersegment revenues, if included in the measure of segment profit or loss reviewed by the chief				

Sl. No.	Technical reference	Particulars	Response			Remarks
		operating decision maker or otherwise regularly provided to the chief operating decision maker.				
		(iii) a measure of segment profit or loss.				
		(iv) total assets and liabilities for which there has been a material change from the amount disclosed in the last annual financial statements and such amounts are regularly provided to the chief operating decision maker.				
		(v) a description of differences from the last annual financial statements in the basis of segmentation or in the basis of measurement of segment profit or loss.				
		(vi) a reconciliation of the total of the reportable segments' measures of profit or loss to the entity's profit or loss before tax expense (tax income) and discontinued operations. However, if an entity allocates to reportable segments items such as tax expense (tax income), the entity may reconcile the total of the segments' measures of profit or loss to profit or				

Sl. No.	Technical reference	Particulars	Response			Remarks
		loss after those items. Material reconciling items shall be separately identified and described in that reconciliation.				
		(h) events after the interim period that have not been reflected in the financial statements for the interim period.				
		(i) the effect of changes in the composition of the entity during the interim period, including business combinations, obtaining or losing control of subsidiaries and long-term investments, restructurings, and discontinued operations. In the case of business combinations, the entity shall disclose the information required by Ind AS 103, *Business Combinations*.				
		(j) for financial instruments, the disclosures about the fair value required by Ind AS 113.91 through .93(h), .94 through .96, .98 and .99 and Ind AS 107.25, .26 and .28 through .30.				
		(k) for entities becoming, or ceasing to be, investment entities, as defined in Ind AS 110, *Consolidated Financial Statements*, the disclosures in Ind AS 112.9B;				
		Disclosure of compliance with Ind AS				

Sl. No.	Technical reference	Particulars	Response			Remarks
18	**Ind AS 34.19**	When an entity's interim financial statement is in compliance with this Standard, ensure that interim financial report disclose that fact. *Practice guidance:* [Ind AS 34.19] An interim financial report shall not be described as complying with Ind AS unless it complies with all of the requirements of Ind AS.				
		Periods for which interim financial statements are required to be presented				
19	**Ind AS 34.20**	Ensure that the interim reports include interim financial statements (condensed or complete) for periods as follows:				
		(a) balance sheet as of the end of the current interim period and a comparative balance sheet as of the end of the immediately preceding financial year.				
		(b) statements of profit or loss for the current interim period and cumulatively for the current financial year to date, with comparative statements of profit or loss for the comparable interim periods (current and year-to-date) of the immediately preceding financial year.				
		(c) statement of changes in equity cumulatively for the current financial year to date, with a comparative statement for the comparable year-to-date period of the				

Sl. No.	Technical reference	Particulars	Response			Remarks
		immediately preceding financial year.				
		(d) statement of cash flows cumulatively for the current financial year to date, with a comparative statement for the comparable year-to-date period of the immediately preceding financial year.				
20	**Ind AS 34.21**	Optional disclosure: Entities whose business is highly seasonal may also report financial information for the twelve months up to the end of the interim period and comparative information for the prior twelve-month period.				
		Disclosure in annual financial statements				
21	**Ind AS 34.26**	When an estimate of an amount reported in an interim period is changed significantly during the final interim period of the financial year but a separate financial report is not published for that final interim period, ensure that the annual financial statements for that financial year disclose the nature and amount of that change in estimate by way of a note. *Practice guidance:* [Ind AS 34.27] (1) Examples include changes in estimate in the final interim period relating to inventory write-downs, restructurings, or impairment losses that were reported in an earlier interim period of the financial year.				

Sl. No.	Technical reference	Particulars	Response			Remarks
		(2) An entity is not required to include additional interim period financial information in its annual financial statements.				

Glossary

Interim financial report	A financial report containing either a complete set of financial statements (as described in Ind AS 1, *Presentation of Financial Statements)*, or a set of condensed financial statements (as described in this Standard) for an interim period.
Interim period	A financial reporting period shorter than a full financial year.
Material or Materiality	Ind AS 1define an item as material if its omission or misstatement Omissions or misstatements of items are material if they could, individually or collectively, influence the economic decisions that users make on the basis of the financial statements. Materiality depends on the size and nature of the omission or misstatement judged in the surrounding circumstances. The size or nature of the item, or a combination of both, could be the determining factor. Assessing whether an omission or misstatement could influence economic decisions of users, and so be material, requires consideration of the characteristics of those users. The Framework for the Preparation and Presentation of Financial Statements issued by the Institute of Chartered Accountants of India states in paragraph 25 that 'users are assumed to have a reasonable knowledge of business and economic activities and accounting and a willingness to study the information with reasonable diligence.' Therefore, the assessment needs to take into account how users with such attributes could reasonably be expected to be influenced in making economic decisions.

CHAPTER 6

Illustrative standalone condensed interim financial statements

This chapter presents an Illustrative condensed standalone financial statement of ABC Limited (a fictional listed company) for the quarter ended 30 September 2016. It illustrates the financial reporting requirements that would apply to such a company under Indian Accounting Standards (Ind AS). These condensed Standalone financial statements have been prepared in accordance with Ind AS 34, Interim Financial Reporting as notified under the Companies (Indian Accounting Standards) Rules, 2015 read with sec 133 of the *Companies Act, 2013* and Division II of Schedule III of the *Companies Act, 2013*. Further, reference has also been made to industry practice and therefore we referred to the condensed interim financial statements prepared by few listed companies and which are available in public domain.

The format is illustrative in nature and should be used in conjunction with the relevant Ind AS and any other accounting/legal pronouncements and legislation, if applicable. Our objective in preparing these Illustrative condensed financial statements is to illustrate one possible approach to financial reporting by an entity engaging in transactions that are typical across a range of non-specialist sectors. However, as with any industry or other sector, this illustration does not envisage every possible transaction and cannot therefore be regarded as comprehensive. Management is responsible for the fair presentation of financial statements and therefore may find other approaches more appropriate for its specific circumstances.

We trust that these illustrative condensed standalone financial statements will help you in preparing your own condensed standalone financial statements in accordance with Ind AS and division II of Schedule III.

ABC Limited

Interim Condensed Standalone Financial Statements for the quarter ended 30 September 2016

ABC Limited

Interim Condensed Standalone Balance Sheet as at 30 September 2016

(INR)

	Note	30 September 2016	31 March 2016	1 April 2015
ASSETS				
Non-current assets				
Property, Plant and Equipment	3	XXX	XXX	XXX
Capital work-in-progress		XXX	XXX	XXX
Other intangible assets	4	XXX	XXX	XXX
Intangible assets under development		XXX	XXX	XXX
Financial Assets				
Investments	5	XXX	XXX	XXX
Trade receivables		XXX	XXX	XXX
Loans	6	XXX	XXX	XXX
Others	7	XXX	XXX	XXX
Deferred tax assets (Net)	17	XXX	XXX	XXX
Income Tax Assets (Net)	17	XXX	XXX	XXX
Other non-current assets	10	XXX	XXX	XXX
Sub total		**XXX**	**XXX**	**XXX**
Current assets				
Inventories		XXX	XXX	XXX
Financial Assets				
Investments	5	XXX	XXX	XXX
Trade receivables	8	XXX	XXX	XXX
Cash and cash equivalents	9	XXX	XXX	XXX
Bank balances other than cash and cash equivalents		XXX	XXX	XXX
Loans	6	XXX	XXX	XXX
Others	7	XXX	XXX	XXX
Current Tax Assets (Net)		XXX	XXX	XXX
Other current assets	10	XXX	XXX	XXX
Sub total		**XXX**	**XXX**	**XXX**
TOTAL ASSETS		**XXX**	**XXX**	**XXX**
EQUITY AND LIABILITIES				
Equity				
Equity Share capital	12	XXX	XXX	XXX
Other Equity		XXX	XXX	XXX

	Note	30 September 2016	31 March 2016	1 April 2015
Total Equity		**XXX**	**XXX**	**XXX**
LIABILITIES				
Non-current Liabilities				
Financial Liabilities				
Other financial liabilities	13	XXX	XXX	XXX
Deferred Tax liabilities (Net)	17	XXX	XXX	XXX
Provisions				
Sub total		**XXX**	**XXX**	**XXX**
Current liabilities				
Financial Liabilities				
Borrowings		XXX	XXX	XXX
Trade payables	14	XXX	XXX	XXX
Other financial liabilities	13	XXX	XXX	XXX
Provisions	16	XXX	XXX	XXX
Other current liabilities	15	XXX	XXX	XXX
Current Tax Liabilities (Net)	17	XXX	XXX	XXX
Sub total		**XXX**	**XXX**	**XXX**
TOTAL EQUITY AND LIABILITIES		**XXX**	**XXX**	**XXX**

The accompanying notes form an integral part of the standalone interim financial statements.

As per our report of even date attached

For XXXXXXXXXXX	**For and on behalf of the Board of Directors**	
Chartered Accountants		
ICAI Firm registration number: XXXXXXXX	Mr A (Chairman)	Mr B (Managing Director)
	Mr C (Chief financial officer)	Mr D (Director)

Per Mr. Z

Partner

Membership No. XXXXXX

Place:

Date:

ABC Limited

Interim Condensed Standalone statement of Profit and Loss for the quarter ended 30 September 2016

(INR)

Particulars	Notes	Three months ended		Six months ended	
		30 Sept 2016	30 Sept 2015	30 Sept 2016	30 Sept 2015
Income					
Revenue from operations	18	XXX	XXX	XXX	XXX
Other income	19	XXX	XXX	XXX	XXX
Total Income (I)		**XXX**	**XXX**	**XXX**	**XXX**
Expenses					
Purchase of traded goods		XXX	XXX	XXX	XXX
(Increase)/decrease in inventories of traded goods		XXX	XXX	XXX	XXX
Employee benefits expense	20	XXX	XXX	XXX	XXX
Finance costs		XXX	XXX	XXX	XXX
Depreciation and amortisation expense	3&4	XXX	XXX	XXX	XXX
Other expenses	20	XXX	XXX	XXX	XXX
Total expenses (II)		**XXX**	**XXX**	**XXX**	**XXX**
Profit before tax and exceptional item (III) [(I)-(II)]		**XXX**	**XXX**	**XXX**	**XXX**
Exceptional item (net of tax) (IV)					
Expected loss on proposed sale of domestic BPO business	25	XXX	XXX	XXX	XXX
Expected loss on exit from other domestic BPO business	26	XXX	XXX	XXX	XXX
Profit before tax after exceptional item (III)-(IV)		**XXX**	**XXX**	**XXX**	**XXX**
Tax expenses					
Current tax	17	XXX	XXX	XXX	XXX
Deferred tax charge	17	XXX	XXX	XXX	XXX
Minimum alternative tax credit entitlement		XXX	XXX	XXX	XXX
Total tax expenses		**XXX**	**XXX**	**XXX**	**XXX**
Profit for the period before exceptional item		**XXX**	**XXX**	**XXX**	**XXX**
Profit for the period after exceptional item		**XXX**	**XXX**	**XXX**	**XXX**

Particulars	Notes	Three months ended		Six months ended	
		30 Sept 2016	30 Sept 2015	30 Sept 2016	30 Sept 2015
Other comprehensive income					
Other comprehensive income to be reclassified to profit or loss in subsequent period					
Net change in fair value of derivatives designated as cash flow hedges (net of tax)		XXX	XXX	XXX	XXX
Exchange differences arising on translating foreign operations		XXX	XXX	XXX	XXX
Disposal of a foreign operation		XXX	XXX	XXX	XXX
Changes in fair values of investments other than equities carried at fair value through OCI		XXX	XXX	XXX	XXX
Changes in fair values of intrinsic value of cash flow hedges		XXX	XXX	XXX	XXX
Changes in fair values of time value of cash flow hedges		XXX	XXX	XXX	XXX
Income tax effect		XXX	XXX	XXX	XXX
Net other comprehensive income to be reclassified to profit or loss in subsequent period		**XXX**	**XXX**	**XXX**	**XXX**
Other comprehensive income not to be reclassified to profit or loss in subsequent period					
Re-measurement gains/(losses) on defined benefit plans	(net of taxes)	XX	XX	XX	XX
Revaluation of land and building (net of tax)		XX	XX	XX	XX
Changes in fair values of equities carried at fair value through OCI		XX	XX	XX	XX
Income tax effect		XX	XX	XX	XX
Net other comprehensive income not to be reclassified to profit or loss in subsequent period		**XX**	**XX**	**XX**	**XX**
Other comprehensive income for the period, net of tax		**XX**	**XX**	**XX**	**XX**
Total comprehensive income for the period		**XXXX**	**XXXX**	**XXXX**	**XXXX**

Particulars	Notes	Three months ended		Six months ended	
		30 Sept 2016	30 Sept 2015	30 Sept 2016	30 Sept 2015
Earnings per equity share (Equity share of par value X each)					
Basic (INR)		XX	XX	XX	XX
Diluted (INR)		XX	XX	XX	XX
Weighted average number of shares – Basic	23	XXXX	XXXX	XXXX	XXXX
Weighted average number of shares – Diluted	23	XXXX	XXXX	XXXX	XXXX

The accompanying notes form an integral part of the standalone interim financial statements.

As per our report of even date attached

For XXXXXXXXXXX

Chartered Accountants

ICAI Firm registration number: XXXXXXXX

Per Mr. Z

Partner

Membership No. XXXXXX

Place:

Date:

For and on behalf of the Board of Directors

Mr A
(Chairman)

Mr B
(Managing Director)

Mr C
(Chief financial officer)

Mr D
(Director)

ABC Limited

Interim Condensed Standalone Statement of changes in equity for the quarter ended 30 September 2016

EQUITY

(INR)

		Other Equity					Other Equity	
		Reserves and Surplus					Items of OCI	
	Equity Share Capital	**Capital Reserve**	**Securities premium reserve**	**Share based payment reserve**	**General reserve**	**Retained earnings**	**Effective portion of cash flow hedge**	**Equity**
As at 1 April 2016	**XXX**	**XXX**	**XXX**	**XXX**	**XXX**	**XXX**	**XXX**	**XXX**
Profit for the period	XXX	XXX	XXX	XXX	XXX	XXX	XXX	**XXX**
Transfer to general reserve	XXX	XXX	XXX	XXX	XXX	XXX	XXX	**XXX**
Exercise of stock options	XXX	XXX	XXX	XXX	XXX	XXX	XXX	**XXX**
Income tax benefit arising on exercise of stock options	XXX	XXX	XXX	XXX	XXX	XXX	XXX	**XXX**
Equity instruments through other comprehensive income	XXX	XXX	XXX	XXX	XXX	XXX	XXX	**XXX**
Increase in share capital on issue of	XXX	XXX	XXX	XXX	XXX	XXX	XXX	**XXX**

		Other Equity					Other Equity	
		Reserves and Surplus					Items of OCI	
	Equity Share Capital	**Capital Reserve**	**Securities premium reserve**	**Share based payment reserve**	**General reserve**	**Retained earnings**	**Effective portion of cash flow hedge**	**Equity**
Effect of share based payments (refer note 12)	XXX	XXX	XXX	XXX	XXX	XXX	XXX	**XXX**
Fair value changes on cash flow hedge	XXX	XXX	XXX	XXX	XXX	XXX	XXX	**XXX**
Dividends	XXX	XXX	XXX	XXX	XXX	XXX	XXX	**XXX**
As at 30 September 2016	**XXX**	**XXX**	**XXX**	**XXX**	**XXX**	**XXX**	**XXX**	**XXX**
As at 1 April 2015	**XXX**	**XXX**	**XXX**	**XXX**	**XXX**	**XXX**	**XXX**	**XXX**
Profit for the period	XXX	XXX	XXX	XXX	XXX	XXX	XXX	**XXX**
Transfer to general reserve	XXX	XXX	XXX	XXX	XXX	XXX	XXX	**XXX**
Exercise of stock options	XXX	XXX	XXX	XXX	XXX	XXX	XXX	**XXX**
Income tax benefit arising on exercise of stock options	XXX	XXX	XXX	XXX	XXX	XXX	XXX	**XXX**

		Other Equity					Other Equity	
		Reserves and Surplus					Items of OCI	
	Equity Share Capital	Capital Reserve	Securities premium reserve	Share based payment reserve	General reserve	Retained earnings	Effective portion of cash flow hedge	Equity
Equity instruments through other comprehensive income	XXX	XXX	XXX	XXX	XXX	XXX	XXX	**XXX**
Increase in share capital on issue of	XXX	XXX	XXX	XXX	XXX	XXX	XXX	**XXX**
Effect of share based payments (refer note 12)	XXX	XXX	XXX	XXX	XXX	XXX	XXX	**XXX**
Fair value changes on cash flow hedge	XXX	XXX	XXX	XXX	XXX	XXX	XXX	**XXX**
Dividends	XXX	XXX	XXX	XXX	XXX	XXX	XXX	**XXX**
As at 30 September 2015	**XXX**	**XXX**	**XXX**	**XXX**	**XXX**	**XXX**	**XXX**	**XXX**

ABC Limited

Interim Condensed Standalone statement of cash flows for six months ended 30 September 2016

(INR)

	Six months ended 30 September 2016	Six months ended 30 September 2015
Cash flow from operating activities		
Profit before tax and exceptional item	**XXX**	**XXX**
Non-Cash Adjustment to reconcile profit before tax to net cash flows:		
Depreciation/amortisation (Net of Provision for loss on a long-term contract)	XXX	XXX
Profit on sale of Property, Plant and Equipment	XXX	XXX
Fair value changes in financial instruments	XXX	XXX
Employee stock compensation expense	XXX	XXX
Interest expense (excluding exchange difference considered as adjustment to borrowing cost)	XXX	XXX
Interest income (excluding fair value changes)	XXX	XXX
Dividend income	XXX	XXX
(Profit)/Loss on sale of investments	XXX	XXX
Effect of exchange rate changes (gain)/loss	XXX	XXX
Operating profit before working capital changes	**XXX**	**XXX**
Decrease/(increase) in trade receivables	XXX	XXX
Decrease/(increase) in loans and advances	XXX	XXX
Decrease/(increase) in other financial assets	XXX	XXX
Decrease/(increase) in inventories	XXX	XXX
Decrease/(increase) in other assets	XXX	XXX
Increase/(decrease) in other financial liabilities	XXX	XXX
Increase/(decrease) in trade payables	XXX	XXX
Increase/(decrease) in provisions	XXX	XXX
Increase/(decrease) in other liabilities	XXX	XXX
Cash generated from/(used in) operations	**XXX**	**XXX**
Direct taxes paid (net of refunds)	XXX	XXX
Net cash flow from operating activities (A)	**XXX**	**XXX**

	Six months ended 30 September 2016	Six months ended 30 September 2015
Cash flow from investing activities:		
Purchase of Property, Plant and Equipment	XXX	XXX
Proceeds from sale of Property, Plant and Equipment	XXX	XXX
Purchase of investments	XXX	XXX
Sale of investments	XXX	XXX
Interest received	XXX	XXX
Dividends received	XXX	XXX
Re-investment of dividend	XXX	XXX
Investments in bank deposits	XXX	XXX
Redemption/maturity of bank deposits	XXX	XXX
Net cash flow from/(used in) investing activities (B)	**XXX**	**XXX**
Cash flow from financing activities		
Proceeds from issue of share capital	XXX	XXX
Proceeds of premium from issue of share capital	XXX	XXX
Repayment of unsecured loans	XXX	XXX
Availment of unsecured loans	XXX	XXX
Interest paid	XXX	XXX
Dividends paid (including tax on dividend)	XXX	XXX
Net cash flow used in financing activities (C)	**XXX**	**XXX**
Net decrease in cash and cash equivalents (A+B+C)	**XXX**	**XXX**
Cash and cash equivalents at the beginning of the period	XXX	XXX
Cash and cash equivalents at the end of the period	**XXX**	**XXX**
Components of cash and cash equivalents		
Cash on hand	XXX	XXX
Balance with banks		
– on current account	XXX	XXX
– on deposit account	XXX	XXX
– unclaimed dividend	XXX	XXX
Total cash and cash equivalents	**XXX**	**XXX**

The accompanying notes form an integral part of the standalone interim financial statements.

As per our report of even date attached

For XXXXXXXXXXX	**For and on behalf of the Board of**	**Directors**
Chartered Accountants		
ICAI Firm registration number: XXXXXXXX	Mr A (Chairman)	Mr B (Managing Director)
	Mr C (Chief financial officer)	Mr D (Director)
Per Mr. Z		
Partner		
Membership No. XXXXXX		

Place:

Date:

ABC Limited

Notes to the Interim Condensed Standalone Financial Statements for the quarter and six months ended 30 September 2016

1. COMPANY OVERVIEW AND SIGNIFICANT ACCOUNTING POLICIES

1.1 Company Overview

ABC Limited ('the Company') is a leading service provider in consulting, technology, outsourcing and other related services. ABC Limited provides a suite of application development and maintenance services, infrastructure outsourcing services and business & knowledge process outsourcing solutions to clients, licensing arrangement, application services and trading of goods.

The Company is a public limited company incorporated and domiciled in India and has its registered office at Mumbai, Maharashtra, India. The company has its primary listings on the Bombay Stock Exchange Limited and National Stock Exchange in India.

The interim financial statements are approved for issue by the Company's Board of Directors on XX October 2016.

1.2 Significant Accounting Policies

1.2.1 Statement of compliance

In accordance with the notification issued by the Ministry of Corporate Affairs, the Company has adopted Indian Accounting Standards (referred to as "Ind AS") notified under the Companies (Indian Accounting Standards) Rules, 2015 with effect from 1 April 2016. Previous period numbers in the financial statements have been restated to Ind AS. In accordance with Ind AS 101, First-time Adoption of Indian Accounting Standard, the Company has presented a reconciliation from the presentation of financial statements under Accounting Standards notified under the Companies (Accounting Standards) Rules, 2006 ("Previous GAAP") to Ind AS notified under the Companies (Indian Accounting Standards) Rules, 2015 as amended by the Companies (Indian Accounting Standards) (Amendment) Rules, 2016, of Shareholders' equity as at 30 September 2015 and of the comprehensive net income for the quarter and six months ended 30 September 2015. Reconciliations and descriptions of the effect of the transition has been summarized in Note 2.2

1.2.2 Basis of preparation of financial statements

These financial statements are prepared in accordance with Indian Accounting Standards (Ind AS) under the historical cost convention on the accrual basis except for certain financial instruments which are measured at fair values and the provisions of the Companies Act , 2013 ('Act') (to the extent notified). Historical cost is generally based on the fair value of the consideration given in exchange for goods and services. The Ind AS are prescribed under Section 133 of the Act read with the Companies (Indian Accounting Standards) Rules, 2015 and Companies (Indian Accounting Standards) Amendment Rules, 2016. These condensed standalone financial statements have been prepared in accordance with Ind AS 34, Interim Financial Reporting as notified under the Companies (Indian Accounting Standards) Rules, 2015 read with Section 133 of the Act.

Accounting policies have been consistently applied except where a newly issued accounting standard is initially adopted or a revision to an existing accounting standard requires a change in the accounting policy hitherto in use.

1.2.3 Business Combinations

The Company accounts for its business combinations under acquisition method of accounting. Acquisition related costs are recognised in profit or loss as incurred. The acquiree's identifiable assets, liabilities and contingent liabilities that meet the condition for recognition are recognised at their fair values at the acquisition date.

Purchase consideration paid in excess of the fair value of net assets acquired is recognised as goodwill. Where the fair value of identifiable assets and liabilities exceed the cost of acquisition, after reassessing the fair values of the net assets and contingent liabilities, the excess is recognised as bargain purchase.

Business combinations arising from transfers of interests in entities that are under the common control are accounted at historical cost. The difference between any consideration given and the aggregate historical carrying amounts of assets and liabilities of the acquired entity are recorded in shareholders' equity.

1.2.4 Use of estimates

The preparation of the condensed standalone financial statements in conformity with Ind AS requires the management to make estimates, judgements and assumptions that affect the reported amounts of assets and liabilities, the disclosure of contingent assets and liabilities on the date of the condensed standalone financial statements and the reported amounts of revenues and expenses for the period reported. Actual results could differ from those estimates. Estimates and underlying assumptions are reviewed on an ongoing basis. Revisions to accounting estimates are recognised in the period in which the estimates are revised and future periods are affected.

Key source of estimation of uncertainty at the date of the financial statements, which may cause a material adjustment to the carrying amounts of assets and liabilities within the next financial year, is in respect of impairment of goodwill, impairment of investments, useful lives of property, plant and equipment, valuation of deferred tax assets and provisions and contingent liabilities.

Impairment of investments

The Company reviews its carrying value of investments carried at amortised cost annually, or more frequently when there is indication for impairment. If the recoverable amount is less than its carrying amount, the impairment loss is accounted for.

Useful lives of property, plant and equipment

The Company reviews the useful life of property, plant and equipment at the end of each reporting period. This reassessment may result in change in depreciation expense in future periods.

Valuation of deferred tax assets

The Company reviews the carrying amount of deferred tax assets at the end of each reporting period. The policy for the same has been explained under Note 1.2.18.

Provisions and contingent liabilities

A provision is recognised when the Company has a present obligation as a result of past event and it is probable than an outflow of resources will be required to settle the obligation, in respect of which the reliable estimate can be made. Provisions (excluding retirement benefits and compensated absences) are not discounted to its present value and are determined based on best estimate required to settle the obligation at the balance sheet date. These are reviewed at each balance sheet date adjusted to reflect the current best estimates. Contingent liabilities are not recognised in the financial statements. A contingent asset is neither recognised nor disclosed in the financial statements.

1.2.5 Revenue recognition

Revenue is recognised to the extent that it is probable that the economic benefits will flow to the Company and the revenue can be reliably measured, regardless of when the payment is being made. Revenue is measured at the fair value of the consideration received or receivable, taking into account contractually defined terms of payment.

Sales tax/ Value Added Tax (VAT)/ Service Tax is not received by the Company on its own account. Rather, it is tax collected on value added to the commodity/service rendered by the seller on behalf of the government. Accordingly, it is excluded from revenue.

The Company derives its revenues primarily from software services & projects, call centre and business & knowledge process outsourcing operations, infrastructure outsourcing services, licensing arrangement, application services and trading of goods.

Revenues from software services & projects comprise income from time-and-material and fixed price contracts. Revenue from time and material contracts is recognized when the services are rendered in accordance with the terms of contracts with clients. Revenue from fixed price contracts is recognized using the percentage-of-completion method, calculated as the proportion of the cost of effort incurred up to the reporting date to estimated cost of total effort.

Revenues from call centre and business & knowledge process outsourcing operations arise from both time-based and unit-priced client contracts. Such revenue is recognized when the services are rendered in accordance with the terms of the contracts with clients.

Revenues from infrastructure outsourcing services arise from time based, unit-priced and fixed price contracts. Revenue from time based and unit-priced is recognized when the services are rendered in accordance with the terms of the contracts with clients. Revenue from fixed price contracts is recognized using the percentage-of-completion method, calculated as the proportion of the cost of effort incurred up to the reporting date to estimated cost of total effort.

License fee revenues are recognised when the general revenue recognition criteria given in Ind AS 18, *Revenue* are met. Revenue from bundled contracts is allocated separately for each element based on their fair values. Maintenance revenue is recognized rateably over the period of underlying maintenance agreements.

Revenue from sale of services is shown as net of applicable discounts and pricing incentives to customer.

Revenues from sale of goods is recognized on transfer of significant risks and rewards where it is probable that economic benefits will flow to the Company and there is neither continuing managerial involvement nor effective control over the goods sold.

Revenue is recognised only when evidence of an arrangement is obtained and the other criteria to support revenue recognition are met, including the price is fixed or determinable, services have been rendered and collectability of the resulting receivables is reasonably assured.

Provisions for estimated losses on incomplete contracts are recorded in the period in which such losses become probable based on the current contract estimates. Unbilled revenue represents revenues in excess of amounts billed to clients as at the balance sheet date. Unearned revenue represents billings in excess of revenues recognized. Deferred contract costs are amortized over the term of the contract.

Advances received for services are reported as liabilities until all conditions for revenue recognition are met. Interest income is recognized based on effective interest rate method.

Dividend income is recognized when the right to receive the dividend is established.

1.2.6 Property, plant and equipment and Intangible assets

Property, plant and equipment are stated at the cost of acquisition or construction less accumulated depreciation and write down for, impairment if any. Direct costs are capitalised until the assets are ready to be put to use. When significant parts of plant and equipment are required to be replaced at intervals, the Company depreciates them separately based on their specific useful lives. All other repair and maintenance costs are recognised in the statement of profit or loss as incurred. Property, plant and equipment purchased in foreign currency are recorded at cost, based on the exchange rate on the date of purchase.

The Company identifies and determines cost of each component/ part of property, plant and equipment separately, if the component/ part has a cost which is significant to the total cost of the property, plant and equipment and has useful life that is materially different from that of the remaining asset.

Advances paid towards the acquisition of property, plant and equipment outstanding at each balance sheet date is classified as capital advances under other non-current assets and the cost of assets not put to use before such date are disclosed under 'Capital work-in-progress'. Subsequent expenditures relating to property, plant and equipment is capitalized only when it is probable that future economic benefits associated with these will flow to the company and the cost of the item can be measured reliably. The cost and related accumulated depreciation are eliminated from the financial statements upon sale or retirement of the asset and the resultant gains or losses are recognized in the statement of profit and loss. Assets to be disposed off are reported at the lower of the carrying value or the fair value less cost to sell.

An item of property, plant and equipment and any significant part initially recognised is derecognised upon disposal or when no future economic benefits are expected from its use or disposal. Any gain or loss arising on de-recognition of the asset (calculated as the difference between the net disposal proceeds and the carrying amount of the asset) is included in the statement of profit and loss when the asset is derecognised.

Intangible assets purchased including acquired in business combination, are measured at cost or fair value as of the date of acquisition, as applicable, less accumulated amortisation and accumulated impairment, if any. The amortisation period and the amortisation method are reviewed at least at each financial year end. Internally generated intangible assets are stated at cost that can be measured reliably during the development phase and capitalised when it is probable that future economic benefits that are attributable to the assets will flow to the Company. The estimated useful life of an identifiable intangible asset is based on a number of factors including the effects of obsolescence, demand, competition, and other economic factors (such as the stability of the industry, and known technological advances), and the level of maintenance expenditures required to obtain the expected future cash flows from the asset.

Research costs are expensed as incurred. Software product development costs are expensed as incurred unless technical and commercial feasibility of the project is demonstrated, future economic benefits are probable, the company has an intention and ability to complete and use or sell the software and the costs can be measured reliably. The costs which can be capitalized include the cost of material, direct labour, overhead costs that are directly attributable to preparing the asset for its intended use. Research and development costs and software development costs incurred under contractual arrangements with customers are accounted as expenses in the statement of profit and loss.

1.2.7 Depreciation and amortisation

Depreciation on property, plant and equipment is calculated on a straight-line basis using the rates arrived at, based on the useful lives estimated by the management. Intangible assets are amortised on a straight line basis over the estimated useful economic life. The useful lives estimated by the management are given below:

(in years)

Asset	Useful life as per Companies Act, 2013	Useful life estimated by the management
Lease hold improvements	10	10 or remaining primary lease term whichever
Buildings	30	40
Plant and machinery	15	10
Furniture and Fixtures	10	12
Office equipment	5	5
Computer equipment	3	3
Vehicles	8	9
Sub-contracting rights	As per Ind AS 38	Useful life of contract term
Others	As per Ind AS 38	Useful life of the asset

In respect of buildings, plant and equipment, furniture and fixtures and vehicles, the management, basis internal assessment of usage pattern believes that the useful lives as mentioned above best represent the period over which management expects to use these assets. Hence the useful lives in respect of these assets are different from the useful lives as prescribed under Part C of Schedule II of the Companies Act 2013.

Project specific assets are depreciated over the period of contract or useful life of the asset, whichever is lower.

The residual values, useful lives and methods of depreciation of property, plant and equipment are reviewed at each financial year end and adjusted prospectively, if appropriate.

1.2.8 Leases

Leases, where the lessor effectively retains substantially all the risks and benefits of ownership of the leased items, are classified as operating leases. Operating lease payments are recognised on a straight line basis over the lease term, unless the lease agreement explicitly states that increase is on account of inflation in the statement of profit and loss.

Profit or loss on sale and lease back arrangements resulting in operating leases are recognized immediately in case the transaction is established at fair value, else, the excess over the fair value is deferred and amortized over the period for which the asset is expected to be used. If the sale price is below fair value, any profit or loss is recognized immediately in the statement of profit and loss.

Leases under which the Company assumes substantially all the risks and rewards of ownership are classified as finance leases. Such assets acquired are capitalised at the fair value of the leased asset or the present value of the minimum lease payments at the inception of the lease, whichever is lower.

For arrangements entered into prior to 1 April 2015, the Company has determined whether the arrangement contains lease on the basis of facts and circumstances existing on the date of transition to Ind AS.

1.2.9 Borrowing costs

Borrowing cost includes interest, amortisation of ancillary costs incurred in connection with the arrangement of borrowings and exchange differences arising from foreign currency borrowings to the extent they are regarded as an adjustment to the interest cost.

Borrowing costs directly attributable to the acquisition, construction or production of an asset that necessarily takes a substantial period of time to get ready for its intended use or sale are capitalized as part of the cost of the respective asset. All other borrowing costs are expensed in the period they occur.

1.2.10 Impairment

a. Financial assets (other than at fair value)

The Company assesses at each date of balance sheet whether a financial asset or a group of financial assets is impaired. Ind AS 109, *Financial Instruments*, requires expected credit losses (ECL) to be measured through a loss allowance. The company recognizes loss allowances using the expected credit loss (ECL) model for the financial assets which are not fair valued through profit or loss. The Company recognises lifetime expected losses for all contract assets and/or all trade receivables that do not constitute a financing transaction. For all other financial assets, ECL are measured at an amount equal to the 12-month ECL or at an amount equal to the life time ECL if the credit risk on the financial asset has increased significantly since initial recognition.

b. Non-financial assets

Property, plant and equipment and intangible assets

Property, plant and equipment and intangible assets with finite life are evaluated for recoverability whenever there is any indication that their carrying amounts may not be recoverable. If any such indication exists, the recoverable amount (i.e. higher of the fair value less cost to sell and the value-in-use) is determined on an individual asset basis unless the asset does not generate cash flows that are largely independent of those from other assets. In such cases, the recoverable amount is determined for the cash generating unit (CGU) to which the asset belongs.

If such assets are considered to be impaired, the impairment to be recognized in the statement of profit and loss is measured by the amount by which the carrying value of the assets exceeds the estimated recoverable amount of the asset. An impairment loss is reversed in the statement of profit and loss if there has been a change in the estimates used to determine the recoverable amount. The carrying amount of the asset is increased to its revised recoverable amount, provided that this amount does not exceed the carrying amount that would have been determined (net of any accumulated amortisation or depreciation) had no impairment loss been recognized for the asset in prior years.

1.2.11 Financial instruments

1.2.11.1 Initial recognition

Financial assets and liabilities are recognised when the Company becomes a party to the contractual provisions of the instrument. Financial assets and liabilities are initially measured at fair value. Transaction costs that are directly attributable to the acquisition or issue of financial assets and financial liabilities (other than financial assets and financial liabilities at fair value through profit or loss) are added to or deducted from the fair value measured on initial recognition of financial asset or financial liability.

1.2.11.2 Subsequent measurement

a. Non-derivative financial instruments

i. Cash and cash equivalents

The Company considers all highly liquid financial instruments, which are readily convertible into known amounts of cash that are subject to an insignificant risk of change in value and having original maturities of three months or less from the date of purchase, to be cash equivalents. Cash and cash equivalents consist of balances with banks which are unrestricted for withdrawal and usage.

ii. Financial assets at amortised cost

Financial assets are subsequently measured at amortised cost if these financial assets are held within a business whose objective is to hold these assets in order to collect contractual cash flows and the contractual terms of the financial asset give rise on specified dates to cash flows that are solely payments of principal and interest on the principal amount outstanding.

iii. Financial assets at fair value through other comprehensive income

Financial assets are measured at fair value through other comprehensive income if these financial assets are held within a business whose objective is achieved by both collecting contractual cash flows and selling financial assets and the contractual terms of the financial asset give rise on specified dates to cash flows that are solely payments of principal and interest on the principal amount outstanding.

The Company has made an irrevocable election to present in other comprehensive income subsequent changes in the fair value of equity investments not held for trading.

iv. Financial assets at fair value through profit or loss

Financial assets are measured at fair value through profit or loss unless it is measured at amortised cost or at fair value through other comprehensive income on initial recognition. The transaction costs directly attributable to the acquisition of financial assets and liabilities at fair value through profit and loss are immediately recognised in statement of profit and loss.

v. Financial liabilities

Financial liabilities are subsequently carried at amortized cost using the effective interest method ,except for contingent consideration recognized in a business combination which is subsequently measured at fair value through profit and loss. For trade and other payables maturing within one year from the balance sheet date, the carrying amounts approximate fair value due to the short maturity of these instruments.

b. Derivative financial instruments

The Company holds derivative financial instruments such as foreign exchange forward contracts to mitigate the risk of changes in exchange rates on foreign currency exposures. The counterparty for these contracts is generally a bank.

i. Financial assets or financial liabilities, at fair value through profit or loss

This category has derivative financial assets or liabilities which are not designated as hedges.

Any derivative that is either not designated a hedge, or is so designated but is ineffective as per Ind AS 109, is categorized as a financial asset or financial liability, at fair value through statement of profit and loss.

Derivatives not designated as hedges are recognized initially at fair value and attributable transaction costs are recognized in net profit in statement of profit and loss when incurred. Subsequent to initial recognition, these derivatives are measured at fair value through profit or loss and the resulting gains or losses are included in statement of profit and loss. Assets/liabilities in this category are presented as current assets/current liabilities if they are either held for trading or are expected to be realized within 12 months after the balance sheet date.

ii. Cash flow hedge accounting

The Company designates certain foreign exchange forward contracts as cash flow hedges to mitigate the risk of foreign exchange exposure on highly probable forecast cash transactions.

When a derivative is designated as a cash flow hedging instrument, the effective portion of changes in the fair value of the derivative is recognized in other comprehensive income and accumulated in the cash flow hedging reserve. Any ineffective portion of changes in the fair value of the derivative is recognized immediately in the net profit in the statement of profit and loss. If the hedging instrument no longer meets the criteria for hedge accounting, then hedge accounting is discontinued prospectively. If the hedging instrument expires or is sold, terminated or exercised, the cumulative gain or loss on the hedging instrument recognized in cash flow hedging reserve till the period the hedge was effective remains in cash flow hedging reserve until the forecasted transaction occurs. The cumulative gain or loss previously recognized in the cash flow hedging reserve is transferred to the net profit in the statement of profit and loss upon the occurrence of the related forecasted transaction. If the forecasted transaction is no longer expected to occur, then the amount accumulated in cash flow hedging reserve is reclassified to net profit in the statement of profit and loss.

1.2.11.3 De-recognition of financial instruments

The Company derecognizes a financial asset when the contractual rights to the cash flows from the financial asset expire or it transfers the financial asset and the transfer qualifies for de-recognition under Ind AS 109. A financial liability (or a part of a financial liability) is derecognized when the obligation specified in the contract is discharged or cancelled or expires.

1.2.11.4 Fair value hierarchy

All assets and liabilities for which fair value is measured or disclosed in the financial statements are categorised within the fair value hierarchy, described as follows, based on the lowest level input that is significant to the fair value measurement as a whole:

- Level 1 — Quoted (unadjusted) market prices in active markets for identical assets or liabilities
- Level 2 — Valuation techniques for which the lowest level input that is significant to the fair value measurement is directly or indirectly observable
- Level 3 — Valuation techniques for which the lowest level input that is significant to the fair value measurement is unobservable

For assets and liabilities that are recognised in the financial statements on a recurring basis, the Company determines whether transfers have occurred between levels in the hierarchy by re-assessing categorisation (based on the lowest level input that is significant to the fair value measurement as a whole) at the end of each reporting period.

1.2.12 *Fair value of financial instruments*

In determining the fair value of its financial instruments, the Company uses a variety of methods and assumptions that are based on market conditions and risks existing at each reporting date. The methods used to determine fair value include discounted cash flow analysis, available quoted market prices and dealer quotes. All methods of assessing fair value result in general approximation of value, and such value may never actually be realized.

1.2.13 *Employee benefits*

1.2.13.1 Gratuity

The Company provides for gratuity, a defined benefit retirement plan ('the Gratuity Plan') covering eligible employees. The Gratuity Plan provides a lump-sum payment to vested employees at retirement, death, incapacitation or termination of employment, of an amount based on the respective employee's salary and the tenure of employment with the Company.

Liabilities with regard to the Gratuity Plan are determined by actuarial valuation, performed by an independent actuary, at each balance sheet date using the projected unit credit method. The company fully contributes all ascertained liabilities to the ABC Limited Employees' Gratuity Fund Trust (the Trust). Trustees administer contributions made to the Trusts and contributions are invested in a scheme with Life Insurance Corporation of India as permitted by laws of India.

The company recognises the net obligation of a defined benefit plan in its balance sheet as an asset or liability. Gains and losses through re-measurements of the net defined benefit liability/(asset) are recognized in other comprehensive income. The actual return of the portfolio of plan assets, in excess of the yields computed by applying the discount rate used to measure the defined benefit obligation is recognized in other comprehensive income. The effect of any plan amendments is recognized in net profits in the statement of profit and loss.

1.2.13.2 Superannuation

Certain employees of ABC are participants in a defined contribution plan. The company has no further obligations to the Plan beyond its monthly contributions which are periodically contributed to a trust fund, the corpus of which is invested with the Life Insurance Corporation of India.

1.2.13.3 Provident fund

Eligible employees of ABC receive benefits from a provident fund, which is a defined benefit plan. Both the eligible employee and the company make monthly contributions to the provident fund plan equal to a specified percentage of the covered employee's salary. The company contributes a portion to the ABC Limited Employees' Provident Fund Trust. The trust invests in specific designated instruments as permitted by Indian law. The remaining portion is contributed to the government administered pension fund. The rate at which the annual interest is payable to the beneficiaries by the trust is being administered by the government. The company has an obligation to make good the shortfall, if any, between the return from the investments of the Trust and the notified interest rate.

1.2.13.4 Compensated absences

The company has a policy on compensated absences which are both accumulating and non-accumulating in nature. The expected cost of accumulating compensated absences is determined by actuarial valuation performed by an independent actuary at each balance sheet date using projected unit credit method on the additional amount expected to be paid/availed as a result of the unused entitlement that has accumulated at the balance sheet date. Expense on non-accumulating compensated absences is recognized in the period in which the absences occur.

1.2.14 Share based payments

The Company measures compensation cost relating to share-based payments using the fair valuation method in accordance with Ind AS 102, *Share-Based Payments*. Compensation expense is amortized over the vesting period of the option on a straight line basis.

The dilutive effect of outstanding options is reflected as additional share dilution in the computation of diluted earnings per share.

1.2.15 Foreign currencies

Functional currency

The functional currency of the company is the Indian rupee. These financial statements are presented in Indian rupees (rounded off to crore; one crore equals ten million).

Transactions and translations

Foreign-currency denominated monetary assets and liabilities are translated into the relevant functional currency at exchange rates in effect at the balance sheet date. The gains or losses resulting from such translations are included in net profit in the statement of profit and loss. Non-monetary assets and non-monetary liabilities denominated in a foreign currency and measured at fair value are translated at the exchange rate prevalent at the date when the fair value was determined. Non-monetary assets and non-monetary liabilities denominated in a foreign currency and measured at historical cost are translated at the exchange rate prevalent at the date of the transaction.

Transaction gains or losses realized upon settlement of foreign currency transactions are included in determining net profit for the period in which the transaction is settled. Revenue, expense and cash-flow items denominated in foreign currencies are translated into the relevant functional currencies using the exchange rate in effect on the date of the transaction.

1.2.16 Income taxes

Income tax expense comprises current tax expense and the net change in the deferred tax asset or liability during the year. Current and deferred tax are recognised in profit or loss, except when they relate to items that are recognised in other comprehensive income or directly in equity, in which case, the current and deferred tax are also recognised in other comprehensive income or directly in equity, respectively.

(i) Current income tax

Current income tax for the current and prior periods are measured at the amount expected to be recovered from or paid to the taxation authorities based on the taxable income for that period. The tax rates and tax laws used to compute the amount are those that are enacted or substantively enacted by the balance sheet date.

(ii) Deferred income tax

Deferred income tax is recognised using the balance sheet approach, deferred tax is recognized on temporary differences at the balance sheet date between the tax bases of assets and liabilities and their carrying amounts for financial reporting purposes, except when the deferred income tax arises from the initial recognition of goodwill or an asset or liability in a transaction that is not a business combination and affects neither accounting nor taxable profit or loss at the time of the transaction.

Deferred income tax assets are recognized for all deductible temporary differences, carry forward of unused tax credits and unused tax losses, to the extent that it is probable that taxable profit will be available against which the deductible temporary differences, and the carry forward of unused tax credits and unused tax losses can be utilized.

The carrying amount of deferred income tax assets is reviewed at each balance sheet date and reduced to the extent that it is no longer probable that sufficient taxable profit will be available to allow all or part of the deferred income tax asset to be utilized.

Deferred income tax assets and liabilities are measured at the tax rates that are expected to apply in the period when the asset is realized or the liability is settled, based on tax rates (and tax laws) that have been enacted or substantively enacted at the balance sheet date.

The company offsets current tax assets and current tax liabilities, where it has a legally enforceable right to set off the recognized amounts and where it intends either to settle on a net basis, or to realize the asset and settle the liability simultaneously. Tax benefits of deductions earned on exercise of employee share options in excess of compensation charged to income are credited to share premium.

1.2.17 Provisions and contingent liabilities

A provision is recognized when an enterprise has a present obligation (legal or constructive) as result of past event and it is probable that an outflow of embodying economic benefits of resources will be required to settle a reliably assessable obligation. Provisions are determined based on best estimate required to settle each obligation at each balance sheet date. If the effect of the time value of money is material, provisions are discounted using a current pre-tax rate that reflects, when appropriate, the risks specific to the liability. When discounting is used, the increase in the provision due to the passage of time is recognised as a finance cost.

Provisions for onerous contracts, i.e. contracts where the expected unavoidable costs of meeting obligations under a contract exceed the economic benefits expected to be received, are recognized when it is probable that an outflow of resources embodying economic benefits will be required to settle a present obligation as a result of an obligating event, based on a reliable estimate of such obligation.

A contingent liability is a possible obligation that arises from past events whose existence will be confirmed by the occurrence or non-occurrence of one or more uncertain future events beyond the control of the Company or a present obligation that is not recognized because it is not probable that an outflow of resources will be required to settle the obligation. A contingent liability also arises in extremely rare cases where there is a liability that cannot be recognized because it cannot be measured reliably. The Company does not recognize a contingent liability but discloses its existence in the condensed standalone financial statements.

1.2.18 Earnings per share

The basic earnings per share is computed by dividing the net profit attributable to equity shareholders for the period by the weighted average number of equity shares outstanding during the period. The number of shares used in computing diluted earnings per share comprises the weighted average shares considered for deriving basic earnings per share, and also the weighted average number of equity shares which could be issued on the conversion of all dilutive potential equity shares. Dilutive potential equity shares are deemed converted as of the beginning of the period, unless they have been issued at a later date. The diluted potential equity shares have been arrived at, assuming that the proceeds receivable were based on shares having been issued at the average market value of the outstanding shares. In computing dilutive earnings per share, only potential equity shares that are dilutive and that would, if issued, either reduce future earnings per share or increase loss per share, are included.

1.2.19 Inventories

Inventory comprises of traded goods and is measured at lower of cost and net realisable value. Cost includes cost of purchase and other costs incurred in bringing the inventories to their present location and condition. Cost is determined on a weighted average basis. Net realisable value is the estimated selling price in the ordinary course of business, less estimated cost necessary to make the sale.

1.2.20 Dividend

Final dividends on shares are recorded as a liability on the date of approval by the shareholders and interim dividends are recorded as a liability on the date of declaration by the company's Board of Directors.

1.2.21 Government Grants

The Company recognizes government grants only when there is reasonable assurance that the conditions attached to them shall be complied with, and the grants will be received. Government grants related to assets are treated as deferred income and are recognized in net profit in the statement of profit and loss on a systematic and rational basis over the useful life of the asset. Government grants related to revenue are recognized on a systematic basis in net profit in the statement of profit and loss over the periods necessary to match them with the related costs which they are intended to compensate

1.2.22 Cash Flow Statement

Cash flows are reported using the indirect method, whereby profit for the period is adjusted for the effects of transactions of a non-cash nature, any deferrals or accruals of past or future operating cash receipts or payments and item of income or expenses associated with investing or financing cash flows. The cash flows from operating, investing and financing activities of the Company are segregated

2. FIRST-TIME ADOPTION OF IND AS

These condensed standalone financial statements, for quarter and six months ended 30 September 2016 have been prepared in accordance with Ind AS. For the year ended 31 March 2016, the Company prepared its annual standalone financial statements in accordance with accounting standards notified under section 133 of the Act, read with with Rule 7 of the Companies (Accounts) Rules, 2014 ('Indian GAAP' or 'previous GAAP').

The transition to Ind AS has resulted in changes in the presentation of the financial statements, disclosures in the notes thereto and accounting policies and principles. The accounting policies set out in note 1 have been applied in preparing the standalone financial statements for the quarter and six months ended 30 September 2016 and the comparative information. An explanation of how the transition from previous GAAP to Ind AS has affected the Company's balance sheet, statement of profit and loss, is set out in note 2.2 (i) and 2.2 (ii). Exemptions on first time adoption of Ind AS availed in accordance with Ind AS 101 have been set out in note 2.1.

2.1 Exemptions applied

Ind AS 101 allows first-time adopters certain exemptions from the retrospective application of certain requirements under Ind AS. The Company has applied the following material exemptions:

- The Company is allowed to apply Ind AS 102, *Share-based payment* to equity instruments that remain unvested as of transition date. The Company has elected to avail this exemption and apply the requirements of Ind AS 102 to all such grants under the 2015 plan (formerly 2011 plan). Accordingly, these options have been measured at fair value as against intrinsic value previously under Indian GAAP. The excess of stock compensation expense measured using fair value over the cost recognized under Indian GAAP using intrinsic value has been adjusted in 'Share Option Outstanding Account', with the corresponding impact taken to the retained earnings as on the transition date.
- Ind AS 103, *Business Combinations* has not been applied to acquisitions, which are considered businesses under Ind AS that occurred before 1 April 2015. Use of this exemption means that the Indian GAAP carrying amounts of assets and liabilities, that are required to be recognised under Ind AS, is their deemed cost at the date of the acquisition. After the date of the acquisition, measurement is in accordance with respective Ind AS. The Company did not recognise or exclude any previously recognised amounts as a result of Ind AS recognition requirements.
- The Company has elected to avail the exemption under Ind AS 101 to use Indian GAAP carrying value as deemed cost at the date of transition for all items of property, plant and equipment as per the statement of financial position prepared in accordance with previous GAAP.

2.2 (i) Reconciliation of equity between previous GAAP and Ind AS

(INR crore)

	31 March 2016	30 Sept 2015	1 April 2015
Equity under previous GAAP	**XXX**	**XXX**	**XXX**
Fair valuation of investments	XX	XX	XX
Fair valuation of forward contracts	XX	XX	XX
Effect of Income tax	XX	XX	XX
Proposed dividend and tax on dividend	XX	XX	XX
Others	XX	XX	XX
Equity as per Ind AS	**XXX**	**XXX**	**XXX**

(ii) Total comprehensive income reconciliation for the quarter ended 30 September 2015.

	Quarter ended 30 September 2015	Six months ended 30 September 2015
Net income under previous GAAP	XXX	**XXX**
Fair valuation of investments	XX	XX
Fair valuation of Forward contracts	XX	XX
Employee benefits	XX	XX
Others	XX	XX
Effect of Income tax	XX	XX
Profit for the quarter under Ind AS	XXX	**XXX**
Other comprehensive income	XX	XX
Total comprehensive income	XXX	**XXX**

Notes to reconciliations between Previous GAAP and Ind AS

(a) Fair valuation of investments

Under previous GAAP, current investments were measured at lower of cost or fair value and long term investments were measured at cost less diminution in value which is other than temporary. Under Ind AS, financial assets other than amortized cost are subsequently measured at fair value.

Investment in Mutual Funds, have been classified as fair value through statement of profit and loss and fair value changes are recognized in the statement of profit and loss.

(b) Fair valuation of forward contracts

Under previous GAAP, in relation to the forward contracts entered into, to hedge the foreign currency risk of the underlying outstanding at the balance sheet date, the exchange difference is calculated and recorded in accordance with paragraphs 36 and 37 of AS 11. Under Ind AS, the aforementioned forward contracts are fair valued through statement of profit and loss and fair value changes are recognized in statement of profit and loss.

(c) Dividend and tax on dividend

Under Ind AS, dividend to holders of equity instruments is recognised as a liability in the period in which the obligation to pay is established. Under Previous GAAP, dividend payable is recorded as a liability in the period to which it relates.

(d) Employee benefits

Under the previous GAAP, actuarial gains and losses were recognized in profit or loss. Under Ind AS, the actuarial gains and losses form part of re-measurement of net defined benefit liability/asset which is recognized in other comprehensive income in the respective periods.

(iii) Cash flow statement: There were no reconciliation items between cash flows prepared under Indian GAAP and those prepared under Indian GAAP and those prepared under Ind AS

3. PROPERTY, PLANT AND EQUIPMENT

Following are the changes in the carrying value of property, plant and equipment for the three months ended 30 September 2016:

(INR crore)

Particulars	Land-leasehold	Buildings	Plant and machinery	Furniture and fixtures	Office equipment	Computer equipment	Furniture and fixtures	Vehicles	Total
Gross carrying value as of 1 July 2016									
Additions									
Deletions									
Gross carrying value as of 30 September 2016									
Accumulated depreciation as of 1 July 2016									
Depreciation									
Accumulated depreciation on deletions									
Accumulated depreciation as of 30 September 2016									
Carrying value as of 30 September 2016									

Following are the changes in the carrying value of property, plant and equipment for the three months ended 30 September 2015:

Particulars	Land-leasehold	Buildings	Plant and machinery	Furniture and fixtures	Office equipment	Computer equipment	Furniture and fixtures	Vehicles	Total
Gross carrying value as of 1 July 2015									
Additions									
Deletions									

Particulars	Land-leasehold	Buildings	Plant and machinery	Furniture and fixtures	Office equipment	Computer equipment	Furniture and fixtures	Vehicles	Total
Gross carrying value as of 30 September 2015									
Accumulated depreciation as of 1 July 2015									
Depreciation									
Accumulated depreciation on deletions									
Accumulated depreciation as of 30 September 2015									
Carrying value as of 30 September 2015									

Following are the changes in the carrying value of property, plant and equipment for the Six months ended 30 September 2016:

(INR crores)

Particulars	Land-leasehold	Buildings	Plant and machinery	Furniture and fixtures	Office equipment	Computer equipment	Furniture and fixtures	Vehicles	Total
Gross carrying value as of 1 July 2016									
Additions									
Deletions									
Gross carrying value as of 30 September 2016									
Accumulated depreciation as of 1 July 2016									
Depreciation									
Accumulated depreciation on deletions									

Particulars	Land-leasehold	Buildings	Plant and machinery	Furniture and fixtures	Office equipment	Computer equipment	Furniture and fixtures	Vehicles	Total
Accumulated depreciation as of 30 September 2016									
Carrying value as of 30 September 2016									

Following are the changes in the carrying value of property, plant and equipment for the Six months ended 30 September 2015:

Particulars	Land-leasehold	Buildings	Plant and machinery	Furniture and fixtures	Office equipment	Computer equipment	Furniture and fixtures	Vehicles	Total
Gross carrying value as of 1 July 2015									
Additions									
Deletions									
Gross carrying value as of 30 September 2015									
Accumulated depreciation as of 1 July 2015									
Depreciation									
Accumulated depreciation on deletions									
Accumulated depreciation as of 30 September 2015									
Carrying value as of 30 September 2015									

Following are the changes in the carrying value of property, plant and equipment for the year ended 31 March 2016:

(INR crore)

Particulars	Land-leasehold	Buildings	Plant and machinery	Furniture and fixtures	Office equipment	Computer equipment	Furniture and fixtures	Vehicles	Total
Gross carrying value as of 1 April 2015									
Additions									
Deletions									
Gross carrying value as of 31 March 2016									
Accumulated depreciation as of 1 April 2015									
Depreciation for the period									
Accumulated depreciation on deletions									
Accumulated depreciation as of 31 March 2016									
Carrying value as of 31 March 2016									
Carrying value as of 1 April 2015									

4. INTANGIBLE ASSETS

Following are the changes in the carrying value of intangible assets for the three months ended 30 September 2016:

Particulars	Sub-contracting rights	Others	Total
Gross carrying value as of 1 July 2016			
Additions			
Deletions			
Gross carrying value as of 30 September 2016			
Accumulated amortisation as of 1 July 2016			
Amortization expense			
Deletions			

Particulars	Sub-contracting rights	Others	Total
Accumulated amortisation as of 30 September 2016			
Carrying value as of 30 September 2016			

Following are the changes in the carrying value of intangible assets for the three months ended 30 September 2015:

Particulars	Sub-contracting rights	Others	Total
Gross carrying value as of 1 July 2015			
Additions			
Deletions			
Gross carrying value as of 30 September 2015			
Accumulated amortisations as of 1 July 2015			
Amortization expense			
Accumulated amortisation on deletions			
Accumulated amortisation as of 30 September 2015			
Carrying value as of 30 September 2015			

Following are the changes in the carrying value of intangible assets for the six months ended 30 September 2016:

Particulars	Sub-contracting rights	Others	Total
Gross carrying value as of 1 July 2016			
Additions			
Deletions			
Gross carrying value as of 30 September 2016			
Accumulated amortisations as of 1 July 2015			
Amortization expense			
Accumulated amortisation on deletions			
Accumulated amortisation as of 30 September 2016			
Carrying value as of 30 September 2016			

Following are the changes in the carrying value of intangible assets for the six months ended 30 September 2015:

Particulars	Sub-contracting rights	Others	Total
Gross carrying value as of 1 July 2015			
Additions			
Deletions			
Gross carrying value as of 30 September 2015			
Accumulated amortisations as of 1 July 2015			
Amortization expense			
Accumulated amortisation on deletions			
Accumulated amortisation as of 30 September 2015			
Carrying value as of 30 September 2015			

Following are the changes in the carrying value of intangible assets for the year ended 31 March 2016:

Particulars	Sub-contracting rights	Others	Total
Gross carrying value as of 1 April 2015			
Additions			
Deletions			
Gross carrying value as of 31 March 2016			
Accumulated amortisations as of 1 July 2015			
Amortization expense			
Accumulated amortisation on deletions			
Accumulated amortisation as of 31 March 2016			
Carrying value as of 31 March 2016			
Carrying value as of 1 April 2015			

5. INVESTMENTS

Particulars	As at		
	30 September 2016	31 March 2016	1 April 2015
Non-current investments			
Equity instruments of subsidiaries	XXX	XXX	XXX
Debentures of subsidiary	XXX	XXX	XXX
Preference securities and equity investments	XXX	XXX	XXX
Tax free bonds	XXX	XXX	XXX
Non convertible debentures	XXX	XXX	XXX
	XXX	**XXX**	**XXX**
Current investments			
Liquid mutual fund units	XXX	XXX	XXX
Government bonds	XXX	XXX	XXX
	XXX	**XXX**	**XXX**
Total carrying value	**XXX**	**XXX**	**XXX**

Particulars	As at		
	30 September 2016	31 March 2016	1 April 2015
Non-current investments			
Unquoted			
Investment carried at cost			
Investments in equity instruments of subsidiaries			
PQR Limited	XXX	XXX	XXX
XXX (XXX and XXX) equity shares of INR 10/- each, fully paid			
ABC Technologies Limited	XXX	XXX	XXX
XXX (XXX) equity shares of INR 10/- each, fully paid			
IPL Technologies	XXX	XXX	XXX
XXX (XXX) equity shares of INR 10/- each, fully paid up			
	XXX	**XXX**	**XXX**
Investment carried at amortised cost			
Investment in debentures of subsidiary			
XYZ Limited			
XXX (XXX) Unsecured redeemable, non-convertible debentures of INR 100 each fully paid up	XXX	XXX	XXX
	XXX	**XXX**	**XXX**
	XXX	**XXX**	**XXX**

Particulars	As at		
	30 September 2016	31 March 2016	1 April 2015
Investment carried at fair value through other comprehensive income (FVOCI)			
Preference securities	XXX	XXX	XXX
Equity instruments	XX	XX	XX
	XXX	**XXX**	**XXX**
Quoted			
Investments carried at amortized cost			
Tax free bonds	XXX	XXX	XXX
	XXX	**XXX**	**XXX**
Investments carried at fair value through other comprehensive income			
Non convertible debentures	**XXX**	**XXX**	**XXX**
Total non-current investments	**XXX**	**XXX**	**XXX**
Current investments			
Unquoted			
Investment carried at fair value through profit or loss			
Liquid mutual funds units			
	XXX	XXX	XXX
	XXX	**XXX**	**XXX**
Quoted			
Investment carried at amortised cost			
Government bonds			
	XXX	**XXX**	**XXX**
	XXX	**XXX**	**XXX**
Total current investment	**XXX**	**XXX**	**XXX**
Total investments	**XXX**	**XXX**	**XXX**
Aggregate amount of quoted investments	XXX	XXX	XXX
Market value of quoted investments (including interest accrued)	XXX	XXX	XXX
Aggregate amount of unquoted investments	XXX	XXX	XXX
Aggregate amount of impairment in value of investments	XXX	XXX	XXX
Investments carried at cost	XXX	XXX	XXX
Investments carried at amortised cost	XXX	XXX	XXX
Investments carried at fair value through other comprehensive income	XXX	XXX	XXX
Investments carried at fair value through profit or loss	XXX	XXX	XXX

6. LOANS

(INR crore)

Particulars	As at		
	30 September 2016	31 March 2016	1 April 2015
Non- Current			
Unsecured, considered good			
Other Loans			
Loans to employees			
	XXX	XXX	XXX
	XXX	**XXX**	**XXX**
Unsecured, considered doubtful			
Loans to employees	**XXX**	**XXX**	**XXX**
Less: Allowance for doubtful loans to employees	**XXX**	**XXX**	**XXX**
Current			
Unsecured, considered good			
Loans to subsidiary	XXX	XXX	XXX
Other Loans			
Loans to employees	XXX	XXX	XXX
	XXX	**XXX**	**XXX**
Total Loans	**XXX**	**XXX**	**XXX**

7. OTHER FINANCIAL ASSETS

Particulars	As at		
	30 September 2016	31 March 2016	1 April 2015
Non current			
Interest receivable	XXX	XXX	XXX
Long-term bank deposits	XXX	XXX	XXX
Security deposits	XXX	XXX	XXX
Rental deposits	XXX	XXX	XXX
	XXX	**XXX**	**XXX**
Current			
Interest receivable	XXX	XXX	XXX
Security deposits	XXX	XXX	XXX
Rental deposits	XXX	XXX	XXX
Unbilled revenues	XXX	XXX	XXX
Foreign exchange forward contracts	XXX	XXX	XXX
Others	XXX	XXX	XXX
	XXX	**XXX**	**XXX**
	XXX	**XXX**	**XXX**

Others include receivables towards sale of mutual funds of ' XXX crores as at 30 September 2016.

8. TRADE RECEIVABLES

Particulars	As at		
	30 September 2016	31 March 2016	1 April 2015
Current			
Unsecured			
Considered good	XXX	XXX	XXX
Considered doubtful	XXX	XXX	XXX
	XXX	**XXX**	**XXX**
Less Allowances for credit losses	XXX	XXX	XXX
	XXX	**XXX**	**XXX**

9. CASH AND CASH EQUIVALENTS

Particulars	As at		
	30 September 2016	31 March 2016	1 April 2015
Balances with banks			
In current	XXX	XXX	XXX
In deposit accounts with original maturity less than three months	XXX	XXX	XXX
Cheques in hand	XXX	XXX	XXX
Cash on hand	XXX	XXX	XXX
Others	XXX	XXX	XXX
Deposits with financial institution	XXX	XXX	XXX
	XXX	**XXX**	**XXX**
Balances with banks in unpaid dividend accounts	XXX	XXX	XXX
Deposit with more than 12 months maturity	XXX	XXX	XXX
Balances with banks held as margin money deposits against guarantees	XXX	XXX	XXX

Cash and cash equivalents as of 30 September 2016, 31 March 2016 and 1 April 2015 include restricted cash and bank balances of INR XXX, INR XXX, INR XXX, respectively. The restrictions are primarily on account of bank balances held as margin money deposits against guarantees and balances held in unpaid dividends bank accounts.

The deposits maintained by the Company with banks and financial institutions comprise of time deposits, which can be withdrawn by the Company at any point without prior notice or penalty on the principal.

10. OTHER ASSETS

Particulars	As at		
	30 September 2016	31 March 2016	1 April 2015
Non-current			
Capital advances	XXX	XXX	XXX
Advances other than capital advance	XXX	XXX	XXX
Prepaid gratuity *(Refer note 22)*	XXX	XXX	XXX
Others			
Prepaid expenses	XXX	XXX	XXX
Prepaid rent	XXX	XXX	XXX
Indirect taxes recoverable	XXX	XXX	XXX
Deferred contract cost	XXX	XXX	XXX
	XXX	**XXX**	**XXX**
Current			
Advances other than capital advance			
Payment to vendors for supply of goods	XXX	XXX	XXX
Others			
Prepaid expenses	XXX	XXX	XXX
Indirect taxes recoverable	XXX	XXX	XXX
Deferred contract cost	XXX	XXX	XXX
	XXX	**XXX**	**XXX**
Total other assets	**XXX**	**XXX**	**XXX**

Deferred contract costs are upfront costs incurred for the contract and are amortized over the term of the contract. Indirect taxes recoverable primarily consist of input tax credits.

11. FINANCIAL INSTRUMENTS

Financial statements by category

The carrying values of financial instruments by categories as of 30 September 2016 were as follows:

(INR crore)

Particulars	Fair value through profit or loss	Derivative instruments in Hedging relationship	Derivative instruments not in Hedging relationship	Amortised Cost	Total
Financial Assets					
Cash and cash equivalents	-	-	-	-	-
Bank balances other than cash and cash equivalents	-	-	-	-	-
Investment	-	-	-	-	-
Equity and preference securities					
Tax free bonds and government bonds					
Liquid mutual fund units					
Redeemable, non-convertible debentures					
Non-convertible debentures					
Trade receivables	-	-	-	-	-
Loans and advances	-	-	-	-	-
Forward cover	-	-	-	-	-
Cash flow hedges	-	-	-	-	-
Other financial assets	-	-	-	-	-
Total	-	-	-	-	-

Particulars	Fair value through profit or loss	Derivative instruments in Hedging relationship	Derivative instruments not in Hedging relationship	Amortised Cost	Total
Financial Liabilities					
Trade Payables	-	-	-	-	-
Forward cover	-	-	-	-	-
Cash flow hedges	-	-	-	-	-
Other financial liabilities	-	-	-	-	-
Total	**-**	**-**	**-**	**-**	**-**

The carrying values of financial instruments by categories as of 31 March 2016 were as follows:

(INR)

Particulars	Fair value through profit or loss	Derivative instruments in Hedging relationship	Derivative instruments not in Hedging relationship	Amortised Cost	Total
Financial Assets					
Cash and cash equivalents	-	-	-	-	-
Bank balances other than cash and cash equivalents	-	-	-	-	-
Investment (other than investment in subsidiary)	-	-	-	-	-
Equity and preference securities					
Tax free bonds and government bonds					
Liquid mutual fund units					
Redeemable, non-convertible debentures					
Non-convertible debentures					

Particulars	Fair value through profit or loss	Derivative instruments in Hedging relationship	Derivative instruments not in Hedging relationship	Amortised Cost	Total
Trade receivables	-	-	-	-	-
Loans and advances	-	-	-	-	-
Forward cover	-	-	-	-	-
Cash flow hedges	-	-	-	-	-
Other financial assets	-	-	-	-	-
Total	-	-	-	-	-
Financial Liabilities					
Trade Payables	-	-	-	-	-
Forward cover	-	-	-	-	-
Cash flow hedges	-	-	-	-	-
Other financial liabilities	-	-	-	-	-
Total	-	-	-	-	-

The carrying values of financial instruments by categories as of 31 March 2016 were as follows:

(INR crores)

Particulars	Fair value through profit or loss	Derivative instruments in instruments not in Hedging relationship	Derivative Hedging relationship	Amortised Cost	Total
Financial Assets					
Cash and cash equivalents	-	-	-	-	-
Bank balances other than cash and cash equivalents	-	-	-	-	-

Particulars	Fair value through profit or loss	Derivative instruments in instruments not in Hedging relationship	Derivative Hedging relationship	Amortised Cost	Total
Investment (other than investment in Subsidiary)	-	-	-	-	-
Equity and preference securities					
Tax free bonds and government bonds					
Liquid mutual fund units					
Redeemable, non-convertible debentures					
Non-convertible debentures					
Trade receivables	-	-	-	-	-
Loans and advances	-	-	-	-	-
Forward cover	-	-	-	-	-
Cash flow hedges	-	-	-	-	-
Other financial assets	-	-	-	-	-
Total	**-**	**-**	**-**	**-**	**-**
Financial Liabilities					
Borrowings	-	-	-	-	-
Trade Payables	-	-	-	-	-
Forward cover	-	-	-	-	-
Cash flow hedges	-	-	-	-	-
Other financial liabilities	-	-	-	-	-
Total	**-**	**-**	**-**	**-**	**-**

Fair value hierarchy:

Particulars	As at 30 September 2016				As at 31 March 2016				As at 1 April 2015			
	Fair value measurements at reporting				Fair value measurements at reporting				Fair value measurements at reporting			
	Total	Level 1	Level 2	Level 3	Total	Level 1	Level 2	Level 3	Total	Level 1	Level 2	Level 3
Assets												
Investment (other than investment in subsidiary)	-	-	-	-	-	-	-	-	-	-	-	-
Derivative instruments												
Cash flow hedges	-	-	-	-	-	-	-	-	-	-	-	-
Forward cover	-	-	-	-	-	-	-	-	-	-	-	-
Liabilities												
Derivative instruments												
Cash flow hedges	-	-	-	-	-	-	-	-	-	-	-	-
Forward cover	-	-	-	-	-	-	-	-	-	-	-	-

12. EQUITY

Equity Share Capital

(INR crore)

Particulars	As at		
	30 September 2016	**31 March 2016**	**1 April 2015**
Authorised			
Equity shares, X/- par value			
XXX (X[(2)]) equity shares	XXX	XXX	XXX
Issued, Subscribed and Paid-Up			
Equity shares, X/- par value [(1)]			
X (X[(2)]) equity shares fully paid-up	XXX	XXX	XXX
	XXX	**XXX**	**XXX**

[(1)] Refer note 23 for details of basic and diluted shares

[(2)] Represents number of shares as of 31 March 2016

The authorised equity shares were XXX and the issued, subscribed and paid-up shares were XXX as of 1 April 2015.

Forfeited shares amounted to INRXXX (INRXXX)

The Company has only one class of shares referred to as equity shares having a par value of INRX. Each holder of equity shares is entitled to one vote per share.

In the period of five years immediately preceding 30 September 2016:

The Company has allotted XXX and XXX fully paid-up shares of face value INRX each during the quarter ended 30 June 2015 and 31 December 2014, pursuant to bonus issue approved by the shareholders through postal ballot.

The Board has increased dividend pay-out ratio from up to 40% to up to 50% of post-tax consolidated profits effective fiscal 2015.

The Board of Directors, in its meeting on (Day Month Year), proposed a final dividend of 'XX per equity share and the same was approved by the shareholders at the Annual General Meeting held on (Day Month Year). The amount was recognized as distributions to equity shareholders during the six months ended 30 September 2016 and the total appropriation was 'XX crore including corporate dividend tax.

The amount of per share dividend recognized as distributions to equity shareholders during the six month ended 30 September 2015 was 'XX per equity share.

The Board of Directors, in their meeting on (Day Month Year), declared an interim dividend of XX per equity share, which would result in a cash outflow of approximately 'XXX crore, inclusive of corporate dividend tax (refer note 2.2 (i) for impact on transition to Ind AS).

In the event of liquidation of the Company, the holders of equity shares will be entitled to receive any of the remaining assets of the company in proportion to the number of equity shares held by the shareholders, after distribution of all preferential amounts.

The details of shareholder holding more than 5% shares as at 30 September 2016, 31 March 2016 and 1 April 2015 are set out below:

(INR crore)

Name of the shareholder	As at 30 September 2016		As at 31 March 2016		As at 1 April 2015	
	Number of shares	% held	Number of shares	% held	Number of shares	% held
DBS	XXX	XX	XXX	XX	XXX	XX
PKM	XXX	XX	XXX	XX	XXX	XX

The reconciliation of the number of shares outstanding and the amount of share capital as at 30 September 2016, 31 March 2016 and 1 April 2016 is set out below:

(INR crore)

Particulars	As at 30 September 2016		As at 31 March 2016		As at 1 April 2015	
	Number of shares	Amount	Number of shares	Amount	Number of shares	Amount
Number of shares at the beginning of the period	XXX	XXX	XXX	XXX	XXX	XXX
Add: Bonus shares issued	XXX	XXX	XXX	XXX	XXX	XXX
Number of shares at the end of the period	**XXX**	**XXX**	**XXX**	**XXX**	**XXX**	**XXX**

Employee Stock Option Plan (ESOP):

2015 Stock Incentive Compensation Plan (the 2015 Plan): SEBI issued the Securities and Exchange Board of India (Share based Employee Benefits) Regulations, 2014 ('SEBI Regulations') which replaced the SEBI ESOP Guidelines, 1999. The 2011 Plan (as explained below) was required to be amended and restated in accordance with the SEBI Regulations. Consequently, to effect this change, the Company put forth the 2015 Stock Incentive Compensation Plan (the 2015 Plan) for approval to the shareholders of the Company. Pursuant to the approval by the shareholders through postal ballot which ended on March 31, 2016, the Board of Directors have been authorised to introduce, offer, issue and allot share-based incentives to eligible employees of the Company and its subsidiaries under the 2015 Plan. The maximum number of shares under the 2015 plan shall not exceed XXX equity shares (this includes XXX equity shares which were held by the Trust towards the 2011 Plan as at March 31, 2016). XXX equity shares will be issued as RSUs at par value and XXX equity shares will be issued as stock options at market price. These instruments will vest over a period of 4 years and the Company expects to grant the instruments under the 2015 Plan over the period of 4 to 7 years.

On 1 August 2016, the company granted XXX RSUs at par value, to employees upto mid management. Further, the company granted XXX Incentive Units (cash-settled) to eligible employees. These instruments will vest equally over a period of 4 years and are subject to continued service. As of 30 September 2016, XXX shares are held by the trust towards 2015 Plan. As of 30 September 2016, XXX Incentive Units were outstanding (net of forfeitures) and the carrying value of the cash liability is less than INR 1 crore.

2011 RSU Plan (the 2011 Plan) now called 2015 Stock Incentive Compensation Plan (the 2015 Plan): The Company had a 2011 RSU Plan which provided for the grant of restricted stock units (RSUs) to eligible employees of the Company. The Board of Directors recommended the establishment of the 2011 Plan to the shareholders on 30 August 2011 and the shareholders approved the recommendation of the Board of Directors on 17 October 2011 through a postal ballot. The maximum aggregate number of shares that may be awarded under the plan was XXX as on date of approval of plan adjusted for bonus shares and the plan was expected to continue in effect for a term of 10 years from the date of initial grant under the plan. The Company has earmarked XXX equity shares for welfare activities of the employees, approved by the shareholders vide postal ballot which ended on 31 March 2016.

The activity in the 2015 Plan (formerly 2011 RSU Plan) for equity-settled share based payment transactions during the three months and six months ended 30 September 2016 is set out below:

Particulars	Three months ended September 30, 2016		Six months ended September 30, 2016	
	Shares arising out of options	Weighted average exercise price (INR)	Shares arising out of Options	Weighted average exercise price (INR)
2015 Plan (Formerly 2011 Plan)				
Outstanding at the beginning	XXX	XX	XXX	XX
Granted	XXX	XX	XXX	XX

Particulars	Three months ended September 30, 2016		Six months ended September 30, 2016	
	Shares arising out of options	**Weighted average exercise price (INR)**	**Shares arising out of Options**	**Weighted average exercise price (INR)**
Forfeited and expired	XXX	XX	XXX	XX
Exercised	XXX	XX	XXX	XX
Outstanding at the end	**XXX**	**XX**	**XXX**	**XX**
Exercisable at the end	-	-	-	-

The activity in the 2015 Plan (formerly 2011 RSU Plan) for equity-settled share based payment transactions during the three months and six months ended 30 September 2015 is set out below:

Particulars	Three months ended September 30, 2016		Six months ended September 30, 2016	
	Shares arising out of options	**Weighted average exercise price (INR)**	**Shares arising out of Options**	**Weighted average exercise price (INR)**
2015 Plan (Formerly 2011 Plan)				
Outstanding at the beginning*	XXX	XX	XXX	XX
Granted	XXX	XX	XXX	XX
Forfeited and expired	XXX	XX	XXX	XX
Exercised	XXX	XX	XXX	XX
Outstanding at the end	**XXX**	**XX**	**XXX**	**XX**
Exercisable at the end	-	-	-	-

During the three months and six months ended 30 September 2016, the weighted average share price of options exercised under the 2015 Plan on the date of exercise was INR XX/- and INR XX/-

During the three months and six months ended 30 September 2015, the weighted average share price of options exercised under the 2015 Plan on the date of exercise was INR XX/-

The weighted average remaining contractual life of RSUs outstanding as of 30 September 2016 and 31 March 2016 under the 2015 Plan was XX years and XX years respectively.

13. OTHER FINANCIAL LIABILITIES

(INR crore)

Particulars	As at		
	30 September 2016	31 March 2016	1 April 2015
Non-current			
Rental deposits	XXX	XXX	XXX
Payable for acquisition of business	XXX	XXX	XXX
	XXX	XXX	XXX
Current			
Unpaid dividends	XXX	XXX	XXX
Others			
Accrued compensation to employees	XXX	XXX	XXX
Accrued expenses	XXX	XXX	XXX
Retention monies	XXX	XXX	XXX
Payable for acquisition of business			
– Deferred consideration	XXX	XXX	XXX
– Contingent consideration	XXX	XXX	XXX
Client deposits	XXX	XXX	XXX
Capital creditors	XXX	XXX	XXX
Compensated absences	XXX	XXX	XXX
Other payables	XXX	XXX	XXX
Foreign currency forward and options contracts	XXX	XXX	XXX
	XXX	XXX	XXX
Total financial liabilities	XXX	XXX	XXX
Financial liability carried at amortized cost	XXX	XXX	XXX
Financial liability carried at fair value through profit or loss	XXX	XXX	XXX
Liability towards acquisition of business on undiscounted basis	XXX	XXX	XXX

14. TRADE PAYABLES

(INR crore)

Particulars	As at		
	30 September 2016	31 March 2016	1 April 2015
Trade payables	XXX	XXX	XXX
	XXX	**XXX**	XXX

15. OTHER LIABILITIES

(INR crore)

Particulars	As at		
	30 September 2016	31 March 2016	1 April 2015
Current			
Unearned revenue	XXX	XXX	XXX
Others			
Withholding taxes and others	XXX	XXX	XXX
Deferred rent	XXX	XXX	XXX
	XXX	**XXX**	**XXX**

16. PROVISIONS

(INR crore)

Particulars	As at		
	30 September 2016	31 March 2016	1 April 2015
Current			
Others			
Post-sales client support and warranties and others	XXX	XXX	XXX
	XXX	**XXX**	**XXX**

Provision for post-sales client support and warranties and others

The movement in the provision for post-sales client support and warranties and others is as follows:

(INR crore)

Particulars	Three months ended September 30, 2016	Six months ended September 30, 2016
Balance at the beginning	XXX	XXX
Provision recognized/(reversed)	XXX	XXX
Provision utilized	XX	XX
Exchange difference	XX	XX
Balance at the end		
	XXX	**XXX**

Provision for post-sales client support and warranties and other provisions are expected to be utilized over a period of 6 months to 1 year.

17. INCOME TAXES

Income tax expense in the statement of profit and loss comprises:

(INR crore)

Particulars	Three months ended 30 September,		Six months ended 30 September ,	
	2016	2015	2016	2015
Current taxes	XXX	XXX	XXX	XXX
Deferred taxes	XXX	XXX	XXX	XXX
Income tax expense	**XXX**	**XXX**	**XXX**	**XXX**

Current tax expense for the three months period ended 30 September 2016 and 30 September 2015 includes reversals (net of provisions) amounting to INRXXX and INRXXX respectively pertaining to prior periods

Current tax expense for the six months period ended 30 September 2016 and 30 September 2015 includes reversals (net of provisions) amounting to INR XXX and INR XXX respectively pertaining to prior periods

Entire deferred income tax for the three months and six months ended 30 September 2016 and 30 September 2015 relates to origination and reversal of temporary differences.

A reconciliation of the income tax provision to the amount computed by applying the statutory income tax rate to the income before income taxes is summarized below:

(INR crore)

Particulars	Three months ended 30 September,		Six months ended 30 September,	
	2016	2015	2016	2015
Profit before income taxes	XXX	XXX	XXX	XXX
Enacted tax rates in India	X%	X%	X%	X%
Computed expected tax expense	XXX	XXX	XXX	XXX
Tax effect due to non-taxable income for Indian tax purposes	(XX)	(XXX)	(XXX)	(XXX)
Overseas taxes	XXX	XXX	XXX	XXX
Tax reversals, overseas and domestic	(XX)	(XX)	(XX)	(XXX)
Effect of exempt non-operating income	(XX)	(XX)	(XX)	(XX)
Effect of unrecognized deferred tax assets	XX	XX	XX	XX
Effect of differential overseas tax rates	(X)	XX	(XX)	XX
Effect of non-deductible expenses	(X)	XX	XX	XX
Additional deduction on research and development expense	XX	(XX)	XX	(XX)
Others	XX	XX	XX	XX
Income tax expense	**XXX**	**XXX**	**XXX**	**XXX**

The applicable Indian statutory tax rate for fiscal 2017 and fiscal 2016 is X%.

The following table provides the details of income tax assets and income tax liabilities as of 30 September 2016, 31 March 2016 and 1 April 2015

(INR crore)

	As at		
	30 September 2016	31 March 2016	1 April 2015
Income tax assets	XXX	XXX	XXX
Current income tax liabilities	XXX	XXX	XXX
Net current income tax assets/ (liability) at the end	**XXX**	**XXX**	**XXX**

The gross movement in the current income tax asset/(liability) for the three months and six months ended 30 September 2016 and 30 September 2015 is as follows:

(INR crore)

Particulars	Three months ended 30 September,		Six months ended 30 September,	
	2016	2015	2016	2015
Net current income tax asset/ (liability) at the beginning	XXX	XXX	XXX	XXX
Income tax paid	XXX	XXX	XXX	XXX
Current income tax expense (refer note 17)	XXX	XXX	XXX	XXX
Income tax on other comprehensive income	XX	XX	XX	XX
Tax benefit on exercise of share based payments	XX	XX	XX	XX
Translation difference	XX	XX	XX	XX
Net current income tax asset/ (liability) at the end	**XXX**	**XXX**	**XXX**	**XXX**

The tax effects of significant temporary differences that resulted in deferred income tax assets and liabilities are as follows:

(INR crore)

Particulars	As at		
	30 September 2016	31 March 2016	1 April 2015
Deferred income tax assets			
Property, plant and equipment	XXX	XXX	XXX
Computer software	XXX	XXX	XXX
Accrued compensation to employees	XXX	XXX	XXX
Trade receivables	XX	XX	XX
Compensated absences	XX	XX	XX
Post sales client support	XX	XX	XX
Others	**XXX**	**XXX**	**XXX**
Total deferred income tax assets	XXX	XXX	XXX
Deferred income tax liabilities			
Branch profit tax	XXX	XXX	XXX
Others	XXX	XXX	XXX
Total deferred income tax liabilities	XXX	XXX	XXX
Deferred income tax assets after set off	XXX	XXX	XX
Deferred income tax liabilities after set off	-	-	-

Deferred tax assets and deferred tax liabilities have been offset wherever the Company has a legally enforceable right to set off current tax assets against current tax liabilities and where the deferred tax assets and deferred tax liabilities relate to income taxes levied by the same taxation authority.

In assessing the realisability of deferred income tax assets, management considers whether some portion or all of the deferred income tax assets will not be realized. The ultimate realization of deferred income tax assets is dependent upon the generation of future taxable income during the periods in which the temporary differences become deductible. Management considers the scheduled reversals of deferred income tax liabilities, projected future taxable income, and tax planning strategies in making this assessment. Based on the level of historical taxable income and projections for future taxable income over the periods in which the deferred income tax assets are deductible, management believes that the Group will realize the benefits of those deductible differences. The amount of the deferred income tax assets considered realizable, however, could be reduced in the near term if estimates of future taxable income during the carry forward period are reduced.

The gross movement in the deferred income tax account for the three months and six months ended 30 September 2016 and 30 September 2015, is as follows:

(INR crore)

Particulars	Three months ended 30 September,		Six months ended 30 September,	
	2016	2015	2016	2015
Net deferred income tax asset at the beginning	XXX	XXX	XXX	XXX
Translation differences	XXX	(XX)	(XX)	(XX)
Credits/(charge) relating to temporary differences (refer note 17)	(X)	XX	XX	(XX)
Temporary differences on other comprehensive income	-	-	-	-
Net deferred income tax asset at the end	**XXX**	**XXX**	**XXX**	**XXX**

The credits relating to temporary differences during the six months ended 30 September 2016 are primarily on account of trade receivable, accrued compensation to employees and compensated absences partially offset by reversal of credits pertaining to property plant and equipment. The charge relating to temporary differences during the six months ended 30 September 2015 are primarily on account of property plant and equipment, trade receivables, accrued compensation to employees partially offset by compensated absences.

18. REVENUE FROM OPERATIONS

(INR crores)

Particulars	Three months ended 30 September,		Six months ended 30 September,	
	2016	2015	2016	2015
Income from services	XXX	XXX	XXX	XXX
Income from software products	XX	XX	XX	XX
	XXX	**XXX**	**XXX**	**XXX**

19. OTHER INCOME

(INR crore)

Particulars	Three months ended 30 September,		Six months ended 30 September,	
	2016	2015	2016	2015
Interest received on financial assets- Carried at amortised cost				
Tax free bonds, government bonds and debentures	XXX	XXX	XXX	XXX
Deposit with Bank and others	XX	XX	XX	XX
Dividend received on investments carried at fair value through profit or loss				
Mutual fund units	**XXX**	**XXX**	**XXX**	**XXX**
Exchange gains/(losses) on foreign currency forward and options contracts	XXX	XXX	XXX	XXX
Exchange gains/(losses) on translation of other assets and liabilities	XX	XX	XX	XX
Miscellaneous income, net	**XXX**	**XXX**	**XXX**	**XXX**
	XXX	**XXX**	**XXX**	**XXX**

20. EXPENSES

(INR crore)

Particulars	Three months ended 30 September		Six months ended 30 September	
	2016	2015	2016	2015
Employee benefit expenses				
Salaries including bonus	XXX	XXX	XXX	XXX
Contribution to provident and other funds	XXX	XXX	XXX	XXX
Share based payments to employees (Refer note 12)	XX	XX	XX	XX
Staff welfare	XX	XX	XX	XX
	XXX	**XXX**	**XXX**	**XXX**
Cost of software packages and others				
For own use	XXX	XXX	XXX	XXX
Third party items bought for service delivery to clients	XXX	XXX	XXX	XXX
	XXX	**XXX**	**XXX**	**XXX**
Other expenses				
Power and fuel	XXX	XXX	XXX	XXX
Brand and Marketing	XXX	XXX	XXX	XXX
Operating lease payments	XXX	XXX	XXX	XXX
Rates and taxes	XXX	XXX	XXX	XXX
Repairs and Maintenance	XXX	XXX	XXX	XXX
Consumables	XXX	XXX	XXX	XXX
Insurance	XXX	XXX	XXX	XXX
Provision for post-sales client support and warranties	XXX	XXX	XXX	XXX
Commission to non-whole time directors	XXX	XXX	XXX	XXX
Allowances for credit losses on financial assets	XXX	XXX	XXX	XXX
Auditor's remuneration				
Statutory audit fees	XXX	XXX	XXX	XXX
Other services	-	-	-	-
Reimbursement of expenses	-	-	-	-
Contributions towards Corporate Social Responsibility	XXX	XXX	XXX	XXX
Others	XXX	XXX	XXX	XXX
	XXX	**XXX**	**XXX**	**XXX**

21. LEASES

Obligations on long-term, non-cancellable operating leases

The lease rentals charged during the period is as under:

(INR crores)

Particulars	Three months ended 30 September		Six months ended 30 September	
	2016	2015	2016	2015
Lease rentals	XX	XX	XXX	XXX

The obligations on long-term, non-cancellable operating leases payable as per the rentals stated in the respective agreements are as follows:

(INR crore)

Future minimum lease payable	As at		
	30 September 2016	31 March 2016	1 April 2015
Not later than 1 year	XXX	XXX	XXX
Later than 1 year and not later than 5 years	XXX	XXX	XXX
Later than 5 years	XXX	XXX	XXX

The operating lease arrangements, are renewable on a periodic basis and for most of the leases extend upto a maximum of ten years from their respective dates of inception and relates to rented premises. Some of these lease agreements have price escalation clauses.

22. EMPLOYEE BENEFITS

a. Gratuity

The following tables set out the funded status of the gratuity plans and the amounts recognised in the Company's financial statements as at 30 September 2016, 31 March 2016 and 1 April 2015:

(INR crore)

Particulars	As at		
	30 September 2016	31 March 2016	1 April 2015
Change in benefit obligations			
Benefit obligations at the beginning Service cost	XXX	XXX	XXX
Interest expense Curtailment gain Transfer of obligation	XXX	XXX	XXX
Remeasurements - Actuarial (gains)/ losses Benefits paid	XXX	XXX	XXX

Particulars	As at		
	30 September 2016	31 March 2016	1 April 2015
Benefit obligations at the end Change in plan assets	**XXX**	**XXX**	**XXX**
Fair value of plan assets at the beginning	XXX	XXX	XXX
Interest income	XXX	XXX	XXX
Transfer of assets	XXX	XXX	XXX
Remeasurements- Return on plan assets excluding amounts included in interest income	XXX	XXX	XXX
Contributions	XXX	XXX	XXX
Benefits paid	XXX	XXX	XXX
Fair value of plan assets at the end	**XXX**	**XXX**	**XXX**
Funded status	XXX	XXX	XXX

Amount for the three months and six months ended 30 September 2016 and 30 September 2015 recognized in the statement of profit and loss under employee benefit expenses.

(INR crore)

Particulars	Three months ended 30 September		Six months ended 30 September	
	2016	2015	2016	2015
Service cost	XXX	XXX	XXX	XX
Net interest on the net defined benefit liability/asset	XXX	XXX	XXX	(X)
Curtailment gain	-	-	-	-
Net gratuity cost	**XXX**	**XXX**	**XXX**	**XXX**

Amount for the three months and six months ended 30 September 2016 and 30 September 2015 recognized in statement of other comprehensive income:

(INR crore)

Particulars	Three months ended 30 September		Six months ended 30 September	
	2016	2015	2016	2015
Remeasurements of the net defined benefit liability/ (asset)	XXX	(X)	XX	XX
Actuarial (gains)/losses (Return)/ loss on plan assets excluding amounts included in the net interest on the net defined benefit liability/(asset)	XX	(X)	(X)	(X)
	XXX	**(XXX)**	**XX**	**XX**

(INR crore)

Particulars	Three months ended 30 September		Six months ended 30 September	
	2016	2015	2016	2015
(Gain)/loss from change in demographic assumptions	-	-	-	-
(Gain)/loss from change in financial assumptions	XX	(XX)	XX	(X)
	XX	**(XX)**	**XX**	**(X)**

The weighted-average assumptions used to determine benefit obligations as at 30 September 2016 31 March 2016 and 1 April 2015 are set out below:

(INR crore)

Particulars	As of		
	30 September 2016	31 March 2016	1 April 2015
Discount rate	XX	XX	XX
Weighted average rate of increase in compensation levels	XX	XX	XX

The weighted-average assumptions used to determine net periodic benefit cost for the three months and six months ended 30 September 2016 and 30 September 2015 are set out below:

(INR crore)

Particulars	Three months ended 30 September		Six months ended 30 September	
	2016	2015	2016	2015
Discount rate	XX	XX	XX	XX
Weighted average rate of increase in compensation levels	XX	XX	XX	XX
Weighted average duration of defined benefit obligation	XX years	XX years	XX years	XX years

Assumptions regarding future mortality experience are set in accordance with the published statistics by the Life Insurance Corporation of India.

The Company assesses these assumptions with its projected long-term plans of growth and prevalent industry standards. The discount rate is based on the government securities yield.

As of 30 September 2016, every percentage point increase/decrease in discount rate will affect our gratuity benefit obligation by approximately INR XX.

As of 30 September 2016, every percentage point increase/decrease in weighted average rate of increase in compensation levels will affect our gratuity benefit obligation by approximately INR XX.

Sensitivity for significant actuarial assumptions is computed by varying one actuarial assumption used for the valuation of the defined benefit obligation by one percentage, keeping all other actuarial assumptions constant.

Gratuity is applicable only to employees drawing a salary in Indian rupees and there are no other foreign defined benefit gratuity plans.

The Company contributes all ascertained liabilities towards gratuity to the ABC Limited Employees' Gratuity Fund Trust. Trustees administer contributions made to the trust. As of 30 September 2016 and 31 March 2016, the plan assets have been primarily invested in insurer managed funds.

Actual return on assets for the three months and six months ended 30 September 2016 and 30 September 2015 were INR XX and INR XX and INR XX and INR XX respectively.

The Company expects to contribute INR XX to the gratuity trusts during the remainder of fiscal 2017.

Maturity profile of defined benefit obligation:

(*In INR*)

Within 1 year	XXX
1-2 year	XXX
2-3 year	XXX
3-4 year	XXX
4-5 year	XXX
5-10 years	XXX

b. Superannuation

The Company contributed INR XX and INR XX to the Superannuation trust during the three months and six months ended 30 September 2016 (INR XX and INR XX during the three months and six months ended 30 September 2015).

c. Provident fund

ABC has an obligation to fund any shortfall on the yield of the trust's investments over the administered interest rates on an annual basis. These administered rates are determined annually predominantly considering the social rather than economic factors and in most cases the actual return earned by the Company has been higher in the past years. The actuary has provided a valuation for provident fund liabilities on the basis of guidance issued by Actuarial Society of India and based on the below provided assumptions there is no shortfall as at 30 September 2016 and 31 March 2016 and 1 April 2015, respectively.

The details of fund and plan asset position are given below:

(INR crore)

Particulars	As of		
	30 September 2016	31 March 2016	1 April 2015
Plan assets at period end, at fair value	XXX	XXX	XXX
Present value of benefit obligation at period end	XXX	XXX	XXX
Asset recognized in balance sheet	-	-	-

The plan assets have been primarily invested in government securities.

Assumptions used in determining the present value obligation of the interest rate guarantee under the Deterministic Approach:

(INR crore)

Particulars	As at		
	30 September 2016	31 March 2016	1 April 2015
Government of India (GOI) bond yield	XX%	XX%	XX%
Remaining term to maturity of portfolio	XX years	XX years	XX years
Expected guaranteed interest rate - First year:	XX%	XX%	XX%
- Thereafter:	XX%	XX%	XX%

The Company contributed INR XX and INR XX during the three months and six months ended 30 September 2016 (INR XX and INR XX during the three months and six months ended 30 September 2015).

The provident plans are applicable only to employees drawing a salary in Indian rupees and there are no other significant foreign defined benefit plans.

Employee benefits cost include:

(INR crore)

Particulars	Three months ended 30 September		Six months ended 30 September	
	2016	2015	2016	2015
Salaries and bonus*	XXX	XXX	XXX	XXX
Defined contribution plans	XX	XX	XX	XX
Defined benefit plans	XX	XX	XX	XX
	XXX	**XXX**	**XXX**	**XXX**

** Includes stock compensation expense of INR XX and INR XX and INR XX and INR XX for the three months and six months ended 30 September 2016 and 30 September 2015, respectively.*

23. RECONCILIATION OF BASIC AND DILUTED SHARES USED IN COMPUTING EARNING PER SHARE

The following is a reconciliation of the equity shares used in the computation of basic and diluted earnings per equity share:

	Three months ended 30 September		Six months ended 30 September	
	2016	2015	2016	2015
Basic earnings per equity share - weighted average number of equity shares outstanding	XXX	XXX	XXX	XXX
Effect of dilutive common equivalent shares - share options outstanding	XXX	-	XXX	-
Diluted earnings per equity share - weighted average number of equity shares and common equivalent shares Outstanding	XXX	XXX	XXX	XXX

24. CONTINGENT LIABILITIES AND COMMITMENTS (TO THE EXTENT NOT PROVIDED FOR)

(INR crore)

Particulars	As at		
	30 September 2016	31 March 2016	1 April 2015
Contingent liabilities :			
Claims against the Company, not acknowledged as debts[(1)]	XXX	XXX	XXX
[Net of amount paid to statutory authorities INRINR XX (*INR INR XX*)]			
Commitments :			
Estimated amount of contracts remaining to be executed on capital contracts and not provided for (net of advances and deposits)	XXX	XXX	XXX

[(1)]Claims against the company not acknowledged as debts as on 30 September 2016 include demand from the Indian Income tax authorities for payment of tax of INR XXX (INR XXX), including interest of INR XXX (INR XXX) upon completion of their tax assessment for fiscal 2007, fiscal 2008, fiscal 2009, fiscal 2010 and fiscal 2011. These demands were paid to statutory tax authorities. The company has filed an appeal with the income tax appellate authorities.

Demand for fiscal 2007, fiscal 2008 and fiscal 2009 includes disallowance of a portion of the deduction claimed by the company under Section 10A of the income Tax Act as determined by the ratio of export turnover to total turnover. The disallowance arose from certain expenses incurred in foreign currency being reduced from export turnover but not reduced from total turnover. Demand for fiscal 2007, fiscal 2008, fiscal 2009, fiscal 2010 and fiscal 2011 also includes disallowance of portion of profit earned outside India from the STP units under section 10A of the Income Tax Act and disallowance of profits earned from SEZ units under section 10AA of the Income Tax Act. The matters for fiscal 2007, fiscal 2008 and fiscal 2009 are pending before the Commissioner of Income Tax (Appeals) Mumbai. The matter for fiscal 2010 and fiscal 2011 is pending before Hon'ble Income Tax Appellate Tribunal (ITAT) Mumbai.

The company is contesting the demand and the management including its tax advisors believes that its position will likely be upheld in the appellate process. The management believes that the ultimate outcome of these proceedings will not have a material adverse effect on the Company's financial position and results of operations.

The company is subject to legal proceedings and claims, which have arisen in the ordinary course of business. The company's management does not reasonably expect that these legal actions, when ultimately concluded and determined, will have a material and adverse effect on the company's results of operations or financial condition.

25. The management has re-assessed the future profitability of long term revenue contract as at 31 March 2016 and accordingly provided for INR XXX (net of tax of INR XXX) towards expected loss as an exceptional item during the year ended 31 March 2016. During the current quarter the loss incurred under this contract has been adjusted against the said provision.

26. SEGMENT REPORTING

Ind AS 108 establishes standards for the way that public business enterprises report information about operating segments and related disclosures about products and services, geographic areas, and major customers. The Company's operations predominantly relate to providing end-to-end business solutions to enable clients to enhance business performance. Based on the "management approach" as defined in Ind AS 108, the Chief Operating Decision Maker (CODM) evaluates the Company's performance and allocates resources based on an analysis of various performance indicators by business segments and geographic segments. Accordingly, information has been presented both along business segments and geographic segments. The accounting principles used in the preparation of the financial statements are consistently applied to record revenue and expenditure in individual segments, and are as set out in the significant accounting policies

The Company has identified Banking and Capital Market, Insurance, Information Technology, Communication and Entertainment and Emerging Industries as primary business segments of the Company. The geographical segments include United States of America (USA), India Asia Pacific (APAC) and Europe, Middle East & Africa (EMEA).

The accounting policies consistently used in the preparation of the financial statements are also applied to record revenue and expenditure in individual segments. Assets, liabilities, revenues and direct expenses in relation to segments are categorised based on items that are individually identifiable to that segment, while other items, wherever allocable, are apportioned to the segments on an appropriate basis. Certain items are not specifically allocable to individual segments as the underlying services are used interchangeably. The Company therefore believes that it is not practical to provide segment disclosures relating to such items, and accordingly such items are separately disclosed as 'unallocated'. Client relationships are driven based on client domicile.

Primary segment information

Three months ended 30 September 2016 and 30 September 2015

(INR crore)

Particulars	Banking and Capital market	Insurance	Information Technology, Communication and Entertainment	Emerging Industries	Total
Revenue from operations	**XXX**	**XXX**	**XXX**	**XXX**	**XXX**
	XXX	XXX	XXX	XXX	XXX
Identifiable operating expenses	XXX	XXX	XXX	XXX	XXX
	XXX	XXX	XXX	XXX	XXX
Allocated expenses	XXX	XXX	XXX	XXX	XXX
	XXX	XXX	XXX	XXX	XXX
Segment operating income	**XXX**	**XXX**	**XXX**	**XXX**	**XXX**
	XXX	XXX	XXX	XXX	XXX
Unallocable expenses					XXX
					XXX
Operating profit					**XXX**
					XXX
Other income, net					XXX
					XXX
Profit before income taxes					**XXX**
					XXX

Particulars	Banking and Capital market	Insurance	Information Technology, Communication and Entertainment	Emerging Industries	Total
Income tax expense					XXX
					XXX
Net profit					**XXX**
					XXX
Depreciation and amortisation					XXX
					XXX
Non cash expenses other than depreciation and amortisation					XXX
					XXX

Six months ended 30 September 2016 and 30 September 2015

(INR crore)

Particulars	Banking and Capital market	Insurance	Information Technology, Communication and Entertainment	Emerging Industries	Total
Revenue from operations	**XXX**	**XXX**	**XXX**	**XXX**	**XXX**
	XXX	*XXX*	*XXX*	*XXX*	*XXX*
Identifiable operating expenses	XXX	XXX	XXX	XXX	XXX
	XXX	*XXX*	*XXX*	*XXX*	*XXX*
Allocated expenses	XXX	XXX	XXX	XXX	XXX
	XX	*XX*	*XX*	*XX*	*XX*
Segment operating income	**XXX**	**XXX**	**XXX**	**XXX**	**XXX**
	XXX	***XXX***	***XXX***	***XXX***	**XXX**
Unallocable expenses					*XXX*
					XXX
Operating profit					**XXX**
					XXX
Other income, net					XXX
					XXX
Profit before income taxes					**XXX**
					XXX
Income tax expense					XXX
					XXX
Net profit					XXX
					XX
Depreciation and amortisation					**XXX**
					XXX
Non-cash expenses other than depreciation and amortisation					**XXX**
					XXX

Geographic segments

Three months ended 30 September 2016 and 30 September 2015

Particulars	North America	Europe	India	Rest of the World	Total
Revenue from operations	XXX	XXX	XXX	XXX	XXX
	XXX	*XXX*	*XXX*	*XXX*	*XXX*
Identifiable operating expenses	XXX	XXX	XXX	XXX	XXX
	XXX	*XXX*	*XXX*	*XXX*	*XXX*
Allocated expenses	XXX	XXX	XXX	XXX	XXX
	XXX	*XXX*	*XXX*	*XXX*	*XXX*
Segment profit	**XXX**	**XXX**	**XXX**	**XXX**	**XXX**
	XXX	***XXX***	***XXX***	***XXX***	***XXX***
Unallocable expenses					XXX
					XXX
Operating profit					XXX
					XXX
Other income, net					XXX
					XXX
Profit before income taxes					**XXX**
					XXX
Income tax expense					XXX
					XXX
Net profit					XXX
					XXX
Depreciation and amortisation					XXX
					XXX
Non-cash expenses other than depreciation and amortisation					XXX
					XXX

Six months ended 30 September 2016 and 30 September 2015

Particulars	North America	Europe	India	Rest of the World	Total
Revenue from operations	XXX	XXX	XXX	XXX	XXX
	XXX	*XXX*	*XXX*	*XXX*	*XXX*
Identifiable operating expenses	XXX	XXX	XXX	XXX	XXX
	XXX	*XXX*	*XXX*	*XXX*	*XXX*
Allocated expenses	XXX	XXX	XXX	XXX	XXX
	XXX	*XXX*	*XXX*	*XXX*	*XXX*
Segment profit	**XXX**	**XXX**	**XXX**	**XXX**	**XXX**
	XXX	***XXX***	***XXX***	***XXX***	***XXX***
Unallocable expenses					XXX
					XXX
Operating profit					XXX
					XXX
Other income, net					XXX
					XXX
Profit before income taxes					**XXX**
					XXX
Income tax expense					XXX
					XXX
Net profit					XXX
					XXX
Depreciation and amortisation					XXX
					XXX
Non-cash expenses other than depreciation and amortisation					XXX
					XXX

Significant clients

No client individually accounted for more than 10% of the revenues in the three months and six months ended 30 September 2016 and 30 September 2015.

27. The comparatives given in condensed standalone financial statement has been compiled by the management after making necessary Ind AS adjustments to the respective audited financial statements under previous GAAP to give a true and fair view in accordance with Ind AS. This has not been subject to any limited review or audit.

As per our report of even date attached

For XXXXXXXXXXX	**For and on behalf of the Board of**	**Directors**
Chartered Accountants		
ICAI Firm registration number: XXXXXXXX	Mr A (Chairman)	Mr B (Managing Director)
	Mr C (Chief financial officer)	Mr D (Director)
Per Mr. Z		
Partner		
Membership No. XXXXXX		

Place:

Date:

Chapter 7

Interim financial reporting by listed companies

In India, Securities and Exchange Board of India (SEBI), the market regulator requires all listed companies to prepare and publish quarterly financial results in the prescribed format within the specified timelines. SEBI has issued a notification dated 2 September 2015 to issue SEBI (Listing Obligations and Disclosure Requirements) Regulations, 2015 (SEBI Listing Regulations). These regulations have been amended on 25 May 2016 vide SEBI (Listing Obligations and Disclosure Requirements) (Amendment) Regulations, 2016 and on 8 July 2016 vide SEBI (Listing Obligations and Disclosure Requirements) (Second Amendment) Regulations, 2016 (the regulations together with the amendments are referred to as "SEBI Listing Regulations" in this publication). The aforesaid regulations provide ease of reference by consolidating into one single document the requirements applicable to various types of securities listed on the stock exchange.

The Regulations are applicable to a listed entity which has listed any of the following designated securities on recognized stock exchange(s):

(a) Specified securities i.e. equity shares and convertible securities listed on main Board, or SME Exchange or Institutional Trading Platform;

(b) Non-convertible debt securities, non-convertible redeemable preference shares, perpetual debt instrument, perpetual non-cumulative preference shares;

(c) Indian depository receipts;

(d) Securitised debt instruments;

(e) Units issued by mutual funds;

(f) Other securities as may be specified by SEBI.

The SEBI Listing Regulations include:

- principles governing disclosures and obligations of listing entities
- common obligations of listed entities
- obligations of listed entities which has listed its specified securities
- duties and obligations of the recognized stock exchange(s)

7.1 INTERIM FINANCIAL RESULTS UNDER THE SEBI LISTING REGULATIONS

The preparation of interim financial results under SEBI Listing Regulations has been divided into two parts:

- **Regulation 33[1] of** Chapter IV, which deals with "Obligations of listed entity which has listed its specified securities" applies to a listed entity which has listed its specified securities on any recognised stock exchange(s) either on the main board or on SME Exchange or on institutional trading platform.
- **Regulation 52[2]** of Chapter V, which deals with "Obligations of listed entity which has listed its non-convertible debt securities or non-convertible redeemable preference shares or both" applies only to a listed entity which has listed its 'Non-convertible Debt Securities' and/or 'Non-Convertible Redeemable Preference Shares' on a recognised stock exchange in accordance with Securities and Exchange Board of India (Issue and Listing of Debt Securities) Regulations, 2008 or Securities and Exchange Board of India (Issue and Listing of Non-Convertible Redeemable Preference Shares) Regulations, 2013 respectively. This also deals with perpetual debt instrument and perpetual non-cumulative preference share listed by banks.

The key requirements and analysis of reg 33 and reg 52 of the SEBI Listing Regulations are discussed in this chapter.

As per a combined reading of reg 33(1)(b) and AS 25/Ind AS 34, quarterly/annual financial results submitted under reg 33 are not 'interim financial report' under AS 25/Ind AS 34. However, due to the specific requirement of the Listing Regulations, such financial results are nevertheless required to comply with the recognition and measurement principles laid down in AS 25/Ind AS 34. The presentation and disclosure requirements contained in AS 25/Ind AS 34 are not required to be applied in respect of quarterly/annual financial results under reg 33 of the SEBI Listing Regulations. These financial results would need to instead comply with the presentation and disclosure requirements of the Listing Regulations (which are different in form and/or content as required by AS 25/Ind AS 34).

As per Implementation Guide on Auditor's Reports under Indian Accounting Standards for Transition Phase issued by the ICAI, the requirement of disclosure of compliance with Ind AS 34 given in paragraph 19 of Ind AS 34 also represents a

[1] Refer **Annexure-VI** at the end for this chapter for text of Regulation-33.

[2] Refer **Annexure-VI** at the end for this chapter for text of Regulation-52.

disclosure requirement and hence would not apply for financial results submitted and published under the Listing Regulations. Paragraph 19 of Ind AS 34 states as below:

> *"Disclosure of compliance with Ind ASs*
>
> *19. If an entity's interim financial report is in compliance with this Standard, that fact shall be disclosed. An interim financial report shall not be described as complying with Ind ASs unless it complies with all of the requirements of Ind ASs."*

7.2 REQUIREMENT OF REGULATION 33

Regulation 33 deals with the requirements related to submission and filing of financial results with SEBI by listed companies which have listed their specified securities.

Filing of quarterly and year to date financial results

The listed entities which have listed their equity shares or convertible securities are required to submit the financial results (quarterly and year-to-date) to the stock exchange within 45 days of the end of each quarter, other than the last quarter. SEBI vide its circular dated 5 July 2016 has provided certain relaxations to companies following Ind AS such as extension of timelines for submission of financial results by one month for the quarters ended June 2016 and September 2016; exemption from comparatives for the quarters ended June 2016, September 2016 and December 2016 and exemption from mandatory requirements of audit/review of the comparatives for the quarter ended June 2016 and September 2016.

Submission of quarterly and year-to-date consolidated financial results

In case the listed entity has subsidiaries, in addition to the requirement to submit quarterly and year-to-date standalone financial results, the listed entity may also submit quarterly/year-to-date consolidated financial results subject to following:

(i) the listed entity shall intimate to the stock exchange, whether or not listed entity opts to additionally submit quarterly/year-to-date consolidated financial results in the first quarter of the financial year and this option shall not be changed during the financial year.

Provided that this option shall also be applicable to listed entity that is required to prepare consolidated financial results for the first time at the end of a financial year in respect of the quarter during the financial year in which the listed entity first acquires the subsidiary.

(ii) in case the listed entity changes its option in any subsequent year, it shall furnish comparable figures for the previous year in accordance with the option exercised for the current financial year.

7.2.1 Uniform accounting practices and accrual accounting policy

The financial results should be prepared on the basis of accrual accounting policy and should be in accordance with uniform accounting practices adopted for all periods.

AS 1, *Disclosure of Accounting Policies* includes accrual as one of the fundamental accounting assumptions that underlie the preparation and presentation of financial statements. Revenues and costs are accrued, that is, recognised as they are earned or incurred (and not as money is received or paid) and recorded in the financial statements of the periods to which they relate.

7.2.2 Recognition and measurement principles

The quarterly and year to date results shall be prepared in accordance with the recognition and measurement principles laid down in AS 25 or Ind AS 34, *Interim Financial Reporting*, as applicable, specified in sec 133 of the *Companies Act, 2013* read with relevant rules framed thereunder or as specified by the Institute of Chartered Accountants of India, whichever is applicable.

For detailed discussion on the key recognition and measurement principles, please refer to *Chapter 2- Accounting framework for companies to which Ind ASs are applicable,* of this publication.

7.2.3 Financial results prepared in accordance with International Financial Reporting Standards

In addition to the financial results prepared as per Generally Accepted Accounting Principles (GAAP) in India, the listed entity may also submit the financial results, as per the International Financial Reporting Standards notified by the International Accounting Standards Board.

7.2.4 Financial results for listed entity which has listed its Indian Depository Receipts (IDRs)

As per SEBI regulations, if a listed entity which has listed its IDRs opts to prepare financial results in accordance with IFRS, then such listed entity shall annex only the summary of significant differences between the Indian GAAP and IFRS.

Further, in case the listed entity which has listed its Indian depository receipts (IDRs) opts to prepare and disclose the financial results as per US GAAP or IFRS, the listed entity shall ensure that the annual, half yearly and/or quarterly results, as required under the laws, rules or regulations of home country shall be audited or subject to limited review by professional accountant or certified public accountant in accordance with the International Standards on Auditing. The auditor's report shall also be prepared in accordance with the International Standards on Auditing.

7.2.5 Auditor having a valid peer review certificate

The listed entity shall ensure that the limited review reports or audit reports submitted to the stock exchange(s) on a quarterly or annual basis are given only by an auditor who has subjected himself to the peer review process of the Institute of Chartered Accountants of India (ICAI) and holds a valid certificate issued by the Peer Review Board of the ICAI.

Example

The first peer review of firm ABC & Co. LLP has been completed in June 2016 and it has received a clean peer review report. However, the certificate is yet to be received from the ICAI. Whether firm ABC & Co. LLP is eligible to be appointed as the auditor under the Listing regulations at the AGM being held in June 2016.

Considering that the reg 33(1)(d) of the listing regulations specifically requires the auditor to hold a valid peer review certificate, the appointment cannot be construed as valid on the basis of only peer review report.

7.2.6 Approval and authentication of financial results

The preparation of financial results is the responsibility of the company and therefore it is essential that it should be duly approved by the board of directors. It requires as below:

(a) The quarterly financial results submitted shall be approved by the board of directors;

Provided that while placing the financial results before the board of directors, the chief executive officer and chief financial officer of the listed entity shall certify that the financial results do not contain any false or misleading statement or figures and do not omit any material fact which may make the statements or figures contained therein misleading.

(b) The financial results submitted to the stock exchange shall be signed by the chairperson or managing director, or a whole time director or in the absence of all of them; it shall be signed by any other director of the listed entity who is duly authorised by the board of director to sign the financial results.

(c) The limited review report shall be placed before the board of directors, at its meeting which approves the financial results, before being submitted to the stock exchange(s).

(d) The annual audited financial results shall be approved by the board of directors of the listed entity and shall be signed in the manner specified in clause (b) above.

7.2.7 Timelines for submission of financial results

Financial results	Prescribed timelines
Quarterly and year to date standalone financial results for Q1, Q2 and Q3	Within 45 days from end of each quarter
Quarterly and year to date consolidated financial results for Q1, Q2 and Q3	Within 45 days from end of each quarter
Half yearly statement of assets and liabilities (as part of standalone or consolidated financial results)	Within 45 from end of each quarter
Annual audited standalone financial results along with audit report and Statement on Impact of Audit Qualifications (applicable only for audit report with modified opinion)/declaration in case of unmodified opinion	Within 60 days from the end of financial year
Annual audited consolidated financial results along with audit report and Statement on Impact of Audit Qualifications (applicable only for audit report with modified opinion)/ Declaration in case of unmodified opinion	Within 60 days from the end of financial year
Audited financial results for last quarter	Within 60 days from the end of the financial year (along with annual audited financial results)

Note: For instruments listed on SME Exchange, need to comply on half yearly basis instead of quarterly.

7.3 REQUIREMENT TO SUBMIT AUDITED/REVIEWED FINANCIAL RESULTS

The listed entity has an option to submit audited or reviewed quarterly and year to date financial results.

- In case the listed entity opts to submit audited financial results, they shall be accompanied by the audit report
- In case the listed entity opts to submit reviewed (unaudited) financial results, they shall be subjected to limited review by the statutory auditors of the listed entity and shall be accompanied by the limited review report. Further, in case of public sector undertakings, the limited review may be undertaken by any practicing Chartered Accountant.

Please refer to *Chapter 4 - Audit and review report on interim financial results.*

7.4 HALF-YEARLY DISCLOSURE OF ASSETS AND LIABILITIES

SEBI (Listing Obligations and Disclosure Requirements) Regulations, 2015 requires that the listed entity should also submit as part of its standalone or consolidated financial results for the half year, a statement of Assets and Liabilities as at the end of the half-year. To be able to take informed decisions, the shareholders/stakeholders of a company not only require information on the financial performance of the company but also its financial health. Thus, inclusion of the Statement of Assets and Liabilities will provide more comprehensive financial information to its users.

7.5 FINANCIAL RESULTS IN CASE OF DEBT LISTED ENTITIES

Regulation 52 of the SEBI Listing Regulations requires a listed entity, which has listed its 'Non-convertible Debt Securities' and/or 'Non-Convertible Redeemable Preference Shares', to prepare and submit un-audited or audited financial results on a half yearly basis within forty five days from the end of the half year to the recognised stock exchange(s).

If the listed entity submits unaudited financial results, they have to be accompanied by limited review report prepared by the statutory auditors.

SEBI has prescribed formats for submitting the half yearly financial results vide circular dated 27 November 2015. The audited results for the year are to be submitted to the recognised stock exchange(s) in the same format as is applicable for half-yearly financial results. SEBI circular dated 10 August 2016 has clarified that existing formats prescribed in SEBI Circular dated 27 November 2015, for disclosure of half yearly and annual financial results, shall continue till the period ending on or before 31 December 2016. For the period ending after 31 December 2016, the disclosure of half yearly and annual financial results, shall be as per the formats as prescribed in Schedule III to the Companies Act, 2013.

If the listed entity intimates in advance to the stock exchange(s) that it will submit to the stock exchange(s) its annual audited results within sixty days from the end of the financial year, then unaudited financial results for the last half year accompanied by limited review report by the auditors need not be submitted to stock exchange(s). However, if the listed entity opts to submit unaudited financial results for the last half year accompanied by limited review report by the auditors, it is also required to submit audited financial results for the entire financial year, as soon as they are approved by the board of directors.

Regulation 52 also requires that the annual audited financial results to be submitted along with the annual audit report and either Form A for audit report with unmodified opinion, or Form B for audit report with modified opinion. On 27 May

2016, SEBI has issued a circular which has dispensed with the existing requirement of filing Form A or Form B for audit report with unmodified or modified opinion respectively and has introduced some additional requirements, which are discussed subsequently in this chapter.

7.6 FORMAT OF STATEMENT OF ASSETS AND LIABILITIES FOR COMPANIES

Annexure IX to the circular dated 30 November 2015 issued by SEBI specifies the format of Statement of Assets and Liabilities for companies (other than banks). The circular states that half-yearly Statement of Assets and Liabilities shall be in the format specified in Annexure IX drawn from Schedule III of the *Companies Act, 2013* or its equivalent formats in other statutes, as applicable.

SEBI issued another circular dated 5 July 2016 on revised formats for financial results and implementation of Ind AS by listed entities wherein is has stated that:

- The existing formats prescribed in SEBI circular dated 30 November 2015 for the unaudited/audited half-yearly balance sheet to be submitted by the listed entities, with the stock exchanges shall continue till the period ending 31 December 2016.
- For the period ending on or after 31 March 2017, the formats for unaudited/audited half-yearly balance sheet to be submitted by the listed entities shall be as per the formats for Balance Sheet as prescribed in Schedule III to the *Companies Act, 2013* (excluding notes and detailed sub-classification). However, banking companies and insurance companies shall follow the formats as prescribed under the respective Act/Regulations as specified by their regulators.

The above circular further specifies in its paragraph 2.6.1 (v) that the format of Balance Sheet for the half-yearly ended 30 September 2016 shall be as per the format for Balance Sheet (excluding notes and detailed sub-classification) as prescribed in Schedule III to the *Companies Act, 2013*. This is applicable for the companies for which first year of adoption of Ind AS is financial year 2016-17 and are preparing Ind AS compliant financial results.

MCA has notified amendments to Schedule III of the *Companies Act, 2013 (2013 Act)* with respect to financial statements in case of Companies whose financial statements are required to comply with the Companies (Indian Accounting Standards) Rules, 2015. These amendments are effective from 06 April 2016. As per the notification, Schedule III of the 2013 Act has been divided into two divisions. The division I (existing Schedule III) will apply to a company whose financial statements are required to comply with the Companies (Accounting Standards) Rules, 2006. The division II will apply to a company whose financial statements are required to comply with the Companies (Indian Accounting Standards) Rules, 2015.

It may be noted that the format of Statement of Assets and Liabilities specified in circular dated 30 November 2015 is based on Division I which applies to a company whose financial statements are required to comply with the Companies (Accounting Standards) Rules, 2006.

However, in view of specific clarification of complying with Schedule III for preparation of Statement of Assets and Liabilities for the half year ended 30 September 2016 (contained in SEBI circular dated 5 July 2016) for companies whose financial statements are required to comply with the Companies (Indian Accounting Standards) Rules, 2015, it would be prudent to follow the format specified in Division II of Schedule III for such companies.

The format for filing of half-yearly Statement of Assets and Liabilities is given in Chapter 11 of this book.

7.7 STATEMENT ON IMPACT OF AUDIT QUALIFICATIONS

The SEBI held its board meeting on 12 March 2016 and through a press release - PR No. 56/2016, approved a revised mechanism to 'review the audit qualifications contained in the audit reports' in order to disseminate the impact of the audit qualifications on the financial statements without any delay. In order to streamline the process, following would be the revised procedure.

(i) Listed entities shall be required to disclose the cumulative impact of all the audit qualifications on relevant financial items in a separate form called 'Statement on Impact of Audit Qualifications' instead of the earlier Form B.

Such disclosure would be in a tabular form along with the annual audited financial results filed in terms of the Listing Regulations.

(ii) In cases where there are no audit qualifications, the earlier requirement of filing Form A signed by top officials/directors of the company and auditors shall not be necessary.

(iii) The management shall have the right to give its views on the audit qualifications in the new form.

(iv) The existing requirement of adjustment in the books of accounts (as per Schedule VIII of the Listing Regulations) of the subsequent year shall not be necessary.

(v) Where the impact of the audit qualification is not quantified by the auditor, the management shall make an estimate. In case the management is unable to make an estimate, it shall provide reasons for the same. In both the scenarios, the auditor shall review and give the comments.

SEBI has issued a circular dated 27 May 2016 to give effect to the above amendments. The circular also prescribed the format as below:

Statement on Impact of Audit Qualifications (for audit report with modified opinion) submitted along-with Annual Audited Financial Results - (*Standalone and Consolidated separately*)

<table>
<tr><th colspan="5">Statement on Impact of Audit Qualifications for the Financial Year ended March 31, ...
[See Regulation 33/52 of the SEBI (LODR) (Amendment) Regulations, 2016]</th></tr>
<tr><td rowspan="9">I.</td><td>Sl. No.</td><td>Particulars</td><td>Audited Figures (as reported before adjusting for qualifications)</td><td>Adjusted Figures (audited figures after adjusting for qualifications)</td></tr>
<tr><td>1.</td><td>Turnover/Total income</td><td>-</td><td>-</td></tr>
<tr><td>2.</td><td>Total Expenditure</td><td>-</td><td>-</td></tr>
<tr><td>3.</td><td>Net Profit/(Loss)</td><td>-</td><td>-</td></tr>
<tr><td>4.</td><td>Earnings Per Share</td><td>-</td><td>-</td></tr>
<tr><td>5.</td><td>Total Assets</td><td>-</td><td>-</td></tr>
<tr><td>6.</td><td>Total Liabilities</td><td>-</td><td>-</td></tr>
<tr><td>7.</td><td>Net Worth</td><td>-</td><td>-</td></tr>
<tr><td>8.</td><td>Any other financial item(s) (as felt appropriate by the management)</td><td>-</td><td>-</td></tr>
<tr><td>II.</td><td colspan="4">Audit Qualification (each audit qualification separately):
(a) Details of Audit Qualification:
(b) Type of Audit Qualification : Qualified Opinion/Disclaimer of Opinion/ Adverse Opinion
(c) Frequency of qualification: Whether appeared first time/repetitive/since how long continuing
(d) For Audit Qualification(s) where the impact is quantified by the auditor, Management's Views:
(e) For Audit Qualification(s) where the impact is not quantified by the auditor:
(i) Management's estimation on the impact of audit qualification;
(ii) If management is unable to estimate the impact, reasons for the same;
(iii) Auditors' Comments on (i) or (ii) above.</td></tr>
</table>

<table>
<tr><th colspan="2">Statement on Impact of Audit Qualifications for the Financial Year ended March 31, ...
[See Regulation 33/52 of the SEBI (LODR) (Amendment) Regulations, 2016]</th></tr>
<tr><td>III.</td><td>Signatories:
• CEO/Managing Director
• CFO
• Audit Committee Chairman
• Statutory Auditor
Place:
Date:</td></tr>
</table>

Few statements on impact of audit qualifications has been included in the **Annexure V** at the end of this chapter.

7.8 CLARIFICATIONS BY STOCK EXCHANGES ON DATE OF APPLICABILITY OF SEBI CIRCULAR

Further to the SEBI circular dated 27 May 2016 on 'Disclosure of the Impact of Audit Qualifications by the Listed Entities' under regulation 33 and regulation 52 of SEBI (Listing and Other Disclosure Requirements) Regulations, 2015 ('Listing Regulations'), National Stock Exchange of India and Bombay Stock Exchange of India have issued circulars (dated 1 June 2016 (refer **Annexures-I and II**)) which provide, *inter alia*, the following operational details for implementing the amendments:

- The listed entities that have already submitted Form A (in case of audit reports with unmodified opinion(s)) for the period ended 31 March 2016 would be considered as sufficient compliance with the aforesaid amendments;
- The listed entities that have not submitted Form A (in case of audit reports with unmodified opinion(s)) for the period ended 31 March 2016 would be required to submit the declaration as mentioned in the aforesaid SEBI circular within 30 days from the date of these circulars duly signed by either CEO/Managing Director/CFO/Audit Committee Chairman;
- All the listed entities (irrespective of having submitted Form B or not in case of modified opinion(s)) for the period ended 31 March 2016 would be required to submit the 'Statement on Impact of Audit Qualifications' within 60 days from the date of these circulars in the format provided in the aforesaid SEBI Circular;
- For all the subsequent annual filings of audited financial results, submission of Form A/Form B as the case may be, would be dispensed

with. Consequently, all listed entities should submit either declaration as mentioned in the aforesaid SEBI circular or 'Statement on Impact of Audit Qualifications', in the prescribed format, within the timelines applicable for submission of annual audited financial results.

Please refer **Annexure III** at the end of this chapter for the concerned SEBI circular.

7.9 REVIEW OF STATEMENT ON IMPACT OF AUDIT QUALIFICATIONS AND ANNUAL AUDIT REPORT

The Statement on Impact of Audit Qualifications (for audit report with modified opinion) and the accompanying annual audit report submitted in terms of reg 33(3)(d), shall be reviewed by the stock exchange(s).

7.10 SPECIFIED DISCLOSURES – PART A OF SCHEDULE IV

Regulations 33 states that the listed entity shall make the disclosures specified in Part A of Schedule IV. Part A of Schedule IV states as below:

- If the auditor has expressed any modified opinion(s) in respect of audited financial results submitted or published under this para, the listed entity shall disclose such modified opinion(s) and cumulative impact of the same on profit or loss, net worth, total assets, turnover/total income, earning per share, total expenditure, total liabilities] or any other financial item(s) which may be impacted due to modified opinion(s), while publishing or submitting such results.
- If the auditor has expressed any modified opinion(s), the management of the listed entity has the option to explain its views on the audit qualifications and the same shall be included in the Statement on Impact of Audit Qualifications (for audit report with modified opinion).
- With respect to audit qualifications where the impact of the qualification is not quantifiable:
  - The management shall make an estimate and the auditor shall review the same and report accordingly; or
  - If the management is unable to make an estimate, it shall provide the reasons and the auditor shall review the same and report accordingly.

  The above shall be included in the statement on impact of audit qualifications (for audit report with modified opinion).

- If the auditor has expressed any modified opinion(s) or other reservation(s) in his audit report or limited review report in respect of the financial results of any previous financial year or quarter which has an impact on the profit or loss of the reportable period, the listed entity shall include as a note to the financial results –
  - how the modified opinion(s) or other reservation(s) has been resolved; or
  - if the same has not been resolved, the reason thereof and the steps which the listed entity intends to take in the matter.

Therefore, on the basis of the above, the auditor would be required to disclose cumulative impact of audit qualification on profit or loss, net worth, total assets turnover/total income for audited financial results. Also, management is required to explain its views on the audit qualifications for inclusion in the 'Statement on Impact of Audit Qualifications'. This raises an issue as to whether the statement also needs to be filed along with quarterly audited results in addition to annual financial results. There is lack of clarity on which guidance may be issued by SEBI to avoid varying interpretations. Pending issuance of any clarification in this regard, the Statement can also be filed for quarterly audited results, if the audit report on such quarterly results is qualified.

7.11 FORMAT OF UNIFORM LISTING AGREEMENT

All listed entities shall be required to execute a "Uniform Listing Agreement" with recognised Stock Exchanges within six months from effective date of the Listing Regulations i.e. 2 September 2015.

SEBI has issued a circular dated 13 October 2015 wherein it has prescribed the requirements of executing a listing agreement with the Stock Exchange under different regulations related with initial issuance of capital, the details of which are as under:

Type of Securities	Regulations	Regulation No.
Specified Securities (Equity & Convertible Securities on Main Board or SME or ITP) or Indian Depository Receipts	Securities and Exchange Board of India (Issue of Capital and Disclosure Requirements) Regulations, 2009	Regulation 109
Non-Convertible Debt Securities	Securities and Exchange Board of India (Issue and Listing of Debt Securities) Regulations, 2008	Regulation 19A
Non-Convertible Redeemable	Securities and Exchange	Regulation 16A

Type of Securities	Regulations	Regulation No.
Preference Shares	Board of India(Issue and Listing of Non-Convertible Redeemable Preference Shares) Regulations, 2013	
Securitised Debt Instruments	Securities and Exchange Board of India (Public Offer and Listing of Securitised Debt Instruments) Regulations, 2008	Regulation 35A
Mutual Funds	Securities and Exchange Board of India (Mutual Funds) Regulations, 1996	Regulation 31B

In order to give effect to the requirements of Regulations mentioned stated above, a simplified listing agreement which is uniform across all types of securities/listed entities is being specified by SEBI which has been included as **Annexure IV** at the end of this chapter.

The circular further provides that a listed entity which has previously entered into agreement(s) with a recognised Stock Exchange(s) to list its securities shall execute a fresh listing agreement with such Stock Exchange within six months of the date of notification of Securities and Exchange Board of India

The circular further clarifies that notwithstanding such novation, any action taken or purported to have been done or taken by the stock exchanges or SEBI, any enquiry or investigation commenced or show-cause notice issued in respect of the existing listing agreement shall be deemed to have been done or taken under the corresponding provisions of the Listing Regulations in force.

7.12 SEBI (INFRASTRUCTURE INVESTMENT TRUSTS) REGULATIONS, 2014, SEBI (REAL ESTATE INVESTMENT TRUSTS) REGULATIONS, 2014 AND THE AMENDMENT REGULATIONS 2016

On 26 September 2014, SEBI notified the SEBI (Infrastructure Investment Trusts) Regulations, 2014 (InvIT Regulations) and SEBI (Real Estate Investment Trusts) Regulations, 2014 (REIT Regulations). On 29 November 2016, SEBI has further issued SEBI (Infrastructure Investment Trusts) (Amendment) Regulations, 2016 and SEBI (Real Estate Investment Trusts) (Amendment) Regulations, 2016 amending InvIT Regulations and REIT Regulations respectively.

InvIT Regulations have prescribed disclosures to be made in an offer document/ placement memorandum along with disclosures to be made to the stock exchanges where the units of an InvIT are listed. The InvIT Regulations also prescribe that the investment manager shall submit a half-yearly report to the designated stock exchange within forty five days from the end of the every half year ending March 31st and September 30th. The mandatory disclosures as per the InvIT Regulations in the half-yearly report include financial statements for the half year (Standalone and consolidated).

REIT Regulations introduced an internationally acclaimed investment structure in India. REIT units are mandatorily required to be listed on recognised stock exchanges in India. Besides, they need to be in dematerialised form. REIT Regulations prescribe that for an REIT raising funds through an initial offer, the units proposed to be offered to the public through such initial offer shall be not less than twenty five per cent. of the total of the outstanding units of the REIT and the units being offered by way of the offer document, if the post issue capital of the REIT calculated at offer price is less than rupees one thousand six hundred crore. The REIT Regulations further prescribe that the manager shall submit a half-yearly report to all unit holders of the REIT with respect to activities of the REIT within forty five days from the end of the half year ending on September 30th. The mandatory disclosures as per the REIT Regulations in the half-yearly report include financial statements for the half year (Standalone and consolidated).

Annexures

Annexure I: NSE Circular dated 1 June 2016 providing disclosure of impact of audit qualifications by the listed entities

Ref No: NSE/CML/2016/09 June 01, 2016

The Company Secretary

All Listed Companies

Dear Sir/Madam,

Sub: Disclosure of the Impact of Audit Qualifications by the Listed Entities under Regulation 33/52 of SEBI (LODR), (Amendment) Regulations, 2016

This is with reference to Notification No. SEBI/LAD-NRO/GN/2016-17/001 dated May 25, 2016 and Circular No. CIR/CFD/CMD/56/2016 dated May 27, 2016 issued by the Securities and Exchange Board of India (SEBI).

The operational details for implementing the amendments shall be as under:

1. The listed entities that have already submitted Form A (in case of audit reports with unmodified opinion(s)) for the period ended March 31, 2016 shall be considered as sufficient compliance with the aforesaid amendments.
2. The listed entities that have NOT submitted Form A (in case of audit reports with unmodified opinion(s)) for the period ended March 31, 2016 shall be required to submit the declaration as mentioned in SEBI Circular CIR/CFD/CMD/56/2016 within 30 days from the date of this circular duly signed by either CEO/Managing Director/CFO/Audit Committee Chairman.
3. All the listed entities (irrespective of having submitted Form B or not in case of modified opinion (s)) for the period ended March 31, 2016 shall be required to submit the 'Statement on Impact of Audit Qualifications' within 60 days from the date of this circular in the format specified in Annexure I.
4. For all the subsequent annual filings of audited financial results, submission of Form A/Form B as the case may be, shall be dispensed with. Consequently, all listed entities shall be required to submit either declaration as mentioned in SEBI Circular CIR/CFD/CMD/56/2016 (in case of audit report with unmodified opinion(s)) or 'Statement on Impact of Audit Qualifications' (in case of modified opinion(s)), in the

format as specified in Annexure I within the timelines applicable for submission of annual audited financial results.

For and on behalf of

National Stock Exchange of India Limited

Kautuk Upadhyay

Manager

Encl: Annexure I

Annexure I

Statement on Impact of Audit Qualifications (for audit report with modified opinion) submitted along-with Annual Audited Financial Results - (*Standalone and Consolidated separately*)

<table>
<tr><th colspan="5">Statement on Impact of Audit Qualifications for the Financial Year ended March 31, ...
[See Regulation 33/52 of the SEBI (LODR) (Amendment) Regulations, 2016]</th></tr>
<tr><td rowspan="5">I.</td><td>Sl. No.</td><td>Particulars</td><td>Audited Figures (as reported before adjusting for qualifications)</td><td>Adjusted Figures (audited figures after adjusting for qualifications)</td></tr>
<tr><td>1.</td><td>Turnover/Total income</td><td>-</td><td>-</td></tr>
<tr><td>2.</td><td>Total Expenditure</td><td>-</td><td>-</td></tr>
<tr><td>3.</td><td>Net Profit/(Loss)</td><td>-</td><td>-</td></tr>
<tr><td>4.</td><td>Earnings Per Share</td><td>-</td><td>-</td></tr>
<tr><td></td><td>5.</td><td>Total Assets</td><td>-</td><td>-</td></tr>
<tr><td></td><td>6.</td><td>Total Liabilities</td><td>-</td><td>-</td></tr>
<tr><td></td><td>7.</td><td>Net Worth</td><td>-</td><td>-</td></tr>
<tr><td></td><td>8.</td><td>Any other financial item(s) (as felt appropriate by the management)</td><td>-</td><td>-</td></tr>
<tr><td>II.</td><td colspan="4">Audit Qualification (each audit qualification separately):</td></tr>
<tr><td></td><td colspan="4">a. Details of Audit Qualification:</td></tr>
<tr><td></td><td colspan="4">b. Type of Audit Qualification : Qualified Opinion/Disclaimer of Opinion/Adverse Opinion</td></tr>
</table>

Statement on Impact of Audit Qualifications for the Financial Year ended March 31, ... **[*See* Regulation 33/52 of the SEBI (LODR) (Amendment) Regulations, 2016]**	
	c. Frequency of qualification: Whether appeared first time/repetitive/since how long continuing
	d. For Audit Qualification(s) where the impact is quantified by the auditor, Management's Views:
	e. For Audit Qualification(s) where the impact is not quantified by the auditor:
	(i) Management's estimation on the impact of audit qualification:
	(ii) If management is unable to estimate the impact, reasons for the same:
	(iii) Auditors' Comments on (i) or (ii) above:
III.	**Signatories:**
	• CEO/Managing Director
	• CFO
	• Audit Committee Chairman
	• Statutory Auditor
	Place:
	Date:

Annexure II: BSE Circular dated 1 June 2016 providing disclosure of impact of audit qualifications by the listed entities

DCS/COMP/04/201617 June 01, 2016

Dear Sir/Madam,

Sub: Disclosure of the Impact of Audit Qualifications by the Listed Entities

This is with reference to Notification No. SEBI/LAD-NRO/GN/2016-17/001 dated May 25, 2016 and Circular No. CIR/CFD/CMD/56/2016 dated May 27, 2016 issued by the Securities and Exchange Board of India (SEBI), which inter-alia:

- Dispensed with the existing requirement of filing Form A or Form B for audit report with unmodified or modified opinion respectively
- Prescribed that for audit reports with unmodified opinion, listed entities should submit a declaration to the stock exchange(s) along with the annual audited financial results
- Prescribed that for audit reports with modified opinion, a statement showing impact of audit qualifications should be filed with the stock exchanges in the mandated format

The operational details for implementing the aforesaid provisions of Regulations 33 and 52 of the SEBI (Listing and Other Disclosure Requirements) Regulations, 2015 ('Listing Regulations') shall be as under:

(1) The listed entities that have already submitted Form A (in case of audit reports with unmodified opinion(s)) for the period ended March 31, 2016 shall be considered as sufficient compliance with the aforesaid amendments.

(2) The listed entities that have NOT submitted Form A (in case of audit reports with unmodified opinion(s)) for the period ended March 31, 2016 shall be required to submit the declaration as mentioned in SEBI Circular CIR/CFD/CMD/56/2016 within 30 days from the date of this circular duly signed by either CEO/Managing Director/CFO/Chairman of the Audit Committee

(3) In the case of audit reports with modified opinion (s) for the period ended March 31, 2016, all the listed entities (including those which have submitted Form B prior to the date of this circular)) shall be required to submit the 'Statement on Impact of Audit Qualifications' within 60 days from the date of this circular in

the format specified in Annexure I of SEBI Circular No. CIR/CFD/CMD/56/2016[1] dated May 27, 2016 (attached).

(4) For all the subsequent annual filings of audited financial results, submission of Form A/Form B as the case may be, shall be dispensed with. Consequently, all listed entities shall be required to submit either declaration in case of audit report with unmodified opinion(s) duly signed by either CEO/Managing Director/CFO/Chairman of the Audit Committee or 'Statement on Impact of Audit Qualifications' in the prescribed format, within the timelines applicable for submission of annual audited financial results.

Listed Companies are required to take note of the said circular and comply accordingly.

Netra Sahani	Arpita Joshi
DGM-Listing Compliance	Associate Manager – Listing Compliance

[1] Attached as **Annexure-III** below.

Annexure III: SEBI CIRCULAR 56/2016 dated 27 May, 2016 providing disclosure of the impact of audit qualifications by the listed entities

CIR/CFD/CMD/56/2016 May 27, 2016

To

All Listed Entities

All Recognized Stock Exchanges

Dear Madam/Sir,

Sub.: Disclosure of the Impact of Audit Qualifications by the Listed Entities

1. SEBI has put in place a mechanism to review the audit qualifications contained in the audit reports of the listed entities. The detailed procedure for the same has been prescribed in Schedule VIII read with Regulation 33 and Regulation 52 of the SEBI (Listing and Other Disclosure Requirements) Regulations, 2015 ('Listing Regulations') and SEBI circular no. CIR/CFD/CMD/15/2015 dated November 30, 2015.

2. In consultation with SEBI Advisory Committees, Institute of Chartered Accountants of India ('ICAI'), Stock Exchanges and Industry Bodies, it has been decided to streamline the existing process as follows:

   (i) to make the listed entities disseminate the cumulative impact of all the audit qualifications in a separate format, simultaneously, while submitting the annual audited financial results to the stock exchanges. This will ensure that the information is available to the investors, without delay, enabling them to take well informed investment decisions;

   (ii) to dispense with the existing requirement of filing Form A or Form B for audit report with unmodified or modified opinion respectively;

   (iii) to dispense with the existing requirement of making adjustment in the books of accounts of the subsequent year.

3. In this context, necessary amendments to the Listing Regulations have already been notified. A copy of the notification is available on the SEBI Website www.sebi.gov.in.

4. The operational details for implementing the aforesaid amendments shall be as under:

   4.1. For audit reports with unmodified opinion, the listed entity shall furnish a declaration to that effect to the stock exchange(s) while submitting the annual audited financial results.

4.2. For audit reports with modified opinion, a statement showing impact of audit qualifications shall be filed with the stock exchanges in a format as specified in **Annexure I**.

4.3. The management of the listed entity shall have the option to explain its views on the audit qualifications;

4.4. Where the impact of the audit qualification is not quantified by the auditor, the management shall make an estimate. In case the management is unable to make an estimate, it shall provide reasons for the same. In both the scenarios, the auditor shall review and give the comments.

4.5. The aforesaid statements on impact of audit qualifications filed by the listed entities shall be a part of regular monitoring by the stock exchanges as specified in Regulation 97 of the Listing Regulations. In case of non-compliance, the stock exchanges shall take action against such entities as deemed fit and report to SEBI on a regular basis.

The stock exchanges shall coordinate with one another in case the scrip is listed on more than one stock exchange.

5. The clause 3 (g) of the aforesaid SEBI circular no. CIR/CFD/CMD/15/2015 dated November 30, 2015 stands deleted.

6. This circular shall be applicable for all the annual audited standalone / consolidated financial results, as applicable, submitted by the listed entities for the period ending on or after March 31,2016.

7. The stock exchanges are advised to ensure compliance with this circular and bring the provisions of this circular to the notice of listed entities and also to disseminate the same on their websites.

8. This circular is being issued in exercise of powers conferred under Section 11 and Section 11A of the Securities and Exchange Board of India Act, 1992 read with Regulation 33, Regulation 52, and Regulation 101 (2) of the Listing Regulations.

9. This circular is available on SEBI website at http://www.sebi.gov.in under the category "Circulars".

Yours faithfully,

Prasanta Mahapatra

General Manager

Compliance and Monitoring Division

Corporation Finance Department

prasantam@sebi.gov.in

Annexure I

Statement on Impact of Audit Qualifications (for audit report with modified opinion) submitted along-with Annual Audited Financial Results - (*Standalone and Consolidated separately*)

Statement on Impact of Audit Qualifications for the Financial Year ended March 31,……………..

[*See* Regulation 33 / 52 of the SEBI (LODR) (Amendment) Regulations, 2016]

I.	Sl. No.	Particulars	Audited Figures (as reported before adjusting for qualifications)	Adjusted Figures (audited figures after adjusting for qualifications)
	1.	Turnover / Total income	-	-
	2.	Total Expenditure	-	-
	3.	Net Profit/(Loss)	-	-
	4.	Earnings Per Share	-	-
	5.	Total Assets	-	-
	6.	Total Liabilities	-	-
	7.	Net Worth	-	-
	8.	Any other financial item(s) (as felt appropriate by the management)		
II.	**Audit Qualification (each audit Qualification separately):**			
	a.	Details of Audit Qualification:		
	b.	Type of Audit Qualification : Qualified Opinion / Disclaimer of Opinion/Adverse Opinion		
	c.	Frequency of qualification: Whether appeared first time / repetitive / since how long continuing		
	d.	For Audit Qualification(s) where the impact is quantified by the auditor, Management's Views:		
	e.	For Audit Qualification(s) where the impact is not quantified by the auditor:		
		(i) Management's estimation on the impact of audit qualification:		
		(ii) If management is unable to estimate the impact, reasons for the same:		
		(iii) Auditors' comments on (i) or (ii) above:		

I.	Sl. No.	Particulars	Audited Figures (as reported before adjusting for qualifications)	Adjusted Figures (audited figures after adjusting for qualifications)
III.	**Signatories:**			
	• CEO/Managing Director			
	• CFO			
	• Audit Committee Chairman			
	• Statutory Auditor			
	Place:			
	Date:			

Annexure IV: SEBI circular dated 13 October 2015 providing format of Uniform Listing Agreement

CIR/CFD/CMD/6/2015 October 13, 2015

To

All Listed Entities

All the Recognised Stock Exchanges

Dear Sir/Madam,

Sub: Format of uniform Listing Agreement

1. The requirement of executing a listing agreement with the Stock Exchange is specified under different regulations related with initial issuance of capital, the details of which are as under:

Type of Securities	Regulation	Regulation No.
Specified Securities (Equity & Convertible Securities on Main Board or SME or ITP) or Indian Depository Receipts	Securities and Exchange Board of India (Issue of Capital and Disclosure Requirements) Regulations, 2009 ("ICDR")	Regulation 109
Non-Convertible Debt Securities	Securities and Exchange Board of India (Issue and Listing of Debt Securities) Regulations, 2008 ("ILDS")	Regulation 19A
Non-Convertible Redeemable Preference Shares	Securities and Exchange Board of India (Issue and Listing of Non-Convertible Redeemable Preference Shares) Regulations, 2013 ("NCRPS")	Regulation 16A
Securitised Debt Instruments	Securities and Exchange Board of India (Public Offer and Listing of Securitised Debt Instruments) Regulations, 2008 ("SDI")	Regulation 35A

Type of Securities	Regulation	Regulation No.
Mutual Funds	Securities and Exchange Board of India (Mutual Funds) Regulations, 1996 ("MF")	Regulation 31B

2. In order to give effect to the requirements of Regulations mentioned at para 1 above, a simplified listing agreement which is uniform across all types of securities/listed entities is being specified under **Annexure I**.

3. A listed entity which has previously entered into agreement(s) with a recognised Stock Exchange(s) to list its securities shall execute a fresh listing agreement with such Stock Exchange within six months of the date of notification of Securities and Exchange Board of India (Listing Obligations and Disclosure Requirements) Regulations, 2015 (Listing Regulations) i.e. September 2, 2015.

   Notwithstanding such novation, any action taken or purported to have been done or taken by the Stock Exchanges or SEBI, any enquiry or investigation commenced or showcause notice issued in respect of the existing listing agreement shall be deemed to have been done or taken under the corresponding provisions of the Listing Regulations in force.

4. This circular is issued in exercise of the powers conferred under sections 11(1) and 11A of the Securities and Exchange Board of India Act1992.

5. This circular is available on SEBI website at www.sebi.gov.in under the categories "Legal Framework" and "Issues and listing", "Mutual Funts", "Corporate Debt Market" "Continuous Disclosure Requirements".

Yours faithfully,

Harini Balaji

General Manager

+91-22-26449372

harinib@sebi.gov.in

Annexure I

LISTING AGREEMENT

This Agreement is made on this .... day of .... by

.... a Company/any other entity duly formed and registered under the relevant Indian Act/statutory enactment of appropriate jurisdiction, including overseas jurisdiction, wherever applicable, and having its registered office at .... (hereinafter called "the Issuer") with the .... (Name of the Stock Exchange) (hereinafter called "the Exchange").

....

WHEREAS:-

(a) It is a requirement of the Exchange that the Issuer shall submit a listing agreement duly executed along with an application for admission and continued admission of the securities to dealings on the Exchange.

(b) *The Issuer is desirous of continuing the listing of its securities on the Exchange

or

The issuer is desirous of listing its securities as mentioned in the application and made part hereof.

(c) The Issuer is desirous of executing this Agreement in compliance with the aforesaid requirement of the Exchange.

NOW THEREFORE in consideration of the aforesaid, the Issuer hereby covenants and agrees with the Exchange as follows:

1. That the Issuer shall comply with the extant provisions of all the applicable statutory enactments governing the issuance, listing and continued listing of securities.

2. That without prejudice to the above clause, the Issuer hereby covenants and agrees that it shall comply with the following:

   (i) the SEBI (Listing Obligations And Disclosure Requirements) Regulations, 2015 and other applicable regulations /guidelines/circulars as may be issued by SEBI from time to time.

   (ii) the relevant byelaws/regulations/circulars/notices/guidelines as may be issued by the Exchange from time to time.

   (iii) such other directions, requirements and conditions as may be imposed by SEBI/Exchange from time to time.

3. That it shall pay listing and such other fees/fines as may be specified/levied by the Exchange from time to time within the prescribed period.

4. That it shall keep intimated the Exchange about change in any information/ details of the issuer.

5. The admission and continued admission of the securities to dealings on the Exchange is subject to the discretion of the Exchange and subject to the powers of the Exchange to prohibit, suspend or withdraw the listing of the securities on the Exchange.

6. That the board of directors or a committee duly authorized by the board of directors of the issuer has passed a resolution for initial listing of the securities on the Exchange at its meeting held on the .... day of .... 20.........(not applicable in cases where the securities are already listed on the Exchange).

7. Both parties agree that earlier listing agreement stands rescinded and novation carried out in accordance with respective regulations (viz. ICDR, ILDS, NCRPS, etc.) shall not affect any right already accrued or liability incurred by either party nor effect any enquiry or investigation or any other action undertaken by the Exchange or SEBI.

This Agreement is duly executed on the day, month and year first mentioned above by the authorized signatories duly authorized by the board of directors or committee thereof in their .... meeting held on .... (date).

SIGNED AND DELIVERED by the within named

.... (Name of the Issuer)

Through its Authorised Signatories

Name(s):

Designation(s):

SIGNED by the authorized signatory of Stock Exchange

Name:

Designation:

**Note: Stock Exchange may strike off whichever is not applicable.*

Information about the Company and Securities

Name of Issuer:	
CIN No.	
Registered office Address	
Corporate office Address	

Telephone No.		**Fax No.**	
Website address		**e-mail id**	

Name of the Company Secretary/ Compliance officer			
Telephone no.		**Fax No.**	
e-mail id			

Securities applied for listing *(Please tick (✓) the appropriate boxes)*	Specified securities (Main Board)	
	Specified securities (SME Exchange)	
	Specified securities (Institutional Trading Platform)	
	Non-convertible debt securities	
	Non-convertible redeemable preference shares	
	Perpetual debt instrument	
	Perpetual non-cumulative preference shares	
	Indian depository receipts	
	Securitized debt instruments	
	Units issued by Mutual Funds	
	Others (Please specify)	

Annexure V: Statement on Impact of Audit Qualifications

ASHOK LEYLAND

July 20, 2016

National Stock Exchange of India Limited
Exchange Plaza,
C-l, Block G, Bandra Kurla Complex
Bandra (E), Mumbai - 400 051

Thru : NEAPS

BSE Limited
Phiroze Jeejeebhoy Towers
Dalai Street
Mumbai - 400 001

Thru : BSE Listing Centre

Dear Sirs,

Disclosure of the Impact of Audit Qualifications - Modified Opinion

The Board of Directors of the Company at their meeting held on May 25, 2016 has approved the audited standalone and consolidated financials statements for the year ended March 31, 2016. The Company along with the financial statements, has submitted Form A (for Audit Report with unmodified opinion) in respect of the Standalone Audited Financial Results and Form B (for Audit Report with modified opinion) in respect of the Consolidated Audited Financial Results to the stock exchanges.

SEBI vide Notification No. SEBI/LAD-NRO/GN/2016-17/001 dated May 25, 2016 and Circular No. CIR/CFD/CMD/56/2016 dated May 27, 2016 and stock exchanges vide circulars dated June 1, 2016 intimated the companies that (irrespective of having submitted Form B or not in case of modified opinion (s)) for the period ended March 31, 2016 shall be required to submit the 'Statement on Impact of Audit Qualifications' within 60 days from the date of this circular in the format specified in Annexure I.

As required vide SEBI Circular CIR/CFD/CMD/56/2016, please find enclosed the Statement on Impact of Audit Qualifications in the specified format

We request you to kindly take the above on record.

Yours faithfully,

for ASHOK LEYLAND LIMITED

N Ramanathan

Company Secretary

Enel : a/a.

ASHOK LEYLAND LIMITED

Reed. Office :1 Sardar Patel Road, Gulndy, Chennai -600 032;
CIN: L34101TIM1948PLC0001Q5
Email id: reachus@asholdevland.cQm

Statement on Impact of Audit Qualifications for the Consolidated Financial Results for the Financial Year ended March 31, 2016 [See Regulation 33 / 52 of the SEBI (LODR) (Amendment) Regulations, 2016]

Rs. Lakhs

	SI.No.	Particulars	Audited Figures (as reported before adjusting for qualifications)	Adjusted. Figures (audited figures after adjusting for qualifications) (Refer ll.e.ii below)
1,	1.	Turnover / Total Income	2,081,058.21	2,081,058.21
	2.	Total Expenditure (including Tax Expense Rs.52,773.80 lakhs)	1,971,181.95	1,971,181.95
	3.	Net Profit / (Loss)*	107,068.34	107,068.34
	4.	Earnings Per Share (in Rs.)	3.76	3.76
	5.	Total Assets	2,296,315.37	2,296,315.37
	6.	Total Liabilities (including Minority Interest)	1,797,098.75	1,797-,098.75
	7.	Net Worth (including revaluation reserve)	499,216.62	499,.216,62
	8.	Any other financials item(s) (as felt appropriate by the management)	Nil	Nil
	*Net Profit / (Loss) includes Share of profit of associates Rs.614.13 lakhs and is net of Minority interest Rs,3,422.05 lakhs			
II	Audit Qualification (each audit qualification separately):			

a. Details of Audit Qualification:

The Holding Company has consolidated the financial statements/ financial information for the year ended March 31, 2016 of three Joint venture companies, which are unaudited and pending approval by the Board of Directors of the respective companies - Refer Note 3 to the consolidated financial results. We are informed that these financial statements are as received from the respective companies, and reflect total assets (net) of Rs.55,125.45 lakhs, total liabilities (net) of Rs.95,020.47 lakhs, total

	SI.No.	Particulars	Audited Figures (as reported before adjusting for qualifications)	Adjusted. Figures (audited figures after adjusting for qualifications) (Refer ll.e.ii below)
		revenue (net) of Rs.17,272,56 lakhs and total expenditure (net) of Rs.101,307.78 lakhs, as considered in the consolidated financial results. We are unable to express an opinion on the said unaudited financial statements/ financial information of the said joint venture companies included in the consolidated financial results of the Holding Company.		
	b.	Type of Audit Qualification : Qualified Opinion / ~~Disclaimer of Opinion/Adverse Opinion~~		
	c.	Frequency of qualification: First time / ~~repetitive/since how long continuing~~		
	d.	For Audit Qualification(s) where the impact is quantified by the auditor, Management's Views Not Applicable		
e.	For Audit Qualification(s) where the impact is not quantified by the auditor: (i) Management's estimation on the Impact of audit qualification: The Consolidated Results of the Company for the year include unaudited financials of three joint venture companies, as received, reflecting total assets (net) of Rs.55,125.45 lakhs, total liabilities (net) of Rs.95,020.47 lakhs, total revenue (net) Rs,17,272.56 lakhs and total expenditure (net) of Rs.101,307.78 lakhs. The said financials are pending approval by the 8oard of Directors of these companies. As the Company is required to submit its consolidated results within 60 days from the end of the financial year to the Stock Exchange, it has considered the said financials, as received from the joint venture companies for the purposes of such consolidation, In the circumstances, it is not possible for the Management to estimate the impact of audit qualification unless the accounts are approved by the respective Board of Directors.			
	(ii) If management is unable to estimate the impact, reasons for the same: Quantification of the variation, if any, can be done only after the financials of these joint venture companies are duly approved by the respective Board of Directors.			
	(iii) Auditors' Comments on (i) or (ii) above: We have reviewed the above and have no comments.			

III. Signatories

For Ashok Leyland Limited
Vinod K Dasari
Managing Director

For Ashok Leyland Limited
Sanjay Kosher
Chairman of Audit Committee

For Ashok Leyland Limited
Gopal Mahadevan
Chief Financial Officer

Chennai
Date: 20/07/2016
Refer our Audit Report dated May 25, 2016 on Consolidated financial results of the Company

For M.S. Krishnaswami & Rajan
Chartered Accountants
Firm's Registration No. 01654S

M.S. Murali
Partner
Membership No. 26455

Chennai
Date: 20/07/2016

For Deloitte Haskins & Sells LLP
Chartered Accountants
Firm's Registration No. 117366W/W-J00018

A. Siddharth Partner
Membership No. 31467

Mumbai
Date: 20/07/2016

GAYATRI PROJECTS LIMITED

Date: 01.08.2016

To,	To,
The General Manager,	**The Secretary,**
The Department of Corporate Relations,	**National Stock Exchange of India Ltd.**
The Bombay Stock Exchange Limited.,	**5th Floor, Exchange Plaza**
25th Floor, Phiroz Jeejeebhoy Towers,	**Plot No.C/1, G Block**
Dalai Street, Mumbai - 400 001	**Bandra Kurla Complex, Bandra (East)**
	Mumbai-400 051.

Dear Sir/Madam,

Sub: Disclosure of the Impact of Audit Qualifications by the Listed Entities under Regulation 33/52 of SEBI (LODR), (Amendment) Regulations, 2016 Reg..,

Ref: NSE Circular dated 1st June, 2016 vide: NSE/CML/2016/09 and BSE Circular dated 1st June, 2016 vide: DCS/COMP/04/2016-17.

....

Pursuant to the SEBI notification no. SEBI/LAD-NRO/GN/2016-17/001 dated May 25, 2016 and Circular No. CIR/CFD/CMD/56/2016 dated May 27, 2016 issued by the Securities and Exchange Board of India (SEBI) on "Disclosure of the Impact of Audit Qualifications by Listed Entities" and circulars issued by NSE and BSE dated 1st June, 2016, we submit herewith enclosed Statement on Impact of Audit Qualifications (in Annexure- I) for the consolidated financial results of the Company for the Financial Year ended 31.03.2016.

Kindly take note on record of the same.

Thanks and Regards

For GAYATRI PROJECTS LIMITED

(CS I.V.LAKSHMI)

Company Secretary & Compliance officer

Membership No. 17607

Annexure I

Statement of Impact of Audit Qualification (for audit report with modified opinion) submitted along-with Annual Audited Financial Results - (Consolidated)

Statement of Impact of Audit Qualification for the Financial Year Ended 31st March 2016 [See Regulation 33/52 of the ESBI (LODR) (Amendment) Regulations, 2016]				
I.	**SI. No.**	**Particulars**	**Audited Figures (As reported before adjusting for qualifications)**	**Adjusted Figures (audited figures after adjusting for qualifications)**
	1	Turnover / Total Income		
	2	Total Expenditure		
	3	Net Profit / (Loss)		
	4	Earnings per Share		
	5	Total Assets		
	6	Total Liabilities		
	7	Net Worth		
	8	Any other financial item(s) / (as felt appropriate by the management)		
II.	Audit Qualification (each audit qualification separately):			
	a.	Details of Audit Qualification: ***The consolidated financial statement of one of the subsidiary company, Gayatri Infra Ventures Ltd (GIVL) as at 31st March, 2016 includes amounts aggregating to Rs.46,06,09,996/- invested in 49,36,850/- equity shares of a jointly controlled entity for which the management has entered into a definitive agreement for divestment of its entire equity shares. As represented to us, the management is in the process of renegotiating the consideration for the sale of investment along with making arrangements for meeting the conditions stipulated. Pending final outcome of the said process, we are unable to comment upon the consequential effects, if any of the said matter on the accompanying financial statements.***		
	b.	Type of Audit Qualification: ***The Independent auditors of a subsidiary company have qualified in their consolidated audit report regarding pending final outcome of***		

		divestment of a jointly controlled entity and consequential effects on the financials ***and the same qualification has been carried in Consolidated Auditors' Report of the company.***
	c.	Frequency of qualification : This is the first financial year in which the above mentioned qualification is appearing.
	d.	For Audit Qualification(s) where the impact is quantified by the auditor, Management's Views: Not Applicable
	e.	For Audit Qualification(s) where the impact is not quantified by the auditor:
	(i)	Management's estimation on the impact of audit qualification: ***Not Applicable***
	(ii)	If management is unable to estimate the impact, reasons for the same: ***As on Balance Sheet date, the purchase consideration for the sale of shares was still under negotiations and was subject to compliance of certain conditions by the SPV [Western UP Tollways Limited (WUPTL)]. As the WUTPL could not fulfil these conditions, the Cube Highways has started renegotiating the sale consideration. Hence, the Management of GIVL could not ascertain the total amount of consideration for the transaction and there by the impact of same could not be ascertained.***
	(iii)	Auditors' Comments on (i) or (ii) above: ***Our qualification in the consolidated financial statements of the company is carried from the auditors' report of the subsidiary company, wherein, the auditors have expressed their inability to comment on the impact of such qualification on the financial statements of the subsidiary for the reasons mentioned therein. Consequently, we are also unable to comment on the impact of such qualification on the consolidated financial statements of the Company.***
III.	Signatories:	
	1.	Mr. T.V. Sandeep Kumar Reddy-Managing Director
	2.	Mr. P. Sreedhar Babu - Chief Financial Officer
	3.	M O S & ASSOCIATES LLP Chartered Accountants, Statutory Auditors of the Company S.V.C. Reddy Partner
	4.	Mr. Ch. HariVittal Rao-Audit Committee Chairman

GONTERMANN-PEIPERS (INDIA) LIMITED

Ref. GPI/SEC/BSE/CSE/2016-17

September 21, 2016

The Manager
Department of Corporate Services
BSE Limited
Phiroze Jeejeebhoy Towers
Dalai Street
Mumbai - 400 001
Ref: Stock Code: 504701

The Secretary
The Calcutta Stock Exchange Limited
7, Lyons Range
Kolkata - 700 001.
Ref: Stock Code: 10017005

Re : Statement on impact of Audit qualifications for the audit report with modified opinion for the financial year 2015-16.

Dear Sir,

Further to our letter No. GPI/SEC/BSE/CSE/2016-17 dated 4th July, 2016. Please find enclosed herewith the modified Statement on impact of Audit Qualifications (for audit report with modified opinion) of the Company for the financial year ended on 31st March, 2016 in terms of Regulation 33(3)(d) of the Securities and Exchange Board of India (Listing Obligations and Disclosure Requirements) (Amendment) Regulations, 2016 as further amended by the SEBI Circular No. CIR/CFD/CMD/56/2016 dated 27th May, 2016, as audited by M/s. V. Malik & Associates, Statutory Auditors of the Company and issued a Report thereon.

You are requested to please consider and take on record.

Thanking you,

Yours faithfully,

For GONTERMANN-PEIPERS (INDIA) LTD.

Prithwi Manas Mitra

Chief Financial Officer

Statement on impact of Audit Qualifications (for audit report with modified opinion (submitted along with Annual Audited Financial Results - (Standalone and Consolidated separately)

Statement on impact of Audit Qualifications for the Financial year end of on Marth 31, 2016
[Regulation 33/52 of the SEBI (LODR) (Amendment) Regulation, 2016]

	SI. No.	Particulars	Audited Figures (as reported before adjusting for qualification) (Rs in Lacs)	Adjusted Figures (Audited figures after adjusting for qualifications) (Rs in Lacs)
I.	1	Turnover/Total Income	9240.77	9240.77
	2	Total Expenditure	12898.14	14541.20
	3	Net Profit/ (Loss)	(3657.37)	5300.43
	4	Earnings Per Share	Rs. (11.38)	Rs. (42)
	5	Total Assets	23279.76	17689.51
	6	Total Liabilities	23279.76	17689.51
	7	Net Worth	(2065.22)	(7655.47)
	8	Tax Expenses	(1126.45)	3947.19
	9	Net Profit / (Loss) after Tax	(2530.92)	(9247.62)
II.	**Audit Qualification (each audit qualification separately)**			
	a.1	**Details of Audit Qualification:-**		
		Long outstanding (i) capital advances (Note No. 12) of Rs. 1,188.51 Lacs (including amount represented as trade receivable) and (ii) advances to suppliers (Note No. 16) of Rs. 454.55 Lacs (including Rs. 288.61 Lacs recoverable from related party) in respect of which no confirmation/acknowledgement, schedule of delivery and agreements are available and in the absence of initiation of concrete steps for recovery/settlement, non-availability of legal tenable rights and doubt about the inability to pay, besides other factors, equivalent provision for advances doubtful for recovery is necessary considering the magnitude of above factors coupled with considerable delay by these parties, non-creation of such provision is contrary to the requirements of Accounting Standard-4, "Contingencies and Events occurring after the Balance Sheet date". Consequently, the loss for the year would be impacted by Rs. 1,643.06 Lacs.		

	SI. No.	Particulars	Audited Figures (as reported before adjusting for qualification) (Rs in Lacs)	Adjusted Figures (Audited figures after adjusting for qualifications) (Rs in Lacs)
	b.1	Type of Audit Qualification : Qualified		
	c.1	Frequency of Qualification : Repetitive		
	d.1	For Audit Qualification(s) where the impact is quantified by the auditor, Managements view As regard long outstanding (i) Capital advances of Rs.1188.51 Lacs (including amount represented as trade receivables) and (ii) advances to suppliers of Rs.454.55 Lacs, the management is confident that the same will be adjusted against supply of materials or realization of advances.		
	e.1	For Audit Qualification(s) where the impact is not quantified by the auditors: N.A.		
		(i) Management's estimation on the impact of audit qualification: N.A.		
		(ii) If Management is unable to estimate the impact, reasons for the same: N.A.		
		(iii) Auditor's Comments on (i) or (ii) above: N.A.		
	a.2	**Details of Audit Qualification:**		
		The company has recognized Net deferred tax asset (DTA) of Rs.3,947.19 Lacs (including Rs. 1,126.45 Lacs for the year) up to 31st March, 2016 on account of unabsorbed depreciation, carried forward business losses and disallowances under Income tax laws (Refer Note No. 11 and 51) based on the future profitability projections made by the management. The company has history of continuous losses for last 5 years and in the absence of virtual certainty supported by convincing evidence along with non-disclosure of nature of evidences supporting its recognition that sufficient taxable income will be available against which such deferred tax assets can be realized in near future, in our opinion, the recognition of deferred tax asset is in contravention to Accounting Standard-22 "Accounting for Taxes on Income" and impacted the loss for the year and financial position to that extent.		
	b.2	Type of Audit Qualification : Qualified Opinion		
	c.2	Frequency of Qualification : Repetitive		
	d.2	For Audit Qualification(s) where the impact is quantified by the auditor, Managements view:- As regards Net Deferred Tax (DTA), based on the future profitability projections, management is confident of achieving the profitability in the coming years and the Company is virtually certain that there would be sufficient taxable income in the future against which the Deferred Tax Asset can be accounted for.		

	Sl. No.	Particulars	Audited Figures (as reported before adjusting for qualification) (Rs in Lacs)	Adjusted Figures (Audited figures after adjusting for qualifications) (Rs in Lacs)
	e.2	For Audit Qualification (s) where the impact is not quantified by the auditors: N.A.		
		(i) Management's estimation on the impact of audit qualification: N.A.		
		(ii) If Management is unable to estimate the impact, reasons for the same: N.A.		
		(iii) Auditor's Comments on (i) or (ii) above: N.A.		
	a.3	**Details of Audit Qualification:** During the year, there are unfilled key positions in the management and non- availability of promoters-cum-directors in India and in view of only one executive director on the Board of the company, Mr. Buddhadeb Duari, independent director, has been authorized to sign the financial statements of the company as at 31st March 2016 for and on behalf of the Board of Directors.		
	b.3	Type of Audit Qualification : Qualified Opinion		
	c.3	Frequency of Qualification : Repetitive		
	d.3	For Audit Qualification(s) where the impact is quantified by the auditor, Managements view:- N.A.		
	e.3	For Audit Qualification (s) where the impact is not quantified by the auditors:		
		(i) Management's estimation on the impact of audit qualification: The qualification given by the Auditors is not quantifiable since it is not a financial qualification.		
		(ii) If Management is unable to estimate the impact, reasons for the same: Management's Comments: During the year, there are no such unfilled Key positions in the management of the Company and regarding non-availability of Promoter- cum-Director, there stands no provision for staying of promoter-cum- director in India in Companies Act, 2013. However, the Promoter-cum- director has attended the Board Meeting of the Company through Video Conferencing which is permissible under Companies Act, 2013.Since and in case of absence of Managing Director & CEO, the Board of Directors of the Company has authorised Mr. Dwijen Lahiri, Whole Time Director and Mr. Buddhadeb Duari, Non-Executive Director to sign the financial statements of the Company on behalf of the Board, which is permissible under Companies Act, 2013.		

	Sl. No.	Particulars	Audited Figures (as reported before adjusting for qualification) (Rs in Lacs)	Adjusted Figures (Audited figures after adjusting for qualifications) (Rs in Lacs)
		(iii) Auditor's Comments on (i) or (ii) above: Mr. Buddhadeb Duari, being a non-executive independent director, does not participate in the day-to-day affairs of the business and is only acting in independent professional capacity. Besides, there are other non-executive non- independent directors present on the Board. Moreover, the Promoters-cum- Directors have attended only the minimum required Board Meetings during past two years.		
	a.4	**Details of Key Emphasis Matters:** **Relating to Complete Erosion of Net Worth** Note No. 34 to the financial statements indicating the basis and factors for complete erosion of net worth of the company on the reporting date: i) incurring heavy negative operating cash flows for the past few years on account of economy slowdown, under-utilization of installed production capacities and paucity of adequate working capital,ii)the company's current liabilities exceed its current assets by Rs. 8025.64 Lacs as at the balance sheet date, resulting into negative working capital gaps, iii)cancellation of term loans by the CDR lenders as envisaged in the CDR scheme, iv)continuously defaulting in repayment of interest and principal on borrowings and, v)non-deposition and delays in deposition of statutory liabilities with Government Exchequer in stipulated time. These conditions, alongwith other matters set forth in the above referred note, indicates the existence of material uncertainty that casts significant doubt about the company's ability to continue functioning as a going concern. However, management's perspective of improved performance/ financial position is largely dependent upon other avenues of raising funds, large confirmed dispatchable orders in hand, company's intention to monetize its identified non-core immovable properties and synergy benefits from ongoing amalgamation process under approval from Hon'ble High Courts and its implementation and accordingly, does not include any adjustments, relating to the recoverability and classification of recorded assets and classification of liabilities, that may be necessary if the entity is unable to continue as a going concern. Under the circumstances, the financial statements of the company have been prepared by the management on a going concern basis and in the opinion of the management no adjustments are considered necessary to the carrying value of its assets and liabilities. **Relating to Non-Confirmation of Balances of Parties** Note No. 38 to the financial statements, relating to pending		

	Sl. No.	Particulars	Audited Figures (as reported before adjusting for qualification) (Rs in Lacs)	Adjusted Figures (Audited figures after adjusting for qualifications) (Rs in Lacs)
		confirmation/ reconciliation of balances in respect of trade receivable and payable, advances to suppliers and from customers, consequential impact whereof cannot be ascertained presently.		
	b.3	Type of Audit Qualification: Emphasis Matters (Our Opinion is Not Qualified in respect of Emphasis		
	C.3	Frequency of Qualification: Repetitive		
	d.3	For Audit Qualification(s) where the impact is quantified by the auditor, Managements view:- N.A.		
	e.3	For Audit Qualification (s) where the impact is not quantified by the auditors:		
		(i) Management's estimation on the impact of audit qualification: **N.A.**		
		(ii) If Management is unable to estimate the impact, reasons for the same: **N.A.**		
		(iii) Auditor's Comments on (i) or (ii) above: **N.A.**		
III.		**Signatories:**		
		• **CEO/ Managing Director**		
		• **CFO**		
		• **Audit Committee Chairman**		
		• **Statutory Auditor**		
	Place : Kolkata			
	Date : 29.07.2016			

LYKA LABS LIMITED

The Dy. General Manager
The Bombay Stock Exchange Ltd
Corporate Relations Department
1st Floor, New Trading Ring,
Rotunda Bldg, P. J. Towers,
Dalai Street, Mumbai - 400 001

Dear Sir,

Script Code: 500259

Sub: Statement of Impact on Audit Qualification

Attached herewith, the Statement of Impact on Audit Qualification in the prescribed format for the Financial year ended on 31st March, 2016.

Kindly take note of same.

Thanking you,

Yours faithfully,

for LYKA LABS LIMITED

P. G. HINDA

COMPANY SECRETARY

Enel: a/a

Statement on Impact of Audit Qualifications (for audit report with modified opinion) submitted along-with Annual Audited Financial Results – *(Standalone and Consolidated separately)*

Rs. In lacs

Statement on Impact of Audit Qualifications for the Financial Year ended March 31, 2016 [See Regulation 33/52 of the SEBI (LODR) Amendment) Regulations. 2016]

	Sr. No.	Particulars	Audited Figures (as reported before adjusting for qualifications)	Adjusted Figures (audited figures after adjusting for qualifications)
I.	1	Turnover/Total income	5726.96	5726.96
	2	Total Expenditure	5197.23	5197.23
	3	Net Profit/(Loss)	482.02	482.02
	4	Earnings Per Share	2.17	2.17
	5	Total Assets	22802.73	22802.73
	6	Total Liabilities	16152.43	16152.43
	7	Net Worth	6650.30	6650.30
	8	Any other financial item(s) (as felt appropriate by the management)		
II.	**Audit Qualification (each audit aualification separately):**			
	a.	**Details of Audit Qualification:** The Auditors at point no.4.2 of notes to their Auditors report qualified that the direct expenditure and allocable indirect expenditures incurred in respect of "new product development and applied research" aggregating to Rs.1313.88 lacs including finance cost of Rs.220.87 lacs which is carried forward under capital work in progress-intangibles.		
	b.	**Type of Audit Qualification: Qualified Opinion**		
	c.	**Frequency of qualification: Repetitive**		
	d.	**For Audit Qualification(s) where the impact is quantified by the auditor, Management's Views:**		
	e.	**For Audit Qualification(s) where the impact is not quantified by the auditor:**		
	(i)	**Management's estimation on the impact of audit qualification:**		
	(ii)	**If management is unable to estimate the impact, reasons for the same:** Lyka has a separate R & D centre at Mumbai which is approved		

	Sr. No.	Particulars	Audited Figures (as reported before adjusting for qualifications)	Adjusted Figures (audited figures after adjusting for qualifications)
	by the Department of Science and Technology, Government of India. It has well equipped laboratories with state of the art equipment to explore development of a wide range of formulations. Like other Pharma companies, Lyka Labs also conducts clinical trials, toxicity studies, stability studies in a phased manner and detailed documentation required for obtaining regulatory approvals is compiled. The period involved could be as much as 8-10 years and result in substantial development costs.			
	The benefit of such substantial development costs by way of product development would accrue over a period of time and therefore such development costs are capitalized, as and when regulatory approvals are obtained and commercial operations commence, to the respective products, or charged to Statement of Profit and Loss in the year in which development is abandoned. During the year, the Company has capitalized Rs.33.22 lacs as "Self-Generated Intangible Assets" upon successful development of respective products and there is no charge to Statement of Profit and Loss as there are no products, development of which is abandoned.			
	(iii) Auditors' Comments on (ii) above: We agree with the reasons stated by the Management.			
III.	**Signatories:**			
	• Narendra I Gandhi (Managing Director)			
	• Yogesh B. Shah (CFO)			
	• Mukul M. Patel (M/s M.A. Parikh & Co. Chartered Accounts-Statutory Auditor)			
	• Ajit Bagadia (Chairman Audit Committee)			
	Place: Mumbai			
	Date: 02 JUL 2016			

Annexure VI: Regulations 33 and 52 of the SEBI (Listing Obligations and Disclosure Requirements) Regulations, 2015

REGULATION 33 RELATED TO FINANCIAL RESULTS

(1) While preparing financial results, the listed entity shall comply with the following:

(a) The financial results shall be prepared on the basis of accrual accounting policy and shall be in accordance with uniform accounting practices adopted for all the periods.

(b) The quarterly and year to date results shall be prepared in accordance with the recognition and measurement principles laid down in Accounting Standard 25 or Indian Accounting Standard 31 (AS 25/ Ind AS 34 – Interim Financial Reporting), as applicable, specified in Section 133 of the Companies Act, 2013 read with relevant rules framed thereunder or as specified by the Institute of Chartered Accountants of India, whichever is applicable.

(c) The standalone financial results and consolidated financial results shall be prepared as per Generally Accepted Accounting Principles in India:

Provided that in addition to the above, the listed entity may also submit the financial results, as per the International Financial Reporting Standards notified by the International Accounting Standards Board.

(d) The listed entity shall ensure that the limited review or audit reports submitted to the stock exchange(s) on a quarterly or annual basis are to be given only by an auditor who has subjected himself to the peer review process of Institute of Chartered Accountants of India and holds a valid certificate issued by the Peer Review Board of the Institute of Chartered Accountants of India.

(e) The listed entity shall make the disclosures specified in Part A of Schedule IV.

(2) The approval and authentication of the financial results shall be done by listed entity in the following manner:

(a) The quarterly financial results submitted shall be approved by the board of directors:

Provided that while placing the financial results before the board of directors, the chief executive officer and chief financial officer of the listed entity shall certify that the financial results do not contain any false or misleading statement or figures and do not omit any material fact which may make the statements or figures contained therein misleading.

(b) The financial results submitted to the stock exchange shall be signed by the chairperson or managing director, or a whole time director or in the absence of all of them; it shall be signed by any other director of the listed entity who is duly authorized by the board of directors to sign the financial results.

(c) The limited review report shall be placed before theboard of directors, at its meeting which approves the financial results, before being submitted to the stock exchange(s).

(d) The annual audited financial results shall be approved by the board of directors of the listed entity and shall be signed in the manner specified in clause (b) of sub- regulation (2).

(3) The listed entity shall submit the financial results in the following manner:

(a) The listed entity shall submit quarterly and year-to-date standalone financial results to the stock exchange within forty-five days of end of each quarter, other than the last quarter.

(b) In case the listed entity has subsidiaries, in addition to the requirement at clause (a) of sub-regulation (3), the listed entity may also submit quarterly/year-to-date consolidated financial results subject to following:

(i) the listed entity shall intimate to the stock exchange, whether or not listed entity opts to additionally submit quarterly/year-to-date consolidated financial results in the first quarter of the financial year and this option shall not be changed during the financial year.

Provided that this option shall also be applicable to listed entity that is required to prepare consolidated financial results for the first time at the end of a financial year in respect of the quarter during the financial year in which the listed entity first acquires the subsidiary.

(ii) in case the listed entity changes its option in any subsequent year, it shall furnish comparable figures for the previous year in accordance with the option exercised for the current financial year.

(c) The quarterly and year-to-date financial results may be either audited or unaudited subject to the following:

(i) In case the listed entity opts to submit unaudited financial results, they shall be subject to limited review by the statutory auditors of the listed entity and shall be accompanied by the limited review report.

Provided that in case of public sector undertakings this limited review may be undertaken by any practicing Chartered Accountant.

(ii) In case the listed entity opts to submit audited financial results, they shall be accompanied by the audit report.

(d) The listed entity shall submit [annual][2] audited standalone financial results for the financial year, within sixty days from the end of the financial year along with the audit report and [Statement on Impact of Audit Qualifications (applicable only][3] for audit report with modified opinion):

Provided that if the listed entity has subsidiaries, it shall, while submitting annual audited standalone financial results also submit annual audited consolidated financial results along with the audit report and [Statement on Impact of Audit Qualifications (applicable only] [4] for audit report with modified opinion)[:] [5]

[Provided further that, in case of audit reports with unmodified opinion(s), the listed entity shall furnish a declaration to that effect to the Stock Exchange(s) while publishing the annual audited financial results.][6]

(e) The listed entity shall also submit the audited financial results in respect of the last quarter along-with the results for the entire financial year, with a note stating that the figures of last quarter are the balancing figures between audited figures in respect of the full financial year and the published year-to-date figures upto the third quarter of the current financial year.

(f) The listed entity shall also submit as part of its standalone or consolidated financial results for the half year, by way of a note, a statement of assets and liabilities as at the end of the half-year.

---

2 Inserted by SEBI (Listing Obligations and Disclosure Requirements) (Amendment) Regulations, 2016, w.e.f. 01.04.2016.

3 Substituted for 'either Form A (for audit report with unmodified opinion) or Form B (' by SEBI (Listing Obligations and Disclosure Requirements) (Amendment) Regulations, 2016, w.e.f. 01.04.2016

4 Substituted for 'either Form A (for audit report with unmodified opinion) or Form B' by SEBI (Listing Obligations and Disclosure Requirements) (Amendment) Regulations, 2016, w.e.f. 01.04.2016

5 Substituted for the symbol '.' by SEBI (Listing Obligations and Disclosure Requirements) (Amendment) Regulations, 2016, w.e.f. 01.04.2016

6 Inserted by SEBI (Listing Obligations and Disclosure Requirements) (Amendment) Regulations, 2016, w.e.f. 01.04.2016.

(4) The applicable formats of the financial results and [Statement on Impact of Audit Qualifications (for audit report with modified opinion)][7] shall be in the manner as specified by the Board [***][8].

(5) For the purpose of this regulation, any reference to — "quarterly/quarter" in case of listed entity which has listed their specified securities on SME Exchange shall be respectively read as — "half yearly/half year" and the requirement of submitting 'year-to-date' financial results shall not be applicable for a listed entity which has listed their specified securities on SME Exchange.

(6) The [Statement on Impact of Audit Qualifications (for audit report with modified opinion)][9] and the accompanying annual audit report submitted in terms of clause (d) of sub-regulation (3) shall be reviewed by the stock exchange(s) [***][10].

(7) [***][11]

---

7 Substituted for 'Form A (for audit report with unmodified opinion) & Form B (for audit report with modified opinion)' by SEBI (Listing Obligations and Disclosure Requirements) (Amendment) Regulations, 2016, w.e.f. 01.04.2016

8 The words 'from time to time' omitted by SEBI (Listing Obligations and Disclosure Requirements) (Amendment) Regulations, 2016, w.e.f. 01.04.2016.

9 Substituted for 'Form B' by SEBI (Listing Obligations and Disclosure Requirements) (Amendment) Regulations, 2016, w.e.f. 01.04.2016

10 The words 'and Qualified Audit Report Review Committee in manner as specified in Schedule VIII' omitted by SEBI (Listing Obligations and Disclosure Requirements) (Amendment) Regulations, 2016, w.e.f. 01.04.2016.

11 Omitted by SEBI (Listing Obligations and Disclosure Requirements) (Amendment) Regulations, 2016, w.e.f. 01.04.2016. Prior to omission, sub regulation (7) read as follows:

'(7) The listed entity shall on the direction issued by the Board, carry out the necessary steps, for rectification of modified opinion and/or submission of revised pro-forma financial results, in the manner specified in Schedule VIII.'

REGULATION 52 RELATED TO FINANCIAL RESULTS

(1) The listed entity shall prepare and submit un-audited or audited financial results on a half yearly basis in the format as specified by the Board within forty five days from the end of the half year to the recognised stock exchange(s).

(2) The listed entity shall comply with following requirements with respect to preparation, approval, authentication and publication of annual and half-yearly financial results:

(a) Un-audited financial results shall be accompanied by limited review report prepared by the statutory auditors of the listed entity or in case of public sector undertakings, by any practising Chartered Accountant, in the format as specified by the Board:

Provided that if the listed entity intimates in advance to the stock exchange(s) that it shall submit to the stock exchange(s) its annual audited results within sixty days from the end of the financial year, un-audited financial results for the last half year accompanied by limited review report by the auditors need not be submitted to stock exchange(s).

(b) Half-yearly results shall be taken on record by the board of directors and signed by the managing director / executive director.

(c) The audited results for the year shall be submitted to the recognised stock exchange(s) in the same format as is applicable for half-yearly financial results.

(d) If the listed entity opts to submit un-audited financial results for the last half year accompanied by limited review report by the auditors, it shall also submit audited financial results for the entire financial year, as soon as they are approved by the board of directors.

(e) Modified opinion(s) in audit reports that have a bearing on the interest payment/ dividend payment pertaining to non-convertible redeemable debentures/ redemption or principal repayment capacity of the listed entity shall be appropriately and adequately addressed by the board of directors while publishing the accounts for the said period.

(3) (a) The annual audited financial results shall be submitted along with the annual audit report and [Statement on Impact of Audit

Qualifications (applicable only][12] for audit report with modified opinion[)][13] [;][14]

[Provided that, in case of audit reports with unmodified opinion, the listed entity shall furnish a declaration to that effect to the Stock Exchange(s) while publishing the annual audited financial results.][15]

(b) The [Statement on Impact of Audit Qualifications (for audit report with modified opinion][16] and the accompanying annual audit report submitted in terms of clause (a) shall be reviewed by the stock exchange(s) [***][17].

(c) [***][18]

(d) The applicable [format][19] of [Statement on Impact of Audit Qualifications (for audit report with modified opinion)][20] shall be [in the manner as][21] specified by the Board [***][22].

(4) The listed entity, while submitting half yearly / annual financial results, shall disclose the following line items along with the financial results:

(a) credit rating and change in credit rating (if any);

(b) asset cover available, in case of non-convertible debt securities;

---

12 Substituted for 'either Form A for audit report with unmodified opinion, or Form B' by SEBI (Listing Obligations and Disclosure Requirements) (Amendment) Regulations, 2016, w.e.f. 01.04.2016.

13 Inserted by SEBI (Listing Obligations and Disclosure Requirements) (Amendment) Regulations, 2016, w.e.f. 01.04.2016.

14 Substituted for the symbol '.' by SEBI (Listing Obligations and Disclosure Requirements) (Amendment) Regulations, 2016, w.e.f. 01.04.2016.

15 Inserted by SEBI (Listing Obligations and Disclosure Requirements) (Amendment) Regulations, 2016, w.e.f. 01.04.2016.

16 Substituted for 'Form B' by SEBI (Listing Obligations and Disclosure Requirements) (Amendment) Regulations, 2016, w.e.f. 01.04.2016.

17 The words 'and the Qualified Audit Report Review Committee in the manner specified in Schedule VIII' omitted by SEBI (Listing Obligations and Disclosure Requirements) (Amendment) Regulations, 2016, w.e.f. 01.04.2016.

18 Omitted by SEBI (Listing Obligations and Disclosure Requirements) (Amendment) Regulations, 2016, w.e.f. 01.04.2016. Prior to omission, sub regulation (3) read as follows:

'The listed entity shall on the direction issued by the Board, carry out the necessary steps, for rectification of modified opinion and/or submission of revised pro-forma financial results, in the manner specified in Schedule VIII'

19 Substituted for 'formats' by SEBI (Listing Obligations and Disclosure Requirements) (Amendment) Regulations, 2016, w.e.f. 01.04.2016

20 Substituted for 'Form A and Form B' by SEBI (Listing Obligations and Disclosure Requirements) (Amendment) Regulations, 2016, w.e.f. 01.04.2016

21 Inserted by SEBI (Listing Obligations and Disclosure Requirements) (Amendment) Regulations, 2016, w.e.f. 01.04.2016.

22 The words 'from time to time' omitted by SEBI (Listing Obligations and Disclosure Requirements) (Amendment) Regulations, 2016, w.e.f. 01.04.2016

(c) debt-equity ratio;

(d) previous due date for the payment of interest/ dividend for non-convertible redeemable preference shares/repayment of principal of non-convertible preference shares/non-convertible debt securities and whether the same has been paid or not; and,

(e) next due date for the payment of interest/ dividend of non-convertible preference shares /principal along with the amount of interest/ dividend of non-convertible preference shares payable and the redemption amount;

(f) debt service coverage ratio;

(g) interest service coverage ratio;

(h) outstanding redeemable preference shares (quantity and value);

(i) capital redemption reserve/debenture redemption reserve;

(j) net worth;

(k) net profit after tax;

(l) earnings per share:

Provided that the requirement of disclosures of debt service coverage ratio, asset cover and interest service coverage ratio shall not be applicable for banks or non-banking financial companies registered with the Reserve Bank of India.

Provided further that the requirement of this sub- regulation shall not be applicable in case of unsecured debt instruments issued by regulated financial sector entities eligible for meeting capital requirements as specified by respective regulators.

(5) While submitting the information required under sub- regulation (4), the listed entity shall submit to stock exchange(s), a certificate signed by debenture trustee that it has taken note of the contents.

(6) The listed entity which has listed its non-convertible redeemable preference shares shall make the following additional disclosures as notes to financials:

(a) profit for the half year and cumulative profit for the year; (b)free reserve as on the end of half year;

(c) securities premium account balance (if redemption of redeemable preference share is to be done at a premium, such premium may be appropriated from securities premium account):

Provided that disclosure on securities premium account balance may be provided only in the year in which non-convertible redeemable preference shares are due for redemption;

(d) track record of dividend payment on non-convertible redeemable preference shares: Provided that in case the dividend has been deferred at any time, then the actual date of payment shall be disclosed;

(e) breach of any covenants under the terms of the non-convertible redeemable preference shares:

Provided that in case a listed entity is planning a fresh issuance of shares whose end use is servicing of the non-convertible redeemable preference shares (whether dividend or principle redemption), then the same shall be disclosed whenever the listed entity decided on such issuances.

(7) The listed entity shall submit to the stock exchange on a half yearly basis along with the half yearly financial results, a statement indicating material deviations, if any, in the use of proceeds of issue of non-convertible debt securities and non-convertible redeemable preference shares from the objects stated in the offer document.

(8) The listed entity shall, within two calendar days of the conclusion of the meeting of the board of directors, publish the financial results and statement referred to in sub-regulation (4), in at least one English national daily newspaper circulating in the whole or substantially the whole of India.

Chapter 8

Ind AS results for equity listed companies

8.1 INTRODUCTION

SEBI vide its circular dated 30 November 2015 has prescribed formats for publishing financial results. The circular further states that companies adopting Ind AS in terms of Companies (Indian Accounting Standards) (Amendment) Rules, 2016 ("Ind AS Rules") notified by the Ministry of Corporate Affairs on 30 March 2016 while publishing quarterly/annual financial results under Regulation 33 of the SEBI (Listing Obligations and Disclosure Requirements) (second amendment) Regulations, 2016, shall ensure that the comparatives filed along with such quarterly/annual financial results are also Ind AS compliant.

SEBI has issued a circular dated 5 July 2016 on revised formats for financial results and implementation of Ind ASs by listed entities. The circular provides various relaxations to the listed entities to which Ind AS Rules are applicable from the accounting periods beginning on or after 1 April 2016. The relaxations pertain to timelines for submitting financial results, comparative periods to be presented and requirement of audit/limited review of comparative figures during the first year of Ind ASs implementation. The highlights of the circular are as follows:

- Existing formats prescribed in SEBI circular dated 30 November 2015 for quarterly financial results will continue till the period ending 31 December 2016;
- For the periods ending on or after 31 March 2017, the formats for quarterly financial results will be as per the formats prescribed in Schedule III to the *Companies Act, 2013*. Banking companies and Insurance companies will follow the formats as prescribed under the respective Acts/Regulations;

The impact of these changes in the quarterly reporting for phase 1 companies (with FY ending 31 March 2017) has been summarised in the below table:

<table>
<tr><th>Sr. No</th><th>Reporting period</th><th>Pre-revised requirement*</th><th>Revised requirements*</th></tr>
<tr><td rowspan="2">1.</td><td rowspan="2">June 2016</td><td>• P& L for quarter ended June 2016
Comparative information:
• P& L for quarter ended June 2015
• P& L for quarter ended Mar 2016
• P& L for year ended Mar 2016 (audited)</td><td>• P& L for quarter ended June 2016
Comparative information:
• P& L for quarter ended June 2015</td></tr>
<tr><td>Timeline: 45 days</td><td>Timeline: 45 days + one month i.e. by 14 September 2016</td></tr>
<tr><td rowspan="2">2.</td><td rowspan="2">September 2016</td><td>• P&L for quarter ended Sep 2016
• P&L for YTD ended Sep 2016
• BS as at Sep 2016
Comparative information:
• P&L for quarter ended June 2016
• P&L for quarter ended Sep 2015
• P&L for YTD ended Sep 2015
• P&L for year ended Mar 2016 (audited)
• BS as at Mar 2016 (audited)</td><td>• P&L for quarter ended Sep 2016
• P&L for YTD ended Sep 2016
• BS as at Sep 2016
Comparative information:
• P&L for quarter ended June 2016
• P&L for quarter ended Sep 2015
• P&L for YTD ended Sep 2015</td></tr>
<tr><td>Timeline: 45 days</td><td>Timeline: 45 days + one month i.e. by 14 December 2016</td></tr>
<tr><td>3.</td><td>December 2016</td><td>• P&L for quarter ended Dec 2016
• P&L for YTD ended Dec 2016</td><td>• P&L for quarter ended Dec 2016
• P&L for YTD ended Dec 2016</td></tr>
</table>

Sr. No	Reporting period	Pre-revised requirement*	Revised requirements*
		Comparative information: • P&L for quarter ended Sep 2016 • P&L for quarter ended Dec 2015 • P&L for YTD ended Dec 2015 • P&L for year ended Mar 2016 (audited)	*Comparative information:* • P&L for quarter ended Sep 2016 • P&L for quarter ended Dec 2015 • P&L for YTD ended Dec 2015
		Timeline: 45 days	**Timeline: 45 days**
4.	March 2017	All periods' information should be audited • P&L for quarter ending Mar 2017 • P&L for year ending Mar 2017 • BS as at Mar 2017 *Comparative information:* • P&L for quarter ended Dec 2016 • P&L for quarter ended Mar 2016 • P&L for year ended Mar 2016 • BS as at Mar 2016	Unchanged
		Timeline: 60 days	**Timeline: 60 days**

* Reporting under Ind AS for the current period should be either subject to limited review (LR) or audited, other than specifically mentioned above:

P&L – Statement of financial results

BS – Statement of Assets and Liabilities)

YTD – Year to date

For listed entities to which Ind AS Rules are applicable in subsequent phases, the relaxations will apply during their corresponding first year of Ind AS implementation;

- For complying with the requirements Ind AS 101, *First time Adoption of Indian Accounting Standards*, a listed entity is required to provide reconciliation of its equity and net profit/loss as follows:
  - (a) For period ending 31 March 2017 - Reconciliation of its equity for the previous year ended 31 March 2016;
  - (b) For period ending 30 September 2016 - The listed entity can submit the reconciliation of its equity for the previous year ended 31 March 2016 but is not mandatory;
  - (c) Reconciliation of its net profit/loss required to be provided only for the corresponding quarter of the previous year;
- If the period for which the comparative information has been provided is shorter or longer than the normal 12-month period (where the entity historically has a year end other than 31 March), the listed entity is required to disclose a suitable note that the comparative amounts are not entirely comparable.

This circular is effective from 5 July 2016 and contents of the circular dated 30 November 2015 stand modified to the extent stated under this circular.

8.2 KEY IMPLEMENTATION ISSUES ARISING FROM SEBI CIRCULAR DATED 5 JULY 2016

8.2.1 Relaxation from audit/review of comparatives limited to quarter ended 30 June 2016 and 30 September 2016

Since relaxations from the requirement for audit or review of comparatives is limited to the quarters ending 30 June 2016 and 30 September 2016, companies will be required to get their comparatives either audited/reviewed by the auditors for the quarter ending 31 December 2016. Further, a company may opt to provide Ind AS compliant comparative for the period ended 31 March 2016 along with financial results for the quarter ended 31 December 2016; in such a situation Ind AS comparatives would be required to be either reviewed or audited by the auditors.

8.2.2 Is it really a relaxation for companies?

Though there is an exemption from audit/review for first two quarters, management needs to exercise a caution to ensure that the financial results provide a true and fair view of affairs of the company. Thus, the relaxation does not relax the responsibility of the management that the comparatives for the year to date 31 December quarter should not include significant adjustments to the quarter ending 30 June 2016 and 30 September 2016.

8.2.3 Are there any relaxations from reconciliations in quarterly financial results

SEBI circular specifies the reconciliations to be provided along with Ind AS quarterly financial results.

SEBI circular dated 5 July states that the listed entities in order to comply with the requirements of paragraph 32 of Ind AS 101 – *First time Adoption of Ind AS*, shall provide a reconciliation of its equity and net profit/loss, in the following manner, for enabling the investors to understand the material adjustments to the Balance Sheet and Statement of Profit and Loss on account of transition from the previous Indian GAAP to Ind-AS:

(i) Reconciliation of its equity for the previous year ended March 31, 2016, shall be provided while submitting the Audited Yearly Balance Sheet for the period ended March 31, 2017.

    Reconciliation of its equity for the previous year ended March 31, 2016, shall be provided in case the listed entity intends to provide the same while submitting the Unaudited/Audited Ind-AS compliant Half-Yearly Balance Sheet for the period ended September 30, 2016.

(ii) Reconciliation of its net profit/loss as mentioned in the Unaudited/Audited quarterly financial results shall be provided only for the corresponding quarter of the previous year.

Thus, relaxation has been given from preparation of equity reconciliation.

8.3 ANALYSIS OF RESULTS OF COMPANIES UNDER IND AS

In this chapter we have analysed the second quarter Ind AS results , i.e. for quarter ended 30 September 2016 announced by the 31 companies out of 50 nifty fifty companies. This chapter analyses the impact of adoption of Ind AS on the profits of these 31 nifty 50 companies and recognises some of the key standards contributing to the impacts on the profit of these companies. The nifty 50 includes 9 financial services companies on which Ind AS is not applicable from 1 April 2016. Therefore, these financial companies are excluded from the analysis of impact on financial information due to transition to Ind AS. The impact of the transition to Ind AS has been analysed by comparing the reported results for the quarter ended 30 September 2015 under the Companies (Accounting Standards) Rules, 2006 with the restated results for the same quarter under Ind AS, that have been published as comparatives for the quarter ended 30 September 2016.

The analysis reveals that there is significant impact on various financial reporting line items that have impacted the profit of companies. The implementation of Ind AS in the second quarter, like the first quarter has been largely impacted by the relaxation provided by SEBI. Most of these companies have presented only the bare minimum information and have availed the exemptions and therefore the impact of the transition on net worth, the transition related choices made and exemptions availed etc. are not evident in published results.

The 31 companies analysed in this publication have been selected from eleven different industrial sectors. The following table summarises the industrial sectors and the number of companies in each industrial sector used for analysis in this publication:

S. No.	Industrial sector	Number of companies
1	Automobile	6
2	Cement & Cement Products	2
3	Consumer Goods	3
4	Energy	5
5	IT	3
6	Media & Entertainment	1
7	Services – Port Operator	1
8	Telecom	2
9	Pharma	5
10	Metal	2
11	Construction	1
Total		**31**

Financial results of the Nifty fifty companies with following attributes are not considered for analysis of impact of Ind AS:

(a) Company with a reconciling item which is very significant quantitatively. This reconciling item could distort the overall impact of other reconciling items on transition to Ind AS.

For example, in the quarter ended 30 September 2016, the effect of transition to Ind AS due to profit on transfer of business of Infosys Limited is 3,036 crores.

(b) Companies with financial year ended 31 March 2016, which was longer or shorter than normal 12 month period.

For example, it was observed that while reporting the quarterly and six-month results ended 30 September 2016:

(i) The previous year ended 31 March 2016, in case of HCL Technologies Limited was a period of nine months from 1 July 2015 to 31 March 2016.

(ii) Similarly, the previous year ended 31 March 2016, in case of Eicher Motors Limited was for a period of fifteen months from 1 January 2015 to 31 March 2016.

How is the analysis performed?

The analysis of impact due to Ind AS on various key captions is based on standalone financial results published by the companies under previous GAAP and Ind AS for the quarter and six-months ended 30 September 2015.

Similarly, based on the Net profit reconciliations presented for the quarter and six-months ended 30 September 2015, we have classified the nature of reconciling item basis the applicability of a particular Ind AS standard. A detailed explanation for the various reconciling items is not provided by many companies, hence our classification is based on the descriptions available in the net profit reconciliations.

The percentage impact on different captions and impact of various Ind ASs on reconciliation are indicative and may change if computed differently and if the number of companies used for financial results is increased.

8.3.1 Impact on key captions of companies for the quarter and six-month ended 30 September 2016 under previous GAAP and Ind AS

Key Captions	Percentage Change	
	Quarter ended 30 September 2016	**Six-month ended 30 September 2016**
Revenue	5.65% ↑	5.81% ↑
EBIDTA	2.49% ↓	1.70% ↓
Finance Cost	7.76% ↑	9.57% ↑
Tax expense	1.74% ↓	2.36% ↓
Profit After Tax	5.44% ↓	4.05% ↓

8.3.2 Impact of various Ind ASs on profits of the companies

The table lists the impact of various Ind ASs on profits of the companies for the quarter and six-month ended 30 September 2015:

(INR In crores)

	Quarter ended 30 September 2015	Six-month ended 30 September 2015
Net profit as per previous GAAP for the quarter ended 30 September 2015	**40,719.13**	**79,606.78**
Adjustments		
Revenue	34.95	164.93
Financial instruments	(2,291.05)	(3,804.15)
Property, plant & equipment	(45.38)	(6.68)
Employee benefits	235.47	245.06
Share-based Payment	(152.02)	(294.84)
Accounting policies, changes in accounting estimates and errors	(102.00)	(99.00)
Others	86.61	530.71
Total adjustments	**(2,233.42)**	**(3,263.96)**
Net profit as per Ind AS for the quarter ended 30 September 2015	**38,485.71**	**76,342.82**

The impact of various standards on transition to Ind AS is presented diagrammatically below:

For the quarter ended 30 September 2015:

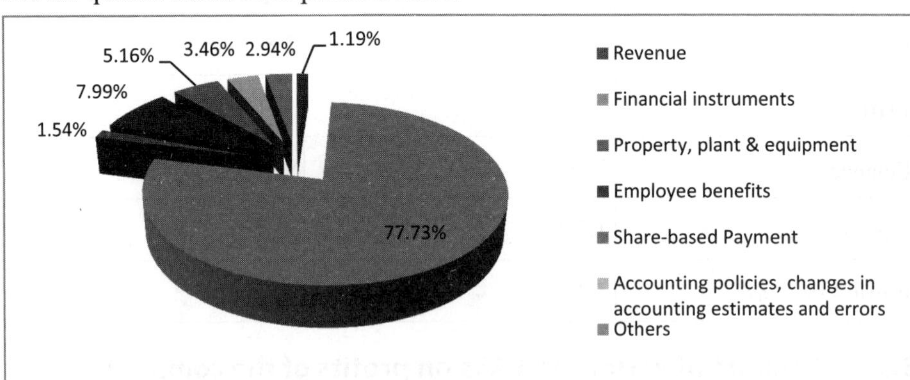

For the six-month ended 30 September 2015:

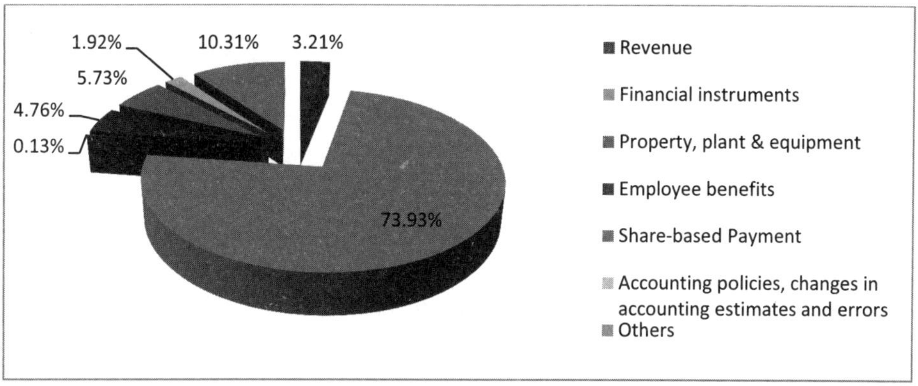

Thus it is evident from the above charts for the quarter and six-month ended September 2015 that adjustments to previous GAAP are primarily due to Ind AS on financial instruments; revenue; property, plant & equipment; employee benefits; share-based payment amongst other standards. Other standards which also impact the profit reconciliation of the companies considered under evaluation are Ind AS on business combination; income taxes; intangible assets; provisions, contingent liabilities and contingent assets; government grant; lease; inventory; the effects of changes in foreign exchange rates; impairment of assets, etc. However, it is to be noted that the reconciling items differ from company to company depending upon the nature of transactions undertaken by the company.

8.3.3 Analysis of impact of Ind AS on various industrial sectors

Revenue for the quarter ended 30 September 2015

Industrial sector	Revenue as per Ind AS	Revenue as per previous GAAP	Increase/(decrease) in revenue	% change in revenue
Automobile (AM)	53,657.02	49,234.60	4,422.42	8.98%
Cement & Cement Products (CP)	8,673.32	7,459.02	1,214.30	16.28%
Consumer Goods (CG)	24,184.04	19,924.32	4,259.72	21.38%
Energy (EN)	122,017.54	118,401.06	3,616.48	3.05%
IT (IT)	37,932.81	37,922.90	9.91	0.03%
Media &	1,021.59	1,021.59	-	0.00%

Industrial sector	Revenue as per Ind AS	Revenue as per previous GAAP	Increase/(decrease) in revenue	% change in revenue
Entertainment (ME)				
Services - Port Operator (SPO)	1,559.67	1,559.68	(0.01)	0.00%
Telecom – TE	10,013.99	10,030.23	(16.24)	-0.16%
Pharma (PH)	12,620.99	12,492.33	128.66	1.03%
Metal (MT)	20,202.64	18,455.68	1,746.96	9.47%
Construction (CO)	14,235.41	13,234.29	1,001.12	7.56%

The impact on revenue for the quarter ended 30 September 2015 is presented below through bar-diagram:

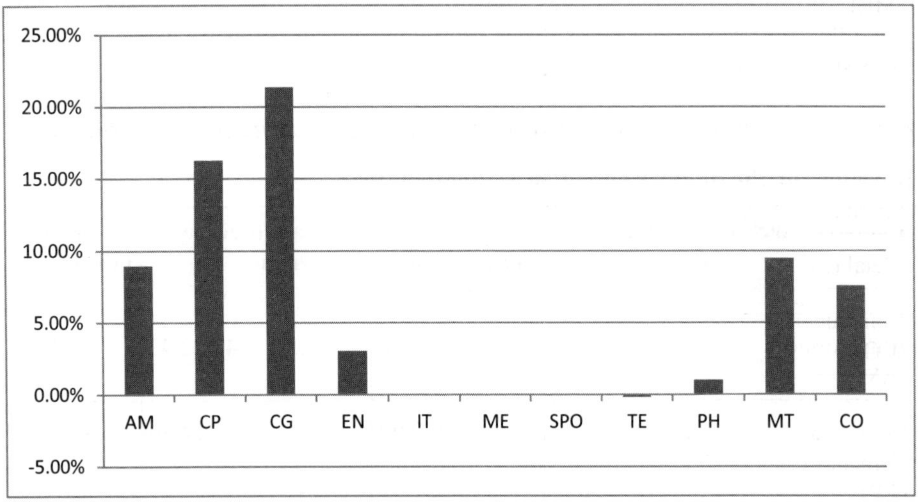

Revenue for the six-month ended 30 September 2015

Industrial sector	Revenue as per Ind AS	Revenue as per previous GAAP	Increase/(decrease) in revenue	% change in revenue
Automobile (AM)	105,415.18	96,914.92	8,500.26	8.77%
Cement & Cement Products (CP)	17,626.28	15,273.25	2,353.03	15.41%
Consumer Goods (CG)	47,938.93	39,555.31	8,383.62	21.19%
Energy (EN)	250,527.00	241,487.68	9,039.32	3.74%
IT (IT)	74,073.52	74,149.75	(76.23)	-0.10%
Media & Entertainment (ME)	1,991.82	1,991.82	-	0.00%
Services - Port Operator (SPO)	2,624.77	2,624.77	-	0.00%
Telecom – TE	20,141.43	20,176.57	(35.14)	-0.17%
Pharma (PH)	25,644.41	25,418.37	226.04	0.89%
Metal (MT)	39,550.69	36,124.66	3,426.03	9.48%
Construction (CO)	25,679.06	23,944.44	1,734.62	7.24%

The impact on revenue for the quarter ended 30 September 2015 is presented below through bar-diagram:

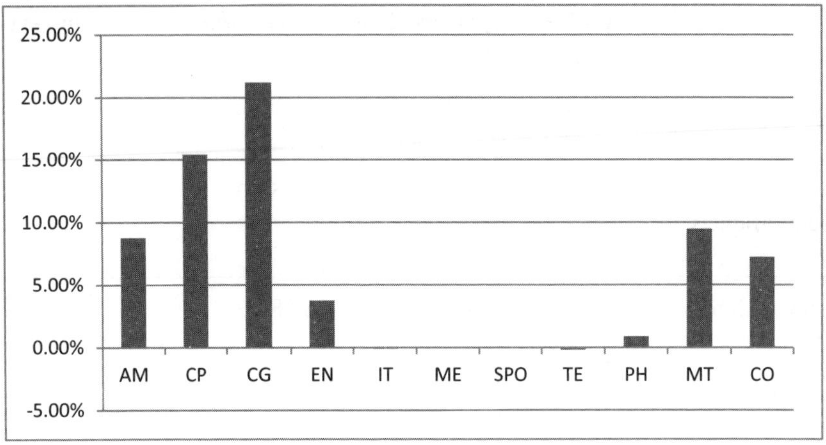

Out of 31 companies taken for analysis, for the quarter ended 30 September 2015, 23 companies have shown a rise in revenue, 6 companies have shown a decline in revenue and 2 companies have shown no change in revenue. Likewise, 8 industrial sectors have shown a rise, 2 industrial sectors have shown a decline and 1 industrial sector have no change in revenue for the aforesaid quarter. Similarly, for the six-month ended 30 September 2015, 21 companies have shown a rise in revenue and 10 companies have shown a decline in revenue. Likewise, 7 industrial sectors have shown a rise, 2 industrial sectors have shown a decline and 2 industrial sectors have no change in revenue for the aforesaid six-month period.

The increase in revenue in general can be attributed to the presentation of revenues gross of excise duty by the companies based on notification issued by BSE and NSE on behalf of SEBI, on 20 September 2016, that 'income from operations' may be disclosed inclusive of excise duty, instead of net of excise duty. Apart from the presentation changes, other adjustments such as revenue deferment, changes in policy etc. have also contributed to the change in revenue.

EBIDTA for the quarter ended 30 September 2015

Industry	EBIDTA as per Ind AS	EBIDTA as per previous GAAP	Increase/ (decrease) in EBIDTA	% change in EBIDTA
Automobile (AM)	8,614.99	7,948.91	666.08	8.38%
Cement & Cement Products (CP)	1,706.78	1,523.76	183.02	12.01%
Consumer Goods	5,909.53	6,052.53	(143.00)	-2.36%

Industry	EBIDTA as per Ind AS	EBIDTA as per previous GAAP	Increase/ (decrease) in EBIDTA	% change in EBIDTA
(CG)				
Energy (EN)	31,291.56	31,242.09	49.47	0.16%
IT (IT)	12,277.20	12,191.85	85.35	0.70%
Media & Entertainment (ME)	253.15	311.80	(58.65)	-18.81%
Services - Port Operator (SPO)	1,471.68	1,452.11	19.57	1.35%
Telecom (TE)	3,417.84	3,563.11	(145.27)	-4.08%
Pharma (PH)	2,692.96	2,660.55	32.41	1.22%
Metal (MT)	3,136.37	5,814.62	(2,678.25)	-46.06%
Construction (CO)	1,640.58	1,499.87	140.71	9.38%

The impact on EBIDTA for the quarter ended 30 September 2015 is presented below through bar-diagram:

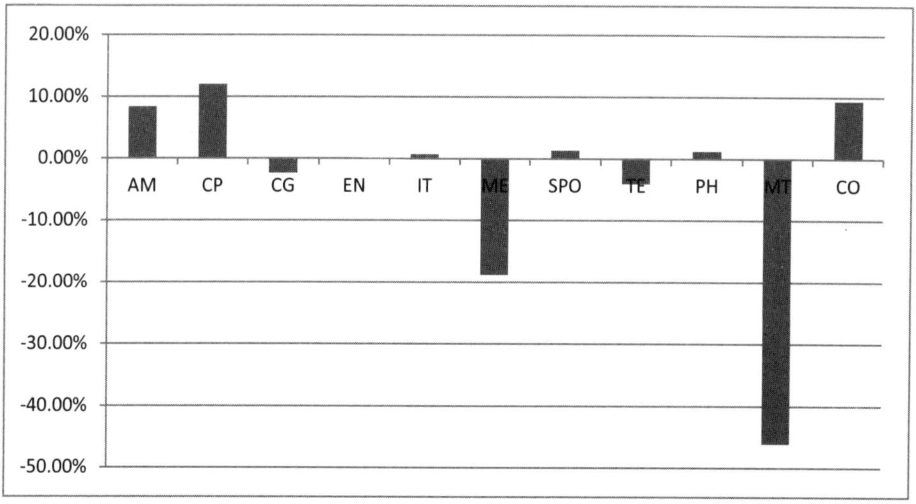

EBIDTA for the six-month ended 30 September 2015

Industrial sector	EBIDTA as per Ind AS	EBIDTA as per previous GAAP	Increase/(decrease) in EBIDTA	% change in EBIDTA
Automobile (AM)	16,990.95	16,299.47	691.48	4.24%
Cement & Cement Products (CP)	3,300.88	3,013.11	287.77	9.55%
Consumer Goods (CG)	11,829.13	12,050.53	(221.40)	-1.84%
Energy (EN)	62,804.83	62,762.79	42.04	0.07%
IT (IT)	23,839.50	23,597.99	241.51	1.02%
Media & Entertainment (ME)	515.37	633.32	(117.95)	-18.62%
Services - Port Operator (SPO)	2,459.94	2,425.47	34.47	1.42%
Telecom (TE)	6,529.43	6,755.79	(226.36)	-3.35%
Pharma (PH)	6,081.32	6,017.20	64.12	1.07%
Metal (MT)	6,064.16	9,323.91	(3,259.75)	-34.96%
Construction (CO)	3,014.32	3,027.93	(13.61)	-0.45%

The impact on EBIDTA for the six-month ended 30 September 2015 is presented below through bar-diagram:

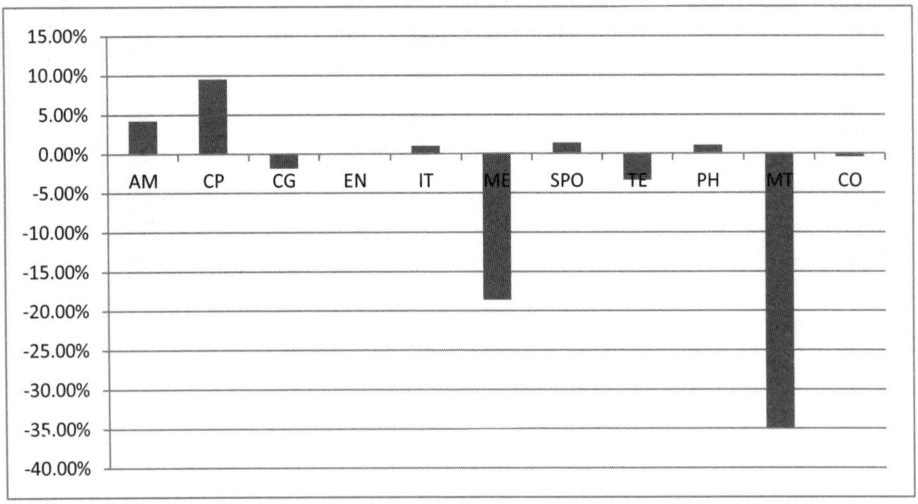

Out of 31 companies taken for analysis, for the quarter and six-month ended 30 September 2015, 21 companies have shown a rise in EBIDTA and 10 companies have shown a decline in EBIDTA. Likewise, 7 industries and 4 industries have shown a rise and decline in EBIDTA respectively for the aforesaid periods.

The change in EBIDTA in general can be attributed to changes in accounting for revenues, financial instruments, employee benefits etc.

Finance Cost for the quarter ended 30 September 2015

Industrial sector	Finance Cost as per Ind AS	Finance Cost as per previous GAAP	Increase/(decrease) in Finance Cost	% change in finance cost
Automobile (AM)	432.33	422.58	9.75	2.31%
Cement & Cement Products (CP)	172.00	144.05	27.95	19.40%
Consumer Goods (CG)	19.36	14.86	4.50	30.28%
Energy (EN)	3,341.50	2,821.10	520.40	18.45%
IT (IT)	201.80	157.24	44.56	28.34%
Media & Entertainment (ME)	6.27	0.09	6.18	6866.67%
Services - Port Operator (SPO)	259.85	264.38	(4.53)	-1.71%
Telecom (TE)	0.43	284.67	(284.24)	-99.85%
Pharma (PH)	264.17	251.04	13.13	5.23%
Metal (MT)	1,060.75	947.23	113.52	11.98%
Construction (CO)	373.99	383.43	(9.44)	-2.46%

The impact on finance cost for the quarter ended 30 September 2015 is presented below through bar-diagram:

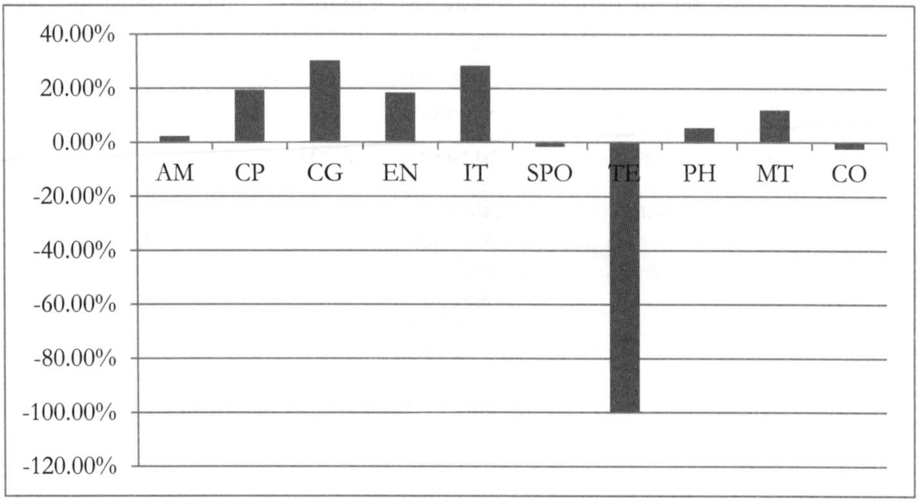

Finance Cost for the six-month ended 30 September 2015

Industrial sector	Finance Cost as per Ind AS	Finance Cost as per previous GAAP	Increase/ (decrease) in Finance Cost	% change in finance cost
Automobile (AM)	927.14	909.21	17.93	1.97%
Cement & Cement Products (CP)	352.87	296.09	56.78	19.18%
Consumer Goods (CG)	37.28	28.18	9.10	32.29%
Energy (EN)	6,384.01	5,424.68	959.33	17.68%
IT (IT)	346.91	300.51	46.40	15.44%
Media & Entertainment (ME)	12.55	0.20	12.35	6175.00%
Services - Port Operator (SPO)	489.71	482.46	7.25	1.50%
Telecom (TE)	349.20	661.13	(311.94)	-47.18%

Industrial sector	Finance Cost as per Ind AS	Finance Cost as per previous GAAP	Increase/ (decrease) in Finance Cost	% change in finance cost
Pharma (PH)	491.75	464.43	27.32	5.88%
Metal (MT)	2,172.17	1,944.88	227.29	11.69%
Construction (CO)	689.43	670.58	18.85	2.81%

The impact on finance cost for the six-month ended 30 September 2015 is presented below through bar-diagram:

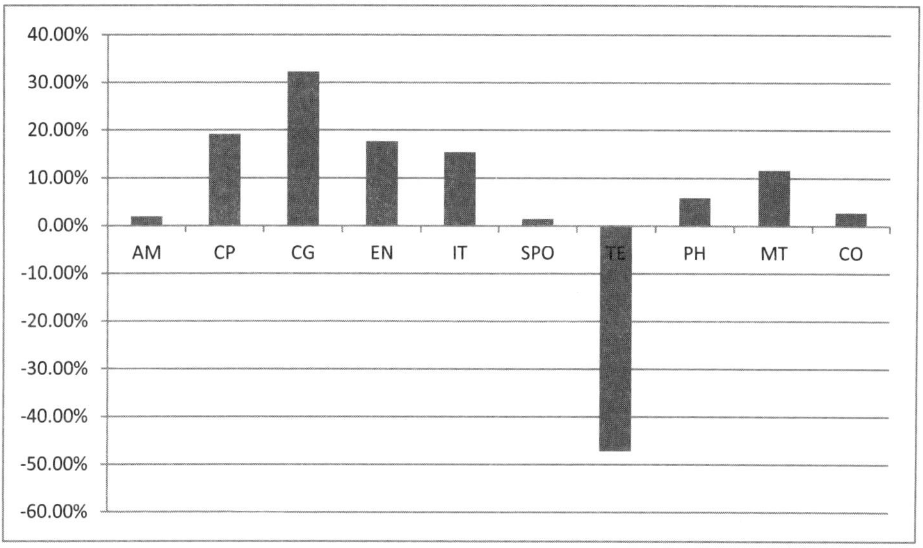

Out of 31 companies taken for analysis, for the quarter ended 30 September 2015, 21 companies have shown a rise in finance cost, 5 companies have shown a decline in finance cost and other 5 companies have shown no change in finance cost. Likewise, 8 industrial sectors and 3 industrial sectors have shown a rise and decline in finance cost respectively for the aforesaid quarter. Similarly, for the six-month ended 30 September 2015, 23 companies have shown a rise in finance cost, 4 companies have shown a decline in finance cost and other 4 companies have shown no change in finance cost. Likewise, 10 industrial sectors and 1 industrial sector have shown a rise and decline in finance cost respectively for the aforesaid six-month period.

The increase in finance cost is generally due to Ind AS 109 on financial instruments which requires various instruments to be classified as debt and also requires recognition of all related finance costs through statement of profit and loss.

Note: *The analysis excludes "Media & Entertainment" industrial sector for presentation in the bar-diagram representing percentage change in finance cost, since percentage change in finance cost for the aforesaid sector is huge as compared to % change for other industrial sectors.*

Tax expense for the quarter ended 30 September 2015

Industry	Tax expense as per Ind AS	Tax expense as per previous GAAP	Increase/(decrease) in Tax expense	% change in tax expense
Automobile (AM)	1,768.23	1,713.62	54.61	3.19%
Cement & Cement Products (CP)	259.97	230.24	29.73	12.91%
Consumer Goods (CG)	1,870.86	1,874.21	(3.35)	-0.18%
Energy (EN)	3,909.68	3,891.08	18.60	0.48%
IT (IT)	2,505.42	2,503.28	2.14	0.09%
Media & Entertainment (ME)	102.09	101.63	0.46	0.45%
Services - Port Operator (SPO)	20.29	18.03	2.26	12.53%
Telecom (TE)	598.90	547.88	51.02	9.31%
Pharma (PH)	435.29	569.29	(134.00)	-23.54%
Metal (MT)	(123.37)	142.83	(266.20)	-186.38%
Construction (CO)	259.47	220.25	39.22	17.81%

The impact on tax expense for the quarter ended 30 September 2015 is presented below through bar-diagram:

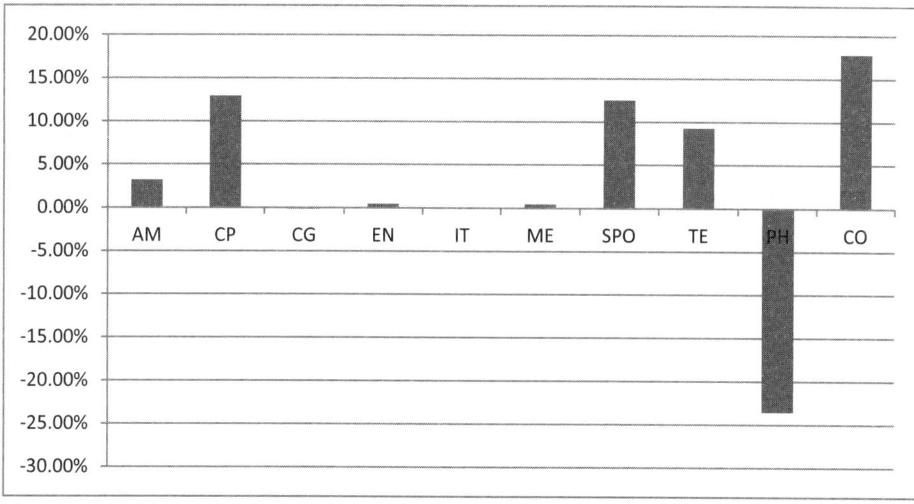

Tax expense for the six-month ended 30 September 2015

Industrial sector	Tax expense as per Ind AS	Tax expense as per previous GAAP	Increase/ (decrease) in tax expense	% change in tax expense
Automobile (AM)	3,461.21	3,452.19	9.02	0.26%
Cement & Cement Products (CP)	554.97	509.62	45.35	8.90%
Consumer Goods (CG)	3,730.34	3,725.55	4.79	0.13%
Energy (EN)	8,797.66	8,889.14	(91.48)	-1.03%
IT (IT)	4,751.83	4,725.88	25.95	0.55%
Media & Entertainment (ME)	205.70	204.80	0.90	0.44%
Services - Port Operator (SPO)	37.90	28.66	9.24	32.24%
Telecom (TE)	1,189.29	1,175.15	14.14	1.20%
Pharma (PH)	1,133.41	1,257.35	(123.94)	-9.86%

Industrial sector	Tax expense as per Ind AS	Tax expense as per previous GAAP	Increase/ (decrease) in tax expense	% change in tax expense
Metal (MT)	147.19	604.31	(457.12)	-75.64%
Construction (CO)	485.77	513.85	(28.08)	-5.46%

The impact on tax expense for the six-month ended 30 September 2015 is presented below through bar-diagram:

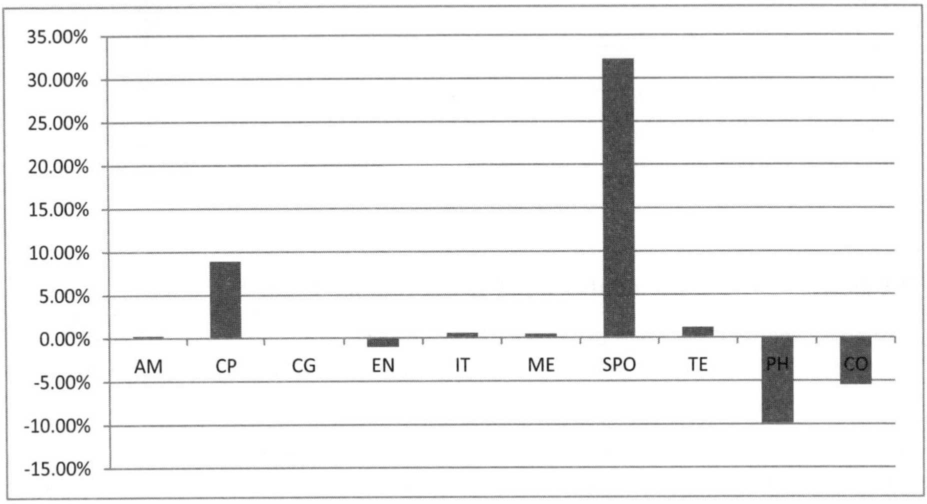

Out of 31 companies taken for analysis, for the quarter and six-month ended 30 September 2015, 19 companies have shown a rise in tax expense and 12 companies have shown a decline in tax expense. Likewise, 8 industrial sectors and 3 industrial sectors have shown a rise and decline in tax expense respectively for the aforesaid periods.

The analysis shows that the change in tax expense is minimal for most of the companies except a few. The change can be generally attributed to reconciling items on transition to Ind AS and deferred tax implications on those items.

Note: The analysis excludes "Metal" industrial sector for presentation in the bar-diagram representing percentage change in tax expense, since percentage change in tax expense for the aforesaid sector is huge as compared to % change for other industrial sectors.

PAT for the quarter ended 30 September 2015

Industrial sectors	PAT as per Ind AS	PAT as per previous GAAP	Increase/(decrease) in PAT	% Change in PAT
Automobile (AM)	4,354.80	3,872.15	482.65	12.46%
Cement & Cement Products (CP)	838.95	732.13	106.82	14.59%
Consumer Goods (CG)	3,615.42	3,757.97	(142.55)	-3.79%
Energy (EN)	16,003.07	16,189.85	(186.78)	-1.15%
IT (IT)	8,859.10	8,797.62	61.48	0.70%
Media & Entertainment (ME)	129.75	195.04	(65.29)	-33.48%
Services - Port Operator (SPO)	1,059.51	1,036.96	22.55	2.17%
Telecom (TE)	1,104.09	1,015.40	88.69	8.73%
Pharma (PH)	1,442.03	1,287.47	154.56	12.00%
Metal (MT)	(165.02)	2,626.19	(2,791.21)	-106.28%
Construction (CO)	1,244.01	1,188.42	55.59	4.68%

The impact on PAT for the quarter ended 30 September 2015 is presented below through bar-diagram:

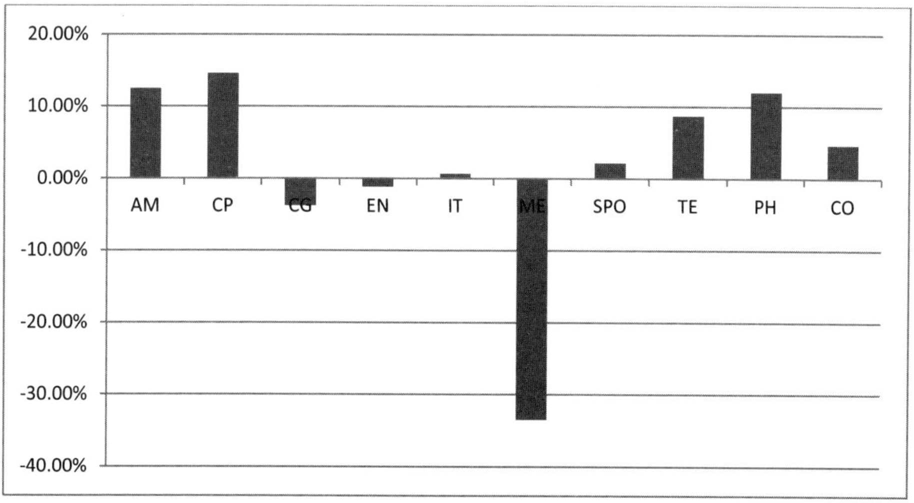

PAT for the six-month ended 30 September 2015

Industrial sectors	PAT as per Ind AS	PAT as per previous GAAP	Increase/ (decrease) in PAT	% change in PAT
Automobile (AM)	8,783.36	8,283.72	499.64	6.03%
Cement & Cement Products (CP)	1,577.47	1,428.69	148.78	10.41%
Consumer Goods (CG)	7,278.21	7,510.36	(232.15)	-3.09%
Energy (EN)	31,753.07	31,893.75	(140.68)	-0.44%
IT (IT)	17,358.20	17,177.48	180.72	1.05%
Media & Entertainment (ME)	267.43	398.63	(131.20)	-32.91%
Services - Port Operator (SPO)	1,675.42	1,656.03	19.39	1.17%
Telecom (TE)	2,186.91	2,174.23	12.68	0.58%
Pharma (PH)	3,334.10	3,172.21	161.89	5.10%
Metal (MT)	321.42	3,981.99	(3,660.57)	-91.93%
Construction (CO)	1,807.23	1,889.39	(82.16)	-4.35%

The impact in PAT for the six-month ended 30 September 2015 is presented below through bar-diagram:

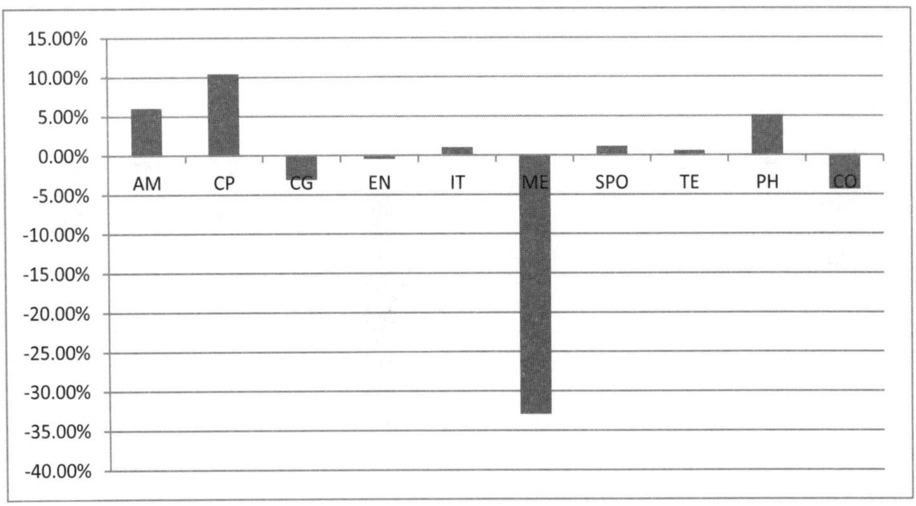

Out of 31 companies taken for analysis, for the quarter ended 30 September 2015, 21 companies have shown a rise in PAT and 10 companies have shown a decline in

PAT. Likewise, 7 industrial sectors and 4 industrial sectors have shown a rise and decline for the aforesaid quarter. Similarly, for the six-month ended 30 September 2015, 19 companies have shown a rise in PAT and 12 companies have shown a decline in PAT. Likewise, 6 industrial sectors and 5 industrial sectors have shown a rise and decline in PAT respectively for the aforesaid six-month period.

On analysis of profit reconciliation, the change in PAT can be attributed mainly to the financial instrument standard for many companies. Other standards which have also contributed to change in PAT include revenue; property, plant and equipment, employee benefits; share-based payment etc.

Note: *The analysis excludes "Metal" industrial sector for presentation in the bar-diagram representing percentage change in PAT, since percentage change in PAT for the aforesaid sector is huge as compared to % change for other industrial sectors.*

Glossary:

Revenue includes other operating income.

EBITDA = Profit before finance cost + Depreciation and amortisation expense

Observations on the financial results published by the companies taken for analysis for the quarter and six-month ended 30 September 2016

(1) Many companies have only given the bare minimum information and have availed all the exemptions granted by SEBI on transition to Ind AS.

(2) Some companies have given the comparative Ind AS compliant balance sheet as at both 31 March 2016 and the date of transition i.e. as at 1 April 2015. Some other companies have only given the comparative Ind AS balance sheet as at 31 March 2016. Other companies have not given the comparative Ind AS balance sheet and have availed the exemption pursuant to the circular dated 5 July 2016 issued by SEBI.

(3) Few companies have provided equity reconciliation and other companies have not provided equity reconciliations.

(4) Most of the companies have presented audited/reviewed Ind AS compliant comparative figures. However, some companies have presented the Ind AS compliant comparative figures which were not reviewed/audited.

Chapter 9

Ind AS results for debt listed companies

With the purpose of providing clarifications and relaxations to listed entities which have listed their debt securities and/or non-cumulative redeemable preference shares ('listed entities') in respect of reporting of financial results, SEBI issued another circular[1] on 10 August 2016. The circular provides similar clarifications and relaxations, as provided in circular dated 5 July 2016 for listed entities publishing financial results under reg 33, for submission of Ind AS compliant half-yearly financial results under reg 52 of the Listing Regulations by the listed entities.

9.1 CLARIFICATIONS AND RELAXATIONS PROVIDED BY THE CIRCULAR DATED 10 AUGUST 2016

9.1.1 For all listed entities (whether Ind AS is applicable or not)

9.1.1.1 Formats for disclosure of half-yearly and annual financial results

- **For period ending on or before 31 December 2016** - Use existing formats prescribed in SEBI circular dated 27 November 2015.
- **For the period ending after 31 December 2016**
  - The formats for balance sheet and statement of profit and loss (excluding notes and detailed sub-classification) as prescribed in Schedule III to the 2013 Act.
  - Banking Companies and Insurance Companies: The formats as prescribed under their respective Acts/Regulations as specified by their Regulators.

The listed entities are required to comply with the Companies (Accounting Standards) Rules, 2006 until Ind AS become applicable to them.

[1] Refer **Annexure-I** at the end of this chapter for the Circular.

9.1.1.2 Periods which are required to be disclosed

For the statement of profit and loss, the figures for the following periods shall be disclosed:

Particulars	6 months (Current 6 months) ended (dd/mm/yyyy)	6 months (Corresponding 6 months in the previous year) ended (dd/mm/yyyy)	Year to Date figures ended (dd/mm/yyyy)	Previous year ended (dd/mm/yyyy)
	Audited/ Unaudited*	Audited/Unaudited*	Audited/ Unaudited*	Audited/ Unaudited*

For the balance sheet, the figures for the following periods shall be disclosed:

Particulars	As at (current half year end/year end date) (dd/mm/yyyy)	As at (previous year end date) (dd/mm/yyyy)
	Audited/Unaudited*	Audited

* Whether the figures are audited or unaudited needs to be clearly specified.

9.1.1.3 Formats for publication of financial results in the newspapers

Regulation 52(8) of the Listing Regulations requires the listed entities to publish the financial results within two calendar days of the conclusion of the meeting of the Board of Directors in at least one English national daily newspaper.

This circular provides such format for publishing the financial results in the newspapers circulating in the whole or substantially the whole of India.

9.1.2 For all listed companies where Ind AS is applicable

9.1.2.1 Relaxations

If the half-yearly/annual financial results are prepared adopting Ind AS, the comparative financial results also need to be Ind AS compliant.

The following relaxations have been provided for the first half year of the adoption of Ind AS:

(i) **Timeline for submitting the financial results**

- extended by one month
- therefore, can be submitted within 75 days from the end of the half year

(ii) **Relaxations in respect of comparative financial results**

For the corresponding half year in the preceding year

- Limited review/audit - **Not mandatory**

  For the preceding full year

- Submission of financial results - **Not mandatory**
- If the listed entity opts to submit - Limited review/audit is **not mandatory**

Where the comparative half-yearly results/comparative full year results are not subjected to limited review or audit

- Disclose that the comparative results have not been subjected to limited review or audit
- Disclose that the management has exercised necessary due diligence to ensure that the said comparative results provide a true and fair view of its affairs.

9.1.2.2 Other clarifications

(i) Reconciliation of equity and net profit/loss

Reconciliation of equity	Reconciliation of net profit/loss
• For the previous year (i.e. for the year immediately before Ind AS adoption), to be provided while submitting the annual financial results for the first year of adoption. • If the listed entity opts to submit comparative full year results along with the financial results for the first half year of the adoption of Ind AS, then such Reconciliation of Equity for the previous year is required to be provided while submitting the aforesaid half-yearly financial results also.	• To be provided only for the corresponding half year in the preceding year.

Thus, listed entity preparing financial statements under Ind AS in the first year of adoption are not required to present the following reconciliations as required by Ind AS 101, *First-time Adoption of Indian Accounting Standards*:

- a reconciliation of equity under previous GAAP to equity under Ind AS at the date of transition to Ind AS;
- a reconciliation of profit or loss under previous GAAP with total comprehensive income in accordance with Ind AS for the comparative annual period ended 31 March 2016;
- explanation of the material adjustments to the statement of cash flows;

- if errors were made under previous GAAP, the distinguishment of correction of those errors from changes in accounting policies.

(ii) If financial statements are prepared for a period different from the normal 12 month period

- The financial results may have comparative information for a shorter or longer period;
- Disclose a suitable note that comparative figures presented in the half-yearly/annual financial results are not entirely comparable.

(iii) If the listed entity faces technical difficulty in disclosure of any specific item in the formats or implementation of the circular

The listed entities should take guidance from relevant provisions of the Ind AS Rules/AS Rules, Schedule III to the 2013 Act and pertinent provisions/guidelines under the relevant Act/Statute under which the listed entity was created, and may make suitable modifications, as applicable. The listed entities should also provide suitable explanations and clarifications, wherever felt necessary.

Annexure-II at the end of this chapter contains the financial results of few companies which have listed their debt securities.

Annexures

Annexure I: SEBI Circular dated 10 August 2016 providing revised formats for financial results

CIR/IMD/DF1/69/2016 August 10, 2016

To

All Listed Entities

All Recognized Stock Exchanges

Dear Sir/Madam,

Sub: Revised Formats for Financial Results and Implementation of Ind AS by listed entities which have listed their debt securities and/or non-cumulative redeemable preference shares

1. SEBI vide Circular No. CIR/IMD/DF1/9/2015 dated November 27, 2015, had prescribed formats for publishing financial results for the entities which have listed their debt securities and/or non-cumulative redeemable preference shares ('**listed entities**').

2. In continuation to SEBI Circular No. "CIR/CFD/FAC/62/2016" dated July 05, 2016, the listed entities are advised to comply with the following:

   Formats for disclosure of financial results:

   2.1. This has reference to the disclosure of half yearly and annual financial results in terms of Regulation 52 (1) of the SEBI (Listing Obligations and Disclosure Requirements) Regulations, 2015 (**'Listing Regulations'**).

   2.2. The existing formats prescribed in SEBI Circular dated November 27, 2015, for disclosure of half yearly and annual financial results, shall continue till the period ending on or before December 31, 2016.

   2.3. For the period ending after December 31, 2016, the disclosure of half yearly and annual financial results, i.e. the Balance Sheet and the Statement of Profit and Loss, shall be as per the formats for Balance Sheet and Statement of Profit and Loss (excluding notes and detailed sub-classification) as prescribed in Schedule III to the Companies Act, 2013. However, Banking Companies and Insurance Companies shall follow the formats as prescribed under their respective Acts/Regulations as specified by their Regulators.

2.4. Until Companies (Indian Accounting Standards) Rules, 2015 ('**Ind AS Rules**') become applicable for a listed entity, the listed entity shall adopt Companies (Accounting Standards) Rules, 2006 ('**AS Rules**') as prescribed by the Ministry of Corporate Affairs ('**MCA**').

2.5. While publishing the financial results as per Paragraph 2.3 above, the listed entities shall disclose the figures relating to the periods as mentioned below:

2.5.1. For the Statement of Profit and Loss, the figures for the following periods shall be disclosed:

Particulars	6 months (Current 6 months) ended (dd/mm/yyyy)	6 months (Corresponding 6 months in the previous year) ended (dd/mm/yyyy)	Year to Date figures ended (dd/mm/yyyy)	Previous year ended (dd/mm/yyyy)
	Audited/ Unaudited*	Audited/ Unaudited*	Audited/Unaudited*	Audited

* Clearly specify whether the figures are audited or unaudited

2.5.2. For the Balance Sheet, the figures for the following periods shall be disclosed:

Particulars	As at (current half year end/year end date) (dd/mm/yyyy)	As at (Previous year end date) (dd/mm/yyyy)
	Audited/Unaudited*	Audited

* Clearly specify whether the figures are audited or unaudited

Formats for publication of financial results:

2.6. The financial results to be published in the newspapers, in terms of Regulation 52 (8) of the Listing Regulations, shall be in the format as prescribed in **Annexure I**.

Implementation of Ind AS:

2.7. Listed entities, adopting the Indian Accounting Standards (hereinafter referred as '**Ind AS**') in terms of Ind AS Rules, while publishing the half yearly/annual financial results under Regulation 52 (1) of the Listing Regulations, shall ensure that the comparative financial results, filed along with the said half yearly/annual financial results, are also Ind AS compliant.

2.8. In order to facilitate smooth transition, the following *relaxations* are being given *for the first half year of the adoption of Ind AS*:

(i) The timeline for submitting the said financial results would be extended by one month (i.e. the said half yearly financial results can be submitted within 75 days from the end of the half year).

(ii) With regard to the comparative financial results for the corresponding half year in the preceding year, the limited review or audit of such comparative half yearly results is not mandatory.

(iii) With regard to the comparative financial results for the preceding full year, the submission of such comparative full year results is not mandatory. However, if the listed entity opts to submit such comparative full year results, then limited review or audit of such comparative full year results is not mandatory

In the aforementioned cases wherein the comparative half yearly results and/or comparative full year results are not subjected to limited review or audit, the listed entity shall disclose with due prominence that the said comparative results have not been subjected to limited review or audit. The listed entity shall further disclose that the management has exercised necessary due diligence to ensure that the said comparative results provide a true and fair view of its affairs.

Clarifications with regard to implementation of Ind AS and other issues:

2.9. The listed entities in order to comply with the requirements of paragraph 32 of Ind AS 101 - 'First time Adoption of Ind AS', shall provide a reconciliation of its equity and net profit/loss, in the following manner, for enabling the investors to understand the material adjustments to the Balance Sheet and Statement of Profit and Loss on account of transition from the previous Indian GAAP to Ind AS:

(i) Reconciliation of Equity for the previous year (i.e. for the year immediately before Ind AS adoption), shall be provided while submitting the annual financial results for the first year of adoption.

Further, if the listed entity opts to submit comparative full year results along with the financial results for the first half year of the adoption of Ind AS in terms of Paragraph 2.8 (iii) above, then such Reconciliation of Equity for the previous year shall be provided while submitting the aforesaid half yearly financial results also.

(ii) Reconciliation of net profit/loss shall be provided only for the corresponding half year in the preceding year.

2.10. In some circumstances, a listed entity may prepare financial statements for a period different from the normal 12 month period (For instance, a listed company may now be required to prepare financial statements for a period different from the normal 12 month period for coinciding with 31st day of March as prescribed under Section 2(41) of the Companies Act, 2013).

In the aforementioned circumstances, the financial results may have comparative information for a shorter or longer period. The listed entity, in such cases, shall disclose a suitable note, with due prominence, that comparative figures presented in the half-yearly/annual financial results are not entirely comparable because of the above reasons.

2.11. In case of any technical difficulty in disclosure of any specific item in the formats or implementation of this circular while publishing the financial results, the listed entities, shall be guided by the relevant provisions of the Ind AS Rules/AS Rules, Schedule III to the Companies Act, 2013 and pertinent provisions/guidelines under the relevant Act/Statute under which the listed entity was created, and may make suitable modifications, as applicable. The listed entities shall also provide suitable explanations and clarifications, wherever felt necessary.

3. This Circular shall come into force with immediate effect and the contents of the Circular No. CIR/IMD/DF1/9/2015 dated November 27, 2015, shall stand modified to the extent stated under this Circular.

4. The Stock Exchanges are advised to bring the provisions of this circular to the notice of listed entities and also to disseminate the same on its website.

5. This Circular is being issued in exercise of powers conferred under Section 11 and Section 11A of the SEBI Act, 1992 read with Regulation 52, Regulation 101 (2) and Regulation 102 of the Listing Regulations.

6. This circular is available on SEBI website at http://www.sebi.gov.in under the category "Circulars".

Yours faithfully,

Richa Goel Agarwal Deputy General Manager

Investment Management Department

richag@sebi.gov.in

Annexure I

Format for publishing financial results in newspapers

[Regulation 52(8), read with Regulation 52(4), of the SEBI (LODR) Regulations, 2015]

Sl. No.	Particulars	Half year ending/ Current Year ended	Corresponding half year ended in the previous year (Applicable only in case of half yearly results)	Previous year ended
1.	Total Income from Operations			
2.	Net Profit/(Loss) for the period (before Tax, Exceptional and/or Extraordinary items#)			
3.	Net Profit/(Loss) for the period before tax (after Exceptional and/or Extraordinary items#)			
4.	Net Profit/(Loss) for the period after tax (after Exceptional and/or Extraordinary items#)			
5.	Total Comprehensive Income for the period [Comprising Profit/(Loss) for the period (after tax) and Other Comprehensive Income (after tax)]			
6.	Paid up Equity Share Capital			
7.	Reserves (excluding Revaluation Reserve)			
8	Net worth			
9	Paid up Debt Capital/Outstanding Debt			
10	Outstanding Redeemable Preference Shares *			

Sl. No.	Particulars	Half year ending/ Current Year ended	Corresponding half year ended in the previous year (Applicable only in case of half yearly results)	Previous year ended
11.	Debt Equity Ratio *			
12.	Earnings Per Share (of Rs. ___/- each) (for continuing and discontinued operations) - 1. Basic: 2. Diluted:			
13.	Capital Redemption Reserve *			
14.	Debenture Redemption Reserve *			
15.	Debt Service Coverage Ratio *			
16.	Interest Service Coverage Ratio *			

Note:

(a) The above is an extract of the detailed format of half yearly/annual financial results filed with the Stock Exchanges under Regulation 52 of the SEBI (Listing and Other Disclosure Requirements) Regulations, 2015. The full format of the half yearly/annual financial results are available on the websites of the Stock Exchange(s) and the listed entity. (URL of the filings).

(b) For the items referred in sub-clauses (a), (b), (d) and (e) of the Regulation 52 (4) of the SEBI (Listing and Other Disclosure Requirements) Regulations, 2015, the pertinent disclosures have been made to the Stock Exchange(s) (specify names of Stock Exchanges) and can be accessed on the URL (specify URL).

(c) The impact on net profit/loss, total comprehensive income or any other relevant financial item(s) due to change(s) in accounting policies shall be disclosed by means of a footnote.

(d) # - Exceptional and/or Extraordinary items adjusted in the Statement of Profit and Loss in accordance with Ind AS Rules/AS Rules, whichever is applicable.

e) * - The pertinent items need to be disclosed if the said disclosure is required as per Regulation 52 (4) of the SEBI (Listing and Other Disclosure Requirements) Regulations, 2015.

Annexure II: Financial results of few companies with listed debt securities

A. RELIANCE HOME FINANCE LIMITED

STATEMENT OF UNAUDITED FINANCIAL RESULTS FOR THE SIX MONTHS ENDED SEPTEMBER 30, 2016

(Rs.in Lacs)

Particulars	Six Months Ended		Year to Date Figures for Six Months Period Ended	Year Ended
	30-Sep-16	30-Sep-15	30-Sep-16	31-Mar-16
	Unaudited	Unaudited	Unaudited	Audited
1. Interest Earned (a+b+c+d)	44,882	34,967	44,882	73,739
(a) Interest on Housing & Other Loans	43,615	34,629	43,615	72,690
(b) Income on investments	938	147	938	669
(c) Interest on balances with Reserve Bank of India and other inter bank funds	-	-	-	-
(d) Others	329	191	329	380
2. Other Income	5,280	3,348	5,280	7,764
3. Total Income (1+2)	50,162	38,315	50,162	81,503
4. Interest Expended	29,438	25,159	29,438	47,457
5. Operating Expenses (i)+(ii)+(iii)+(iv)+(v)	13,076	5,729	13,076	19,165
(i) Employees cost	3,520	2,998	3,520	7,102
(ii) Marketing cost	805	640	805	1,366
(iii) Amortised DSA Commission	571	478	571	1,060
(iv) Legal and Professional fees	1,060	580	1,060	991
(v) Other operating expenses	7,120	1,033	7,120	8,646
6. Total Expenditure (4+5) excluding provisions and contingencies	42,514	30,888	42,514	66,622
7. Operating Profit before Provisions and Contingencies (3-6)	7,648	7,427	7,648	14,880
8. Provisions (other than tax) and Contingencies	1,463	544	1,463	1,211
9. Exceptional Items	-	_	-	-
10. Profit (+)/ Loss (-) from Ordinary Activities before tax (7-8-9)	6,185	6,883	6,185	13,669
11. Tax expense (Including Deferred Tax)	2,000	2,393	2,000	4,995
12. Net Profit(+)/ Loss(-) from Ordinary Activities	4,185	4,490	4,185	8,674

Particulars	Six Months Ended		Year to Date Figures for Six Months Period Ended	Year Ended
	30-Sep-16	30-Sep-15	30-Sep-l6	31-Mar-16
	Unaudited	Unaudited	Unaudited	Audited
after tax (10-11)				
13. Extraordinary items (net of tax expense)	-	-	-	-
14. Net Profit (+)/ Loss (-) for the period (12-13)	4,185	4,490	4,185	8,674
15. Paid-up equity share capital (face value of Rs.10/-)	6,582	6,582	6,582	6,582
16. Reserves excluding Revaluation Reserves (As per Balance Sheet of previous accounting year)				55,430
17. Analytical Ratios				
(i) Capital Adequacy Ratio	14.08%	16.52%	14.08%	16.34%
(ii) Earnings Per Share (EPS)(Not Annualised) (In Rupees)	6.36	6.82	6.36	13.18
18) NPA Ratios				
a) Gross/Net NPA				
(i) Gross NPA	11,673	5,979	11,673	6,561
(ii) Net NPA	9,289	4,647	9,289	5,010
b) % of Gross/Net NPA				
(i) % of Gross NPA/ Gross Loans & Advances	1.48%	1.01%	1.48%	0.97%
(ii) % of Net NPA/ Net Loans & Advances	1.18%	0.79%	1.18%	0.74%
c) Return on Assets (Not Annualised) [PBT/Total Assets]	0.68%	1.07%	0.68%	1.78%

Notes:

1. The previous period/year's figures have been regrouped and reclassified wherever necessary.
2. The Company is mainly engaged in the housing finance business and all other activities revolve around the main business of the Company. Further all activities are conducted within India and as such there is no separate reportable segment as specified in Accounting Standard (AS-17) on "Segment Reporting", in terms of Companies (Accounts) Rules, 2014.
3. The above results were reviewed by the Audit Committee. The Board of Directors at its meeting held on October 22, 2016 approved the above results and its release.

4. The financial results for the six months' period ended September 30, 2016 of the company have been subjected to a "Limited Review" by the Statutory Auditor of the Company.

5. The Board of Directors of the Company at its Meeting held on June 20, 2016 has considered and approved a Scheme of Arrangement ("the Scheme") under Sections 391 to 394 of the Companies Act, 1956 ("the Scheme") between India Debt Management Private Limited ("Demerged Company") and the Company. As per the Scheme, credit business of the demerged company would be transferred to the Company from the Appointed Date.

   The Appointed Date for the Scheme is March 31, 2016. The Scheme is subject to requisite approvals, including sanction of the Hon'ble High Court of Judicature of Bombay.

6. The Board of Directors of the Company at their meeting held on September 13, 2016 have decided, subject to regulatory approvals, to list the equity shares of the Company on the Stock Exchanges and to allot 49% stake in the Company to shareholders of Reliance Capital Limited in the ratio of 1:1.

7. Secured Non-convertible Debentures amounting to Rs. 86,700 lacs are secured by way of first pari passu legal mortgage and charge over the premises situated at Bharuch and additional pari passu charge by way of hypothecation on the present and future books debts/receivables, outstanding money (loan book), receivable claims of the Company with other secured lenders, except those book debts and receivables charged/ to be charged in favour of National Housing Bank for refinance availed/ to be availed from them, of Home Finance Business subject to maintenance of minimum asset coverage of 100% of issue amount.

8. Additional information as per Para 52 (3) of Chapter V of SEBI (Listing Obligations and Disclosure Requirements) Regulations, 2015

(a) Credit rating

Nature of Rating	Rating
Long Term Secured NCD Issue	BWR AA+
Subordinated Tier II Unsecured NCD	BWR AA+
Subordinated Debt	CARE AA
Principal Protected Market linked Debentures	CARE PP-MLD AA+

(b) Debt-Equity ratio as on September 30, 2016 13:19

(c) Debenture redemption reserve Nil

As the Company is registered with National Housing Bank as a Housing Finance Company under Section 29A of the National Housing Bank Act, 1987, no DRR is required in place of privately placed debentures in terms of Rule 18(7)(b)(ii) of Companies (Share Capital and Debentures) Rules, 2014

(d) Net worth as on September 30, 2016 Rs. 60,092 lacs

(e) Details of listed debentures

(*Rs, in Lacs*)

ISIN	Previous Due Dates for payment of #		Next Due Date for payment of			
	Interest	**Principal**	**Interest Due Date**	**Interest Amount**	**Principal Due Date**	**Principal Amount**
INE217K07026	26-May-16	-	26-Nov-16	102	-	-
INE217K07034	ll-Jun-16	-	ll-Dec-16	5	-	-
INE217K07042	3-Jul-l 6		3-Jan-17	76	.	-
INE217K07059	8-Jul-16	_	8-Jan-17	126	-	-
INE217K07083	4-Apr-16	4-Apr-1.6	-		-	-
INE217K07117	27-Apr~16	-	27-Oct-I6	5	-	-
INE217K07125	29-Apr-16	-	-	-	-	-
INE217K07141	3-Jun-16	-	-	-		-
INE217K07158	4-Jun-16	-	4-Dec-16	23	-	-
INE217K07166	7-Jun-16	-	-	-	-	-
INE217K07174	10-Jun-16		-	-	-	-
1NE217K07182	13-Jun-16			-	-	-
INE217K07190	19-Jun-16		-		-	-
INE217K07208	5-JuM6	-	5-Jan-17	118	-	-
INE217K07208	5-Jul-16	-	5-Jan-17	24		-
INE217K07216	26-Jul-16	-	26-Jan-17	72	-	-
INE21.7K07224	22-Aug-16	22-Aug-16	-	_	-	-
INE21.7K07232	31-JuM6	-	31-Jan-17	75	31-Jan-17	1,500
INE217K07240	28-Sep-16	-	28-Mar-17	8	-	-
INE217K07257	15-May-16	-	15-Nov-16	74		-
INE217K07273	19-Jun-16	-	-	-	-	-
INE217K07265	27-jun-16	-		-	-	-
INE217K07281	-	-	1.6-Oct-16	98	-	-
INE217K07315	26-Sep-16	-	26-Mar-17	67	-	-
INE217K07323	-	-	27-Mar-17	182	-	-
INE217K07349	-	-	3-Oct-16	13	3-Oct-16	315
INE217K07380	-	-	27-Jan-17	48	27-Jan-17	325
INE217K07430	22-Sep-16	-	22-Mar-17	68	-	-
INE217K07497	28-Apr-16	-	28-Oct-16	88	-	-
INE217K07505	-	-	21-Mar-17	91	21-Mar-17	7,500
INE217K07521	-	-	15-Dec-16	221	-	-
INE217K07646	-	-	8-Mar-17	450	-	-
INE217K07661		-	16-Mar-17	90	-	-
INE217K07737	-	-	ll-Oct-16	177	-	.
INE217K07752		-	26-Oct-16	110	-	-
INE217K07778	-	-	6-Nov-16	67	-	-
INE217K07828	-	-	24-Dec-16	110		-

ISIN	Previous Due Dates for payment of #		Next Due Date for payment of			
	Interest	Principal	Interest Due Date	Interest Amount	Principal Due Date	Principal Amount
INE217K07836	-	-	24-Dec-1.6	133	-	-
INE217K07869	.	-	20-Jar»-17	89	-	-
INE217K08016	18-Sep-16	-	-	-	-	-
INE217K08016	18-Sep-16	-	-	-	-	-
INE217K08024	21.-Sep-16	-		-	-	_
INE217K08032	24.-Sep-'16	-	-	-	-	-
INE217K08032	24-Sep-16	-		-	-	.
INE217K08040	18-Sep-16	-	-	-	-	-
INE217K08057	-		4-Oct-16	156	-	-
INE217K08065	10-Apr-16	-	10-Oct-16	104	-	-
INE217K08065	10-Apr-16	-	lO-Oct-1.6	52	-	-
INE217K08073	18-Apr-16	-	18-Oct-16	52	-	-
INE217K08081	26-May-16	-	26-NOV-16	26	-	-
INE217K08107	.	-	7-Feb-17	150	-	-
INE217K08115	14-May-1.6	-	-	-	-	-
INE217K08123	29-May-16	-	-	-	-	-
INE217K08131	9~Jun-16	-		-	-	-
INE217K08149	12-Jun-16	-	-	-	-	-
INE217K08156	15-Jun~16	-	-	-	-	-
INE217K08164	29-Jun-16	-	-	-	-	-
INE217K08172	l-Jul-16	-	-	-		-
INE217K08180	3-Jul-16	-	-	-		-
INE217K08198	21-Aug-16	-	-	-	-	-
INE217K08206	24-Au g-16	-	-	-	-	-
INE217K08214	15-Sep-16	-	-	-	-	-
INE217K08222	.		21-Jan-17	136	-	-
INE217K08230	_	-	10-Feb-17	27	-	-
INE217K07307	-	-	6-Feb-17	Market Linked Debentures	6-Feb-17	500
INE217K07448	-	-	28-Oct-16		28-Oct-16	105
INE217K07539	-	-	17-Mar-17		17-Mar-17	200

All payments have been made on the respective due dates

Place: Mumbai

Date: October 22, 2016

B. BRIGADE PROPERTIES PRIVATE LIMITED

Unaudited Financial results for the half-year ended September 30, 2016

(*Rs. in lakhs*)

	Particulars	6 months ended 30/09/2016 (Unaudited]	Corresponding 6 months ended in the previous year 30/09/2015 (Refer Note 7 below)	Year to date figures for the current period ended 30/09/2016 (Refer Note 7 below)	Previous accounting year ended 31/03/2016 (Refer Note 7 below)
1	**Income from operations**				
	(a) Sales/ income from operations	8,777	4,686	8,777	20,958
	(b) Other operating income	-		-	*
	Total income from Operations (net)	**8,777**	**4,686**	**8,777**	**20,958**
2	**Expenditure**				
	(a) (Increase)/ decrease in inventories of work-in-progress	1,803	(4,458)	1,803	(262)
	(b) Land purchase cost	-	1,381		1,393
	(c) Cost of project materials consumed	327	265	327	1,394
	(d) Sub-contracting charges	1,920	3,861	1,920	7,860
	(e) Employee cost	7	2	7	5
	(f) Depreciation and amortization expense	7	11	7	18
	(g) Other expenditure	668	1,012	668	1,708
	Total Expenses	**4,732**	**2,074**	**4,732**	**12,116**
3	**Profit from Operations before Other Income, Finance Cost and**	**4,045**	**2,612**	**4,045**	**8,842**
4	**Exceptional Items (1-2)**				
	Other income	260	169	260	400
5	**Profit before Finance Cost and Exceptional Items (3+4)**	**4,305**	**2,781**	**4,305**	**9,242**
6	Finance Costs	2,220	2,481	2,220	4,649
7	Exceptional items	-		-	
8	**Profit from ordinary activities before tax (S-6-7)**	**2,085**	**300**	**2,085**	**4,593**
9	Tax expense	699	81	699	1,563
10	**Profit from ordinary activities after tax (8-9)**	**1,386**	**219**	**1,386**	**3,030**
11	Extraordinary items (net of tax expenses)				

	Particulars	6 months ended 30/09/2016 (Unaudited]	Corresponding 6 months ended in the previous year 30/09/2015 (Refer Note 7 below)	Year to date figures for the current period ended 30/09/2016 (Refer Note 7 below)	Previous accounting year ended 31/03/2016 (Refer Note 7 below)
12	**Net profit for the period (10-11)**	**1,386**	**219**	**1,386**	**3,030**
13	Paid-up equity share capital (Face value per share - Rs. 10)	214	214	214	214
14	Paid-up debt capital (refer note 6)	20,727	25,242	20,727	19,491
15 16	Reserves excluding revaluation reserves as per balance sheet of previous accounting year Debenture redemption reserve	461	301	461	3,255 349
17	Earnings Per Share (EPS) - (in Rs.) (not annualised, face value Rs.10) a) Basic Class A equity shares				
	Class B equity shares	56.58	10.53	56.58	145.68
	Class C equity shares	79.43	10.98	79.43	151.92
	b) Diluted (refer note 4) Class A equity shares				
	Class B equity shares	3.20	0.55	3.20	7.09
	Class C equity shares	7.77	1.05	7.77	16.67
18	Debt equity ratio (refer note 5)	5.64	8.55	5.64	8.20
19	Debt service coverage ratio (DSCR) (refer note 5)	0.59	0.56	0.59	0.63
20	Interest service coverage ratio (ISCR) (refer note 5)	1.98	0.95	1.98	1.93

Notes to the financial results for the half year ended September 30, 2016:

1. Brigade Properties Private Limited ('the Company' or 'BPPL') had issued 490 A Series Non-Convertible Debentures (NCD) of Rs. 10,00,000 each on March 20, 2015 which were listed on BSE Limited ('BSE') on March 30, 2015

2. The above unaudited financial results of the Company for the half year ended September 30, 2016 have been reviewed by the Audit Committee and taken on record at the meeting of the Board of Directors of the Company held on October 27, 2016. The statutory auditors of the Company have carried out limited review of the above unaudited financial results of the Company for the half year ended September 30, 2016.

3. The company has adopted Indian Accounting Standards prescribed under section 133 of the Companies Act, 2013 ("Ind AS") from April 1, 2016 and all the periods presented in the accompanying financial results and other financial information have been prepared in accordance with recognition and measurement principles laid down in Ind AS and discloses information required to be disclosed in terms of Regulation 52 of SEBI (Listing Obligations and Disclosure Requirements) Regulations, 2015 (as amended).

The Company has also prepared a reconciliation of the net profit for the corresponding periods under the previously applicable General Accepted Accounting Principles ("previous GAAP") with the total comprehensive income as reported in these financial results under Ind AS. The net profit reconciliation for the half year ended September 30, 2015 and the year ended March 31, 2016 for the financial results are presented below:

(*Rs. in lakhs*)

Particular	**Half year ended 30/09/201S**	**Year ended 31/03/2016**
Net profit as per previous GAAP	363	3,031
Fair valuation of financial assets	11	27
Accounting for compound financial instruments	(229)	(29)
Tax expense impact of above adjustments	74	1
Net profit as per Ind AS (A)	219	3,030
Other comprehensive income	-	
Total (B)	-	-
Total comprehensive income (A+B)	219	3,030

The Company has also prepared a reconciliation of equity for the previous year under the previous GAAP with the equity as reported under IND AS. The equity reconciliation as at March 31, 2016, is presented below:

Particulars	**As at 31/03/2016**
Equity as per previous GAAP	**4,689**
1. Fair Valuation of financial assets (net of tax)	151
II. Accounting for compound financial instruments (net of tax)	(377)
Equity as per Ind-AS	**4,463**

4. In accordance with the Indian Accounting Standard (IND AS) - 33 Earnings Per Share, specified under Section 133 of the Companies Act 2013, read with relevant rules issued thereunder, there are certain class of securities which are anti-dilutive and hence the impact of those securities has been ignored in the computation of diluted EPS.

5. (a) DSCR represents profit/ loss from operations before interest expense (net of interest inventorised and charged to statement of profit and loss), exceptional items and tax expenses/ interest expense (gross of interest inventorised and charged to statement of profit and loss) plus principal repayment of loan funds during the period.

   (b) ISCR represents profit/ loss from operations before interest expense (net of interest inventorised and charged to statement of profit and loss), exceptional items and tax expenses/ interest expense (gross of interest inventorised and charged to statement of profit and loss).

(c) Debt equity ratio represents debt [long-term borrowings, short-term borrowings and current maturity of long-term borrowings and interest accrued (included in other financial liabilities)]/ equity [equity share capital + other equity (including retained earnings and debenture redemption reserve)].

6. Paid up debt capital represents outstanding non-convertible debentures, debt portion of compulsorily convertible debentures and debt portion of optionally convertible debentures issued by the Company and interest outstanding thereon (excluding short term borrowings).

7. The Ind AS financial results and other financial information for the half year ended September 30, 2015 and year ended March 31, 2016 have been compiled by the Company's management after making necessary adjustments to give a true and fair view of the results in accordance with Ind AS. This information has not been subject to any limited review or audit.

8. Figures pertaining to previous period have been regrouped or reclassified, wherever necessary, to conform to the classification adopted in the current period.

For and on behalf of the Board of Directors of

Brigade Properties Private Limited

K. Suresh

Director

Place : Bengaluru, India

Date : October 27, 2016

C. RELIANCE JIO INFOCOMM LIMITED UNAUDITED FINANCIAL RESULTS FOR HALF YEAR ENDED 30TH SEPTEMBER 2016

(Rs. in crore, except per share data)

Sr. No	Particulars	Six months ended 30.09.2016	Corresponding six months ended in the previous year 30.09.2015	Year to date figures for period ended 30.09.2016	Previous accounting year ended 31.03.2016
		Unaudited	**Unaudited**	**Unaudited**	**Unaudited**
1	Sales/Income from Operations	0.02	0.02	0.02	0.04
	Total	**0.02**	**0.02**	**0.02**	**0.04**
2	**Expenditure**				
(a)	License Fees, Network and Other Operating Expenses	1.37	0.80	1.37	1.64
(b)	Employee Cost	2.57	2.14	2.57	4.08
(c)	Depreciation and amortisation expense	2.39	2.15	2.39	4.33
(d)	Other Expenditure	7.36	7.53	7.36	15.66
	Total	13.69	12.62	13.69	25.71
3	**(Loss) from Operations before Other Income, Interest and Exceptional Items (1-2)**	**(13.67)**	**(12.60)**	**(13.67)**	**(25.67)**
4	Other Income	0.66	0.88	0.66	3.11
5	**(Loss) before Interest & Exceptional Items (3+4)**	**(13.01)**	**(11.72)**	**(13.01)**	**(22.56)**
6	Interest	0.56	0.89	0.56	1.43
7	Exceptional items	-	-	-	-
8	**(Loss) from Ordinary activities before tax (5)-(6+7)**	**(13.57)**	**(12.61)**	**(13.57)**	**(23.99)**
9	Tax expense	-	-	-	-
10	**Net (Loss) from ordinary activities after tax (8-9)**	**(13.57)**	**(12.61)**	**(13.57)**	**(23.99)**
11	Extraordinary Items (net of tax expense Rs.Nil)	-	-	-	-
12	**Net (Loss) for the period (10-11)**	**(13.57)**	**(12.61)**	**(13.57)**	**(23.99)**
13	Paid-up Equity Share Capital (Face value of the Equity	45,000.00	30,000.00	45,000.00	45,000.00

Sr. No	Particulars	Six months ended 30.09.2016	Corresponding six months ended in the previous year 30.09.2015	Year to date figures for period ended 30.09.2016	Previous accounting year ended 31.03.2016
		Unaudited	Unaudited	Unaudited	Unaudited
	Share Rs.10 each) Paid-up Preference Capital (Face value of the Preference	125.00	125.00	125.00	125.00
14	Share Rs.10 each) Paid-up Debt Capital	45,461.84	30,426.79	45,461.84	33,178.58
15	Reserves excluding Revaluation Reserves as per Balance	-	-	-	(74.69)
16	Sheet Debenture Redemption Reserve (Refer Note 9)	–	–	–	–
17	Earning Per Share (EPS) - Not annualised-(Rs.) (a) Basic	(0.003)	(0.004)	(0.003)	(0.01)
	(b) Diluted	(0.003)	(0.004)	(0.003)	(0.01)
18	Debt Equity Ratio (Refer Note 7)	1.01	1.01	1.01	0.74
19	Debt Service Coverage Ratio (Refer Note 8)	-	-	-	-
20	Interest Service Coverage Ratio (Refer Note 8)	-	-	-	-
21	Net worth	45,036.74	30,061.69	45,036.74	45,050.31

Notes:

1. Results for the half year ended 30th September, 2016 are in compliance with the Indian Accounting Standards (Ind AS) notified by the Ministry of Corporate Affairs. Results for the half year ended 30th September, 2015 and previous year ended 31st March, 2016 have been restated to comply with Ind AS to make them comparable.

2. In accordance with the conditions of the Unified License, the Company, on 1st September, 2016, intimated the Department of Telecommunication ("DoT") and Telecom Regulatory Authority of India ('TRAI"), regarding the commencement of wireless telecommunication services from 5th September, 2016. The Company also informed DoT and TRAI that the Company will not be charging its subscribers for domestic voice / messages and data usage till 31st December, 2016. The Company, in accordance with the Accounting Standards, will commence amortization / depreciation of the cost of the Project and will cease to capitalize the expenses on the Project when the assets are available for use in the manner as intended by the Management, i.e. when all the Quality of Service parameters set by the Management are met.

3. The DoT, Government of India conducted an auction for spectrum in the month of March 2015. Under the said auction, the Company has received provisional allocation of spectrum for 20 years in the 800 MHz band and 1800 MHz band in 13 Service Areas. The results of the auction are subject to the final outcome of a number of matters, wherein the lead petition is titled Reliance Telecom Ltd. & Anr. v. Union of India & Anr. Transfer Case (Civil) No. 43 of 2015, which are reserved for orders in the Hon'ble Supreme Court of India.

4. The Company has received approval from DoT, Government of India, for transaction with Reliance Communications Limited towards change in allotment of agreed spectrum in the 850 MHz band in 13 Service Areas as per provisions of the Agreement for Change in Spectrum Allotment between the companies dated 18th January 2016.

5. The Company has successfully acquired the right to use 269.2 MHz (Uplinking+Downlinking) spectrum in 800 MHz, 1800 MHz and 2300 MHz bands across all 22 Service Areas in India in the spectrum auction conducted by DoT, Government of India in October 2016, The payment to be made for the right to use spectrum for a period of 20 years is Rs. 13,672 crore.

6. The Company has adopted Ind AS with effect from 1st April, 2016 with comparatives being restated. Accordingly the impact of transition has been provided in the Opening Reserves as at 1st April, 2015 and all the periods presented have been restated accordingly. The Company is required to apply Ind AS in its first annual financial statements for the year ending 31st March, 2017. Consequently, further transition adjustments may be required to the financial statements as at 31st March, 2016 including those arising from new or revised standards or interpretations issued by the Ministry of Corporate Affairs or changes in use of one or more optional exemptions from full retrospective application of certain Ind AS.

RECONCILATION OF PROFIT BETWEEN IND AS AND INDIAN GAAP FOR EARLIER PERIODS AND AS AT 31ST MARCH 2016

(Rs. in crore)

Nature of Adjustment	**Profit Reconciliation**	
	For half year ended	**For year ended**
	30 Sep'15	**31 Mar'16**
Net (Loss) as per Indian GAAP	(12.48)	(23.88)
Adjustments for		
Fair valuation of Investments (refer note below)	(0.13)	(0.11)
Net (Loss) as per Ind AS	(12.61)	(23.99)

Note

Fair value of Investments - Under the Ind AS, the Investments have been accounted at fair value through Profit and Loss. Under Indian GAAP the same was recorded at cost or market value whichever is lower.

7. Formula used for computation of ratios:

   Debt Equity Ratio = Debt/Equity. Equity includes Preference Share Capital for the purpose of calculation of Debt Equity Ratio.

8. Debt capital comprises debentures, term loans and other short term borrowings taken by the Company towards implementation of Digital Services Project which is under implementation and hence Debt Service Coverage Ratio and Interest Service Coverage Ratio are not applicable.

9. Debenture Redemption Reserve will be created at the year end subject to availability of profits.

10. During the period, the Company has issued 300 crore 9% Non-Cumulative Optionally Convertible Preference Shares ('OCPS') of Rs. 10/- each for cash, at a premium of Rs. 40 per OCPS aggregating Rs. 15,000 crore to Reliance Industries Limited, the holding company and received Rs. 3,600 crore till 30th September, 2016 as Share application money. Shares have been subsequently allotted on 3rd October, 2016.

11. Details of Non Convertible Debentures are as

S No.	Particulars	Previous Due Date (01st Apr 2016 to 30th Sep 2016)		Next Due Date (01st Oct 2016 to 31st Mar 2017)	
		Principal	Interest	Principal	Interest
1	PPD1	-	15th Sep 2016	-	-
2	PPD2	-	-	-	04th Oct 2016
3	PPD3	-	16th June 2016	-	-
4	PPD4	‘	-	-	18th Nov 2016
5	PPD5 (Option 1)	-	-	-	23rd Jan 2017
6	PPD5 (Option 2)	-	-	-	23rd Jan 2017
7	PPD6	-	1st Aug 2016	-	-
8	PPD7 (Option 1)	-	3rd Aug 2016	-	-
9	PPD8	-	2nd May 2016, 1st Aug 2016	-	31st Oct 2016, 30th Jan 2017

All the interest due were paid on due dates.

12. Credit rating and change in credit rating (if any):

The Company has retained its credit ratings of "AAA (SO)/ Stable" by CRISIL and "CARE AAA (SO)" by CARE for series PPD 1 and series PPD 2 and "CRISIL AAA/ Stable" by CRISIL and "ICRA AAA/ Stable" by ICRA Limited for all other series.

13 The Non-Convertible Debentures of the Company aggregating Rs. 12,500 crore as at 30th September, 2016 are secured by way of Pari Passu charge on the Company's certain movable properties and the asset cover thereof exceeds hundred percent of the principal amount of the said debentures.

14 The Audit Committee has reviewed the above results and the Board of Directors have approved the above results and its release at their respective meetings held on 19th and 20th October, 2016 respectively. The Statutory Auditors of the Company have carried out a Limited Review of the results for the half year ended 30th September, 2016.

15 The figures for the previous period/year have been restated/regrouped wherever necessary, to make them comparable.

For Reliance Jio Infocom Limited

Place: Mumbai Sanjay Mashruwala

Date: 20th October, 2016 Managing Director

DIN : 01259774

Chapter 10

Disclosures in case of listed insurance & banking companies

SEBI had issued circular dated 30 November 2015 which provided formats for publishing financial results by listed companies. Subsequently, SEBI issued circular on Revised Formats for Financial Results and Implementation of Ind AS, dated 05 July 2016 which provided that for the period ending on or after 31 March 2017, the formats for unaudited/audited quarterly financial results to be submitted by the listed entities, with the stock exchanges, should be as prescribed in Schedule III to the Companies Act, 2013. However, Banking Companies and Insurance Companies should follow the formats as prescribed under the respective Acts/Regulations as specified by their Regulators.

In view of the recent listing by insurance companies, SEBI, in consultation with Insurance Regulatory and Development Authority of India (IRDAI), has now clarified that:

- The insurance companies should submit the following disclosures for quarters ending 30 September 2016 and 31 December 2016 in the format as specified by IRDAI:
    - Format for quarterly financial results;
    - Format for reporting of segment wise revenue, results and capital employed along with the quarterly results.
- With respect to the format for newspaper publishing purpose (standalone/consolidated), the insurance companies should continue to follow the format as specified under the relevant circulars issued earlier by SEBI. Additional disclosures may also be made as prescribed by IRDAI.

Accordingly, IRDAI has issued a circular on 25 October 2016 which provides following formats for compliance with the requirements of the SEBI Listing Regulations, 2015:

- Quarterly financial results;
- Reporting of segment wise revenue, results and capital employed along with the quarterly results;
- Limited review reports to be given by auditors;

- In case of audited financial reports, the audit report to be given by auditors;
- Financial results published in the newspapers in terms of Regulation 47(1)(b) of SEBI Listing Regulations, 2015.

The IRDAI circular further states that the other requirements specified under the relevant circulars issued earlier by SEBI will continue to apply to insurance companies. Please refer to **Annexure-I** at the end of this chapter for IRDAI circular.

The provisions of the SEBI Listing Regulations, 2015 are applicable to all listed companies including listed banks. Therefore, if a bank has listed its specified securities (equity shares and convertible securities), it needs to comply with the provisions of reg 33 of the SEBI Listing Regulations, 2015 for publishing quarterly financial results.

Similarly, if a bank has listed its non-convertible debt securities or non-convertible redeemable preference shares, it needs to comply with the requirements of reg 52 of the SEBI Listing Regulations, 2015. It may be noted that Chapter V, which includes reg 52, is also applicable to "perpetual debt instrument" and "perpetual non-cumulative preference share" listed by banks.

However, SEBI has issued formats of financial results for listed banks under both reg 33 and reg 52, which are different from the formats of financial results for other companies.

Please refer to **Annexure-II** at the end of this chapter for the financial results of few banking and insurance companies as available on the website of the stock exchange.

Annexures

Annexure I: IRDA circular dated 25 October 2016 providing formats for publishing financial results by Life Insurance companies

IRDA/F&I/REG/CIR/208/10/2016

October 25,2016

To

All Listed Life Insurance Companies

Madam/ Sir,

Formats for publishing financial results as required by the SEBI (Listing Obligations and Disclosure Requirements) Regulations, 2015 (LODR Regulations, 2015)

SEBI circular No. CIR/CFD/CMD/15/2015 dated Nov 30, 2015 provides for formats for publishing financial results by listed companies.

2. It was further specified by SEBI vide circular No. CIR/CFD/FAC/62/2016 dated July 05, 2016 as under:

   "For the period ending on or after March 31, 2017, the formats for Unaudited/Audited quarterly financial results to be submitted by the Listed Entities, with the stock exchanges, shall be as prescribed in Schedule III to the Companies Act, 2013. However, Banking Companies and Insurance Companies shall follow the formats as prescribed under the respective Acts/Regulations as specified by their Regulators."

3. Further vide circular reference CIR/CFD/DIL/115/2016 dated October 24, 2016, it has been clarified in the context of Para 2above that

   (a) The insurance companies (life and non-life) shall submit the following disclosures for quarters ending 30th September, 2016 and 31st December, 2016 in the format as specified by IRDAI:

      (i) Format for quarterly financial results

      (ii) Format for Reporting of Segment wise Revenue, Results and Capital Employed along with the quarterly results

(b) With respect to the format for Newspaper Publishing Purpose (Standalone/Consolidated), the insurance companies shall continue to follow the format as specified under the aforesaid circulars issued by SEBI. Additional disclosures may also be made as prescribed by IRDAI.

5. Accordingly, the following formats are prescribed herewith to ensure compliance with the requirements of SEBI under LODR Regulations, 2015:

(i) The quarterly financial results shall be presented in the format prescribed at Annexure I

(ii) Reporting of Segment wise Revenue, Results and Capital Employed along with the quarterly results shall be presented in the format prescribed at Annexure II

(iii) Limited review reports shall be given by auditors in the format prescribed in Annexure III

(iv) In case of audited financial reports, the audit report shall be given by the auditors in the format given in Annexure IV

(v) The financial results published in the newspapers in terms of Regulation 47(1)(b) of LODR Regulations, 2015 shall be in the format prescribed in Annexure V

The other requirements specified under the aforesaid SEBI circulars shall continue to apply to insurance companies.

6. This circular is issued with the limited purpose of enabling listed life insurance companies to meet the disclosure requirements of SEBI under LODR Regulations, 2015. These requirements do not in any manner, modify the disclosure requirements or the manner of preparation of financial statements as required under the Insurance Act, 1938; the IRDAI Act, 1999 and the Regulations framed thereunder.

Yours faithfully,

Member (F&I)

Annexure I

(Pursuant to the Regulation 33 of the SEBI (Listing Obligations and Disclosure Requirements) Regulations, 2015 read with IRDAI Circular reference: IRDA/F&I/REG/CIR/208/10/2016 dated 25th October 2016)

Format for submission of Unaudited / Audited financial results by Life Insurance Companies to be filed with Stock Exchanges

Statement of Standalone / Consolidated Unaudited / Audited Results for the Quarter and months ended (dd/mm/yyyy) OR for the Year Ended (dd/mm/yyyy)

(Rs. in Lakhs)

Sl. No.	Particulars		3months ended	Preceding 3 months ended	Corresponding 3 months ended in the previous year	Year to date for current period ended	Year to date for the previous year ended	Previous year ended
			(dd/mm/yyyy)	(dd/mm/yyyy)	(dd/mm/yyyy)	(dd/mm/yyyy)	(dd/mm/yyyy)	(dd/mm/yyyy)
			Audited/ unaudited[1]	Audited/ unaudited[1]	Audited/ unaudited[1]	Audited/ unaudited[1]	Audited/ unaudited[1]	Audited/ unaudited[1]
POLICYHOLDERS' A/C								
1	Gross premium income							
	(a)	First Year Premium						
	(b)	Renewal Premium						
	(c)	Single Premium						
2	Net premium income[2]							
3	Income from investments (Net)[3]							
4	Other income[4]							
5	Transfer of funds from Shareholders' A/c							
6	**Total (2 to 5)**							
7	Commission on							
	(a)	First Year Premium						
	(b)	Renewal Premium						
	(c)	Single Premium						
8.	Net Commission[2]							
9	Operating Expenses							

	related to insurance business (a + b)[5]:						
	(a) Employees remuneration and welfare expenses						
	(b) Other operating expenses						
10	**Expenses of Management (8+9)**						
11	Provisions for doubtful debts (including bad debts written off)						
12	Provisions for diminution in value of investments						
13	Service tax charge on linked charges						
14	Provision for taxes						
15	Benefits Paid [6](Net)[2]						
16	Change in actuarial liability						
17	Total (10+11+12+13+ 14+15+16)						
18	**Surplus/Deficit (6-17)**						
19	Appropriations						
	(a) Transferred to Shareholders A/c						
	(b) Funds for Future Appropriations						
20	Details of Surplus/Deficit						
	(a) Interim bonus paid						
	(b) Allocation of bonus to policyholders						
	(c) Surplus shown in the Revenue Account						
	Total Surplus						
SHAREHOLDERS' A/C							
21	Transfer from Policyholders' Account						
22	Total income under Shareholders' Account						
	(a) Investment Income						

	(b)	Other income 4						
23	Expenses other than those related to insurance business							
24	Transfer of funds to Policyholders' A/c							
25	Provisions for doubtful debts (including write off)							
26	Provisions for diminution in value of investments							
27	**Profit/ (loss) before tax**							
28	Provisions for tax							
29	**Profit/(loss) after tax and before Extraordinary Items**							
30	Extraordinary Items (Net of tax expenses) (if applicable)							
31	Profit/ (loss) after tax and Extraordinary Items							
32	Dividend per share (Rs.):							
	(a)	**Interim Dividend**						
	(b)	**Final Dividend**						
33	Profit/(Loss) carried to Balance Sheet							
34	Paid up equity share capital							
35	Reserve & Surplus (excluding Revaluation Reserve)							
36	Fair Value Change Account and Revaluation Reserve (Shareholders)							
37	**Total Assets:**							
	(a)	**Investments:**						
		- Shareholders'						
		- Policyholders Fund excluding Linked Assets						
		- Assets held to cover Linked						

		Liabilities						
	(b)	Other Assets (Net of current liabilities and provisions)						
38	**Analytical Ratios7:**							
	(i)	Solvency Ratio						
	(ii)	Expenses of Management Ratio						
	(iii)	Policyholder's liabilities to shareholders' fund						
	(iv)	Earnings per share (Rs.):						
		a) Basic and diluted EPS before extraordinary items (net of tax expense) for the period (not to be annualized)						
		b) Basic and diluted EPS after extraordinary items (net of tax expense) for the period (not to be annualized)						
	(v)	NPA ratios: (for policyholders' fund)						
		a) Gross &Net NPAs						
		b) % of Gross & Net NPAs						
	(vi)	Yield on Investments (on policyholders' fund)						
		A. Without unrealised gains						
		B. With unrealised gains						
	(vii)	NPA ratios: (for shareholders' fund)						

		a) Gross & Net NPAs					
		b) % of Gross & Net NPAs					
	(viii)	Yield on Investments (on shareholders' fund)					
		A. Without unrealised gains					
		B. With unrealised gains					
	(ix)	Persistency Ratio					
	(x)	Conservation Ratio					
	(xi)	Percentage of shares held by Government of India (in case of public sector insurance companies)					

Foot Note:	
1.	Strike out whichever is not applicable
2.	Net of reinsurance
3.	Net of amortisation and losses (including capital gains)
4.	Note specifying nature of other income to be given if the amount of other income exceeds 10% of total premium income
5.	Any expense contributing more than 10% of the expense of management needs to be shown separately
6.	Inclusive of interim bonus, if any
7.	Analytical ratios have to be calculated as per definition given in IRDAI Analytical ratios disclosures

Annexure II

(Pursuant to the Regulation 33 of the SEBI (Listing Obligations and Disclosure Requirements) Regulations, 2015 read with IRDA Circular reference: IRDAI /F&I / REG/CIR/ 208 / 10/ 2016 dated 25th October 2016)

Format for Reporting of Segment[1] wise Revenue, Results and Capital Employed along with the quarterly results

							(Rs. in Lakhs)
Sl. No.	**Particulars**	**3 months ended**	**Preceding 3 months ended**	**Corresponding 3 months ended in the previous year**	**Year to date for current period ended**	**Year to date for the previous year ended**	**Previous year ended**
		(dd/mm/yyyy)	**(dd/mm/yyyy)**	**(dd/mm/yyyy)**	**(dd/mm/yyyy)**	**(dd/mm/yyyy)**	**(dd/mm/yyyy)**
		Audited/ unaudited[2]	**Audited/ unaudited[2]**	**Audited/ unaudited[2]**	**Audited/ unaudited[2]**	**Audited/ unaudited[2]**	**Audited/ unaudited[2]**
1	***Segment Income:***						
	(a) Segment A:						
	Net Premium						
	Income from Investments[3]						
	Transfer of Funds from shareholders' account						
	Other Income						
	(b) Segment B:						
	Net Premium						
	Income from Investments[3]						
	Transfer of Funds from shareholders' account						
	Other Income						
	(c) Segment………..						
	(d) Unallocated						
2	**Segment Surplus/ Deficit (net of transfer from shareholders' A/c) :**						
	(a) Segment A:						
	(b) Segment B:						

	(c) Segment						
	(d) Unallocated						
3	**Segment Assets:**						
	(a) Segment A:						
	(b) Segment B:						
	(c)Segment						
	(d) Unallocated						
4	**Segment Policy Liabilities:**						
	(a) Segment A:						
	(b) Segment B:						
	(c) Segment						
	(d) Unallocated						

Footnotes:	
1.	Segments include:
a.	Linked Policies: (i) Life (ii) General Annuity and Pension (iii) Health (iv) Variable
b.	Non-Linked
	1. Non-Participating Policies: (i) Life (ii) General Annuity and Pension (iii) Health (iv) Variable
	2. Participating Policies : (i) Life (ii) General Annuity and Pension (iii) Health (iv) Variable
c.	Variable insurance shall be further segregated into Life, General Annuity and Pension and Health where any such segment contributes ten per cent or more of the total premium of an insurer.
2.	Strike out whichever is not applicable
3.	Net of Provisions for diminution in value of investments
Other disclosures*:	
	Details of Shareholder complaints pending at the beginning of the year, received and disposed off during the year and lying unresolved at the end of the period/year are required to be furnished.
	*These disclosures are not required to be audited

Annexure III

Format for the Limited Review Report

Review Report to ....

We have reviewed the accompanying statement of unaudited financial results of .... (Name of the Company) for the quarter and period ended............. This statement is the responsibility of the Company's Management and has been approved by the Board of Directors. Our responsibility is to issue a report on these financial statements based on our review.

We conducted our review of the Statement in accordance with the Standard on Review Engagements (SRE) 2410, "*Review of Interim Financial Information Performed by the Independent Auditor of the Entity*", issued by the Institute of Chartered Accountants of India. This standard requires that we plan and perform the review to obtain moderate assurance as to whether the financial statements are free of material misstatement. A review is limited primarily to inquiries of Company personnel and analytical procedures applied to financial data and thus provide less assurance than an audit. We have not performed an audit and accordingly, we do not express an audit opinion.

Based on our review conducted as above, nothing has come to our attention that causes us to believe that the accompanying statement of unaudited financial results prepared in accordance with the applicable accounting standards, accounting and presentation principles as prescribed in the relevant provisions of the Insurance Act, 1938 (the "Insurance Act"), the Insurance Regulatory and Development Authority Act, 1999 (the "IRDA Act") and IRDA (Preparation of Financial Statements and Auditors' Report of Insurance Companies) Regulations, 2002; orders/directions/circulars issued by the Insurance Regulatory and Development Authority of India ("IRDAI"/"the Authority") to the extent applicable and other recognized accounting practices and policies has not disclosed the information required to be disclosed in terms of Regulation 33 of the SEBI (Listing Obligations and Disclosure Requirements) Regulations, 2015 including the manner in which it is to be disclosed, or that it contains any material misstatement.

Other Matters

The actuarial valuation of liabilities for life policies in force is the responsibility of the Company's Appointed Actuary (the "Appointed Actuary"). The actuarial valuation of these liabilities for life policies in force and for policies in respect of which premium has been discontinued but liability exists as at XXX has been duly certified by the Appointed Actuary and in his opinion, the assumptions for such valuation are in accordance with the guidelines and norms issued by the IRDAIand the Institute of Actuaries of India in concurrence with the Authority. We have relied upon the Appointed Actuary's certificate in this regard during our review of the valuation of liabilities for life policies in force and for policies in respect of which premium has been discontinued but liability exists, as contained in the statement of unaudited financial results.

For XYZ & Co. Chartered Accountants Signature
(Name of the member signing the audit report)
(Designation)[1]
(Membership Number)

Place of signature
Date

[1] Partner or proprietor, as the case may be.

Annexure IV

When an Unmodified Opinion is expressed on the Quarterly financial results

Auditor's Report on Quarterly Financial Results and Year to Date Results of the Company pursuant to the Regulation 33 of the SEBI (Listing Obligations and Disclosure Requirements) Regulations, 2015 read with IRDA Circular reference: IRDAI/F&I/REG/CIR/208/10/2016 dated 25th October 2016

To The Board of Directors of

.... (Name of the company)

We have audited the accompanying quarterly financial results of .... (Name of the company) for the quarter ended .... (date of the quarter end) and the year to date financial results for the period .... to ...., being submitted by the Company pursuant to the requirement of Regulation 33 of the SEBI (Listing Obligations and Disclosure Requirements) Regulations, 2015and IRDA Circular reference: IRDAI /F&I / REG/CIR/ 208 / 10/ 2016 dated 25th October 2016. These quarterly financial results as well as the year to date financial results have been prepared on the basis of the interim financial statements, which are the responsibility of the Company's management and have been approved by the Board of Directors on XXXX.

Our responsibility is to express an opinion on these financial results and year to date financial results based on our audit of such interim financial statements, which have been prepared in accordance with the recognition and measurement principles laid down in Accounting Standard ('AS') 25, "Interim Financial Reporting", specified under Section 133 of the Companies Act, 2013 ("the Act") read with Rule 7 of the Companies (Accounts) Rules, 2014 issued thereunder, including the relevant provisions of the Insurance Act, 1938 (the "Insurance Act"), the Insurance Regulatory and Development Authority Act, 1999 (the "IRDA Act") and other accounting principles generally accepted in India, to the extent considered relevant and appropriate for the purpose of quarterly financial results as well as the year to date financial results and which are not inconsistent with the accounting principles as prescribed in the Insurance Regulatory and Development Authority (Preparation of Financial Statements and Auditors' Report of Insurance Companies) Regulations, 2002 (the "Regulations") and orders/directions/circulars issued by the Insurance Regulatory and Development Authority of India ("IRDAI") to the extent applicable.

We conducted our audit in accordance with the auditing standards generally accepted in India. Those standards require that we plan and perform the audit to obtain reasonable assurance about whether the financial results are free of material misstatements. An audit includes examining, on a test basis, evidence supporting the amounts disclosed as financial results. An audit also includes assessing the accounting principles used and significant estimates made by management. We believe that our audit provides a reasonable basis for our opinion.

In our opinion and to the best of our information and according to the explanations given to us these quarterly financial results as well as the year to date results:

(i) are presented in accordance with the requirements of Regulation 33 of the SEBI (Listing Obligations and Disclosure Requirements) Regulations, 2015 and IRDAI IRDA Circular reference: IRDAI/F&I/REG/CIR/208/10/2016 dated 25th October 2016 in this regard; and

(ii) give a true and fair view of the net profit and other financial information for the quarter ended ……………………… (date of the quarter end) as well as the year to date results for the period …………… to ……………………

Other Matters

The actuarial valuation of liabilities for life policies in force is the responsibility of the Company's Appointed Actuary (the "Appointed Actuary"). The actuarial valuation of these liabilities for life policies in force and for policies in respect of which premium has been discontinued but liability exists as at ……………………… (date of the quarter end) has been duly certified by the Appointed Actuary and in his opinion, the assumptions for such valuation are in accordance with the guidelines and norms issued by the Insurance Regulatory and Development Authority of India ("IRDAI"/"Authority") and the Institute of Actuaries of India in concurrence with the Authority. We have relied upon the Appointed Actuary's certificate in this regard for forming our opinion on the valuation of liabilities for life policies in force and for policies in respect of which premium has been discontinued but liability exists, as contained in the interim financial statements of the Company.

For XYZ & Co.

Chartered Accountants

Signature (Name of the member signing the audit report)

(Designation)

(Membership Number)

Place of signature

Annexure V

Format for Insurance Companies: Newspaper Publishing Purpose (Standalone/Consolidated)

[See Regulation 47(1)(b) of the SEBI (LODR) Regulations, 2015 read with IRDAI Circular Reference IRDA/F&I/REG/CIR/208/10/2016 dated 25th October 2016]

Sl. No.	Particulars	Quarter ending/Current Year ending	Year to date Figures/Previous Year ending	Corresponding 3 months ended in the previous year
1.	Premium Income (Gross) (Refer note (d))			
2.	Net Profit/(Loss) for the period (before Tax Exceptional and / or Extra ordinary items#)			
3.	Net Profit/(Loss) for the period before tax(after Exceptional and/or Extraordinary items#) (Refer note (e))			
4.	Net Profit/(Loss) for the period after tax (after Exceptional and/or Extraordinary items#)			
5.	Total Comprehensive Income for the period [Comprising Profit/ (Loss) for the period(after tax) and Other Comprehensive Income (after tax)] Refer note (f))			
6.	Equity Share Capital			
7.	Reserves (excluding Revaluation Reserve) as shown in the Audited Balance Sheet of the previous year (Refer note (g))			
8.	Earnings Per Share (of Rs._/- each) (for continuing and discontinued operations)-			

	1. Basic: 2. Diluted:			

Note:

(a) This format is modified to reflect the terminology used in the Insurance Act/ IRDAI Regulations.

(b) The above is an extract of the detailed format of Quarterly/Annual Financial Results filed with the Stock Exchanges under Regulation 33 of the SEBI (Listing and Other Disclosure Requirements) Regulations, 2015.The full format of the Quarterly/Annual Financial Results are available on the websites of the Stock Exchange (s) and the listed entity.(URL of the filings).

(c) The impact on net profit/loss of total comprehensive income or any other relevant financial item(s) due to change (s) in accounting policies shall be disclosed by means of a footnote.

(d) Premium income should be gross of reinsurance and net of service tax

(e) Net Profit/(Loss) before tax, for the period would be Profit before tax as appearing in Profit and Loss Account (Shareholders' account)

(f) Line item no. 5 needs to be disclosed when Ind-AS becomes applicable for Insurance Companies.

(g) Reserves need to be shown excluding Revaluation reserve and fair value change account.

(h) #-Exceptional and /or Extraordinary items adjusted in the Statement of Policyholders' and Shareholders' account in accordance with Ind-AS Rules/ AS Rules, whichever is applicable

Annexure II: Financial results of few banking and insurance companies as available on the website of the stock exchange

A. ICICI PRUDENTIAL LIFE INSURANCE COMPANY LIMITED

Statement of Standalone Audited Results for the quarter and half year ended September 30, 2016

(INR in Lakhs)

Sr No.		Particulars	Three months ended			Six months ended		Year Ended
			September 30, 2016	June 30, 2016	September 30, 2015	September 30, 2016	September 30, 2015	March 31, 2016
			(Audited)	(Audited)	(Audited)	(Audited)	(Audited)	(Audited)
POLICYHOLDERS' A/C								
1	Gross premium income							
	(a)	First Year Premium	152,898	92,344	126,722	245,242	210,538	492,438
	(b)	Renewal Premium	352,132	230,044	305,065	582,176	494,315	1,239,864
	(c)	Single Premium	41,828	33,606	88,730	75,434	127,006	184,137
2	Net premium income[1]		542,253	350,879	516,092	893,132	823,577	1,899,870
3	Income from investments: (Net)[2]		370,941	535,638	(53,218)	906,579	(44,782)	120,837
4	Other income		1,534	1,394	478	2,928	958	2,088
5	Transfer of funds from Shareholders' A/c		(319)	528	-	209	-	
6	Total (2 to 5)		914,409	888,439	463,352	1,802,848	779,753	2,022,795
7	Commission on							
		First Year Premium	10,991	8,022	9,255	19,013	15.515	37,441
	(b)	Renewal Premium	7,093	4,359	6,141	11,452	9,783	24,023
	(c)	Single Premium	207	192	94	399	120	534
8	Net Commission[1]		18,291	12,573	15,490	30,864	25,418	61,998
	Operating Expenses related to insurance business (a + b +c):							
	(a)	Employees	20,246	18,745	18,902	38,991	36,827	73,501

Sr No.	Particulars		Three months ended			Six months ended		Year Ended
			September 30, 2016	June 30, 2016	September 30, 2015	September 30, 2016	September 30, 2015	March 31, 2016
			(Audited)	(Audited)	(Audited)	(Audited)	(Audited)	(Audited)
		remuneration and welfare expenses						
	(b)	Administration support expenses	13,677	13,620	13,749	27,297	9	45,279
	(c)	Other operating expenses	20,404	22,836	16,245	43,242	29,677	70,055
10	Expenses of Management (8+9)		72,618	67,774	64,386	140,394	117,518	250,833
11	Provisions for doubtful debts (including write off)		157	246	215	403	439	516
12	Provisions for diminution in value of investments		-	139	462	139	462	1,264
13	Service tax charge on linked charges		10,519	9,037	8,602	19,556	16,171	34,650
14	Provision for taxes (a+b)		3,559	42	191	3,600	371	7,035
	(a)	Current tax	3,559	40	190	3,598	368	7,029
	(b)	Deferred tax	-	2	1	2	3	6
15	Benefits Paid [3] (Net)[1]		417,013	292,806	330,877	709,819	662,070	1,242,742
16	Change in actuarial liability		378,964	495,696	33,138	874,659	(70,362)	351,548
17	Total (10+11 + 12 + 13+14+15+16)		882,830	865,740	437,871	1,748,570	726,669	1,888,588
18	Surplus/Deficit as a result of Actuarial Valuation (6- 17)		31,579	22,699	25,481	54,278	53,084	134,207
19	Appropriations							
	(a)	Transferred to Shareholders	31,391	24,970	28,067	56,361	54,887	120,764
	(b)	Funds for Future Appropriations	188	(2,271)	(2,586)	(2,083)	(1,803)	13,443
20	Details of Surplus/ (Deficit)							
	(a)	Interim bonus paid	761	676	390	1,437	858	1,874
	(b)	Allocation of	-	-	-	-	-	32,212

Sr No.	Particulars	Three months ended			Six months ended		Year Ended
		September 30, 2016	June 30, 2016	September 30, 2015	September 30, 2016	September 30, 2015	March 31, 2016
		(Audited)	(Audited)	(Audited)	(Audited)	(Audited)	(Audited)
	bonus to policyholders						
	(c) Surplus shown in the Revenue Account	31,579	22,699	25,481	54,278	53,084	134,207
	Total Surplus	32,340	23,375	25,871	55,715	53,942	168,293
SHAREHOLDERS'A/C							
21	Transfer from Policyholders' Account	31,391	24,970	28,067	56,361	54,887	120,764
22	Total income under Shareholders' Account						
	(a) Investment Income	12,775	19,550	15,833	32,325	32,687	59,958
	(b) Other income	17	18	8	35	13	
23	Expenses other than those related to insurance less business	962	734	728	1,696	1,621	3,126
24	Transfer of funds to Policyholders A/c	(319)	528	-	209	-	
25	Provisions for doubtful debts (including write off)	-	-	-	-	-	
26	Provisions for diminution in value of investments	-	-	439	-	439	439
27	Profit/ (loss) before tax	43,540	43,276	42,741	86,816	85,527	177,157
28	Provisions for tax (a+b)	1,662	2,777	1,243	4,439	4,348	12,111
	(a) Current tax	1,662	2,777	1,243	4,439	4,348	12,111
	(b) Deferred tax	-	-	-		-	
29	Profit/(loss) after tax and before extraordinary items	41,878	40,499	41,498	82,377	81,179	165,046
30	Extraordinary Items (Net of tax expenses)	-	-	-	-		-
31	Profit / (loss) after tax and extraordinary items	41,878	40,499	41,498	82,377	81,179	165,046
32	Dividend per share						

Sr No.	Particulars		Three months ended			Six months ended		Year Ended
			September 30, 2016	June 30, 2016	September 30, 2015	September 30, 2016	September 30, 2015	March 31, 2016
			(Audited)	(Audited)	(Audited)	(Audited)	(Audited)	(Audited)
	(INR) (Nominal Value INR 10 per share:							
	(a)	Interim Dividend	1.75	2.10	2.10	3.85	4.20	6.30
	(b)	Final Dividend	-	-	-		-	2.10
33	Profit/(Loss) carried to Balance Sheet		71,216	65,563	13,614	71,216	13,614	25,077
34	Reserve & Surplus (excluding Revaluation Reserve)		413,141	405,121	352,232	413,141	352,232	364,051
35	Fair value Change Account and revaluation reserve (Shareholders)		26,983	25,816	29,113	26,983	29,113	25,187

1 *Net of reinsurance*

2 *Net of amortisation and losses (including capital gains)*

3 *Inclusive of interim bonus*

ICICI Prudential Life Insurance Company Limited
Standalone Balance Sheet

(INR in Lakhs)

Particulars	As at			
	September 30, 2016	June 30, 2016	March 31, 2016	September 30, 2015
	(Audited)	(Audited)	(Audited)	(Audited)
Sources of funds				
Shareholders' funds:				
Share capital	143,532	143,287	143,232	143,196
Share application money	-	167	8	91
Reserve and surplus	413,239	405,219	364,150	352,232
Credit/[debit] fair value change account	26,885	25,717	25,088	29,113
Sub - total	**583,656**	**574,390**	**532,478**	**524,632**
Borrowings	-	-	-	-
Policyholders' funds :				
Credit/debit fair value change account	147,310	131,249	97,123	99,823
Revaluation reserve - Investment property	5,771	5,771	5,771	5,621
Policy liabilities (A) + (B) + (C)	10,429,609	10,050,646	9,554,951	9,133,040
Non unit liabilities (mathematical reserves) (A)	2,235,229	2,113,750	2,025,479	1,822,503

Particulars	As at			
	September 30, 2016	June 30, 2016	March 31, 2016	September 30, 2015
	(Audited)	(Audited)	(Audited)	(Audited)
Provision for linked liabilities (fund reserves) (B)	7,802,590	7,557,134	7,199,029	7,011,104
(a) Provision for linked liabilities	6,776,982	6,570,146	6,508,250	6,163,292
(b) Credit/(debit) fair value change account (Linked)	1,025,608	986,988	690,779	847,812
Funds for discontinued policies (C)	391,790	379,762	330,443	299,433
(a) Discontinued on account of non-payment of premium	391,321	379,528	330,274	299,433
(b) Other discontinuance	339	234	169	-
(c) Credit/(debit) fair value change account	130	-	-	-
Total linked liabilities (B) + (C)	8,194,380	7,936,896	7,529,472	7,310,537
Sub - total	10,582,690	10,187,666	9,657,845	9,238,484
Funds for Future Appropriations				
Linked	84	82	108	154
Non linked	64,024	63,838	66,083	50,792
Sub - total	**64,108**	**63,920**	**66,191**	**50,946**
Total	**11,230,454**	**10,825,976**	**10,256,514**	**9,814,062**
Application of funds				
Investments				
Shareholders'	573,748	554,684	621,567	563,635
Policyholders'	2,429,550	2,297,204	2,151,562	1,951,307
Asset held to cover linked liabilities	8,194,464	7,936,979	7,529,579	7,310,691
Loans	5,893	5,014	4,427	3,167
Fixed assets - net block	21,009	21,323	21,954	21,499
Deferred tax asset - Refer note 9 of schedule 16	5	5	7	11
Current assets				
Cash and Bank balances	7,671	6,320	20,021	11,520
Advances and Other assets	179,327	187,824	127,508	131,469
Sub-Total (A)	186,998	194,144	147,529	142,989
Current liabilities	179,351	174,798	182,138	141,455
Provisions	1,862	8,579	37,973	37,782
Sub-Total (B)	181,213	183,377	220,111	179,237
Net Current Assets (C) = (A-B)	5,785	10,767	(72,582)	(36,248)
Miscellaneous expenditure (to the extent not written-off or adjusted)	-	-	-	-
Debit Balance in Profit & Loss Account (Shareholders' account)	-	-	-	-
Total	**11,230,454**	**10,825,976**	**10,256,514**	**9,814,062**
Contingent liabilities	20,947	19,875	20,065	20,110

ICICI Prudential Life Insurance Company Limited

Statement of Analytical ratios (Standalone) for the quarter and half year ended September 30, 2016

	Particulars	Three months ended/As at			Six months ended/As at		Year Ended/ As at March 31, 2016
		September 30, 2016	June 30, 2016	September 30, 2015	September 30, 2016	September 30, 2015	
		(Audited)	(Audited)	(Audited)	(Audited)	(Audited)	(Audited)
Analytical Ratios:'							
(i)	Solvency Ratio:	305.9%	320.5%	328.2%	305.9%	328.2%	320.0%
(ii)	Expenses of management ratio	13.3%	19.0%	12.4%	15.6%	14.1%	13.1%
(iii)	Policyholder's liabilities to shareholders' fund	1824.2%	1784.8%	1770.7%	1824.2%	1770.7%	1826.2%
(iv)	Earnings per share (INR):						
	a) Basic EPS before and after extraordinary items (net of tax expense) for the period (not annualized for three/six months)	2.92	2.83	2.90	5.75	5.67	11.53
	b) Diluted EPS before and after extraordinary items (net of tax expense) for the period (not annualized for three/six months)	2.92	2.82	2.89	5.74	5.66	11.51
(v)	NPA ratios: (for policyholders' fund)						
	a) Gross & Net NPAs	NIL	NIL	NIL	NIL	NIL	NIL
	b) % of Gross & Net NPAs	NIL	NIL	NIL	NIL	NIL	NIL
(vi)	Yield on Investments (On Policyholders' fund)						
	A. Without unrealised gains						
	- Non Linked						
	Par	9.5%	9.2%	8.6%	9.3%	9.1%	8.7%
	Non Par	8.6%	8.0%	8.4%	8.3%	8.5%	8.1%
	- Linked						
	Non Par	14.9%	9.9%	10.4%	12.4%	12.7%	9.1%
	B. With unrealised gains						
	- Non Linked						

	Particulars	Three months ended/As at			Six months ended/As at		Year Ended/ As at March 31, 2016
		September 30, 2016	June 30, 2016	September 30, 2015	September 30, 2016	September 30, 2015	
		(Audited)	(Audited)	(Audited)	(Audited)	(Audited)	(Audited)
	Par	28.5%	18.3%	13.7%	23.4%	5.3%	5.7%
	Non Par	26.0%	18.0%	13.5%	22.0%	5.9%	5.8%
	- Linked						
	Non Par	15.1%	26.9%	(6.5%)	20.9%	(4.9%)	(2.1%)
(vii)	NPA ratios: (for shareholders' fund)						
	a) Gross & Net NPAs	NIL	NIL	NIL	NIL	NIL	NIL
	b) % of Gross & Net NPAs	NIL	NIL	NIL	NIL	NIL	NIL
(viii)	Yield on Investments (on Shareholders' A/c)						
	A. Without unrealised gains	9.4%	14.4%	11.1%	12.0%	11.7%	10.6%
	B. With unrealised gains	17.8%	15.4%	10.0%	16.6%	5.4%	5.8%
(ix)	Persistency Ratio[2]						
	13th month	78.6%	77.3%	79.1%	82.1%	81.0%	82.4%
	25th month	70.8%	68.9%	69.7%	72.5%	68.0%	71.2%
	37th month	64.1%	60.0%	60.9%	62.9%	63.5%	61.6%
	49th month	58.3%	56.0%	59.6%	61.1%	77.8%	62.2%
	61st month	54.9%	55.5%	19.2%	65.6%	15.6%	46.0%
(x)	Conservation Ratio						
	Par Life	88.5%	87.4%	88.9%	88.1%	88.1%	88.3%
	Par Pension	91.5%	96.2%	94.0%	94.1%	91.3%	92.8%
	Non Par	94.0%	93.4%	96.0%	93.8%	97.6%	96.1%
	Non Par Variable	NA	NA	NA	NA	NA	NA
	Non Par Variable Pension	NA	NA	NA	NA	NA	NA
	Annuity Non Par	NA	NA	NA	NA	NA	NA
	Health	87.7%	89.1%	89.3%	88.3%	90.7%	90.6%
	Linked	78.1%	82.1%	85.3%	79.6%	85.0%	82.5%

1 *Analytical ratios have been calculated as per definition given in IRDAI Analytical ratios disclosure*

2 *Calculations are in accordance with the IHDA circular IHDA/A C T/CIR/MISC/035/01/2014 dated January 23, 201A.*

a) *Persistency ratios for the quarter ending September 30, 2016 have been calculated on September 30, 2016 for the policies issued in June to August period of the relevant years. For example, the 13th month persistency for quarter ending September 30, 2016 is calculated for policies issued from June 1, 2015 to August 31,2015.*

b) *Persistency ratios for the quarter ending June 30, 2016 have been calculated on July 31,2016 for the policies issued in April to June period of the relevant years. For example, the 13th month persistency for quarter ending June 30, 2016 is calculated for policies issued from April 1,2015 to June 30, 2015.*

c) *Persistency ratios for the quarter ending September 30, 2015 have been calculated on October 31, 2015 for the policies issued in July to September period of the relevant years. For example, the 13th month persistency for quarter ending September 30, 2015 is calculated for policies issued from July 1,2014 to September 30, 2014.*

d) Persistency ratios for year ending September 30, 2016 have been calculated on September 30, 2016 for the policies issued in September to August period of the relevant years. For example, the 13th month persistency for year ending September 30, 2016 is calculated for policies issued from September 1,2014 to August 31,2015.

e) Persistency ratios for the year ending September 30, 2015 have been calculated on October 31, 2015 for the policies issued in October to September period of the relevant years. For example, the 13th month persistency for year ending September 30, 2015 is calculated for policies issued from October 1, 2013 to September 30, 2014.

f) Persistency ratios for the year ending March 31, 2016 have been calculated on April 30, 2016 for the policies issued in April to March period of the relevant years. For example, the 13th month persistency for year ending March 31, 2016 is calculated for policies issued from April 1,2014 to March 31,2015.

g) Group policies and policies under micro insurance products are excluded.

ICICI Prudential Life Insurance Company Limited

Segment[1] Reporting (Standalone) for the quarter and half year ended September 30, 2016

(INR in Lakhs)

Sr No.	Particulars	Three months ended/As at			Six months ended/As at		Year Ended/ As at March 31, 2016
		September 30, 2016	June 30, 2016	September 30, 2015	September 30,2016	September 30,2015	
		(Audited)	(Audited)	(Audited)	(Audited)	(Audited)	(Audited)
1	*Segment Income:*						
	Segment A: Per life						
	Net Premium	57,454	41,910	47,869	99,364	78,400	213,968
	Income from investments [2]	18,100	16,293	12,279	34,393	25,240	52,125
	Transfer of Funds from shareholders' account		-	-	-	-	
	Other income	194	182	172	376	358	801
	Segment B: Par pension						
	Net Premium	467	609	510	1,076	1,143	3,575
	income from investments[2]	2,268	2,219	2,464	4,488	6,332	10,813
	Transfer of Funds from shareholders' account	-	-		-	-	
	Other income	2	2	2	4	6	11
	Segment C: Non Par						
	Net Premium	71,972	48,461	62,196	120,433	98,204	231,483
	income from investments[2]	20,561	17,903	16,147	38,463	31,549	63,355
	Transfer of Funds from shareholders' account						-
	Other income	275	231	235	506	475	1,035
	Segment D: Non Par						

Sr No.	Particulars	Three months ended/As at			Six months ended/As at		Year Ended/ As at March 31, 2016
		September 30, 2016	June 30, 2016	September 30, 2015	September 30,2016	September 30,2015	
		(Audited)	(Audited)	(Audited)	(Audited)	(Audited)	(Audited)
	Variable						
	Net Premium	3,386	4,144	-	7,530		-
	income from investments[2]	95	2	-	97		-
	Transfer of Funds from shareholders' account	(343)	528	-	185		-
	Other income	-	.	-	-	-	-
	Segment E: Non Par Variable Pension						
	Net Premium	1,299	-		1,299	-	
	income from investments[2]	17	-		17	-	
	Transfer of Funds from shareholders' account	24	-		24	-	
	Other income	-	-		-	-	
	Segment F: Annuity Non Par						
	Net Premium	5,784	4,314	4,846	10,098	9,224	18,675
	income from investments[2]	5,774	4,790	4,426	10,564	8,790	17,902
	Transfer of Funds from shareholders' account	-					
	Other income	-	-	-	-	-	1
	Segment G: Health						
	Net Premium	252	210	295	462	535	1,162
	income from investments [2]	125	117	158	241	286	519
	Transfer of Funds from shareholders' account	-	-	-	-	-	
	Other income		1	-	1	1	2
	Segment H: Linked						
	Net Premium	401,639	251,231	400,376	652,870	636,071	1,431,007
	income from investments[2]	324,001	494,175	(89,154)	818,177	(117,441)	(25,141)
	Transfer of Funds from shareholders' account				-		
	Other income	1,063	978	69	2,041	118	238

Sr No.	Particulars	Three months ended/As at			Six months ended/As at		Year Ended/ As at March 31, 2016
		September 30, 2016	June 30, 2016	September 30, 2015	September 30,2016	September 30,2015	
		(Audited)	(Audited)	(Audited)	(Audited)	(Audited)	(Audited)
	Shareholders						
	Income from investments[2]	12,775	19,551	15,394	32,325	32,247	59,518
	Other income	17	18	8	35	13	-
2	Segment Surplus/ (Deficit) (net of transfer from shareholders' A/c)						
	Segment A: Par life	2,433	(248)	1,417	2,185	2,251	12,879
	Segment B: Par pension	648	902	119	1,550	1,002	3,035
	Segment C: Non Par	12,582	1,733	10,777	14,315	20,498	45,462
	Segment D: Non Par Variable	343	(528)	-	(185)	-	-
	Segment E: Non Par Variable Pension	(24)	-	-	(24)	-	-
	Segment F: Annuity Non Par	2,197	1,152	556	3,349	1,360	14,973
	Segment G: Health	521	313	427	834	930	3,409
	Segment H: Linked	13,198	18,847	12,185	32,045	27,043	54,449
	Shareholders	10,168	16,057	13,431	26,225	26,292	44,282
3	Segment Assets:						
	Segment A: Par life	872,547	818,990	672,879	872,547	672,879	774,869
	Segment B: Par pension	114,451	114,529	120,273	114,451	120,273	111,506
	Segment C: Non Par	1,149,238	1,077,967	890,252	1,149,238	890,252	1,012,810
	Segment D: Non Par Variable	7,643	4,608		7,643	-	
	Segment E: Non Par Variable Pension	1,323	-		1,323		
	Segment F: Annuity Non Par	221,856	216,166	214,037	221,856	214,037	211,860
	Segment G: Health	2,850	3,106	5,119	2,850	5,119	3,219
	Segment H: Linked	8,276,890	8,016,220	7,386,870	8,276,890	7,386,870	7,609,772
	Shareholders	583,656	574,390	524,632	583,656	524,632	532,478
4	*Segment Policy Liabilities:*						
	Segment A: Par life	872,547	818,990	672,879	872,547	672,879	774,869
	Segment B: Par pension	114,451	114,529	120,273	114,451	120,273	111,506
	Segment C: Non Par	1,149,238	1,077,967	890,252	1,149,238	890,252	1,012,810

Sr No.	Particulars	Three months ended/As at			Six months ended/As at		Year Ended/ As at March 31, 2016
		September 30, 2016	June 30, 2016	September 30, 2015	September 30,2016	September 30,2015	
		(Audited)	(Audited)	(Audited)	(Audited)	(Audited)	(Audited)
	Segment D: Non Par Variable	7,643	4,608		7,643	-	-
	Segment E: Non Par Variable Pension	1,323	-		1,323	-	-
	Segment F: Annuity Non Par	221,856	216,166	214,037	221,856	214,037	211,860
	Segment G: Health	2,850	3,106	5,119	2,850	5,119	3,219
	Segment H: Linked	8,276,890	8,016,220	7,386,870	8,276,890	7,386,870	7,609,772

Footnotes:

1 *Segments includes as under:*

a. *Linked Policies*

b. *Non-Linked*

1. *Non-Participating Policies: (i) Life (ii) General Annuity and Pension (Hi) Health (iv) Variable*
2. *Participating Policies: (i) Life (ii) General Annuity and Pension (iii) Health (iv) Variable*

c. *Variable insurance shall be further segregated into Life, General Annuity and Pension and Health where any such segment contributes ten per cent or more of the total premium of the Company.*

2 *Net of Provisions for diminution in value of investments*

Other disclosures:

Status of Shareholders Complaints for the six months ended September 30, 2016:

Sr No.	Particulars	Number
1	No. of investor complaints pending at the beginning of period	0
2	No. of investor complaints received during the period	13
3	No. of investor complaints disposed off during the period	10
4	No. of investor complaints remaining unresolved at the end of the period	3*

* *These are SEBI SCORES Complaints and were redressed and there were no complaints which remained unattended/pending for more than 20 days.*

Notes:

1. The above financial results have been approved by the Board of Directors at its meeting held on October 25, 2016.
2. The financial statements have been prepared in accordance with Accounting Standard (AS) 25 on 'Interim Financial Reporting'.
3. In view of seasonality of Industry, the financial results for the quarter are not indicative of full year's expected performance.
4. During the quarter ended September 30, 2016, the Company completed the Initial Public Offering (IPO) through an offer for sale of 181,341,058 equity shares of INR 10 each at a price of INR 334 per equity share, by ICICI Bank Limited, the

Holding Company, aggregating upto INR 6,057 crores. The equity shares of the Company were listed on National Stock Exchange of India Limited and Bombay Stock Exchange Limited on September 29, 2016.

5. The Company has declared an interim dividend of INR 1.75 per equity share (including special dividend of INR 0.65 per equity share) of face value of INR 10 each for the quarter ended September 30, 2016.
6. During the quarter ended September 30, 2016, the Company has allotted 2,454,834 equity shares of face value of INR 10 each pursuant to exercise of employee stock options.
7. The above financial results are audited by the joint statutory auditors, B S R & Co. LLP, Chartered Accountants and Walker Chandiok & Co LLP, Chartered Accountants.
8. In accordance with requirements of IRDAI Master Circular on Preparation of Financial Statements and Filing of Returns, the Company will publish the financials in the newspaper and on the company's website latest by November 9, 2016.

For and on behalf of the Board of Directors

Place: Mumbai — Sandeep Batra

Date: October 25, 2016 — Executive Director

DIN: 03620913

B. AXIS BANK LIMITED

UNAUDITED FINANCIAL RESULTS FOR THE HALF YEAR ENDED 30TH SEPTEMBER, 2016

(INR in lacs)

Particulars	For the quarter ended 30.09.2016	For the quarter ended 30.06.2016	For the quarter ended 30.09.2015	For the half year ended 30.09.2016	For the half year ended 30.09.2015	For the year ended 31.03.2016
	(Unaudited)	(Unaudited)	(Unaudited)	(Unaudited)	(Unaudited)	(Audited)
1. Interest earned (a)+|b)+(c)+(d)	11,159,11	11,113,90	9,959,61	22,273,01	19,895,75	40,988,04
(a) Interest/discount on advances/bills	8,386,18	8,319,81	7,344,01	16,705,99	14,417,79	30,040,56
(b) income on Investments	2,380,58	2,436,28	2,188,87	4,816,86	4,663,97	9,377,59
(c) Interest on balances with Reserve Bank of India and other inter-bank funds	76,75	57,59	91,59	134,34	162,65	295,25
(d) Others	315,60	300,22	335,14	615,82	651,34	1,274,64
2. Other income (Refer note 3)	2,539,66	2,738,28	2,041,40	5,277,94	4,339,67	9,371,46
3. TOTAL INCOME (1+2)	13,698,77	13,852,18	12,001.01	27,550,95	24,235,42	50,359,50
4. Interest Expended	6,645,24	6,596,98	5,897,52	13,242,22	11,777,43	24,155,07
5. Operating expenses (i)+(ii)	2,953,35	2,785,83	2,475,54	5,739,18	4,737,97	10,100,82
(i) Employees cost	988,83	963,18	829,31	1,952,01	1,638,59	3,376,01
(ii) Other operating expenses	1,964,52	1,822,65	1,646,23	3,787,17	3,099,38	6,724,81
6. TOTAL EXPENDITURE (4+5) (Excluding Provisions and Contingencies)	9,598,59	9,382,81	8,373,06	18,981,40	16,515,40	34,255,89
7. OPERATING PROFIT (3-6) (Profit before Provisions and Contingencies)	4,100,18	4,469,37	3,627,95	8,569,55	7,720,02	16,103,61
8. Provisions (other than tax) and Contingencies (Net)	3,622,74	2,117,17	707,17	5,739,91	1,828,94	3,709,86
9. Exceptional Items	-	-	-	-	-	-
10. Profit/(Loss) from Ordinary Activities before Tax (7-8-9)	477,44	2,352.20	2,920,78	2,829,64	5.891.08	12.393,75
11. Tax expense	158,36	796,67	1,005,14	955,03	1,997,00	4,170,09
12. Net Profit/(Loss) from Ordinary Activities after Tax (10-11)	319,08	1,555,53	1,915,64	1,874,61	3,894,08	8,223,66
13. Extraordinary Items (net of tax expense)			.	.	.	
14. Net Profit/(loss) for the period (12- 13)	319,08	1,555,53	1,915,64	1,874,61	3,894,08	8,223,66

Particulars	For the quarter ended 30.09.2016	For the quarter ended 30.06.2016	For the quarter ended 30.09.2015	For the half year ended 30.09.2016	For the half year ended 30.09.2015	For the year ended 31.03.2016
	(Unaudited)	(Unaudited)	(Unaudited)	(Unaudited)	(Unaudited)	(Audited)
15. Paid-up equity share capita! (Face value *f2/-* per share)	477,95	477,46	475,59	477,95	475,59	*476.57*
16. Reserves excluding revaluation reserves						52,688,34
17. Analytical Ratios						
(i) Percentage of Shares held by Government of India	NIL	NIL	NIL	NIL	NIL	NIL
(ii) Capital Adequacy Ratio (Basel III)	14.78%	15.30%	14.37%	14.78%	14.37%	15.29%
(iii) Earnings per Share (EPS) for the period/year (before and after extraordinary items) Basic Diluted	1.34 1.33	6.52 6.49	8.06 8.00	7.85 7.81	16.40 16.27	34.59 34.40
(iv) NPA Ratios						
(a) Amount of Gross Non Performing Assets	16,378.65	9,553,17	4,451,11	16,378,65	4,451,11	6,087,51
(b) Amount of Net Non Performing Assets	7,761,15	4,010,23	1,543,62	7,761,15	1,543,62	2,522,14
(c) % of Gross NPAs	4.17	2.54	1.38	4.17	1.38	1.67
(d) % of Net NPAs	2.02	1.08	0.48	2.02	0.48	0.70
(v) Return on Assets (annualized)	0.23	1.19	1.64	0.70	1.71	1.72

Notes:

1. Statement of Assets and Liabilities of the Bank as on 30th September, 2016 is given below.

(INR in lacs)

Particulars	As on 30.09.2016	As on 30.09.2015
	(Unaudited)	(Unaudited)
CAPITAL AND LIABILITIES		
Capital	477,95	475,59
Reserves and Surplus	53,345,37	48.416,51
Deposits	380,187,16	324,101,08
Borrowings	100,414,68	84,352,07
Other Liabilities and Provisions	23,225.27	19,179,56
TOTAL	**557,650,43**	**476,524,81**
ASSETS		
Cash and Balances with Reserve Bank of India	19,081,14	16,798,38

Particulars	As on 30.09.2016 (Unaudited)	As on 30.09.2015 (Unaudited)
Balances with Banks and Money at Call and Short Notice	18,125,33	13,034,09
Investments	124,589,93	113,681,02
Advances	353,169,94	298,065,59
Fixed Assets	3,592,70	2,588,05
Other Assets	39,091,39	32,357,68
TOTAL	**557,650,43**	**476,524,81**

2. The Bank has presented mark-to-market gain or loss on foreign exchange and derivative contracts on gross basis as against the erstwhile policy of presenting the same on net basis. Consequent to the change, the balance of other assets and other liabilities is higher by INR 5,900.59 crores and INR 3,800.25 crores as on 30th September, 2016 and 30th September, 2015 respectively. The aforesaid change in presentation has no impact on the profit of the bank for the period ended on 30th September, 2016 and 30lh September, 2015.
3. 'Other income' includes gains from securities' transactions, commission earned from guarantees/letters of credit, fees earned from providing services to customers, selling of third party products, ATM sharing fees.
4. During the quarter ended 30th September, 2016, the Bank allotted 2,481,440 equity shares pursuant to the exercise of options under its Employee Stock Option Scheme.
5. In accordance with RBI circular DBR.No.BP.BC.1/21.06.201/2015-16 dated 1st July, 2015 on 'Basel III Capital Regulations' and RBI circular DBR.No.BP.BC.80/21.06.201/2014-15 dated 31st March, 2015 on 'Prudential Guidelines on Capital Adequacy and Liquidity Standards Amendments', banks are required to make Pillar 3 disclosures including leverage ratio and liquidity coverage ratio under the Basel III framework. The Bank has made these disclosures .which are available on its website at the following link: http://www.axisbank.com/investor-corner/basellll-disclosures.aspx. The disclosures have not been subjected to audit or limited review by the statutory auditors of the Bank.
6. The above results have been approved by the Board of Directors of the Bank at its meeting held at Mumbai today.
7. These results for the half year ended 30th September, 2016 have been subjected to a "Limited Review" by the statutory auditors of the Bank.
8. Previous period figures have been regrouped and reclassified, where necessary, to make them comparable with current period figures.

Axis Bank Limited Segmental Results

(INR in lacs)

		For the quarter ended 30.09.2016	For the quarter ended 30.06.2016	For the quarter ended 30.09.2015	For the half year ended 30.09.2016	For the half year ended 30.09.2015	For the year ended 31.03.2016
		(Unaudited)	**(Unaudited)**	**(Unaudited)**	**(Unaudited)**	**(Unaudited)**	**(Audited)**
1	Segment Revenue						
A	Treasury	15,749,07	16,108,51	15,686,51	31,857,58	28,584,70	60,190,66
B	Corporate/Wholesale Banking	6,079,75	6,123,17	5,649,35	12,202,92	11,179,34	23,348,42
C	Retail Banking	9,586,64	9,123,57	8,469,11	18,710,21	16,315,82	33,987,96
D	Other Banking Business	236,39	158,19	208,23	394,58	368,91	894,73
	Total	**31,651,85**	**31,513,44**	**30,013,20**	**63,165,29**	**56,448,77**	**1,18,421,77**
	Less: Inter segment revenue	17,953,08	17,661,26	18,03 2,19	35,614,34	32,213,35	68.062,27
	income from Operations	13,698,77	13,852,18	12,001,01	27,550,95	24,235,42	50,359,50
2	**Segment Results After Provisions & Before Tax**						
A	Treasury	(39,67)	1,025,10	376,16	985,43	1,679,41	3,305,54
B	Corporate/Wholesale Banking	(708,00)	446,98	1,632,92	(261,02)	2,644,02	5,559,66
C	Retail Banking	1,016,82	749,17	727,56	1,765,99	1,246,63	2,742,56
D	Other Banking Business	208,29	130,95	184,14	339,24	321,02	785,99
	Total Profit Before Tax	**477,44**	**2,352,20**	**2,920,78**	**2,829,64**	**5,891,08**	**12,393,75**
3	**Segment Assets**						
A	Treasury	1,89,671,86	1,81,922,94	1,68,461,18	1,89,671,86	1,68,461,18	1,79,902,25
B	Corporate/Wholesale Banking	1,96,274,91	1,95,047,26	1,66,973,18	1,96,274,91	1,66,973,18	1,90,831,82
C	Retail Banking	1,67,576,66	1,59,658,95	1,37,908,47	1,67,576,66	1,37,908,47	1,56,657,98
D	Other Banking Business	690,88	727,04	817,91	690,88	817,91	731,53
E	Unallocated	3,436,12	2,294,13	2,364,07	3,436,12	2,364,07	2,343,44
	Total	**5,57,650,43**	**5,39,650,32**	**4,76,524,81**	**5,57,650,43**	**4,76,524,81**	**5,30,467,02**
4	**Segment Liabilities**						
A	Treasury	1,85,737,08	1,87,613,36	1,57,789,62	1,85,737,08	1,57,789,62	1,74,301,51
B	Corporate/Wholesale Banking	87,016,98	77,837,71	74,563,44	87,016,98	74,563,44	90,433,40
C	Retail Banking	2,30,935,66	2,19,239,96	1,95,157,36	2,30,935,66	1,95,157,36	2,12,526,77
E	Unallocated	108,56	65,21	91,02	108,56	91,02	17,74

		For the quarter ended 30.09.2016	For the quarter ended 30.06.2016	For the quarter ended 30.09.2015	For the half year ended 30.09.2016	For the half year ended 30.09.2015	For the year ended 31.03.2016
		(Unaudited)	(Unaudited)	(Unaudited)	(Unaudited)	(Unaudited)	(Audited)
	Capital and Other Reserves	53,823,32	54,870,62	48,892,10	53,823,32	48,892,10	53,164,91
	Total	5,57,650,43	5,39,650,32	4,76,524,81	5,57,650,43	4,76,524,81	5,30,467,02

Note: Previous period figures have been regrouped and reclassified, where necessary, to make them comparable with current period figures.

For and on behalf of the Board

SHIKHA SHARMA
MD & CEO

Place: Mumbai

Date: 25th October, 2016

C. BANK OF BARODA

(INR in lacs)

Sr No		Particulars	Quarter Ended			Half Year Ended		Year Ended
			30.09.2016	30.06.2016	30.09.2015	30.09.2016	30.09.2015	31.03.2016
			Reviewed	Reviewed	Reviewed	Reviewed	Reviewed	Audited
1		Interest earned (a)+(b)+(c)+(d)	1048517	1043352	1115636	2091869	2243285	4406127
	(a)	Interest /discount on advances / bills	683974	716208	771193	1400182	1574464	2979623
	(b)	Income on investments	253289	249496	273935	502785	529800	1067322
	(c)	Interest on balances with Reserve Bank of India and other inter bank funds	39178	32492	29121	71670	58726	130592
	(d)	Others	72076	45156	41387	117232	80295	228590
2		Other Income	156143	144439	114404	300582	211127	499886
3		Total Income (1 + 2)	1204660	1187791	1230040	2392451	2454412	4906013
4		Interest Expended	705907	706243	791189	1412150	1572876	3132143
5		Operating Expenses (a)+ (b)+ (C)	229733	214599	205149	444332	427639	892313
	(a)	Employees cost	116850	110812	104398	227662	238906	497802
	(b)	Rent, Taxes & Lighting	25740	20118	22160	45858	40528	86202
	(c)	Other operating expenses	87143	83669	78591	170812	148205	308309
6		Total Expenditure (4+5) excluding provisions and contingencies	935640	920842	996338	1856482	2000515	4024456
7		Operating Profit (3-6) before Provisions and Contingencies	269020	266949	233702	535969	453897	881557
8		Provisions (other than tax) and Contingencies	179584	200407	189170	379991	249144	1551365
		of which provisions for Non-peforming Asset	163045	198644	184380	361689	241162	1376591
9		Exceptional Items	0	0	0	0	0	0
10		Profit (+)/Loss (-) from Ordinary Activities before tax (7-8-9)	89436	66542	44532	155978	204753	(669808)
11		Provision for Taxes	34224	24180	32084	58404	87090	(130253)
12		Net Profit (+) / Loss (-) from Ordinary Activities after tax (10-11)	55212	42362	12448	97574	117663	(539555)
13		Extraordinary items (net of tax expenses)	0	0	0	0	0	0

Sr No		Particulars	Quarter Ended			Half Year Ended		Year Ended
			30.09.2016	30.06.2016	30.09.2015	30.09.2016	30.09.2015	31.03.2016
			Reviewed	Reviewed	Reviewed	Reviewed	Reviewed	Audited
14		Net Profit (+)/Loss (-) for the period (12-13)	55212	42362	12448	97574	117663	(539555)
15		Paid-up equity share capital (Face Value of INR 2 each)	46209	46209	46209	46209	46209	46209
16		Reserve excluding Revaluation Reserve	-	-	-	-	-	3561068
17		Analytical Ratios						
	i)	Percentage of shares held by Government of India	59.24	59.24	59.24	59.24	59.24	59.24
	ii)	Capital Adequacy Ratio(%) -Basel-Ill	12.94	13.07	12.51	12.94	12.51	13.17
	a	CET 1 Ratio (%)	10.09	10.19	9.42	10.09	9.42	10.29
	b	Additional Tier 1 Ratio (%)	0.50	0.51	0.50	0.50	0.50	0.50
	iii)	Earnings Per Share						
		Basic and diluted EPS before and after Extraordinary items, net of tax expenses (not annualized) [in INR]	2.39	1.84	0.56	4.23	5.32	(23.89)
	iv)	NPA Ratios						
	(a)	Gross NPA	4294925	4299168	2371033	4294925	2371033	4052104
		Net NPA	1934195	2078377	1279782	1934195	1279782	1940646
	(b)	% of Gross NPA	11.35	11.15	5.56	11.35	5.56	9.99
		% of Net NPA	5.46	5.73	3.08	5.46	3.08	5.06
	v)	Return on Assets (annualized) %	0.33	0.25	0.07	0.29	0.33	(0.78)

Notes forming part of the un-audited financial results for the Quarter/Half Year Ended 30th September, 2016

1. The above financial results have been reviewed by the Audit Committee of Board in their meeting held on 11th November, 2016 and approved by the Board of Directors in their meeting held on 11th November, 2016. The same have been subjected to Limited Review by the Statutory Central Auditors of the Bank, in line with the guidelines issued by Reserve Bank of India and as per the requirement of listing agreement with Stock Exchanges.
2. The above results for the quarter/half year ended 30th September 2016 have been prepared, following the same accounting policy as those followed in the annual financial statements for the year ended 31st March, 2016.
3. The financial results for the quarter ended 30th Sept 2016 have been arrived at after considering provision for Non-performing Assets, Standard Assets, Restructured Assets and depreciation/provision for Investments on the basis of prudential norms and specific guidelines issued by the RBI. The Bank has made provision @ 20% on the Secured Sub-standard Advances as against the Regulatory requirement of 15%.

4. On review of NPA advances portfolio, bank has made additional provision of INR 829 Crs during the quarter, over and above the IRAC norms.

5. In terms of RBI Circular DBOD,BP.BC.2/21.06.201/2013-14 dated 01.07.2013, Banks are required to make Pillar 3 disclosure under Basel III Capital Regulations, These details are being made available on our website "www.bankofbaroda.com". These disclosures have not been subjected to Audit by the auditors.

6. The bank has approved SDR proposals of INR 2370 Crs during this quarter in terms of RBI guidelines issued in this regard and made provision of INR 118.50 Crs as on 30.09.2016.

   Further in respect of provision for mark to market requirements on equity portion and 15% on residual loan portion, the bank has decided to provide such provision in equal installments over the four quarters from the date of conversion of Debt into Equity in terms of RBI circular dated 25.02.2016.

7. Non Performing Loan Provisioning Coverage Ratio is 62.95 % as on 30th September 2016.

8. A penalty of INR 22.29 lacs was imposed by overseas regulators (Kenya and Oman) for deviation in prudential / other guidelines during the quarter which has been fully provided / paid.

9. Details of Investor's complaints for the quarter ended 30.09.2016: Pending at Beginning: 0; Received: 169; Disposed off: 169; Closing: 0

10. Statement of Assets & Liabilities is as under:-

(INR in Lacs)

	As on 30th September 2016	As on 30th September 2015
	Reviewed	**Reviewed**
CAPITAL & LIABILITIES		
Capital	46209	46209
Reserves and Surplus	4033967	4284971
Deposits	56753124	61245779
Borrowings	3272225	3526651
Other Liabilities and Provisions	2094112	2049676
TOTAL	66199638	71153286
ASSETS		
Cash and Balances with Reserve Bank of India	2073220	2396807
Balances with Banks and Money at Call and Short Notice	12001769	11081021
Investments	13605567	13738084
Advances	35414960	41489978
Fixed Assets	601971	300410
Other Assets	2502151	2146987
TOTAL	66199638	71153286

11 The figures of previous period have been regrouped / rearranged, wherever necessary, so as to make them comparable with those of the current period.

Segment reporting for the Quarter/Half Year Ended 30th September, 2016

Part A - Business Segments

(INR in lacs)

Sr. No.	Particulars	Quarter Ended			Half Year Ended		Year Ended
		30.09.2016	30.06.2016	30.09.2015	30.09.2016	30.09.2015	31.03.2016
		Reviewed	Reviewed	Reviewed	Reviewed	Reviewed	Audited
1	Segment Revenue						
	(a) Treasury Operations	416481	396212	388164	812693	749797	1553437
	(b) Wholesale Banking	475974	487760	523422	963734	1086255	2186743
	(c) Retail Banking	281927	294248	318403	576175	618233	1091807
	(d)Other Banking Operations	30278	9571	51	39849	127	74026
	Total Revenue	1204660	1187791	1230040	2392451	2454412	4906013
2	Segment Results						
	(a) Treasury Operations	110583	102292	62881	212875	116785	255375
	(b) Wholesale Banking	(42788)	(22977)	(36150)	(65765)	68364	(594386)
	(c) Retail Banking	57746	36242	68265	93988	141215	(147955)
	(d)Other Banking Operations	22711	7321	41	30032	100	56938
	Total	148252	122878	95037	271130	326464	(4300281
	Unallocated Expenditure	58816	56336	50505	115152	121711	239780
	Profit before Tax	89436	66542	44532	155978	204753	(669808)
	Provision for Tax	34224	24180	32084	58404	87090	(130253)
	Net Profit	55212	42362	12448	97574	117663	(539555)
3	Segment Assets						
	(a) Treasury Operations	28822704	27650758	27899457	28822704	27899457	26412307
	(b) Wholesale Banking	26176036	28629382	32111537	26176036	32111537	29353737
	(c) Retail Banking	10137647	8807699	10377606	10137647	10377606	10090113
	(d)Other Banking Operations	0	0	0		0	0
	(e) Unallocated	1063251	1082917	764686	1063251	764686	1281490
	Total Assets	66199638	66170756	71153286	66199638	71153286	67137647
4	Segment Liabilities						
	(a) Treasury Operations	27046233	25956329	26201186	27046233	26201186	24830858
	(b) Wholesale Banking	24562691	26874983	30156872	24562691	30156872	27596168
	(c) Retail Banking	9512819	8267966	9745909	9512819	9745909	9485962
	(d) Other Banking Operations	0	0	0	0	0	0

Sr. No.	Particulars	Quarter Ended			Half Year Ended		Year Ended
		30.09.2016	30.06.2016	30.09.2015	30.09.2016	30.09.2015	31.03.2016
		Reviewed	Reviewed	Reviewed	Reviewed	Reviewed	Audited
	(e) Unallocated	997718	1016557	718139	997718	718139	1204760
	Total Liabilities	62119461	62115835	66822106	62119461	66822106	63117748
5	Capital Employed						
	(a) Treasury Operations	1776471	1694429	1698271	1776471	1698271	1581449
	(b) Wholesale Banking	1613345	1754399	1954665	1613345	1954665	1757569
	(c) Retail Banking	624828	539733	631697	624828	631697	604151
	(d) Other Banking Operations	0	0	0	0	0	0
	(e) Unallocated	65533	66360	46547	65533	46547	76730
	Total Capital Employed	4080177	4054921	4331180	4080177	4331180	4019899

Segment reporting for the Quarter/Half Year Ended 30th September, 2016

Part - B: Geographic Segments

Sr. No	Particulars	Quarter Ended			Half Year Ended		Year Ended
		30.09.2016	30.06.2016	30.09.2015	30.09.2016	30.09.2015	31.03.2016
		Reviewed	Reviewed	Reviewed	Reviewed	Reviewed	Audited
1	Revenue						
	(a) Domestic	1075134	1059327	1098668	2134461	2197963	4397454
	(b) International	129526	128464	131372	257990	256449	508559
	Total	1204660	1187791	1230040	2392451	2454412	4906013
2	Assets						
	(a) Domestic	44955635	44554179	47282492	44955635	47282492	44388112
	(b) International	21244003	21616577	23870794	21244003	23870794	22749536
	Total	66199638	66170756	71153286	66199638	71153286	67137648

Notes on Segment Reporting:

1 As per guidelines of the RBI on compliance with Accounting Standards, the Bank has adopted “Treasury Operations”, Wholesale, Retail and “Other Banking Operations” as Primary business segments and “Domestic” and International as secondary/geographic segments for the purpose of compliance with AS-17 on Segment Reporting issued by ICAI.

2 Segment revenue represents revenue from external customers.

3 Capital employed for each segment has been allocated proportionate to the assets of the segment.

4 The figures of previous period / year have been regrouped / rearranged wherever necessary so as to make them comparable with those of the current period.

Place : Mumbai

Date : 11th November 2016

D. HDFC Bank Limited

FINANCIAL RESULTS FOR THE QUARTER AND HALF YEAR ENDED SEPTEMBER 30, 2016

(INR in lacs)

		Quarter ended 30.09.2016	Quarter ended 30.06.2016	Quarter ended 30.09.2015	Half year ended 30.09.2016	Half year ended 30.09.2015	Year ended 31.03.2016
	Particulars	**Unaudited**	**Unaudited**	**Unaudited**	**Audited**	**Audited**	**Audited**
1	Interest Earned (a)+(b)+(c)+(d)	1706994	1651602	1477252	3358596	2881358	6022145
	a) Interest / discount on advances / bills	1290136	1247081	1094834	2537217	2139548	4482766
	b) Income on Investments	381807	380924	339767	762731	667901	1412003
	c) Interest on balances with Reserve Bank of India and other inter bank funds	13967	4021	17466	17988	25317	36161
	d) Others	21084	19576	25165	40660	48592	91195
2	Other Income	290095	280661	255176	570756	501367	1075172
3	**TOTAL INCOME (1)+(2)**	**1997089**	**1932263**	**1732428**	**3929352**	**3382725**	**7097317**
4	Interest Expended	907635	873458	B09162	1781093	1574391	3262993
5	Operating Expenses (i)+(ii)	486999	476886	418977	963885	819056	1697969
	i) Employees cost	165721	158517	141397	324238	277298	570220
	ii) Other operating expenses	321278	318369	277580	639647	541756	1127749
6	**TOTAL EXPENDITURE (4)+(5) (excluding Provisions &**	**1394634**	**1350344**	**1228139**	**2744978**	**2393447**	**4960962**
7	Contingencies)	602455	581919	504289	1184374	989278	2136355
S	Operating Profit before Provisions and Contingencies (3)-(6) Provisions (other than tax) and Contingencies	74899	86673	68129	161572	140928	272561
9	Exceptional Items	-	-	-	-	-	-
10	Profit / (Loss) from Ordinary Activities before tax (7)-(8)-(9)	527556	495246	436160	1022802	848350	1863794
11	Tax Expense	182023	171355	149215	353378	291833	634171
12	Net Profit / (Loss) from Ordinary Activities after tax (10)-(11)	345533	323891	286945	659424	556517	1229623
13	Extraordinary items (net of tax expense)		-	-	-	-	-
14	Net Profit / (Loss) for the period (12)-(13)	345533	323891	286945	669424	556517	1229623
15	Paid up equity share capital (Face Value of INR 21/- each)	50913	50701	50364	50913	50364	50564

	Particulars	Quarter ended 30.09.2016	Quarter ended 30.06.2016	Quarter ended 30.09.2015	Half year ended 30.09.2016	Half year ended 30.09.2015	Year ended 31.03.2016
		Unaudited	Unaudited	Unaudited	Audited	Audited	Audited
16	Reserves excluding revaluation reserves						7217213
17	**Analytical Ratios** (i) Percentage of shares held by Government of India	Nil	Nil	Nil	Nil	Nil	Nil
	(ii) Capital Adequacy Ratio	15.4%	15.5%	15.5%	15.4%	15.5%	15.5%
	(iii) Earnings per share (INR) (a) Basic EPS before & after extraordinary items (net of tax expense) -not annualized	13.6	12.8	11.5	26.4	22.2	48.8
	(b) Diluted EPS before & after extraordinary items (net of tax	13.4	12.6	11.3	26.1	21.9	48.3
	expense) - not annualized (iv) NPA Ratios (a) Gross NPAs	506904	492089	382777	506904	382777	439283
	(b) Net NPAs	146885	149339	103768	148885	103768	132037
	(c) % of Gross NPAs to Gross Advances	1.02%	1.04%	0.91%	1.02%	0.91%	0.94%
	(d) % of Net NPAs to Net Advances	0.30%	0.32%	0.25%	0.30%	0.25%	0.28%
	(v) Return on assets (average) - not annualized	0.5%	0.5%	0.5%	0.9%	0.9%	1.9%

Segment information in accordance with the Accounting Standard on Segment Reporting (AS 17) of the operating segments of the Bank is as under:

(INR in lacs)

Particulars	Quarter ended 30.09.2016	Quarter ended 30.06.2016	Quarter ended 30.09.2015	Half year ended 30.09.2016	Half year ended 30.09.2015	Year ended 31.03.2016
	Unaudited	Unaudited	Unaudited	Audited	Audited	Audited
1 Segment Revenue a) Treasury	502595	502324	427215	1004919	847824	18264B8
b) Retail Banking	1651316	1585264	1470256	3236580	2866325	5925234
c) Wholesale Banking	790352	761527	671954	1551879	1330116	2716239
d) Other Banking Operations	212645	194967	178406	407612	336054	755442
e) Unallocated **Total**	**3156908**	**3044082**	**2747831**	**6200990**	**5380319**	**11223403**
Less: Inter Segment Revenue	1159819	1111819	1015403	2271638	1997594	4126086
Income from Operations	**1997089**	**1932263**	**1732428**	**3929352**	**33B2725**	**7097317**
2 Segment Results a) Treasury	26834	49173	27092	76007	60256	148921
b) Retail Banking	200731	189469	180064	390200	344406	785503
c) Wholesale Banking	259949	232716	187341	492665	387549	788720
d) Other Banking Operations	74350	58521	75298	132871	127526	283227

Particulars	Quarter ended 30.09.2016	Quarter ended 30.06.2016	Quarter ended 30.09.2015	Half year ended 30.09.2016	Half year ended 30.09.2015	Year ended 31.03.2016
	Unaudited	Unaudited	Unaudited	Audited	Audited	Audited
e) Unallocated	(34308)	(34633)	(33635)	(68941)	(71387)	(142577)
Total Profit Before Tax	**527556**	**495246**	**436160**	**1022602**	**848350**	**1863794**
3 Segment Assets						
a) Treasury	25186101	24266067	20370868	25186101	20370868	20338147
b) Retail Banking	28268880	25255629	23257355	28268880	23257355	25269065
c) Wholesale Banking	22697228	22318870	20039762	22697228	20039762	22624265
d) Other Banking Operations	2214545	2204164	1877149	2214545	1877149	2163306
e) Unallocated	515941	465278	454713	515941	454713	489774
Total	**78882695**	**75510008**	**65999847**	**78882695**	**65999847**	**70884557**
4 Segment Liabilities						
a) Treasury	7305597	6048990	4202613	7305597	4202613	4538987
b) Retail Banking	48817836	46701569	41342011	48817836	41342011	44831340
c) Wholesale Banking	12602207	12807800	11509677	12682207	11509677	12042552
d) Other Banking Operations	287794	264259	233866	287794	233866	247631
e) Unallocated	1733535	2050833	1883969	1733535	1883969	1956270
Total	**70826969**	**67873451**	**59172136**	**70B26969**	**59172136**	**63616780**
5 Capital Employed (Segment Assets-Segment Liabilities) a) Treasury	17880504	16217077	16168255	17880504	16168255	15799160
b) Retail Banking	(20548956)	(20445940)	(1B084656)	(20548956)	(18084656)	(19562275)
c) Wholesale Banking	10015021	9511070	8530085	10015021	6530085	10581713
d) Other Banking Operations	1926751	1939905	1643283	1926751	1643283	1915675
e) Unallocated	(1217594)	(1585555)	(1429256)	(1217594)	(1429256)	(1466496)
Total	**8055726**	**7636557**	**6827711**	**8055726**	**6827711**	**7267777**

Business Segments have been identified and reported taking into account the target customer profile, the nature of products and services, the differing risks and returns, the organisation structure, the internal business reporting system and the guidelines prescribed by RBI.

Notes:

1 Statement of Assets and Liabilities as on September 30, 2016 is given below.

(INR in lacs)

Particulars	As at 30.09.2016	As at 30,09.2015	As at 31.03.2016
CAPITAL AND LI ABILITIES	**Audited**	**Audited**	**Audited**
Capital	50913	50384	50564
Reserves and Surplus	8004813	6777347	7217213
Deposits	59173061	50690866	54642419
Borrowings	7703851	5230736	5301848
Other Liabilities and Provisions	3950057	3250534	3672513
Total	**78882695**	**65999847**	**70884557**
ASSETS			
Cash and Balances with Reserve Bank of India	2862972	2570396	3005831
Balances with Banks and Money at Call and Short notice	1787833	778444	886053
Investments	20665262	17128133	16388578
Advances	49441784	41854097	46459396
Fixed Assets	351225	321165	334315
Other Assets	3773619	3347612	3810384
Total	**78882695**	**65999847**	**70884557**

2 The above results have been approved by the Board of Directors at its meeting held on October 25, 2016. The results for the half year ended September 30, 2016 have been audited by the Statutory Auditors of the Bank. An unqualified report has been issued by them thereon.

3 The Bank has followed the same significant accounting policies in the preparation of these financial results as those followed in the annual financial statements for the year ended March 31, 2016.

4 During the quarter and half year ended September 30, 2016, the Bank allotted 10501700 and 17447200 shares respectively pursuant to the exercise of options under the approved employee stock option schemes.

5 RBI circular DBQD.No.BP.BC.1/21.06.201/2015-16 dated July 1, 2015 on 'Basel III Capital Regulations' read together with the RBI circular D8R.No.BP.BC.80/21.06.201/2014-15 dated March 31. 2015 on 'Prudential Guidelines on Capital Adequacy and Liquidity Standards - Amendments' requires banks to make applicable Pillar 3 disclosures including leverage ratio and liquidity coverage ratio under the Basel III Framework. These disclosures are available on the Bank's website at the following link: http:/www.hdfcbank.com/aboutus/basel_disctosures/default.htm. The disclosures have not been subjected to audit or limited review.

6 Other income relates to income from non-fund based banking activities including commission, fees, earnings from foreign exchange and derivative transactions, profit and loss (including revaluation) from investments and recoveries from accounts written off.

7 As at September 30, 2016, the total number of branches (including extension counters) and ATM network stood at 4548 branches and 12016 ATMs respectively.

8 Figures of the previous period have been regrouped/reclassified wherever necessary to conform to current period's classification.

9 INR 10 lac = INR 1 million INR 10 million = INR 1 crore

Place: Mumbai

Date : October 25, 2016

Chapter 11

Formats for filing financial results

SEBI has issued circular dated 30 November 2015 which prescribes the formats for preparation of interim financial results under reg 33 of the SEBI Listing Regulations.

SEBI has also issued circular dated 27 November 2015 which prescribes the formats for preparation of interim financial results under reg 52 SEBI Listing Regulations.

This chapter contains formats for the following:

- Formats for interim financial results under regulation 33;
- Formats for interim financial results under regulation 52.

11.1 FORMATS FOR INTERIM FINANCIAL RESULTS UNDER REGULATION 33

11.1.1 Format for submission of Unaudited/Audited interim financial results for companies other than banks for quarter ending 30 June 2016, 30 September 2016 and 31 December 2016

Part I	**(INR in___)**
Statement of Standalone / Consolidated Unaudited / Audited Results for the Quarter and Months Ended dd/mm/yyyy OR for the Year	**Ended dd/mm/yyyy**

Particulars	**3 months ended (dd/mm/ yyyy)**	**Preceding 3 months ended (dd/mm/ yyyy)**	**Correspon ding 3 months ended in the previous year (dd/mm/ yyyy)**	**Year to date figures for current period ended (dd/mm/yy yy)**	**Year to date figures for the previous year ended d/mm/ yyyy)**	**Previous year ended (dd/mm/ yyyy)**
(Refer Notes Below)	(Unaudited) /(Audited)	(Unaudited) /(Audited)	(Unaudited) /(Audited)	(Unaudited) /(Audited)	(Unaudited) /(Audited)	(Audited)
1. Income from Operations (a) Net Sales/Income from Operations (Net of excise duty) (b) Other Operating Income						

Particulars	3 months ended (dd/mm/ yyyy)	Preceding 3 months ended (dd/mm/ yyyy)	Correspon ding 3 months ended in the previous year (dd/mm/ yyyy)	Year to date figures for current period ended (dd/mm/yy yy)	Year to date figures for the previous year ended d/mm/ yyyy)	Previous year ended (dd/mm/ yyyy)
(Refer Notes Below)	(Unaudited) /(Audited)	(Unaudited) /(Audited)	(Unaudited) /(Audited)	(Unaudited) /(Audited)	(Unaudited) /(Audited)	(Audited)
Total income from Operations (net)						
2. Expenses (a) Cost of Materials consumed (b) Purchase of stock-in-trade (c) Changes in inventories of finished goods, work-in-progress and stock-in-trade (d) Employee benefits expense (e) Depreciation and amortisation expense (f) Other expenses(Any item exceeding 10% of the total expenses relating to continuing operations to be shown separately) **Total Expenses**						
3. Profit / (Loss) from operations before other income, finance costs and exceptional items (1-2)						
4. Other Income						
5. Profit / (Loss) from ordinary activities before finance costs and exceptional items (3 ± 4)						
6. Finance Costs						
7. Profit / (Loss) from ordinary activities after finance costs but before exceptional items (5 ± 6)						
8. Exceptional Items						
9.Profit / (Loss) from ordinary activities before tax (7 ± 8)						
10. Tax expense						
11.Net Profit / (Loss) from ordinary activities after tax (9 ± 10)						
12. Extraordinary items (net of tax INR expense _____ Lakhs)						
13. Net Profit / (Loss) for the period (11 ± 12)						
14. Share of Profit / (loss) of associates *						
15. Minority Interest*						
16. Net Profit/(Loss) after taxes, minority interest and share of profit / (loss) of associates (13 ± 14 ± 15) *						
17. Paid-up equity share capital (Face Value of the Share shall be indicated)						

Particulars	3 months ended (dd/mm/ yyyy)	Preceding 3 months ended (dd/mm/ yyyy)	Corresponding 3 months ended in the previous year (dd/mm/ yyyy)	Year to date figures for current period ended (dd/mm/yy yy)	Year to date figures for the previous year ended d/mm/ yyyy)	Previous year ended (dd/mm/ yyyy)
(Refer Notes Below)	(Unaudited) /(Audited)	(Unaudited) /(Audited)	(Unaudited) /(Audited)	(Unaudited) /(Audited)	(Unaudited) /(Audited)	(Audited)
18. Reserve excluding Revaluation Reserves as per balance sheet of previous accounting year						
19.i Earnings Per Share (before extraordinary items) (of INR__/- each) (not annualised): (a) Basic (b) Diluted **19.ii Earnings Per Share (after extraordinary items) (of INR___/- each) (not annualised):** (a) Basic (b) Diluted See accompanying note to the Financial Results						

* Applicable in the case of consolidated results.

Note:

- Profit/loss from discontinuing operations, if any, included in the above shall be disclosed separately with details thereof.
- A company which presents quarterly financial results in accordance with Ind AS 34 Interim Financial Reporting (applicable under Companies (Indian Accounting Standards) Rules, 2015) for the period covered by its first Ind AS financial statement shall comply with the requirements of paragraph 32 of Ind AS 101 – First time Adoption of Indian Accounting Standard.

11.1.2 Format for interim financial results for banks for quarter ending 30 June 2016, 30 September 2016 and 31 December 2016

(INR in ____)

Particulars	3 months ended (dd/mm/ yyyy)	Previous 3 months ended (dd/mm/ yyyy)	Corresponding 3 months ended in the previous year (dd/mm/ yyyy)	Year to date figures for current period ended (dd/mm/ yyyy)	Year to date figures for the previous year ended (dd/mm/ yyyy)	Previous accounting year ended (dd/mm/ yyyy)
	Audited/ Unaudited*	**Audited/ Unaudited***	**Audited/ Unaudited***	**Audited/ Unaudited***	**Audited/ Unaudited***	**Audited/ Unaudited***
1. Interest earned (a)+(b)+(c)+(d)						
(a) Interest/ discount on advances/bills						

Particulars	3 months ended (dd/mm/ yyyy)	Previous 3 months ended (dd/mm/ yyyy)	Corresponding 3 months ended in the previous year (dd/mm/ yyyy)	Year to date figures for current period ended (dd/mm/ yyyy)	Year to date figures for the previous year ended (dd/mm/ yyyy)	Previous accounting year ended (dd/mm/ yyyy)
	Audited/ Unaudited*	Audited/ Unaudited*	Audited/ Unaudited*	Audited/ Unaudited*	Audited/ Unaudited*	Audited/ Unaudited*
(b) Income on investments						
(c) Interest on balances with Reserve Bank of India and other interbank funds						
(d) Others						
2. Other Income						
3. Total Income (1+2)						
4. Interest Expended						
5. Operating Expenses (i)+(ii)						
(i) Employees cost						
(ii) Other operating expenses (All items exceeding 10% of the total expenditure excluding interest expenditure may be shown separately)						
6. Total Expenditure ((4+5) excluding provisions and contingencies						
7. Operating Profit before Provisions and Contingencies (3-6)						
8. Provisions (other than tax) and Contingencies						
9. Exceptional Items						
10. Profit (+)/ Loss (-) from Ordinary Activities before tax (7-8-9)						
11. Tax expense						
12. Net Profit(+)/ Loss(-) from Ordinary Activities after tax (10-11)						
13. Extraordinary items (net of tax expense) (if applicable)						
14. Net Profit (+)/ Loss (–) for the period((12- 13)						
15. Paid-up equity share capital (Face Value of the Share shall be indicated)						
16. Reserves excluding Revaluation Reserves (as per balance sheet of previous accounting year)						
17. Analytical Ratios						
(i) Percentage of shares held by Government of India						

Particulars	3 months ended (dd/mm/ yyyy)	Previous 3 months ended (dd/mm/ yyyy)	Corresponding 3 months ended in the previous year (dd/mm/ yyyy)	Year to date figures for current period ended (dd/mm/ yyyy)	Year to date figures for the previous year ended (dd/mm/ yyyy)	Previous accounting year ended (dd/mm/ yyyy)
	Audited/ Unaudited*	Audited/ Unaudited*	Audited/ Unaudited*	Audited/ Unaudited*	Audited/ Unaudited*	Audited/ Unaudited*
(ii) Capital Adequacy Ratio						
(iii) Earnings Per Share (EPS) (a) Basic and diluted EPS before Extraordinary items (net of tax expense) for the period, for the year to date and for the previous year (not to be annualized) (b) Basic and diluted EPS after Extraordinary items for the period, for the year to date and for the previous year (not to be annualized)						
(ii) NPA Ratios (a) Gross/Net NPA (b) % of Gross/Net NPA (c) Return on Assets						

* Strike off whichever is not applicable Notes (as per RBI requirements)

1. Employee cost under operating expenses to include all forms of consideration given by the bank in exchange for services rendered by employees. It should also include provisions for post-employment benefits such as gratuity, pension, other retirement benefits, etc.

2. A company which presents quarterly financial results in accordance with Ind AS 34 Interim Financial Reporting (applicable under Companies (Indian Accounting Standards) Rules, 2015) for the period covered by its first Ind AS financial statement shall comply with the requirements of paragraph 32 of Ind AS 101 – First time Adoption of Indian Accounting Standard.

11.1.3 Format for interim financial results for manufacturing, trading and service companies, which propose to follow functional (secondary) classification of expenditure in the annual profit and loss account

(INR In ____)

S. No	Particulars	3 months ended (dd/mm/ yyyy)	Previous 3 months ended (dd/mm/yyyy)	Corresponding 3 months ended in the previous year (dd/mm/ yyyy)	Year to date figures for current period ended (dd/mm/ yyyy)	Year to date figures for the previous year ended (dd/mm/ yyyy)	Previous accounting year ended (dd/mm/ yyyy)
		Audited/ Unaudited*	Audited/ Unaudited*	Audited/ Unaudited*	Audited/ Unaudited*	Audited/ Unaudited*	Audited/ Unaudited*
1	Net Income from sales/services						
2	Cost of sales/services (a) Increase/decrease in						

S. No	Particulars	3 months ended (dd/mm/ yyyy)	Previous 3 months ended (dd/mm/yyyy)	Corresponding 3 months ended in the previous year (dd/mm/ yyyy)	Year to date figures for current period ended (dd/mm/ yyyy)	Year to date figures for the previous year ended (dd/mm/ yyyy)	Previous accounting year ended (dd/mm/ yyyy)
		Audited/ Unaudited*	Audited/ Unaudited*	Audited/ Unaudited*	Audited/ Unaudited*	Audited/ Unaudited*	Audited/ Unaudited*
	stock in trade and work in progress (b) Consumption of raw materials (c) Purchase of traded goods (d) Other expenditure						
3	Gross Profit (1-2)						
4	General Administrative Expenses						
5	Selling and Distribution Expenses						
6	Depreciation						
7	Operating Profit before interest (3) – (4+5+6)						
8	Interest						
9	Exceptional Items						
10	Operating Profit after interest and Exceptional Items (7-8-9)						
11	Other Income						
12	Profit (+)/Loss (-) from Ordinary Activities before tax (10-11)						
13	Tax Expense						
14	Net Profit (+)/ Loss (-) from Ordinary Activities after tax (12-13)						
15	Extraordinary items (net of tax expense)						
16	Net Profit (+)/ Loss(-) for the period (14-15)						
17	Paid-up equity share capital (Face value of the Share shall be indicated)						
18	Reserves excluding Revaluation Reserves (as per balance sheet) of previous accounting year						
19	Earnings Per Share (EPS) (a) Basic and diluted EPS before Extraordinary items for the period, for the year to date and for the previous year (not to be						

S. No		Particulars	3 months ended (dd/mm/ yyyy)	Previous 3 months ended (dd/mm/yyyy)	Corresponding 3 months ended in the previous year (dd/mm/ yyyy)	Year to date figures for current period ended (dd/mm/ yyyy)	Year to date figures for the previous year ended (dd/mm/ yyyy)	Previous accounting year ended (dd/mm/ yyyy)
			Audited/ Unaudited*	Audited/ Unaudited*	Audited/ Unaudited*	Audited/ Unaudited*	Audited/ Unaudited*	Audited/ Unaudited*
		annualized)						
	(b)	Basic and diluted EPS after Extraordinary items for the period, for the year to date and for the previous year (not to be annualized)						

* strike off whichever is notapplicable

Note:

- Total expenditure incurred on:

  (1) Employee Cost or

  (2) Any item of expenditure which exceeds 10% of the total expenditure, shall be given as a note.

- A company which presents quarterly financial results in accordance with Ind AS 34 Interim Financial Reporting (applicable under Companies (Indian Accounting Standards) Rules, 2015) for the period covered by its first Ind AS financial statement shall comply with the requirements of paragraph 32 of Ind AS 101 – First time Adoption of Indian Accounting Standard.

11.1.4 Format for interim financial results for quarter ending 31 March 2017 onwards

SEBI circular dated 5 July 2016 states that for the period ending on or after 31 March 2017:

(a) The formats for unaudited/audited quarterly financial results to be submitted by the listed entities, with the stock exchanges, shall be as per the formats for as prescribed in Schedule III to *the Companies Act, 2013* (excluding notes and detailed sub-classification).

(b) Banking companies and insurance companies shall follow the formats as prescribed under the respective Acts/Regulations as specified by their Regulators.

11.2 FORMATS FOR INTERIM FINANCIAL RESULTS UNDER REGULATION 52

11.2.1 Format for half yearly interim financial results for companies other than banks and NBFCs till the period ending 31 December 2016

(INR in Lacs)

Particulars	6 months ended (dd/mm/yyyy)	Corresponding 6 months ended in the previous year (dd/mm/yyyy)	Year to Date Figures for Current Period Ended (dd/mm/yyyy)	Previous accounting year ended (dd/mm/yyyy)
	Audited/ Unaudited*	Audited/ Unaudited*	Audited / Unaudited*	Audited /Unaudited*
1. (a) Net Sales/Income from Operations (b) Other Operating Income				
2. Expenditure (a) Increase/decrease in stock in trade and work inprogress (b) Consumption of raw materials (c) Purchase of traded goods (d) Employees cost (e) Depreciation (f) Other expenditure (g) Total (Any item exceeding 10% of the total expenditure to be shown separately)				
3. Profit from Operations before Other Income, Interest and Exceptional Items (1–2)				
4. Other Income				
5. Profit before Interest & Exceptional Items (3+4)				
6. Interest				
7. Exceptional items				
8. Profit (+)/ Loss (-) from Ordinary Activities before tax (3) - (4+5+6)				
9. Tax expense				
10. Net Profit (+)/ Loss (-) from Ordinary Activities after tax (7-8)				
11. Extraordinary Items (net of tax expense INR____)				
12. Net Profit(+)/ Loss(-) for the				

Particulars	6 months ended (dd/mm/yyyy)	Corresponding 6 months ended in the previous year (dd/mm/yyyy)	Year to Date Figures for Current Period Ended (dd/mm/yyyy)	Previous accounting year ended (dd/mm/yyyy)
	Audited/ Unaudited*	Audited/ Unaudited*	Audited / Unaudited*	Audited /Unaudited*
period (9-10)				
13. Paid-up equity share capital (Face Value of the Share shall be indicated)				
14. Paid up Debt Capital				
15. Reserves excluding Revaluation Reserves as per balance sheet of previous accounting year				
16. Debenture Redemption Reserve				
17. Earnings Per Share (EPS)				
18. Debt Equity Ratio				
19. Debt Service Coverage Ratio				
20. Interest Service Coverage Ratio				

Note: Suggested definition for Coverage Ratios: ISCR = Earnings before Interest and Tax / Interest Expense. DSCR = Earnings before Interest and Tax/ (Interest + Principal Repayment). Formula used for actual computation of the ratios shall be disclosed in the footnotes.

11.2.2 Format for half yearly interim financial results for banks and NBFCs till the period ending 31 December 2016

(INR in lacs)

Particulars	6 months ended (dd/mm/yyyy)	Corresponding 6 months ended in the previous year (dd/mm/yyyy)	Year to Date Figures for Current Period Ended (dd/mm/yyyy)	Previous accounting year ended (dd/mm/yyyy)
	Audited/ Unaudited*	Audited/ Unaudited*	Audited / Unaudited*	Audited /Unaudited*
1. Interest earned (a)+(b)+(c)+(d)				
(a) Interest/disc. on advances/ bills				
(b) Income on investments				
(c) Interest on balances with Reserve Bank of India and other interbank funds				
(d) Others				
2. Other Income				
3. Total Income (1+2)				

Particulars	6 months ended (dd/mm/yyyy)	Corresponding 6 months ended in the previous year (dd/mm/yyyy)	Year to Date Figures for Current Period Ended (dd/mm/yyyy)	Previous accounting year ended (dd/mm/yyyy)
	Audited/ Unaudited*	**Audited/ Unaudited***	**Audited / Unaudited***	**Audited /Unaudited***
4. Interest Expended				
5. Operating Expenses (i)+(ii)				
(i) Employees cost				
(ii) Other operating expenses (All items exceeding 10% of the total expenditure excluding interest expenditure may be shown separately)				
6. Total Expenditure ((4+5) excluding provisions and contingencies				
7. Operating Profit before Provisions and Contingencies (3-6)				
8. Provisions (other than tax) and Contingencies				
9. Exceptional Items				
10. Profit (+)/ Loss (-) from Ordinary Activities before tax (7-8-9)				
11. Tax expense				
12. Net Profit(+)/ Loss(-) from Ordinary Activities after tax (10-11)				
13. Extraordinary items (net of tax expense)				
14. Net Profit (+)/ Loss (–) for the period (12-13)				
15. Paid-up equity share capital (Face Value of the Share shall be indicated)				
16. Reserves excluding Revaluation Reserves (as per balance sheet of previous accounting year)				
17. Analytical Ratios				
(i) Capital Adequacy Ratio				
(ii) Earnings Per Share (EPS)				
18) NPA Ratios (a) Gross/Net NPA (b) % of Gross/Net NPA (c) Return on Assets				

*strike off whichever is not applicable

Notes (as per RBI requirements)

1. Employee cost under Operating expenses to include all forms of consideration given by the bank in Exchange for services rendered by employees. It should also include provisions for post-employment benefits such as gratuity, pension, other retirement benefits, etc.
2. Extraordinary items as defined in Accounting Standard 5 as income or expenses that arise from the ordinary activities of the enterprise and therefore, are not expected to recur frequently or regularly.

11.2.3 Format for half yearly interim financial results for manufacturing, trading and service companies, which have followed functional (secondary) classification of expenditure in the annual profit and loss account published in the most recent annual report or which proposed to follow such classification for the current financial year

(INR in lakh)

Particulars	3 months ended (dd/mm/yyyy)	Corresponding 3 months ended in the previous year (dd/mm/yyyy)	Year to Date Figures for Current Period Ended (dd/mm/yyyy)	Year to Date Figures for the previous year ended (dd/mm/yyyy)	Previous accounting year ended (dd/mm/yyyy)
	Audited/ Unaudited*	Audited/ Unaudited*	Audited / Unaudited*	Audited / Unaudited*	Audited /Unaudited *
1. Net Income from Sales and Services					
2. Cost of sales/services (a) Increase/decrease in stock in trade and work in progress (b) Consumption of raw materials (c) Purchase of traded goods (d) Other expenditure					
3. Gross Profit (1-2)					
4. General Administrative Expenses					
5. Selling and Distribution Expenses					
6. Depreciation					
7. Operating Profit before interest (3) – (4+5+6)					
8. Interest					

Particulars	3 months ended (dd/mm/yyyy)	Corresponding 3 months ended in the previous year (dd/mm/yyyy)	Year to Date Figures for Current Period Ended (dd/mm/yyyy)	Year to Date Figures for the previous year ended (dd/mm/yyyy)	Previous accounting year ended (dd/mm/yyyy)
	Audited/ Unaudited*	**Audited/ Unaudited***	**Audited / Unaudited***	**Audited / Unaudited***	**Audited /Unaudited ***
9. Exceptional Items					
10. Operating Profit after interest and Exceptional Items (7-8-9)					
11. Other Income					
12. Profit (+)/Loss (-) from Ordinary Activities before tax (10-11)					
13. Tax Expenses					
14. Net Profit (+)/ Loss (-) from Ordinary Activities after tax (12-13)					
15. Extraordinary items (net of tax expense)					
16. Profit (+)/Loss(-) for the period(14-15)					
17. Paid-up equity share capital (Face Value of the Share shall be indicated)					
18. Paid up Debt Capital					
19. Reserves excluding Revaluation Reserves as per balance sheet of previous accounting year					
20. Debenture Redemption Reserve					
21. Earnings Per Share (EPS)					
22. Debt Equity Ratio					
23. Debt Service Coverage Ratio					
24. Interest Service Coverage Ratio					

*Strike of whichever is not applicable

Notes:

(1) Total expenditure incurred on (1) Employee Cost or (2) Any item of expenditure which exceeds 10% of the total expenditure, shall be given as a note.

(2) Suggested definition for Coverage Ratios: ISCR = Earnings before Interest and Tax/Interest Expense. DSCR = Earnings before Interest and Tax/ (Interest + Principal

Repayment). Formula used for actual computation of the ratios shall be disclosed in the footnotes.

11.2.4 Format for interim financial results for quarter ending 31 March 2017 onwards

SEBI circular dated 10 August 2016 states that for the period ending on or after 31 December 2016:

(a) the formats for half yearly and annual financial results shall be as per the formats prescribed in Schedule III to the *Companies Act, 2013* (excluding notes and detailed sub-classification).

(b) Banking companies and insurance companies shall follow the formats as prescribed under their respective Acts/Regulations as specified by their Regulators.

Other clarification

SEBI had issued a circular dated 30 November 2015, wherein, it was prescribed that 'revenue from operations' may be disclosed net of excise duty. Subsequently, as per Schedule III of the *Companies Act, 2013*, which was notified on 6 April 2016, revenue from sale of products should be disclosed inclusive of excise duty. SEBI issued a circular dated 5 July 2016, wherein as per clause 2.9 it was clarified that in case of any technical difficulty in the interpretation of any specific item in the formats or implementation of this circular while publishing the financial results, the listed entities shall be guided by the relevant provisions of the Ind-AS Rules / AS Rules and Schedule III to the *Companies Act, 2013* and may make suitable modifications, as applicable.

However, it is seen that some companies have been disclosing 'revenue from operations' including excise duty and some companies have been disclosing 'revenue from operations' excluding excise duty in their financial results for the quarter ended 30 June 2016.

It is desirable that companies follow a uniform approach with regard to disclosure of 'revenue from operations'. In view thereof, SEBI has issued the following clarification:

'Income from Operations', as mentioned in the formats for publishing financial results prescribed in the circular dated 30 November 2015, may be disclosed inclusive of excise duty, instead of net of excise duty, as specified in the Companies Act, 2013. Listed Companies are required to take note of the said clarification and comply accordingly.

Annexures

Annexure I: Schedule III to the Companies Act, 2013

MINISTRY OF CORPORATE AFFAIRS
NOTIFICATION

New Delhi, 6th April, 2016

G.S.R. 404(E).—In exercise of the powers conferred by sub section (1) of section 467 of the Companies Act, 2013 (18 of 2013), the Central Government hereby makes the following amendments to Schedule III of the said Act with effect from the date of publication of this notification in the Official Gazette, namely:-

2. In the Companies Act, 2013 (hereinafter referred to as the principal Act) in Schedule III, for the heading "General instructions for preparation of Balance Sheet and Statements of Profit and Loss of a Company" the following shall be substituted, namely:-

"Division I

Financial Statements for a company whose Financial Statements are required to comply with the Companies (Accounting Standards) Rules, 2006.

GENERAL INSTURCTIONS FOR PREPARATION OF BALANCE SHEET AND STATEMENT OF PROFIT AND LOSS OF A COMPANY".

3. In the principal Act, in Schedule III, at the end, the following shall be inserted, namely:-

"Division II

Financial Statements for a company whose financial statements are drawn up in compliance of the Companies (Indian Accounting Standards) Rules, 2015.

GENERAL INSTURCTIONS FOR PREPARATION OF FINANCIAL STATEMENTS OF A COMPANY REQUIRED TO COMPLY WITH Ind AS

1. Every company to which Indian Accounting Standards apply, shall prepare its financial statements in accordance with this Schedule or with such modification as may be required under certain circumstances.

2. Where compliance with the requirements of the Act including Indian Accounting Standards (except the option of presenting assets and liabilities in the order of liquidity as provided by the relevant Ind AS) as applicable to the companies

require any change in treatment or disclosure including addition, amendment, substitution or deletion in the head or sub-head or any changes inter se, in the financial statements or statements forming part thereof, the same shall be made and the requirements under this Schedule shall stand modified accordingly.

3. The disclosure requirements specified in this Schedule are in addition to and not in substitution of the disclosure requirements specified in the Indian Accounting Standards. Additional disclosures specified in the Indian Accounting Standards shall be made in the Notes or by way of additional statement or statements unless required to be disclosed on the face of the Financial Statements. Similarly, all other disclosures as required by the Companies Act, 2013 shall be made in the Notes in addition to the requirements set out in this Schedule.

4. (i) Notes shall contain information in addition to that presented in the Financial Statements and shall provide where required-

   (a) narrative descriptions or disaggregations of items recognised in those statements; and

   (b) information about items that do not qualify for recognition in those statements.

   (ii) Each item on the face of the Balance Sheet, Statement of Changes in Equity and Statement of Profit and Loss shall be cross-referenced to any related information in the Notes. In preparing the Financial Statements including the Notes, a balance shall be maintained between providing excessive detail that may not assist users of Financial Statements and not providing important information as a result of too much aggregation.

5. Depending upon the turnover of the company, the figures appearing in the Financial Statements shall be rounded off as below:

Turnover	Rounding off
(i) less than one hundred crore rupees	To the nearest hundreds, thousands, lakhs or millions, or decimals thereof.
(ii) one hundred crore rupees or more	To the nearest, lakhs, millions or crores, or decimals thereof.

Once a unit of measurement is used, it should be used uniformly in the Financial Statements.

6. Financial Statements shall contain the corresponding amounts (comparatives) for the immediately preceding reporting period for all items shown in the Financial Statements including Notes except in the case of first Financial Statements laid before the company after incorporation.

7. Financial Statements shall disclose all 'material' items, i.e., the items if they could, individually or collectively, influence the economic decisions that users make on the basis of the financial statements. Materiality depends on the size or

nature of the item or a combination of both, to be judged in the particular circumstances.

8. For the purpose of this Schedule, the terms used herein shall have the same meanings assigned to them in Indian Accounting Standards.

9. Where any Act or Regulation requires specific disclosures to be made in the standalone financial statements of a company, the said disclosures shall be made in addition to those required under this Schedule.

Note: This Schedule sets out the minimum requirements for disclosure on the face of the Financial Statements, i.e., Balance Sheet, Statement of Changes in Equity for the period, the Statement of Profit and Loss for the period (The term 'Statement of Profit and Loss' has the same meaning as 'Profit and Loss Account') and Notes. Cash flow statement shall be prepared, where applicable, in accordance with the requirements of the relevant Indian Accounting Standard.

Line items, sub-line items and sub-totals shall be presented as an addition or substitution on the face of the Financial Statements when such presentation is relevant to an understanding of the company's financial position or performance or to cater to industry or sector-specific disclosure requirements or when required for compliance with the amendments to the Companies Act, 2013 or under the Indian Accounting Standards.

PART I

BALANCE SHEET

Name of the Company……………………….

Balance Sheet as at ………………………

(Rupees in...........)

	Particulars	Note No.	Figures as at the end of current reporting period	Figures as at the end of the previous reporting period
	1	2	3	4
(1)	**ASSETS** **Non-current assets**			
	(a) Property, Plant and Equipment (b) Capital work-in-progress (c) Investment Property (d) Goodwill (e) Other Intangible assets (f) Intangible assets under development (g) Biological Assets other than bearer plants (h) Financial Assets (i) Investments (ii) Trade receivables (iii) Loans (iv) Others (to be specified) (i) Deferred tax assets (net) (j) Other non-current assets			
(2)	**Current assets** (a) Inventories (b) Financial Assets (i) Investments (ii) Trade receivables (iii) Cash and cash equivalents (iv) Bank balances other than (iii) above (v) Loans (vi) Others (to be specified) (c) Current Tax Assets (Net) (d) Other current assets			
	Total Assets			

	Particulars	Note No.	Figures as at the end of current reporting period	Figures as at the end of the previous reporting period
	1	2	3	4
	EQUITY AND LIABILITIES			
	Equity			
	(a) Equity Share capital			
	(b) Other Equity			
	LIABILITIES			
(1)	**Non-current liabilities**			
	(a) Financial Liabilities			
	(i) Borrowings			
	(ii) Trade payables			
	(iii) Other financial liabilities (other than those specified in item (b), to be specified)			
	(b) Provisions			
	(c) Deferred tax liabilities (Net)			
(2)	(d) Other non-current liabilities			
	Current liabilities			
	(a) Financial Liabilities			
	(i) Borrowings			
	(ii) Trade payables			
	(iii) Other financial liabilities (other than those specified in item (c)			
	(b) Other current liabilities			
	(c) Provisions			
	(d) Current Tax Liabilities (Net)			
	Total Equity and Liabilities			

See accompanying notes to the financial statements

STATEMENT OF CHANGES IN EQUITY

Name of the Company……………………..

Statement of Changes in Equity for the period ended ……………………

A. Equity Share Capital

(Rupees in.................)

Balance at the beginning of the reporting period	Changes in equity share capital during the year	Balance at the end of the reporting period

B. Other Equity

	Share application money pending allotment	Equity component of compound financial instruments	Reserves and Surplus				Debt instruments through Other Comprehensive Income	Equity Instruments through Other Comprehensive Income	Effective portion of Cash Flow Hedges	Revaluation Surplus	Exchange differences on translating the financial statements of a foreign operation	Other items of Other Comprehensive Income (specify nature)	Money received against share warrants	Total
			Capital Reserve	Securities Premium Reserve	Other Reserves (specify nature)	Retained Earnings								
Balance at the beginning of the reporting period														
Changes in accounting policy or prior period errors														
Restated balance at the beginning of the reporting period														
Total Comprehensive Income for the year														
Dividends														
Transfer to retained earnings														
Any other														

	Share application money pending allotment	Equity component of compound financial instruments	Reserves and Surplus				Debt instruments through Other Comprehensive Income	Equity Instruments through Other Comprehensive Income	Effective portion of Cash Flow Hedges	Revaluation Surplus	Exchange differences on translating the financial statements of a foreign operation	Other items of Other Comprehensive Income (specify nature)	Money received against share warrants	Total
			Capital Reserve	Securities Premium Reserve	Other Reserves (specify nature)	Retained Earnings								
change (to be specified)														
Balance at the end of the reporting period														

Note: Remeasurment of defined benefit plans and fair value changes relating to own credit risk of financial liabilities designated at fair value through profit or loss shall be recognised as a part of retained earnings with separate disclosure of such items alongwith the relevant amounts in the Notes.

Notes:

GENERAL INSTRUCTIONS FOR PREPARATION OF BALANCE SHEET

1. An entity shall classify an asset as current when-
   - (a) it expects to realise the asset, or intends to sell or consume it, in its normal operating cycle;
   - (b) it holds the asset primarily for the purpose of trading;
   - (c) it expects to realise the asset within twelve months after the reporting period; or
   - (d) the asset is cash or a cash equivalent unless the asset is restricted from being exchanged or used to settle a liability for at least twelve months after the reporting period.

   An entity shall classify all other assets as non-current.
2. The operating cycle of an entity is the time between the acquisition of assets for processing and their realisation in cash or cash equivalents. When the entity's normal operating cycle is not clearly identifiable, it is assumed to be twelve months.
3. An entity shall classify a liability as current when-
   - (a) it expects to settle the liability in its normal operating cycle;
   - (b) it holds the liability primarily for the purpose of trading;

(c) the liability is due to be settled within twelve months after the reporting period; or

(d) it does not have an unconditional right to defer settlement of the liability for at least twelve months after the reporting period. Terms of a liability that could, at the option of the counterparty, result in its settlement by the issue of equity instruments do not affect its classification.

An entity shall classify all other liabilities as non-current.

4. A receivable shall be classified as a 'trade receivable' if it is in respect of the amount due on account of goods sold or services rendered in the normal course of business.

5. A payable shall be classified as a 'trade payable' if it is in respect of the amount due on account of goods purchased or services received in the normal course of business.

6. A company shall disclose the following in the Notes:

A. Non-Current Assets

I. Property, Plant and Equipment :

(i) Classification shall be given as:

(a) Land

(b) Buildings

(c) Plant and Equipment

(d) Furniture and Fixtures

(e) Vehicles

(f) Office equipment

(g) Bearer Plants

(h) Others (specify nature)

(ii) Assets under lease shall be separately specified under each class of assets.

(iii) A reconciliation of the gross and net carrying amounts of each class of assets at the beginning and end of the reporting period showing additions, disposals, acquisitions through business combinations and other adjustments and the related depreciation and impairment losses or reversals shall be disclosed separately.

II. Investment Property:

A reconciliation of the gross and net carrying amounts of each class of property at the beginning and end of the reporting period showing additions, disposals, acquisitions through business combinations and other adjustments and the related depreciation and impairment losses or reversals shall be disclosed separately.

III Goodwill:

A reconciliation of the gross and net carrying amount of goodwill at the beginning and end of the reporting period showing additions, impairments, disposals and other adjustments.

IV. Other Intangible assets:

(i) Classification shall be given as:

(a) Brands or trademarks

(b) Computer software

(c) Mastheads and publishing titles

(d) Mining rights

(e) Copyrights, patents, other intellectual property rights, services and operating rights

(f) Recipes, formulae, models, designs and prototypes

(g) Licenses and franchises

(h) Others (specify nature)

(ii) A reconciliation of the gross and net carrying amounts of each class of assets at the beginning and end of the reporting period showing additions, disposals, acquisitions through business combinations and other adjustments and the related amortization and impairment losses or reversals shall be disclosed separately.

V. Biological Assets other than bearer plants:

A reconciliation of the carrying amounts of each class of assets at the beginning and end of the reporting period showing additions, disposals, acquisitions through business combinations and other adjustments shall be disclosed separately.

VI. Investments:

(i) Investments shall be classified as:

(a) Investments in Equity Instruments;

(b) Investments in Preference Shares;

(c) Investments in Government or trust securities;

(d) Investments in debentures or bonds;

(e) Investments in Mutual Funds;

(f) Investments in partnership firms; or

(g) Other investments (specify nature).

Under each classification, details shall be given of names of the bodies corporate that are-

(i) subsidiaries,

(ii) associates,

(iii) joint ventures, or

(iv) structured entities,

in whom investments have been made and the nature and extent of the investment so made in each such body corporate (showing separately investments which are partly-paid). Investments in partnership firms alongwith names of the firms, their partners, total capital and the shares of each partner shall be disclosed separately.

(ii) The following shall also be disclosed:

(a) Aggregate amount of quoted investments and market value thereof;

(b) Aggregate amount of unquoted investments; and

(c) Aggregate amount of impairment in value of investments.

VII. Trade Receivables:

(i) Trade receivables shall be sub-classified as:

(a) Secured, considered good;

(b) Unsecured considered good; and

(c) Doubtful.

(ii) Allowance for bad and doubtful debts shall be disclosed under the relevant heads separately.

(iii) Debts due by directors or other officers of the company or any of them either severally or jointly with any other person or debts due by firms or private companies respectively in which any director is a partner or a director or a member should be separately stated.

VIII. Loans:

(i) Loans shall be classified as-

(a) Security Deposits;

(b) Loans to related parties (giving details thereof); and

(c) Other loans (specify nature).

(ii) The above shall also be separately sub-classified as-

(a) Secured, considered good;

(b) Unsecured, considered good; and

(c) Doubtful.

(iii) Allowance for bad and doubtful loans shall be disclosed under the relevant heads separately.

(iv) Loans due by directors or other officers of the company or any of them either severally or jointly with any other persons or amounts due by firms or private companies respectively in which any director is a partner or a director or a member should be separately stated.

IX. Bank deposits with more than 12 months maturity shall be disclosed under 'Other financial assets';

X. Other non-current assets: Other non-current assets shall be classified as-

(i) Capital Advances; and

(ii) Advances other than capital advances;

(1) Advances other than capital advances shall be classified as:

(a) Security Deposits;

(b) Advances to related parties (giving details thereof); and

(c) Other advances (specify nature).

(2) Advances to directors or other officers of the company or any of them either severally or jointly with any other persons or advances to firms or private companies respectively in which any director is a partner or a director or a member should be separately stated. In case advances are of the nature of a financial asset as per relevant Ind AS, these are to be disclosed under 'other financial assets' separately.

(iii) Others (specify nature).

B. Current Assets

I. Inventories:

(i) Inventories shall be classified as-

(a) Raw materials;

(b) Work-in-progress;

(c) Finished goods;

(d) Stock-in-trade (in respect of goods acquired for trading);

(e) Stores and spares;

(f) Loose tools; and

(g) Others (specify nature).

(ii) Goods-in-transit shall be disclosed under the relevant sub-head of inventories.

(iii) Mode of valuation shall be stated.

II. Investments:

(i) Investments shall be classified as-

(a) Investments in Equity Instruments;

(b) Investment in Preference Shares;

(c) Investments in government or trust securities;

(d) Investments in debentures or bonds;

(e) Investments in Mutual Funds;

(f) Investments in partnership firms; and

(g) Other investments (specify nature).

Under each classification, details shall be given of names of the bodies corporate that are-

(i) subsidiaries,

(ii) associates,

(iii) joint ventures, or

(iv) structured entities,

in whom investments have been made and the nature and extent of the investment so made in each such body corporate (showing separately investments which are partly-paid).

(ii) The following shall also be disclosed-

(a) Aggregate amount of quoted investments and market value thereof;

(b) Aggregate amount of unquoted investments;

(c) Aggregate amount of impairment in value of investments.

III. Trade Receivables:

(i) Trade receivables shall be sub-classified as:

(a) Secured, considered good;

(b) Unsecured considered good; and

(c) Doubtful.

(ii) Allowance for bad and doubtful debts shall be disclosed under therelevant heads separately.

(iii) Debts due by directors or other officers of the company or any of them either severally or jointly with any other person or debts due by firms or private companies respectively in which any director is a partner or a director or a member should be separately stated.

IV. Cash and cash equivalents: Cash and cash equivalents shall be classified as-

a. Balances with Banks (of the nature of cash and cash equivalents);

b. Cheques, drafts on hand;

c. Cash on hand; and

d. Others (specify nature).

V. Loans:

(i) Loans shall be classified as:

(a) Security deposits;

(b) Loans to related parties (giving details thereof); and

(c) Others (specify nature).

(ii) The above shall also be sub-classified as-

(a) Secured, considered good;

(b) Unsecured, considered good; and

(c) Doubtful.

(iii) Allowance for bad and doubtful loans shall be disclosed under the relevant heads separately.

(iv) Loans due by directors or other officers of the company or any of them either severally or jointly with any other person or amounts due by firms or private companies respectively in which any director is a partner or a director or a member shall be separately stated.

VI. Other current assets (specify nature): This is an all-inclusive heading, which incorporates current assets that do not fit into any other asset categories. Other current assets shall be classified as-

(i) Advances other than capital advances

(1) Advances other than capital advances shall be classified as:

(a) Security Deposits;

(b) Advances to related parties (giving details thereof);

(c) Other advances (specify nature).

(2) Advances to directors or other officers of the company or any of them either severally or jointly with any other persons or advances to firms or private companies respectively in which any director is a partner or a director or a member should be separately stated.

(ii) Others (specify nature)

C. Cash and Bank balances: The following disclosures with regard to cash and bank balances shall be made:

(a) Earmarked balances with banks (for example, for unpaid dividend) shall be separately stated.

(b) Balances with banks to the extent held as margin money or security against the borrowings, guarantees, other commitments shall be disclosed separately.

(c) Repatriation restrictions, if any, in respect of cash and bank balances shall be separately stated.

D. Equity

I. Equity Share Capital: For each class of equity share capital:

(a) the number and amount of shares authorised;

(b) the number of shares issued, subscribed and fully paid, and subscribed but not fully paid;

(c) par value per share;

(d) a reconciliation of the number of shares outstanding at the beginning and at the end of the period;

(e) the rights, preferences and restrictions attaching to each class of shares including restrictions on the distribution of dividends and the repayment of capital;

(f) shares in respect of each class in the company held by its holding company or its ultimate holding company including shares held by subsidiaries or associates of the holding company or the ultimate holding company in aggregate;

(g) shares in the company held by each shareholder holding more than five per cent. shares specifying the number of shares held;

(h) shares reserved for issue under options and contracts or commitments for the sale of shares or disinvestment, including the terms and amounts;

(i) for the period of five years immediately preceding the date at which the Balance Sheet is prepared-

- aggregate number and class of shares allotted as fully paid up pursuant to contract without payment being received in cash;
- aggregate number and class of shares allotted as fully paid up by way of bonus shares; and
- aggregate number and class of shares bought back;

(j) terms of any securities convertible into equity shares issued along with the earliest date of conversion in descending order starting from the farthest such date;

(k) calls unpaid (showing aggregate value of calls unpaid by directors and officers);

(l) forfeited shares (amount originally paid up).

II. Other Equity:

(i) 'Other Reserves' shall be classified in the notes as-

(a) Capital Redemption Reserve;

(b) Debenture Redemption Reserve;

(c) Share Options Outstanding Account; and

(d) Others– (specify the nature and purpose of each reserve and the amount in respect thereof); (Additions and deductions since last balance sheet to be shown under each of the specified heads)

(ii) Retained Earnings represents surplus i.e. balance of the relevant column in the Statement of Changes in Equity;

(iii) A reserve specifically represented by earmarked investments shall disclose the fact that it is so represented;

(iv) Debit balance of Statement of Profit and Loss shall be shown as a negative figure under the head 'retained earnings'. Similarly, the balance of 'Other Equity', after adjusting negative balance of retained earnings, if any, shall be shown under the head 'Other Equity' even if the resulting figure is in the negative; and

(v) Under the sub-head 'Other Equity', disclosure shall be made for the nature and amount of each item.

E. Non-Current Liabilities

I. Borrowings:

(i) borrowings shall be classified as-

(a) Bonds or debentures

(b) Term loans

(I) from banks

(II) from other parties

(c) Deferred payment liabilities

(d) Deposits

(e) Loans from related parties

(f) Long term maturities of finance lease obligations

(g) Liability component of compound financial instruments

(h) Other loans (specify nature);

(ii) borrowings shall further be sub-classified as secured and unsecured. Nature of security shall be specified separately in each case.

(iii) where loans have been guaranteed by directors or others, the aggregate amount of such loans under each head shall be disclosed;

(iv) bonds or debentures (along with the rate of interest, and particulars of redemption or conversion, as the case may be) shall be stated in descending order of maturity or conversion, starting from farthest redemption or conversion date, as the case may be. Where bonds/debentures are redeemable by installments, the date of maturity for this purpose must be reckoned as the date on which the first installment becomes due;

(v) particulars of any redeemed bonds or debentures which the company has power to reissue shall be disclosed;

(vi) terms of repayment of term loans and other loans shall be stated; and

(vii) period and amount of default as on the balance sheet date in repayment of borrowings and interest shall be specified separately in each case.

III. Provisions: The amounts shall be classified as-

(a) Provision for employee benefits; and

(b) Others (specify nature).

IV. Other non-current liabilities;

(a) Advances; and

(b) Others (specify nature).

F. Current Liabilities

I. Borrowings:

(i) Borrowings shall be classified as-

(a) Loans repayable on demand

(I) from banks

(II) from other parties

(b) Loans from related parties

(c) Deposits

(d) Other loans (specify nature);

(ii) borrowings shall further be sub-classified as secured and unsecured. Nature of security shall be specified separately in each case;

(iii) where loans have been guaranteed by directors or others, the aggregate amount of such loans under each head shall be disclosed;

(iv) period and amount of default as on the balance sheet date in repayment of borrowings and interest, shall be specified separately in each case.

II. Other Financial Liabilities: Other Financial liabilities shall be classified as-

(a) Current maturities of long-term debt;

(b) Current maturities of finance lease obligations;

(c) Interest accrued;

(d) Unpaid dividends;

(e) Application money received for allotment of securities to the extent refundable and interest accrued thereon;

(f) Unpaid matured deposits and interest accrued thereon;

(g) Unpaid matured debentures and interest accrued thereon; and

(h) Others (specify nature).

'Long term debt' is a borrowing having a period of more than twelve months at the time of origination

III. Other current liabilities:

The amounts shall be classified as-

(a) revenue received in advance;

(b) other advances (specify nature); and

(c) others (specify nature);

IV. Provisions: The amounts shall be classified as-

(i) provision for employee benefits; and

(ii) others (specify nature).

G. The presentation of liabilities associated with group of assets classified as held for sale and non-current assets classified as held for sale shall be in accordance with the relevant Indian Accounting Standards (Ind ASs).

H. Contingent Liabilities and Commitments:

(to the extent not provided for)

(i) Contingent Liabilities shall be classified as-

(a) claims against the company not acknowledged as debt;

(b) guarantees excluding financial guarantees; and

(c) other money for which the company is contingently liable.

(ii) Commitments shall be classified as-

(a) estimated amount of contracts remaining to be executed on capital account and not provided for;

(b) uncalled liability on shares and other investments partly paid; and

(c) other commitments (specify nature).

I. The amount of dividends proposed to be distributed to equity and preference shareholders for the period and the related amount per share shall be disclosed separately. Arrears of fixed cumulative dividends on irredeemable preference shares shall also be disclosed separately.

J. Where in respect of an issue of securities made for a specific purpose the whole or part of amount has not been used for the specific purpose at the Balance Sheet date, there shall be indicated by way of note how such unutilised amounts have been used or invested.

7. When a company applies an accounting policy retrospectively or makes a restatement of items in the financial statements or when it reclassifies items in its financial statements, the company shall attach to the Balance Sheet, a "Balance Sheet" as at the beginning of the earliest comparative period presented.

8. Share application money pending allotment shall be classified into equity or liability in accordance with relevant Indian Accounting Standards. Share application money to the extent not refundable shall be shown under the head Equity and share application money to the extent refundable shall be separately shown under 'Other financial liabilities'.

9. Preference shares including premium received on issue, shall be classified and presented as 'Equity' or 'Liability' in accordance with the requirements of the relevant Indian Accounting Standards. Accordingly, the disclosure and presentation requirements in this regard applicable to the relevant class of equity or liability shall be applicable *mutatis mutandis* to the preference shares. For instance, redeemable preference shares shall be classified and presented under 'non-current liabilities' as 'borrowings' and the disclosure requirements in this regard applicable to such borrowings shall be applicable *mutatis mutandis* to redeemable preference shares.

10. Compound financial instruments such as convertible debentures, where split into equity and liability components, as per the requirements of the relevant Indian Accounting Standards, shall be classified and presented under the relevant heads in 'Equity' and 'Liabilities'

11. Regulatory Deferral Account Balances shall be presented in the Balance Sheet in accordance with the relevant Indian Accounting Standards.

PART II

STATEMENT OF PROFIT AND LOSS

Name of the Company……………………….

Statement of Profit and Loss for the period ended ……………………………

(Rupees in…………)

	Particulars	**Note No.**		**Figures for the current reporting period**		**Figures for the previous reporting period**
I	Revenue From Operations					
II	Other Income					
III	Total Income (I+II)					
IV	**EXPENSES** Cost of materials consumed					
	Purchases of Stock-in-Trade					
	Changes in inventories of finished goods, Stock-in - Trade and work-in-progress					
	Employee benefits expense					
	Finance costs					
	Depreciation and amortization expense					
	Other expenses					
	Total expenses (IV)					
V	Profit/(loss) before exceptional items and tax (I- IV)					
VI	Exceptional Items					
VII	Profit/(loss) before tax (V-VI)					
VIII	Tax expense: (1) Current tax (2) Deferred tax					
IX	Profit (Loss) for the period					

	Particulars	**Note No.**		**Figures for the current reporting period**		**Figures for the previous reporting period**
	from continuing operations (VII-VIII)					
X	Profit/(loss) from discontinued operations					
XI	Tax expense of discontinued operations					
XII	Profit/(loss) from Discontinued operations (after tax) (X-XI)					
XIII	Profit/(loss) for the period (IX+XII)					
XIV	Other Comprehensive Income A (i) Items that will not be reclassified to profit or loss (ii) Income tax relating to items that will not be reclassified to profit or loss B (i) Items that will be reclassified to profit or loss (ii) Income tax relating to items that will be reclassified to profit or loss					
XV	Total Comprehensive Income for the period (XIII+XIV)(Comprising Profit (Loss) and Other Comprehensive Income for the period)					

	Particulars	Note No.		Figures for the current reporting period		Figures for the previous reporting period
XVI	Earnings per equity share (for continuing operation): (1) Basic (2) Diluted					
XVII	Earnings per equity share (for discontinued operation): (1) Basic (2) Diluted					
XVIII	Earnings per equity share(for discontinued & continuing operations) (1) Basic (2) Diluted					

See accompanying notes to the financial statements

Notes:

GENERAL INSTRUCTIONS FOR PREPARATION OF STATEMENT OF PROFIT AND LOSS

1. The provisions of this Part shall apply to the income and expenditure account, in like manner as they apply to a Statement of Profit and Loss.
2. The Statement of Profit and Loss shall include:
   (1) Profit or loss for the period;
   (2) Other Comprehensive Income for the period.
   The sum of (1) and (2) above is 'Total Comprehensive Income'.
3. Revenue from operations shall disclose separately in the notes
   (a) sale of products (including Excise Duty);
   (b) sale of services; and
   (c) other operating revenues.
4. Finance Costs: Finance costs shall be classified as-
   (a) interest;
   (b) dividend on redeemable preference shares;
   (c) exchange differences regarded as an adjustment to borrowing costs; and

(d) other borrowing costs (specify nature).

5 Other income: Other income shall be classified as-

(a) interest Income ;

(b) dividend Income; and

(c) other non-operating income (net of expenses directly attributable to such income).

6. Other Comprehensive Income shall be classified into-

(A) Items that will not be reclassified to profit or loss

(i) Changes in revaluation surplus;

(ii) Remeasurements of the defined benefit plans;

(iii) Equity Instruments through Other Comprehensive Income;

(iv) Fair value changes relating to own credit risk of financial liabilities designated at fair value through profit or loss;

(v) Share of Other Comprehensive Income in Associates and Joint Ventures, to the extent not to be classified into profit or loss; and

(vi) Others (specify nature).

(B) Items that will be reclassified to profit or loss;

(i) Exchange differences in translating the financial statements of a foreign operation;

(ii) Debt Instruments through Other Comprehensive Income;

(iii) The effective portion of gains and loss on hedging instruments in a cash flow hedge;

(iv) Share of Other Comprehensive Income in Associates and Joint Ventures, to the extent to be classified into profit or loss; and

(v) Others (specify nature).

7. Additional Information: A Company shall disclose by way of notes, additional information regarding aggregate expenditure and income on the following items:

(a) employee Benefits expense [showing separately (i) salaries and wages, (ii) contribution to provident and other funds, (iii) share based payments to employees, (iv) staff welfare expenses].

(b) depreciation and amortisation expense;

(c) any item of income or expenditure which exceeds one per cent of the revenue from operations or Rs.10,00,000, whichever is higher, in addition to the consideration of 'materiality' as specified in clause 7 of the General Instructions for Preparation of Financial Statements of a Company;

(d) interest Income;

(e) interest Expense;

(f) dividend income;

(g) net gain or loss on sale of investments;

(h) net gain or loss on foreign currency transaction and translation (other than considered as finance cost);

(i) payments to the auditor as (a) auditor, (b) for taxation matters, (c) for company law matters, (d) for other services, (e) for reimbursement of expenses;

(j) in case of companies covered under section 135, amount of expenditure incurred on corporate social responsibility activities; and

(k) details of items of exceptional nature;

8. Changes in Regulatory Deferral Account Balances shall be presented in the Statement of Profit and Loss in accordance with the relevant Indian Accounting Standards.

PART III

GENERAL INSTRUCTIONS FOR THE PREPARATION OF CONSOLIDATED FINANCIAL STATEMENTS

1. Where a company is required to prepare Consolidated Financial Statements, i.e., consolidated balance sheet, consolidated statement of changes in equity and consolidated statement of profit and loss, the company shall *mutatis mutandis* follow the requirements of this Schedule as applicable to a company in the preparation of balance sheet, statement of changes in equity and statement of profit and loss. In addition, the consolidated financial statements shall disclose the information as per the requirements specified in the applicable Indian Accounting Standards notified under the Companies (Indian Accounting Standards) Rules 2015, including the following, namely:-

(i) Profit or loss attributable to 'non-controlling interest' and to 'owners of the parent' in the statement of profit and loss shall be presented as allocation for the period. Further, 'total comprehensive income' for the period attributable to 'non-controlling interest' and to 'owners of the parent' shall be presented in the statement of profit and loss as allocation for the period. The aforesaid disclosures for 'total comprehensive income' shall also be made in the statement of changes in equity. In addition to the disclosure requirements in the Indian Accounting Standards, the aforesaid disclosures shall also be made in respect of 'other comprehensive income'.

(ii) 'Non-controlling interests' in the Balance Sheet and in the Statement of Changes in Equity, within equity, shall be presented separately from the equity of the 'owners of the parent'.

(iii) Investments accounted for using the equity method.

2. In Consolidated Financial Statements, the following shall be disclosed by way of additional information:

Name of the entity in the Group	Net Assets, i.e., total assets minus total liabilities		Share in profit or loss		Share in other comprehensive income		Share in total comprehensive income	
	As % of consolidated net assets	Amount	As % of consolidated profit or loss	Amount	As % of consolidated other comprehensive income	Amount	As % of total comprehensive income	Amount
Parent								
Subsidiaries								
Indian 1.								
2.								
3.								
.								
.								
Foreign 1.								
2.								
3.								
.								
.								
Non-controlling Interests in all subsidiaries								
Associates (Investment as per the equity method)								
Indian 1.								
2.								
3.								
.								
.								
Foreign 1.								
2.								
3.								
.								
.								
Joint Ventures(investment as per the equity method)								
Indian 1.								
2.								

Name of the entity in the Group	Net Assets, i.e., total assets minus total liabilities		Share in profit or loss		Share in other comprehensive income		Share in total comprehensive income	
3.								
.								
.								
Foreign 1.								
2.								
3.								
.								
.								
Total								

3. All subsidiaries, associates and joint ventures (whether Indian or foreign) will be covered under consolidated financial statements.

4. An entity shall disclose the list of subsidiaries or associates or joint ventures which have not been consolidated in the consolidated financial statements along with the reasons of not consolidating.

[F. No. 17/62/2015-CL-V]

Note: Schedule III of the Companies Act, 2013 came into force with effect from the 1st April, 2014 *vide* Notification S.O. 902(E), dated 26-3-2014.

Appendix I

Accounting Standard (AS) 25

Interim Financial Reporting

(*This Accounting Standard includes paragraphs set in* ***bold italic*** *type and plain type, which have equal authority. Paragraphs in bold italic type indicate the main principles. This Accounting Standard should be read in the context of its objective and the General Instructions contained in part A of the Annexure to the Notification.*)

Objective

The objective of this Standard is to prescribe the minimum content of an interim financial report and to prescribe the principles for recognition and measurement in a complete or condensed financial statements for an interim period. Timely and reliable interim financial reporting improves the ability of investors, creditors, and others to understand an enterprise's capacity to generate earnings and cash flows, its financial condition and liquidity.

Scope

1. ***This Standard does not mandate which enterprises should be required to present interim financial reports, how frequently, or how soon after the end of an interim period. If an enterprise is required or elects to prepare and present an interim financial report, it should comply with this Standard.***

2. A statute governing an enterprise or a regulator may require an enter- prise to prepare and present certain information at an interim date which may be different in form and/or content as required by this Standard. In such a case, the recognition and measurement principles as laid down in this Standard are applied in respect of such information, unless otherwise

3. The requirements related to cash flow statement, complete or condensed, contained in this Standard are applicable where an enterprise prepares and presents a cash flow statement for the purpose of its annual financial report.

Definitions

4. The following terms are used in this Standard with the meanings specified:

    4.1 ***Interim period is a financial reporting period shorter than a full financial year.***

4.2 ***Interim financial report** means a financial report containing either a complete set of financial statements or a set of condensed financial statements (as described in this Standard) for an interim period.*

5. During the first year of operations of an enterprise, its annual financial reporting period may be shorter than a financial year. In such a case, that shorter period is not considered as an interim period.

Content of an Interim Financial Report

6. A complete set of financial statements normally includes:

   (a) balance sheet;

   (b) statement of profit and loss;

   (c) cash flow statement; and

   (d) notes including those relating to accounting policies and other statements and explanatory material that are an integral part of the financial statements.

7. In the interest of timeliness and cost considerations and to avoid repetition of information previously reported, an enterprise may be required to or may elect to present less information at interim dates as compared with its annual financial statements. The benefit of timeliness of presen- tation may be partially offset by a reduction in detail in the information provided. Therefore, this Standard requires preparation and presentation of an interim financial report containing, as a minimum, a set of condensed financial statements. The interim financial report containing condensed financial statements is intended to provide an update on the latest annual financial statements. Accordingly, it focuses on new activities, events, and circumstances and does not duplicate information previously reported.

8. This Standard does not prohibit or discourage an enterprise from presenting a complete set of financial statements in its interim financial report, rather than a set of condensed financial statements. This Standard also does not prohibit or discourage an enterprise from including, in condensed interim financial statements, more than the minimum line items or selected explanatory notes as set out in this Standard. The recognition and measurement principles set out in this Standard apply also to complete financial statements for an interim period, and such statements would include all disclosures required by this Standard (particularly the selected disclosures in paragraph 16) as well as those required by other Accounting Standards.

Minimum Components of an Interim Financial Report

9. ***An interim financial report should include, at a minimum, the following components:***

   (a) ***condensed balance sheet;***

   (b) ***condensed statement of profit and loss;***

(c) condensed cash flow statement; and

(d) selected explanatory notes.

Form and Content of Interim Financial Statements

10. If an enterprise prepares and presents a complete set of financial statements in its interim financial report, the form and content of those statements should conform to the requirements as applicable to annual complete set of financial statements.

11. If an enterprise prepares and presents a set of condensed financial statements in its interim financial report, those condensed statements should include, at a minimum, each of the headings and sub-headings that were included in its most recent annual financial statements and the selected explanatory notes as required by this Standard. Additional line items or notes should be included if their omission would make the condensed interim financial statements misleading.

12. If an enterprise presents basic and diluted earnings per share in its annual financial statements in accordance with Accounting Standard (AS) 20, Earnings Per Share, basic and diluted earnings per share should be presented in accordance with AS 20 on the face of the statement of profit and loss, complete or condensed, for an interim

13. If an enterprise's annual financial report included the consolidated financial statements in addition to the parent's separate financial statements, the interim financial report includes both the consolidated financial statements and separate financial statements, complete or condensed.

14. Illustration 1 attached to the Standard provides illustrative formats of condensed financial statements.

Selected Explanatory Notes

15. A user of an enterprise's interim financial report will ordinarily have access to the most recent annual financial report of that enterprise. It is, therefore, not necessary for the notes to an interim financial report to provide relatively insignificant updates to the information that was already reported in the notes in the most recent annual financial report. At an interim date, an explanation of events and transactions that are significant to an understanding of the changes in financial position and performance of the enterprise since the last annual reporting date is more useful.

16. An enterprise should include the following information, as a minimum, in the notes to its interim financial statements, if material and if not disclosed elsewhere in the interim financial report:

(a) a statement that the same accounting policies are followed in the interim financial statements as those followed in the most recent annual financial statements or, if those policies have been changed, a description of the nature and effect of the change;

(b) ***explanatory comments about the seasonality of interim operations;***

(c) ***the nature and amount of items affecting assets, liabilities, equity, net income, or cash flows that are unusual because of their nature, size, or incidence (see paragraphs 12 to 14 of Accounting Standard (AS) 5, Net Profit or Loss for the Period, Prior Period Items and Changes in Accounting Policies);***

(d) ***the nature and amount of changes in estimates of amounts reported in prior interim periods of the current financial year or changes in estimates of amounts reported in prior financial years, if those changes have a material effect in the current interim period;***

(e) ***issuances, buy-backs, repayments and restructuring of debt, equity and potential equity shares;***

(f) ***dividends, aggregate or per share (in absolute or percentage terms), separately for equity shares and other shares;***

(g) ***segment revenue, segment capital employed (segment assets minus segment liabilities) and segment result for business segments or geographical segments, whichever is the enterprise's primary basis of segment reporting (disclosure of segment information is required in an enterprise's interim financial report only if the enterprise is required, in terms of AS 17, Segment Reporting, to disclose segment information in its annual financial statements);***

(h) ***material events subsequent to the end of the interim period that have not been reflected in the financial statements for the interim period;***

(i) ***the effect of changes in the composition of the enterprise during the interim period, such as amalgamations, acquisition or disposal of subsidiaries and long-term investments, restructurings, and discontinuing operations; and***

(j) ***material changes in contingent liabilities since the last annual balance sheet date.***

The above information should normally be reported on a financial year- to-date basis. However, the enterprise should also disclose any events or transactions that are material to an understanding of the current interim period.

17. Other Accounting Standards specify disclosures that should be made in financial statements. In that context, financial statements mean complete set of financial statements normally included in an annual financial report and sometimes included in other reports. The disclosures required by those other Accounting Standards are not required if an enterprise's interim financial report includes only condensed financial statements and selected explanatory notes rather than a complete set of financial statements.

Periods for which Interim Financial Statements are required to be presented

18. ***Interim reports should include interim financial statements (condensed or complete) for periods as follows:***

(a) ***balance sheet as of the end of the current interim period and a comparative balance sheet as of the end of the immediately preceding financial year;***

(b) ***statements of profit and loss for the current interim period and cumulatively for the current financial year to date, with comparative statements of profit and loss for the comparable interim periods (current and year-to-date) of the immediately preceding financial year;***

(c) ***cash flow statement cumulatively for the current financial year to date, with a comparative statement for the comparable year- to-date period of the immediately preceding financial year.***

19. For an enterprise whose business is highly seasonal, financial infor- mation for the twelve months ending on the interim reporting date and comparative information for the prior twelve-month period may be useful. Accordingly, enterprises whose business is highly seasonal are encouraged to consider reporting such information in addition to the information called

20. Illustration 2 attached to the Standard illustrates the periods required to be presented by an enterprise that reports half-yearly and an enterprise that reports quarterly.

Materiality

21. ***In deciding how to recognise, measure, classify, or disclose an item for interim financial reporting purposes, materiality should be assessed in relation to the interim period financial data. In making assessments of materiality, it should be recognised that interim measurements may rely on estimates to a greater extent than measurements of annual financial data.***

22. The Preface to the Statements of Accounting Standards states that "The Accounting Standards are intended to apply only to items which are material". The Framework for the Preparation and Presentation of Financial Statements, issued by the Institute of Chartered Accountants of India, states that "information is material if its misstatement (i.e., omission or erroneous statement) could influence the economic decisions of users taken on the basis of the financial information".

23. Judgement is always required in assessing materiality for financial reporting purposes. For reasons of understandability of the interim figures, materiality for making recognition and disclosure decision is assessed in relation to the interim period financial data. Thus, for example, unusual or extraordinary items, changes in accounting policies or estimates, and prior period items are recognised and disclosed based on materiality in relation to interim period data. The overriding objective is to ensure that an interim financial report includes all information that is relevant to understanding an

Disclosure in Annual Financial Statements

24. An enterprise may not prepare and present a separate financial report for the final interim period because the annual financial statements are presented. In such a case, paragraph 25 requires certain disclosures to be made in the annual financial statements for that financial year.

25. ***If an estimate of an amount reported in an interim period is changed significantly during the final interim period of the financial year but a separate financial report is not prepared and presented for that final interim period, the nature and amount of that change in estimate should be disclosed in a note to the annual financial statements for that financial year.***

26. Accounting Standard (AS) 5, Net Profit or Loss for the Period, Prior Period Items and Changes in Accounting Policies, requires disclosure, in financial statements, of the nature and (if practicable) the amount of a change in an accounting estimate which has a material effect in the current period, or which is expected to have a material effect in subsequent periods. Paragraph 16(d) of this Standard requires similar disclosure in an interim financial report. Examples include changes in estimate in the final interim period relating to inventory write-downs, restructurings, or impairment losses that were reported in an earlier interim period of the financial year. The disclosure required by the preceding paragraph is consistent with AS 5 requirements and is intended to be restricted in scope so as to relate only to the change in estimates. An enterprise is not required to include additional interim period financial information in its annual financial statements.

Recognition and Measurement

Same Accounting Policies as Annual

27. ***An enterprise should apply the same accounting policies in its interim financial statements as are applied in its annual financial statements, except for accounting policy changes made after the date of the most recent annual financial statements that are to be reflected in the next annual financial statements. However, the frequency of an enterprise's reporting (annual, half-yearly, or quarterly) should not affect the measurement of its annual results. To achieve that objective, measurements for interim reporting purposes should be made on a year-to-date basis.***

28. Requiring that an enterprise apply the same accounting policies in its interim financial statements as in its annual financial statements may seem to suggest that interim period measurements are made as if each interim period stands alone as an independent reporting period. However, by providing that the frequency of an enterprise's reporting should not affect the measurement of its annual results, paragraph 27 acknowledges that an interim period is a part of a financial year. Year-to-date measurements may involve changes in estimates of amounts reported in prior interim periods of the current financial year. But the principles for

recognising assets, liabi- lities, income, and expenses for interim periods are the same as in annual financial statements.

29. To illustrate:

(a) the principles for recognising and measuring losses from inven- tory write-downs, restructurings, or impairments in an interim period are the same as those that an enterprise would follow if it prepared only annual financial statements. However, if such items are recognised and measured in one interim period and the estimate changes in a subsequent interim period of that financial year, the original estimate is changed in the subsequent interim period either by accrual of an additional amount of loss or by reversal of the previously recognised amount;

(b) a cost that does not meet the definition of an asset at the end of an interim period is not deferred on the balance sheet date either to await future information as to whether it has met the definition of an asset or to smooth earnings over interim periods within a financial year; and

(c) income tax expense is recognised in each interim period based on the best estimate of the weighted average annual income tax rate expected for the full financial year. Amounts accrued for income tax expense in one interim period may have to be adjusted in a subsequent interim period of that financial year if the estimate of the annual income tax rate changes.

30. Under the Framework for the Preparation and Presentation of Financial Statements, recognition is the "process of incorporating in the balance sheet or statement of profit and loss an item that meets the definition of an element and satisfies the criteria for recognition". The definitions of assets, liabilities, income, and expenses are fundamental to recognition, both at annual and interim financial reporting dates.

31. For assets, the same tests of future economic benefits apply at interim dates as they apply at the end of an enterprise's financial year. Costs that, by their nature, would not qualify as assets at financial year end would not qualify at interim dates as well. Similarly, a liability at an interim reporting date must represent an existing obligation at that date, just as it must at an annual reporting date.

32. Income is recognised in the statement of profit and loss when an increase in future economic benefits related to an increase in an asset or a decrease of a liability has arisen that can be measured reliably. Expenses are recognised in the statement of profit and loss when a decrease in future economic benefits related to a decrease in an asset or an increase of a liability has arisen that can be measured reliably. The recognition of items in the balance sheet which do not meet the definition of assets or liabilities is not allowed.

33. In measuring assets, liabilities, income, expenses, and cash flows reported in its financial statements, an enterprise that reports only annually is able to take into account information that becomes available throughout the financial year. Its measurements are, in effect, on a year-to-date basis.

34. An enterprise that reports half-yearly, uses information available by mid-year or shortly thereafter in making the measurements in its financial statements for the first six-month period and information available by year- end or shortly thereafter for the twelve-month period. The twelve-month measurements will reflect any changes in estimates of amounts reported for the first six-month period. The amounts reported in the interim financial report for the first six-month period are not retrospectively adjusted. Paragraphs 16(d) and 25 require, however, that the nature and amount of any significant changes in estimates bedisclosed.

35. An enterprise that reports more frequently than half-yearly, measures income and expenses on a year-to-date basis for each interim period using information available when each set of financial statements is being prepared. Amounts of income and expenses reported in the current interim period will reflect any changes in estimates of amounts reported in prior interim periods of the financial year. The amounts reported in prior interim periods are not retrospectively adjusted. Paragraphs 16(d) and 25 require, however, that the nature and amount of any significant changes in estimates be disclosed.

Revenues Received Seasonally or Occasionally

36. Revenues that are received seasonally or occasionally within a financial year should not be anticipated or deferred as of an interim date if anticipation or deferral would not be appropriate at the end of the enterprise's financial year.

37. Examples include dividend revenue, royalties, and government grants. Additionally, some enterprises consistently earn more revenues in certain interim periods of a financial year than in other interim periods, for example, seasonal revenues of retailers. Such revenues are recognised when they occur.

Costs Incurred Unevenly During the Financial Year

38. Costs that are incurred unevenly during an enterprise's financial year should be anticipated or deferred for interim reporting purposes if, and only if, it is also appropriate to anticipate or defer that type of cost at the end of the financial year.

Applying the Recognition and Measurement principles

39. Illustration 3 attached to the Standard illustrates application of the general recognition and measurement principles set out in paragraphs 27 to 38.

Use of Estimates

40. The measurement procedures to be followed in an interim financial report should be designed to ensure that the resulting information is reliable and that all material financial information that is relevant to an understanding of the financial position or performance of the enterprise is appropriately disclosed. While measurements in both annual and interim financial reports are often based on reasonable estimates, the preparation of interim financial reports generally will require a greater use of estimation methods than annual financial reports.

41. Illustration 4 attached to the Standard illustrates the use of estimates in interim periods.

Restatement of Previously Reported Interim Periods

42. ***A change in accounting policy, other than one for which the transition is specified by an Accounting Standard, should be reflected by restating the financial statements of prior interim periods of the current financial year.***

43. One objective of the preceding principle is to ensure that a single accounting policy is applied to a particular class of transactions throughout an entire financial year. The effect of the principle in paragraph 42 is to require that within the current financial year any change in accounting policy be applied retrospectively to the beginning of the financial year.

Transitional Provision

44. On the first occasion that an interim financial report is presented in accordance with this Standard, the following need not be presented in respect of all the interim periods of the current financial year:

(a) comparative statements of profit and loss for the comparable interim periods (current and year-to-date) of the immediately preceding financial year; and

(b) comparative cash flow statement for the comparable year-to-date period of the immediately preceding financial year.

Illustration 1

Illustrative Format of Condensed Financial Statements

This illustration which does not form part of the Accounting Standard, provides illustrative format of condensed financial statements. Its purpose is to illustrate the application of the Accounting Standard to assist in clarifying its meaning.

Paragraph 11 of the Accounting Standard provides that if an enterprise prepares and presents a set of condensed financial statements in its interim financial report, those condensed statements should include, at a minimum, each of the headings and sub-headings that were included in its most recent annual financial statements and the selected explanatory notes as required by the Standard. Additional line items or notes should be included if their omission would make the condensed interim financial statements misleading.

The purpose of the following illustrative format is primarily to illustrate the requirements of paragraph 11 of the Standard. It may be noted that these illustrative formats are subject to the requirements laid down in the Standard including those of paragraph 11.

Illustrative Format of Condensed Financial Statements for an enterprise other than a bank

(A) Condensed Balance Sheet

	Figures at the end of the current interim period	Figures at the end of the previous accounting year
I. Sources of Funds		
1. Capital		
2. Reserve and surplus		
3. Minority interests (in case of consolidated financial statements)		
4. Loan funds: (a) Secured loans (b) Unsecured loans		
Total		
II. Application of Funds		
1. Fixed assets (a) Tangible fixed assets (b) Intangible fixed assets		
2. Investments		
3. Current assets, loans and advances (a) Inventories (b) Sundry debtors (c) Cash and bank balances (d) Loans and advances (e) Others		
Less: Current liabilities and provisions (a) Liabilities (b) Provisions		
Net Current assets		
4. Miscellaneous expenditure to the extent not written off or adjusted		
5. Profit and loss account		
Total		

(B) Condensed Statement of Profit and Loss

	Three months ended	Corresponding three months of the previous accounting year	Year-to-date figures for current period	Year-to-date figures for the previous year
1. Turnover				
2. Other Income				
Total				
3. Changes in inventories of finished goods and work in progress				
4. Cost of raw materials and consumables used				
5. Salaries, wages and other staff costs				
6. Other expenses				
7. Interest				
8. Depreciation and amortisations				
Total				
9. Profit or loss from ordinary activities before tax				
10. Extraordinary items				
11. Profit or loss before tax				
12. Tax expense				
13. Profit or loss after tax				
14. Minority Interests (in case of consolidated financial statements)				
15. Net profit or loss for the period				
Earnings Per Share 1. Basic Earnings Per Share 2. Diluted Earnings Per Share				

(C) Condensed Cash Flow Statement

	Year-to-date figures for the current period	Year-to-date figures for the previous year

	Year-to-date figures for the current period	Year-to-date figures for the previous year
1. Cash flows from operating activities		
2. Cash flows from investing activities		
3. Cash flows from financing activities		
4. Net increase/(decrease) in cash and cash equivalents		
5. Cash and cash equivalents at beginning of period		
6. Cash and cash equivalents at end of period		

(D) Selected Explanatory Notes

This part should contain selected explanatory notes as required by para- graph 16 of this Standard.

Illustrative Format of Condensed Financial Statements for a Bank

(A) Condensed Balance Sheet

	Figures at the end of the current interim period	Figures at the end of the previous accounting year
I. Capital and Liabilities		
1. Capital		
2. Reserve and surplus		
3. Minority interests (in case of consolidated financial statements)		
4. Deposits		
5. Borrowings		
6. Other liabilities and provisions		
Total		
II. Assets		
1. Cash and balances with Reserve Bank of India		
2. Balances with banks and money at call and short notice		
3. Investments		
4. Advances		
5. Fixed assets		

	Figures at the end of the current interim period	Figures at the end of the previous accounting year
(a) Tangible fixed assets (b) Intangible fixed assets		
6. Other Assets		
Total		

(B) Condensed Statement of Profit and Loss

	Three months ended	Corresponding three months of the previous accounting year	Year-to-date figures for current period	Year-to-date figures for the previous year
1. Interest earned (a) Interest/discount on advances/bills (b) Interest on Investments (c) Interest on balances with Reserve Bank of India and other inter banks funds (d) Others				
2. Other Income				
Total Income				
1. Interest expended				
2. Operating expenses (a) Payments to and provisions for employees (b) Other operating expenses				
3. Total expenses (excluding provisions and contingencies)				
4. Operating profit (profit before provisions and contingencies)				
5. Provisions and contingencies				
6. Profit or loss from ordinary activities before tax				
7. Extraordinary items				
8. Profit or loss before tax				
9. Tax expense				
10. Profit or loss after tax				
11. Minority Interests (in case of consolidated financial statements)				

	Three months ended	Corresponding three months of the previous accounting year	Year-to-date figures for current period	Year-to-date figures for the previous year
12. Net profit or loss for the period				
Earnings Per Share 1. Basic Earnings Per Share 2. Diluted Earnings Per Share				

(C) Condensed Cash Flow Statement

	Year-to-date figures for the current period	Year-to-date figures for the previous year
1. Cash flows from operating activities		
2. Cash flows from investing activities		
3. Cash flows from financing activities		
4. Net increase/(decrease) in cash and cash equivalents		
5. Cash and cash equivalents at beginning of period		
6. Cash and cash equivalents at end of period		

(D) Selected Explanatory Notes

This part should contain selected explanatory notes as required by paragraph 16 of this Standard.

Illustration 2

Illustration of Periods Required to Be Presented

This illustration which does not form part of the Accounting Standard, Illustrates application of the principles in paragraphs 18 and 19. Its purpose is to illustrate the application of the Accounting Standard to assist

Enterprise Preparing and Presenting Interim Financial Reports Half- Yearly

1. An enterprise whose financial year ends on 31 March, presents financial statements (condensed or complete) for following periods in its half-yearly interim financial report as of 30 September 2001:

Balance Sheet:		
As at	30 September 2001	31 March 2001
Statement of Profit and Loss:		
6 months ending	30 September 2001	30 September 2000
Cash Flow Statement[1]:		
6 months ending	30 September 2001	30 September 2000

Enterprise Preparing and Presenting Interim Financial Reports Quarterly

2. An enterprise whose financial year ends on 31 March, presents financial statements (condensed or complete) for following periods in its interim financial report for the second quarter ending 30 September 2001:

Balance Sheet:		
As at	30 September 2001	31 March 2001
Statement of Profit and Loss:		
6 months ending	30 September 2001	30 September 2000
3 months ending	30 September 2001	30 September 2000
Cash Flow Statement:		
6 months ending	30 September 2001	30 September 2000

Enterprise whose business is highly seasonal Preparing and Presenting Interim Financial Reports Quarterly

3. An enterprise whose financial year ends on 31 March, may present financial statements (condensed or complete) for the following periods in its interim financial report for the second quarter ending 30 September 2001:

Balance Sheet:		
As at	30 September 2001	31 March 2001
		30 September 2000
Statement of Profit and Loss:		

[1] It is assumed that the enterprise prepares a cash flow statement for the purpose of its Annual Report.

6 months ending	30 September 2001	30 September 2000
3 months ending	30 September 2001	30 September 2000
12 months ending	30 September 2001	30 September 2000
Cash Flow Statement:		
6 months ending	30 September 2001	30 September 2000
12 months ending	30 September 2001	30 September 2000

Illustration 3

Illustration of Applying the Recognition and Measurement Principles

This illustration which does not form part of the Accounting Standard, illustrates application of the general recognition and measurement principles set out in paragraphs 27-38 of this Standard. Its purpose is to illustrate the application of the Accounting Standard to assist in clarifying its meaning.

Gratuity and Other Defined Benefit Schemes

1. Provisions in respect of gratuity and other defined benefit schemes for an interim period are calculated on a year-to-date basis by using the actuarially determined rates at the end of the prior financial year, adjusted for significant market fluctuations since that time and for significant curtailments, settlements, or other significant one-time events.

Major Planned Periodic Maintenance or Overhaul

2. The cost of a major planned periodic maintenance or overhaul or other seasonal expenditure that is expected to occur late in the year is not anticipated for interim reporting purposes unless an event has caused the enterprise to have a present obligation. The mere intention or necessity to incur expenditure related to the future is not sufficient to give rise to an obligation.

Provisions

3. This Standard requires that an enterprise apply the same criteria for recognising and measuring a provision at an interim date as it would at the end of its financial year. The existence or non-existence of an obligation to transfer economic benefits is not a function of the length of the reporting period. It is a question of fact subsisting on the reporting date.

Year-End Bonuses

4. The nature of year-end bonuses varies widely. Some are earned simply by continued employment during a time period. Some bonuses are earned based on monthly, quarterly, or annual measure of operating result. They may be purely discretionary, contractual, or based on years of historical precedent.

5. A bonus is anticipated for interim reporting purposes if, and only if, (a) the bonus is a legal obligation or an obligation arising from past practice for which the

enterprise has no realistic alternative but to make the payments, and (b) a reliable estimate of the obligation can be made.

Intangible Assets

6. An enterprise will apply the definition and recognition criteria for an intangible asset in the same way in an interim period as in an annual period. Costs incurred before the recognition criteria for an intangible asset are met are recognised as an expense. Costs incurred after the specific point in time at which the criteria are met are recognised as part of the cost of an intangible asset. "Deferring" costs as assets in an interim balance sheet in the hope that the recognition criteria will be met later in the financial year is not justified.

Other Planned but Irregularly Occurring Costs

7. An enterprise's budget may include certain costs expected to be incurred irregularly during the financial year, such as employee training costs. These costs generally are discretionary even though they are planned and tend to recur from year to year. Recognising an obligation at an interim financial reporting date for such costs that have not yet been incurred generally is not consistent with the definition of a liability.

Measuring Income Tax Expense for Interim Period

8. Interim period income tax expense is accrued using the tax rate that would be applicable to expected total annual earnings, that is, the estimated average annual effective income tax rate applied to the pre-tax income of the interim period.

9. This is consistent with the basic concept set out in paragraph 27 that the same accounting recognition and measurement principles should be applied in an interim financial report as are applied in annual financial statements. Income taxes are assessed on an annual basis. Therefore, interim period income tax expense is calculated by applying, to an interim period's pre-tax income, the tax rate that would be applicable to expected total annual earnings, that is, the estimated average annual effective income tax rate. That estimated average annual income tax rate would reflect the tax rate structure expected to be applicable to the full year's earnings including enacted or substantively enacted changes in the income tax rates scheduled to take effect later in the financial year. The estimated average annual income tax rate would be re-estimated on a year-to-date basis, consistent with paragraph 27 of this Standard. Paragraph 16(d) requires

10. To the extent practicable, a separate estimated average annual effective income tax rate is determined for each governing taxation law and applied individually to the interim period pre-tax income under such laws. Similarly, if different income tax rates apply to different categories of income (such as capital gains or income earned in particular industries), to the extent practicable a separate rate is applied to each individual category of interim period pre-tax income. While that degree of precision is desirable, it may not be achievable in all cases, and a weighted average of rates across such governing taxation laws or across

categories of income is used if it is a reasonable approximation of the effect of using more specific rates.

11. As illustration, an enterprise reports quarterly, earns Rs. 150 lakhs pre- tax profit in the first quarter but expects to incur losses of Rs 50 lakhs in each of the three remaining quarters (thus having zero income for the year), and is governed by taxation laws according to which its estimated average annual income tax rate is expected to be 35 per cent. The following table shows the amount of income tax expense that is reported in each quarter:

(Amount in Rs. lakhs)

	1st Quarter	2nd Quarter	3rd Quarter	4th Quarter	Annual
Tax Expense	52.5	(17.5)	(17.5)	(17.5)	0

Difference in Financial Reporting Year and Tax Year

12. If the financial reporting year and the income tax year differ, income tax expense for the interim periods of that financial reporting year is measured using separate weighted average estimated effective tax rates for each of the income tax years applied to the portion of pre-tax income earned in each of those income tax years.

13. To illustrate, an enterprise's financial reporting year ends 30 September and it reports quarterly. Its year as per taxation laws ends 31 March. For the financial year that begins 1 October, Year 1 ends 30 September of Year 2, the enterprise earns Rs 100 lakhs pre-tax each quarter. The estimated weighted average annual income tax rate is 30 per cent in Year 1 and 40 per cent in Year 2.

(Amount in Rs. lakhs)

Quarter Ending 31 Dec. Year 1	Quarter Ending 31 Mar. Year 1	Quarter Ending 30 June Year 2	Quarter Ending 30 Sep. Year 2	Year Ending 30 Sep.
	Year 2			

Tax Deductions/Exemptions

14. Tax statutes may provide deductions/exemptions in computation of income for determining tax payable. Anticipated tax benefits of this type for the full year are generally reflected in computing the estimated annual effective income tax rate, because these deductions/exemptions are calculated on an annual basis under the usual provisions of tax statutes. On the other hand, tax benefits that relate to a one-time event are recognised in computing income tax expense in that interim period, in the same way that special tax rates applicable to particular categories of income are not

Tax Loss Carry forwards

15. A deferred tax asset should be recognised in respect of carryforward tax losses to the extent that it is virtually certain, supported by convincing evidence, that future taxable income will be available against which the deferred tax assets can be realised. The criteria are to be applied at the end of each interim period and, if they are met, the effect of the tax loss carryforward is reflected in the computation of the estimated average annual effective income tax rate.

16. To illustrate, an enterprise that reports quarterly has an operating loss carryforward of Rs 100 lakhs for income tax purposes at the start of the current financial year for which a deferred tax asset has not been recognised. The enterprise earns Rs 100 lakhs in the first quarter of the current year and expects to earn Rs 100 lakhs in each of the three remaining quarters. Excluding the loss carryforward, the estimated average annual income tax rate is expected to be 40 per cent. The estimated payment of the annual tax on Rs. 400 lakhs of earnings for the current year would be Rs. 120 lakhs {(Rs. 400 lakhs - Rs. 100 lakhs) x 40%}. Considering the loss carryforward, the estimated average annual effective income tax rate would be 30% {(Rs. 120 lakhs/Rs. 400 lakhs) x 100}. This average annual effective income tax rate would be applied to earnings of each quarter. Accordingly, tax expense would be as follows:

(Amount in Rs. lakhs)

	1st Quarter	**2nd Quarter**	**3rd Quarter**	**4th Quarter**	**Annual**
Tax Expense	30.00	30.00	30.00	30.00	120.00

Contractual or Anticipated Purchase Price Changes

17. Volume rebates or discounts and other contractual changes in the prices of goods and services are anticipated in interim periods, if it is probable that they will take effect. Thus, contractual rebates and discounts are anticipated but discretionary rebates and discounts are not anticipated because the resulting liability would not satisfy the conditions of recognition, viz., that a liability must be a present obligation whose settlement is expected to result in an outflow of resources.

Depreciation and Amortisation

18. Depreciation and amortisation for an interim period is based only on assets owned during that interim period. It does not take into account asset acquisitions or disposals planned for later in the financial year.

Inventories

19. Inventories are measured for interim financial reporting by the same principles as at financial year end. AS 2 on Valuation of Inventories, establishes standards for recognising and measuring inventories. Inventories pose particular problems at any financial reporting date because of the need to determine inventory quantities, costs, and net realisable values. Nonetheless,

the same measurement principles are applied for interim inventories. To save cost and time, enterprises often use estimates to measure inventories at interim dates to a greater extent than at annual reporting dates. Paragraph 20 below provides an example of how to apply the net realisable value test at an interim date.

Net Realisable Value of Inventories

20. The net realisable value of inventories is determined by reference to selling prices and related costs to complete and sell the inventories. An enterprise will reverse a write-down to net realisable value in a subsequent interim period as it would at the end of its financial year.

Foreign Currency Translation Gains and Losses

21. Foreign currency translation gains and losses are measured for interim financial reporting by the same principles as at financial year end in accordance with the principles as stipulated in AS 11 on The Effects of Changes in Foreign Exchange Rates.

Impairment of Assets

22. Accounting Standard on Impairment of Assets[2] requires that an impairment loss be recognised if the recoverable amount has declined below carrying amount.

23. An enterprise applies the same impairment tests, recognition, and reversal criteria at an interim date as it would at the end of its financial year. That does not mean, however, that an enterprise must necessarily make a detailed impairment calculation at the end of each interim period. Rather, an enterprise will assess the indications of significant impairment since the end of the most recent financial year to determine whether such a calculation is needed.

Illustration 4

Examples of the Use of Estimates

This illustration which does not form part of the Accounting Standard, illustrates application of the principles in this Standard. Its purpose is to illustrate the application of the Accounting Standard to assist inclarifying its meaning.

1. **Provisions:** Determination of the appropriate amount of a provision (such as a provision for warranties, restructuring costs, gratuity, etc.) may be complex and often costly and time-consuming. Enterprises sometimes engage outside experts to assist in annual calculations. Making similar estimates at interim dates often involves updating the provision made in the preceding annual financial statements rather than engaging outside experts to do a new calculation.

---

2 Accounting Standard (AS) 28, 'Impairment of Assets', specifies the requirements relating to impairment of assets.

2. **Contingencies:** Measurement of contingencies may involve obtaining opinions of legal experts or other advisers. Formal reports from independent experts are sometimes obtained with respect to contingencies. Such opinions about litigation, claims, assessments, and other contingencies and uncer- tainties may or may not be needed at interim dates.

3. **Specialised industries:** Because of complexity, costliness, and time involvement, interim period measurements in specialised industries might be less precise than at financial year end. An example is calculation of insurance reserves by insurance companies.

Appendix II

Indian Accounting Standard (Ind AS) 34

Interim Financial Reporting

*(This Indian Accounting Standard includes paragraphs set in **bold** type and plain type, which have equal authority. Paragraphs in bold type indicate the main principles.)*

Objective

The objective of this Standard is to prescribe the minimum content of an interim financial report and to prescribe the principles for recognition and measurement in complete or condensed financial statements for an interim period. Timely and reliable interim financial reporting improves the ability of investors, creditors, and others to understand an entity's capacity to generate earnings and cash flows and its financial condition and liquidity.

Scope

1 This Standard does not mandate which entities should be required to publish interim financial reports, how frequently, or how soon after the end of an interim period. However, governments, securities regulators, stock exchanges, and accountancy bodies often require entities whose debt or equity securities are publicly traded to publish interim financial reports[1]. This Standard applies if an entity is required or elects to publish an interim financial report in accordance with Indian Accounting Standards (Ind ASs). [Refer Appendix 1]

2 Each financial report, annual or interim, is evaluated on its own for conformity to Ind ASs. The fact that an entity may not have provided interim financial reports during a particular financial year or may have provided interim financial reports that do not comply with this Standard does not prevent the entity's annual financial statements from conforming to Ind ASs if they otherwise do so.

3 If an entity's interim financial report is described as complying with Ind ASs, it must comply with all of the requirements of this Standard. Paragraph 19 requires certain disclosures in that regard.

[1] Unaudited Financial Results required to be prepared and presented under Clause 41 of Listing Agreement with stock exchanges is not an 'Interim Financial Report' as defined in paragraph 4 of this Standard

Definitions

4 **The following terms are used in this Standard with the meanings specified:**

Interim period **is a financial reporting period shorter than a full financial year.**

Interim financial report **means a financial report containing either a complete set of financial statements (as described in Ind AS 1,** ***Presentation of Financial Statements,*** **or a set of condensed financial statements (as described in this Standard) for an interim period.**

Content of an interim financial report

5 Ind AS 1 defines a complete set of financial statements as including the following components:

(a) a balance sheet as at the end of the period ;

(b) a statement of profit and loss for the period;

(c) a statement of changes in equity for the period;;

(d) a statement of cash flows for the period;

(e) notes, comprising a summary of significant accounting policies and other explanatory information;

(ea) comparative information in respect of the preceding period as specified in paragraphs 38 and 38A of Ind AS 1; and

(f) a balance sheet as at the beginning of the preceding period when an entity applies an accounting policy retrospectively or makes a retrospective restatement of items in its financial statements, or when it reclassifies items in its financial statements in accordance with paragraphs 40A–40D of Ind AS 1.

6 In the interest of timeliness and cost considerations and to avoid repetition of information previously reported, an entity may be required to or may elect to provide less information at interim dates as compared with its annual financial statements. This Standard defines the minimum content of an interim financial report as including condensed financial statements and selected explanatory notes. The interim financial report is intended to provide an update on the latest complete set of annual financial statements. Accordingly, it focuses on new activities, events, and circumstances and does not duplicate information previously reported.

7 Nothing in this Standard is intended to prohibit or discourage an entity from publishing a complete set of financial statements (as described in Ind AS 1) in its interim financial report, rather than condensed financial statements and selected explanatory notes. Nor does this Standard prohibit or discourage an entity from including in condensed interim financial statements more than the minimum line items or selected explanatory notes as set out in this Standard. The recognition and measurement guidance in this Standard applies also to complete financial statements for an interim period, and such statements would include all of the

disclosures required by this Standard (particularly the selected note disclosures in paragraph 16A) as well as those required by other Ind ASs.

Minimum components of an interim financial report

8 **An interim financial report shall include, at a minimum, the following components:**

(a) **a condensed balance sheet ;**

(b) **a condensed statement of profit and loss;**

(c) **a condensed statement of changes in equity;**

(d) **a condensed statement of cash flows; and**

(e) **selected explanatory notes.**

8A **[Refer Appendix 1]**

Form and content of interim financial statements

9 **If an entity publishes a complete set of financial statements in its interim financial report, the form and content of those statements shall conform to the requirements of Ind AS 1 for a complete set of financial statements.**

10 **If an entity publishes a set of condensed financial statements in its interim financial report, those condensed statements shall include, at a minimum, each of the headings and subtotals that were included in its most recent annual financial statements and the selected explanatory notes as required by this Standard. Additional line items or notes shall be included if their omission would make the condensed interim financial statements misleading.**

11 **In the statement that presents the components of profit or loss for an interim period, an entity shall present basic and diluted earnings per share for that period when the entity is within the scope of Ind AS 33, *Earnings per Share.***

11A **[Refer Appendix 1]**

12 [Refer Appendix 1]

13 [Refer Appendix 1]

14 An interim financial report is prepared on a consolidated basis if the entity's most recent annual financial statements were consolidated statements. The parent's separate financial statements are not consistent or comparable with the consolidated statements in the most recent annual financial report. If an entity's annual financial report included the parent's separate financial statements in addition to consolidated financial statements, this Standard neither requires nor prohibits the inclusion of the parent's separate statements in the entity's interim financial report.

Significant events and transactions

15 An entity shall include in its interim financial report an explanation of events and transactions that are significant to an understanding of the changes in financial

position and performance of the entity since the end of the last annual reporting period. Information disclosed in relation to those events and transactions shall update the relevant information presented in the most recent annual financial report.

15A A user of an entity's interim financial report will have access to the most recent annual financial report of that entity. Therefore, it is unnecessary for the notes to an interim financial report to provide relatively insignificant updates to the information that was reported in the notes in the most recent annual financial report.

15B The following is a list of events and transactions for which disclosures would be required if they are significant: the list is not exhaustive.

(a) the write-down of inventories to net realisable value and the reversal of such a write-down;

(b) recognition of a loss from the impairment of financial assets, property, plant and equipment, intangible assets, assets arising from contracts with customers, or other assets, and the reversal of such an impairment loss;

(c) the reversal of any provisions for the costs of restructuring;

(d) acquisitions and disposals of items of property, plant and equipment;

(e) commitments for the purchase of property, plant and equipment;

(f) litigation settlements;

(g) corrections of prior period errors;

(h) changes in the business or economic circumstances that affect the fair value of the entity's financial assets and financial liabilities, whether those assets or liabilities are recognised at fair value or amortised cost;

(i) any loan default or breach of a loan agreement that has not been remedied on or before the end of the reporting period;

(j) related party transactions;

(k) transfers between levels of the fair value hierarchy used in measuring the fair value of financial instruments;

(l) changes in the classification of financial assets as a result of a change in the purpose or use of those assets; and

(m) changes in contingent liabilities or contingent assets.

15C Individual Ind ASs provide guidance regarding disclosure requirements for many of the items listed in paragraph 15B. When an event or transaction is significant to an understanding of the changes in an entity's financial position or performance since the last annual reporting period, its interim financial report should provide an explanation of and an update to the relevant information included in the financial statements of the last annual reporting period.

16-18 [Refer Appendix 1]

Other Disclosures

16A In addition to disclosing significant events and transactions in accordance with paragraphs 15–15C, an entity shall include the following information, in the notes to its interim financial statements, if not disclosed elsewhere in the interim financial report. The information shall normally be reported on a financial year-to-date basis.

(a) a statement that the same accounting policies and methods of computation are followed in the interim financial statements as compared with the most recent annual financial statements or, if those policies or methods have been changed, a description of the nature and effect of the change.

(b) explanatory comments about the seasonality or cyclicality of interim operations.

(c) the nature and amount of items affecting assets, liabilities, equity, net income or cash flows that are unusual because of their nature, size or incidence.

(d) the nature and amount of changes in estimates of amounts reported in prior interim periods of the current financial year or changes in estimates of amounts reported in prior financial years.

(e) issues, repurchases and repayments of debt and equity securities.

(f) dividends paid (aggregate or per share) separately for ordinary shares and other shares[2].

(g) the following segment information (disclosure of segment information is required in an entity's interim financial report only if Ind AS 108, *Operating Segments,* requires that entity to disclose segment information in its annual financial statements):

(i) revenues from external customers, if included in the measure of segment profit or loss reviewed by the chief operating decision maker or otherwise regularly provided to the chief operating decision maker.

(ii) intersegment revenues, if included in the measure of segment profit or loss reviewed by the chief operating decision maker or otherwise regularly provided to the chief operating decision maker.

(iii) a measure of segment profit or loss.

(iv) a measure of total assets and liabilities for a particular reportable segment if such amounts are regularly provided to

[2] Here 'ordinary' shares refer to 'equity' shares

the chief operating decision maker and if there has been a material change from the amount disclosed in the last annual financial statements for that reportable segment.

(v) a description of differences from the last annual financial statements in the basis of segmentation or in the basis of measurement of segment profit or loss.

(vi) a reconciliation of the total of the reportable segments' measures of profit or loss to the entity's profit or loss before tax expense (tax income) and discontinued operations. However, if an entity allocates to reportable segments items such as tax expense (tax income), the entity may reconcile the total of the segments' measures of profit or loss to profit or loss after those items. Material reconciling items shall be separately identified and described in that reconciliation.

(h) events after the interim period that have not been reflected in the financial statements for the interim period.

(i) the effect of changes in the composition of the entity during the interim period, including business combinations, obtaining or losing control of subsidiaries and long-term investments, restructurings, and discontinued operations. In the case of business combinations, the entity shall disclose the information required by Ind AS 103, *Business Combinations.*

(j) for financial instruments, the disclosures about fair value required by paragraphs 91–93(h), 94–96, 98 and 99 of Ind AS 113, *Fair Value Measurement,* and paragraphs 25, 26 and 28–30 of Ind AS 107, *Financial Instruments: Disclosures.*

(k) for entities becoming, or ceasing to be, investment entities, as defined in Ind AS 110, *Consolidated Financial Statements*, the disclosures in Ind AS 112, *Disclosure of Interests in Other Entities* paragraph 9B.

(l) the disaggregation of revenue from contracts with customers required by paragraphs 114–115 of Ind AS 115, *Revenue from Contracts with Customers.*

Disclosure of compliance with Ind ASs

19 If an entity's interim financial report is in compliance with this Standard, that fact shall be disclosed. An interim financial report shall not be described as complying with Ind ASs unless it complies with all of the requirements of Ind ASs.

Periods for which interim financial statements are required to be presented

20 Interim reports shall include interim financial statements (condensed or complete) for periods as follows:

(a) **balance sheet as of the end of the current interim period and a comparative balance sheet as of the end of the immediately preceding financial year.**

(b) **statements of profit and loss for the current interim period and cumulatively for the current financial year to date, with comparative statements of profit and loss for the comparable interim periods (current and year-to-date) of the immediately preceding financial year.**

(c) **statement of changes in equity cumulatively for the current financial year to date, with a comparative statement for the comparable year-to-date period of the immediately preceding financial year.**

(d) **statement of cash flows cumulatively for the current financial year to date, with a comparative statement for the comparable year-to-date period of the immediately preceding financial year.**

21 For an entity whose business is highly seasonal, financial information for the twelve months up to the end of the interim period and comparative information for the prior twelve-month period may be useful. Accordingly, entities whose business is highly seasonal are encouraged to consider reporting such information in addition to the information called for in the preceding paragraph.

22 [Refer Appendix 1]

Materiality

23 In deciding how to recognise, measure, classify, or disclose an item for interim financial reporting purposes, materiality shall be assessed in relation to the interim period financial data. In making assessments of materiality, it shall be recognised that interim measurements may rely on estimates to a greater extent than measurements of annual financial data.

24 Ind AS 1 and Ind AS 8, *Accounting Policies, Changes in Accounting Estimates and Errors,* define an item as material if its omission or misstatement could influence the economic decisions of users of the financial statements. Ind AS 1 requires separate disclosure of material items, including (for example) discontinued operations, and Ind AS 8 requires disclosure of changes in accounting estimates, errors, and changes in accounting policies. The two Standards do not contain quantified guidance as to materiality.

25 While judgement is always required in assessing materiality, this Standard bases the recognition and disclosure decision on data for the interim period by itself for reasons of understandability of the interim figures. Thus, for example, unusual items, changes in accounting policies or estimates, and errors are recognised and disclosed on the basis of materiality in relation to interim period data to avoid misleading inferences that might result from non-disclosure. The overriding goal is to ensure that an interim financial report includes all information that is relevant to understanding an entity's financial position and performance during the interim period.

Disclosure in annual financial statements

26 **If an estimate of an amount reported in an interim period is changed significantly during the final interim period of the financial year but a separate financial report is not published for that final interim period, the nature and amount of that change in estimate shall be disclosed in a note to the annual financial statements for that financial year.**

27 Ind AS 8 requires disclosure of the nature and (if practicable) the amount of a change in estimate that either has a material effect in the current period or is expected to have a material effect in subsequent periods. Paragraph 16A(d) of this Standard requires similar disclosure in an interim financial report. Examples include changes in estimate in the final interim period relating to inventory write-downs, restructurings, or impairment losses that were reported in an earlier interim period of the financial year. The disclosure required by the preceding paragraph is consistent with the Ind AS 8 requirement and is intended to be narrow in scope—relating only to the change in estimate. An entity is not required to include additional interim period financial information in its annual financial statements.

Recognition and measurement

Same accounting policies as annual

28 **An entity shall apply the same accounting policies in its interim financial statements as are applied in its annual financial statements, except for accounting policy changes made after the date of the most recent annual financial statements that are to be reflected in the next annual financial statements. However, the frequency of an entity's reporting (annual, half-yearly, or quarterly) shall not affect the measurement of its annual results. To achieve that objective, measurements for interim reporting purposes shall be made on a year-to-date basis.**

29 Requiring that an entity apply the same accounting policies in its interim financial statements as in its annual statements may seem to suggest that interim period measurements are made as if each interim period stands alone as an independent reporting period. However, by providing that the frequency of an entity's reporting shall not affect the measurement of its annual results, paragraph 28 acknowledges that an interim period is a part of a larger financial year. Year-to-date measurements may involve changes in estimates of amounts reported in prior interim periods of the current financial year. But the principles for recognising assets, liabilities, income, and expenses for interim periods are the same as in annual financial statements.

30 To illustrate:

(a) the principles for recognising and measuring losses from inventory write-downs, restructurings, or impairments in an interim period are the same as those that an entity would follow if it prepared only annual financial statements. However, if such items are recognised and measured in one interim period and the estimate changes in a subsequent interim period of that financial year, the original estimate is changed in the subsequent interim period either by accrual of an additional amount of loss or by reversal of the previously recognised amount;

(b) a cost that does not meet the definition of an asset at the end of an interim period is not deferred in the balance sheet either to await future information as to whether it has met the definition of an asset or to smooth earnings over interim periods within a financial year; and

(c) income tax expense is recognised in each interim period based on the best estimate of the weighted average annual income tax rate expected for the full financial year. Amounts accrued for income tax expense in one interim period may have to be adjusted in a subsequent interim period of that financial year if the estimate of the annual income tax rate changes.

31 Under the *Framework for the Preparation and Presentation of Financial Statements in accordance with Indian Accounting Standards* (the *Framework*) issued by the Institute of Chartered Accountants of India, recognition is the 'process of incorporating in the balance sheet or statement of profit and loss an item that meets the definition of an element and satisfies the criteria for recognition'. The definitions of assets, liabilities, income, and expenses are fundamental to recognition, at the end of both annual and interim financial reporting periods.

32 For assets, the same tests of future economic benefits apply at interim dates and at the end of an entity's financial year. Costs that, by their nature, would not qualify as assets at financial year-end would not qualify at interim dates either. Similarly, a liability at the end of an interim reporting period must represent an existing obligation at that date, just as it must at the end of an annual reporting period.

33 An essential characteristic of income (revenue) and expenses is that the related inflows and outflows of assets and liabilities have already taken place. If those inflows or outflows have taken place, the related revenue and expense are recognised; otherwise they are not recognised. The *Framework* says that 'expenses are recognised in the statement of profit and loss when a decrease in future economic benefits related to a decrease in an asset or an increase of a liability has arisen that can be measured reliably… [The] *Framework* does not allow the recognition of items in the balance sheet which do not meet the definition of assets or liabilities.'

34 In measuring the assets, liabilities, income, expenses, and cash flows reported in its financial statements, an entity that reports only annually is able to take into account information that becomes available throughout the financial year. Its measurements are, in effect, on a year-to-date basis.

35 An entity that reports half-yearly uses information available by mid-year or shortly thereafter in making the measurements in its financial statements for the first six-month period and information available by year-end or shortly thereafter for the twelve-month period. The twelve-month measurements will reflect

possible changes in estimates of amounts reported for the first six-month period. The amounts reported in the interim financial report for the first six-month period are not retrospectively adjusted. Paragraphs 16A(d) and 26 require, however, that the nature and amount of any significant changes in estimates be disclosed.

36 An entity that reports more frequently than half-yearly measures income and expenses on a year-to-date basis for each interim period using information available when each set of financial statements is being prepared. Amounts of income and expenses reported in the current interim period will reflect any changes in estimates of amounts reported in prior interim periods of the financial year. The amounts reported in prior interim periods are not retrospectively adjusted. Paragraphs 16A(d) and 26 require, however, that the nature and amount of any significant changes in estimates be disclosed.

Revenues received seasonally, cyclically, or occasionally

37 Revenues that are received seasonally, cyclically, or occasionally within a financial year shall not be anticipated or deferred as of an interim date if anticipation or deferral would not be appropriate at the end of the entity's financial year.

38 Examples include dividend revenue, royalties, and government grants. Additionally, some entities consistently earn more revenues in certain interim periods of a financial year than in other interim periods, for example, seasonal revenues of retailers. Such revenues are recognised when they occur.

Costs incurred unevenly during the financial year

39 Costs that are incurred unevenly during an entity's financial year shall be anticipated or deferred for interim reporting purposes if, and only if, it is also appropriate to anticipate or defer that type of cost at the end of the financial year.

40 [Refer Appendix 1]

Use of estimates

41 The measurement procedures to be followed in an interim financial report shall be designed to ensure that the resulting information is reliable and that all material financial information that is relevant to an understanding of the financial position or performance of the entity is appropriately disclosed. While measurements in both annual and interim financial reports are often based on reasonable estimates, the preparation of interim financial reports generally will require a greater use of estimation methods than annual financial reports.

42 [Refer Appendix 1]

Restatement of previously reported interim periods

43 A change in accounting policy, other than one for which the transition is specified by a new Ind AS, shall be reflected by:

(a) restating the financial statements of prior interim periods of the current financial year and the comparable interim periods of any prior financial years that will be restated in the annual financial statements in accordance with Ind AS 8; or

(b) when it is impracticable to determine the cumulative effect at the beginning of the financial year of applying a new accounting policy to all prior periods, adjusting the financial statements of prior interim periods of the current financial year, and comparable interim periods of prior financial years to apply the new accounting policy prospectively from the earliest date practicable.

44 One objective of the preceding principle is to ensure that a single accounting policy is applied to a particular class of transactions throughout an entire financial year. Under Ind AS 8, a change in accounting policy is reflected by retrospective application, with restatement of prior period financial data as far back as is practicable. However, if the cumulative amount of the adjustment relating to prior financial years is impracticable to determine, then under Ind AS 8 the new policy is applied prospectively from the earliest date practicable. The effect of the principle in paragraph 43 is to require that within the current financial year any change in accounting policy is applied either retrospectively or, if that is not practicable, prospectively, from no later than the beginning of the financial year.

45 To allow accounting changes to be reflected as of an interim date within the financial year would allow two differing accounting policies to be applied to a particular class of transactions within a single financial year. The result would be interim allocation difficulties, obscured operating results, and complicated analysis and understandability of interim period information.

Appendix A

Interim Financial Reporting and Impairment

This appendix is an integral part of the Ind AS.

Background

1 An entity is required to assess goodwill for impairment at the end of each reporting period, and, if required, to recognise an impairment loss at that date in accordance with Ind AS 36. However, at the end of a subsequent reporting period, conditions may have so changed that the impairment loss would have been reduced or avoided had the impairment assessment been made only at that date. This appendix provides guidance on whether such impairment losses should ever be reversed.

2 The appendix addresses the interaction between the requirements of Ind AS 34 and the recognition of impairment losses on goodwill in Ind AS 36, and the effect of that interaction on subsequent interim and annual financial statements.

Issue

3 Ind AS 34 paragraph 28 requires an entity to apply the same accounting policies in its interim financial statements as are applied in its annual financial statements. It also states that 'the frequency of an entity's reporting (annual, half-yearly, or quarterly) shall not affect the measurement of its annual results. To achieve that objective, measurements for interim reporting purposes shall be made on a year- to-date basis.'

4 Ind AS 36 paragraph 124 states that 'An impairment loss recognised for goodwill shall not be reversed in a subsequent period.'

5-6 [Refer Appendix 1]

7 The appendix addresses the following issue:

> Should an entity reverse impairment losses recognised in an interim period on goodwill if a loss would not have been recognised, or a smaller loss would have been recognised, had an impairment assessment been made only at the end of a subsequent reporting period?

Accounting Principle

8 An entity shall not reverse an impairment loss recognised in a previous interim period in respect of goodwill.

9 An entity shall not extend this accounting principle by analogy to other areas of potential conflict between Ind AS 34 and other Indian Accounting Standards.

Appendix B

References to matters contained in other Indian Accounting Standards

This Appendix is an integral part of the Ind AS.

1 Appendix C, Levies, contained in Ind AS 37, Provisions, Contingent Liabilities and Contingent Assets.

Appendix 1

Note: This Appendix is not a part of the Indian Accounting Standard. The purpose of this Appendix is only to bring out the major differences, if any, between Indian Accounting Standard (Ind AS) 34 and the corresponding International Accounting Standard (IAS) 34, Interim Financial Reporting, and IFRIC 10, Interim Financial Reporting and Impairment, issued by the International Accounting Standards Board.

Comparison with IAS 34, *Interim Financial Reporting, and IFRIC 10*

1 With regard to preparation of statement of profit and loss, International Accounting Standard (IAS) 34, *Interim Financial Reporting*, provides option either to follow single statement approach or to follow two statement approaches. But, Ind AS 34 allows only single statement approach on the lines of Ind AS 1, *Presentation of Financial Statements,* which also allows only single statement approach. Paragraphs 8A and 11A of IAS 34 which provides the option are deleted. In order to maintain consistency with paragraph numbers of IAS 34, the paragraph numbers are retained in Ind AS 34.

2 Different terminology is used in Ind AS 34 eg, the term 'balance sheet' is used instead of 'Statement of financial position' and 'Statement of Profit and Loss' is used instead of 'Statement of comprehensive income' or 'Statement of profit or loss and other comprehensive income'.

3 Last sentence of paragraph 1 of IAS 34 is deleted in Ind AS 34 since it is felt that the requirement to present interim financial report should be governed by the relevant law or regulation and not by way of an encouragement through an Accounting Standard.

4 The following paragraph numbers appear as 'Deleted' in IAS 34. In order to maintain consistency with paragraph numbers of IAS 34, the paragraph numbers are retained in Ind AS 34:

(i) paragraph 13

(ii) paragraph16

(iii) paragraphs17-18

(iv) paragraphs 5-6 of Appendix A

5 Paragraph 12 of IAS 34 making reference to Implementation Guidance included in IAS 1 has been deleted in Ind AS 34, as Implementation Guidance is not an

integral part of IAS 1. In order to maintain consistency with paragraph numbers of IAS 34, the paragraph number is retained in Ind AS 34.

6 Following paragraphs making references to Illustrative examples which are not integral part of IAS 34 have been deleted in Ind AS 34. The paragraph numbers have been retained in Ind AS 34 in order to maintain consistency with paragraph numbers of IAS 34:

(i) Paragraph 22 making reference to Illustration A of 'Illustrative Examples' illustrating the periods required to be presented by an entity that reports half yearly and an entity that reports quarterly.

(ii) Paragraph 40 making reference to Illustration B of 'Illustrative Examples' illustrating the general recognition and measurement principles set out in paragraphs 28-39.

(iii) Paragraph 42 making reference to Illustration C of 'Illustrative Examples' illustrating the use of estimates in interim periods.